Diasporic Intimacies

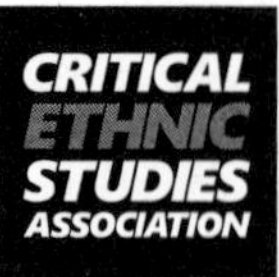

Critical Insurgencies

A Book Series of the Critical Ethnic Studies Association

Series Editors: Jodi A. Byrd and Michelle M. Wright

Critical Insurgencies features activists and scholars, as well as artists and other media makers, who forge new theoretical and political practices that unsettle the nation-state, neoliberalism, carcerality, settler colonialism, Western hegemony, legacies of slavery, colonial racial formations, gender binaries, and ableism, and challenge all forms of oppression and state violence through generative future imaginings.

About CESA The Critical Ethnic Studies Association organizes projects and programs that engage ethnic studies while reimagining its futures. Grounded in multiple activist formations within and outside institutional spaces, CESA aims to develop an approach to intellectual and political projects animated by the spirit of decolonial, antiracist, antisexist, and other global liberationist movements. These movements enabled the creation of ethnic studies and continue to inform its political and intellectual projects.

www.criticalethnicstudies.org

Diasporic Intimacies

Queer Filipinos and Canadian Imaginaries

EDITED BY

Robert Diaz, Marissa Largo, and Fritz Pino

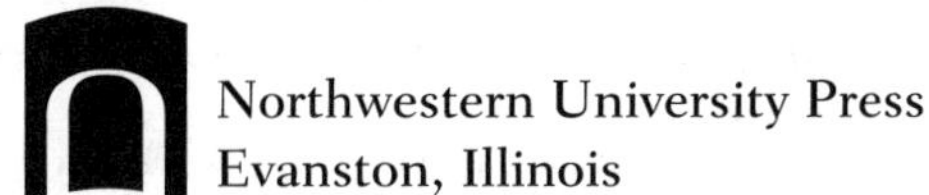

Northwestern University Press
Evanston, Illinois

Northwestern University Press
www.nupress.northwestern.edu

Printed in the United States of America

10 9 8 7 6 5 4 3 2 1

Library of Congress Cataloging-in-Publication Data

Names: Diaz, Robert, Jr., editor. | Largo, Marissa, editor. | Pino, Fritz, editor.
Title: Diasporic intimacies : Queer Filipinos and Canadian imaginaries /
   edited by Robert Diaz, Marissa Largo, and Fritz Pino.
Other titles: Critical insurgencies.
Description: Evanston, Illinois : Northwestern University Press,
   2018. | Series: Critical insurgencies | Papers from a conference held
   January 2015 at Ontario College of Art and Design University, Ontario,
   Canada. | Includes bibliographical references.
Identifiers: LCCN 2017038018 | ISBN 9780810136526 (cloth : alk.
   paper) | ISBN 9780810136519 (pbk. : alk. paper) | ISBN 9780810136533
   (e-book)
Subjects: LCSH: Filipinos—Canada—Social conditions. | Sexual
   minorities—Canada—Social conditions. | Sexual minority community—
   Canada. | Canada—Ethnic relations—21st century. | Cultural pluralism—
   Canada.
Classification: LCC F1035.F48 D53 2018 | DDC 306.760899921071—dc23
LC record available at https://lccn.loc.gov/2017038018

CONTENTS

Part 1. Historical Flashpoints

Part 2. Diasporic Art as Queer Intervention

Part 3. Transnational Imaginaries and the Ruse of Belonging

Part 4. Mourning, Militancy, and Queer Critique

and Jacinto Largo for their support throughout her life. She would also like to thank the Filipinx Canadian cultural workers who create change and widen horizons for the community through their respective practices. This book is an embodiment of the hopes, aspirations, and visions that they nurture everyday.

Fritz Pino would like to thank Fidencio and Loreta Pino and Philip Garvez for their unconditional love and support. He also would like to thank his long time friends Kayla Valiente, Paula Gerinea, Domz Sabanal, Jae Bellot, and Jean Vecina for their encouragement, care, and generosity to share their homes for writing, thinking, eating, and laughing.

The "Stuff" of Queer Horizons and Other Utopic Pursuits

Robert Diaz

"Punta ka ha" ("Hope you can come"). I heard this phrase repeatedly over the course of living and working in Canada for five years. Whether said to me in Toronto, Winnipeg, Calgary, Montreal, or Vancouver, this phrase always seemed to possess hints of *lambing* (a Tagalog term that means "warmth" or "endearment"). *Lambing* saturated the many gatherings I attended in these cities, gatherings as quotidian as house parties and barbecues in parks, or as extravagant as art exhibits, singing contests, and beauty pageants. During these events, I witnessed many Filipinos/as share their collective memories, pains, and yearnings as diasporic subjects. By coming together, community members often negotiated, alleviated, and resisted the challenges they faced. One chilly January evening, I heard this phrase again as PJ Alafriz, Melanya Liwanag Aguila, and Lisa Valencia-Svensson (members of the queer feminist group Babaylan featured in this collection) invited me to their joint birthday celebration at Music Box. Music Box is a bar located in Toronto's "Bathurst and Wilson" area. "Bathurst and Wilson" derives its name from the cross street in the northern part of the city which has a high concentration of Filipino businesses and residents. This area functions as an important point of convergence, as community celebrations, festivals, and parades are often held there. I thus accepted my friends' invitation not only because I was excited to see them. I was also curious to find out why a group of out queer *pinays* would decide to celebrate a significant occasion in this part of the city instead of "Church and Wellesley," which is historically its gay district.

I arrived early to find a mostly empty bar. As I walked in, I was immediately filled with memories of familiar spaces I've navigated outside of Canada. Music Box specifically reminded me of bars I've been to in Manila. Advertisements for Filipino businesses were scattered throughout the space. The bar's menu featured typical Filipino fare such as San Miguel beer, different kinds of *pulutan* (snacks), and popular dishes like *pancit* (a noodle dish), *lechon kawali* (fried pork belly), and *crispy pata* (fried pork knuckles). The music playing on the sound system vacillated between famous ballads from the 1980s and 1990s and contemporary American pop—a familiar soundscape to many diasporic Filipinos. As the space began to fill up, I noticed that most of the incoming patrons were women, trans men, and non-gender-conforming Filipinos/as. Surprised, I turned to Melanya and asked whether there was an event planned for that evening. She nonchalantly replied, "Oh, it's also *Pardz* Night." *Pardz* Night or women's night, I soon learned, was a gathering held a couple of times a year since the early 1990s. Its organizers (Marinel Lozano and PJ Alfariz) brought together lesbian, queer, and trans-identified Filipinos/as so that they could mingle, network, and have fun amid the various demands of their daily life.

Pardz derives from *pare*, a male-gendered noun that roughly translates in colloquial speech to "brother," "dude," or "comrade." In Filipino popular culture, *pare* is traditionally ascribed to men and often imagined through heteronormative representations of masculinity and male virility. *Pardz* Night's attendees queer and unsettle *pare*'s normative nomenclatures. Through collective performances of camp, butchness, and hyperbolic masculinity, they retranslate *Pardz* as a necessary tool for subtending the gendered and classed protocols of masculinity, kinship, and intimacy that often discipline their interactions. These protocols fail to account for their experiences in Canada. Similar to how the term *tibo* has been reframed and reclaimed by lesbian and trans communities in the diaspora, *Pardz* Night is sustained by willful, even subversive efforts to pursue alternative forms of collectivity amid the inequities that many queer and trans people experience—within and outside the Filipino community.[1] This is especially relevant since many of *Pardz* Night's attendees migrated to Canada through the live-in caregiver program. Its demographic thus reflects the gendered migration and labor schemes that continue to shape the larger Filipino/a community, schemes which have prioritized service and care work.[2]

Pardz Night always features a performance, such as a fashion show, drag king contest, karaoke sing-off, or dance-off. On this particular evening, the main competition was a dance contest that pitted people from different age groups against each other. Groups were divided according to their twenties, thirties, forties, and fifties (and beyond). As I watched the night's competitors gyrate and dance with abandon, I was struck by the palpable pleasure that their performance of abandonment often possessed. I was moved by the collective spirit that such abandonment animated. Their collective spirit, it seemed to me, came out of years of being with, laughing with, and dancing with each other. Their being together seemed to index a longer history of community-building often absent in mainstream representations of LGBTQ history, whether in Toronto specifically or in Canada generally.

I begin my introduction with this quotidian gathering—a queer birthday party in a bar removed from the city's mainstream gay district—because it embodies the political and theoretical interventions that the authors, scholars, and artists featured in this collection seek to make. How might *Pardz* Night offer us a different queer genealogy, history, and archive in Canada? How might centering on the experiences of queer women, migrants, and racialized minorities challenge dominant understandings of "mainstream" LGBTQ community in the city? How might *Pardz* Night, with all its joy and frivolity, inform a different understanding of intimacy, pleasure, and resistance amid the limited forms of sexuality made legible by the state and by other institutional articulations of tolerance? How might this event speak to, and critique, the systemic ways in which sexually marginalized Filipinos/as have had to pursue different forms of social engagement, despite the various ways in which policies on migration, multiculturalism, and inclusion have defined their relationship to the spaces they inhabit? *Diasporic Intimacies: Queer Filipinos and Canadian Imaginaries* engages with these and other similar questions in order to imagine queer Filipino/a archives, topographies, and temporalities anew. By focusing on the aesthetic, the sonic, and the performative, the contributors of this collection demonstrate that alongside systemic inequalities, queer longings and imaginaries abound, with force and with resistant potential.

Queerness as this volume envisions it does not only refer to identitarian notions of sexual and racial marginality. Rather, queerness indexes a panoply of nonnormative filiations, intimacies, and affects that proliferate alongside Canadian identificatory regimes. Jose Muñoz reminds us that queerness is not just a subjectivity but is also a means for building ethical relations with the world. Queerness is that "thing that tells us that the world is not enough, that indeed something is missing."[3] Queerness is a tactic for animating aesthetic practices and performances of world-making which insist that our "now" is not necessarily our "future."[4] For Muñoz, queerness is a "horizon," a utopic futurity that we both sense and create. Such a "horizon" is made up of differently situated investments, gestures, pleasures, and desires culled from the debris of our past that may be reoriented, reimagined, and reactivated in unexpected ways to craft a more humane and just world. Returning to *Pardz* Night, this event is not only queer because it is populated by sexually marginalized individuals. It is also queer because it willfully enacts different modes of community-building through pleasures that cannot be easily framed within normalized versions of family, kinship, and collectivity. It is queer because its version of coming together necessarily recites and refashions diasporic articulations of sexuality, masculinity, and solidarity. As I opened myself to the invitation of "*punta ka ha*," I not only agreed to visit a bar in Toronto. I also agreed to visit the other elsewheres that make up the daily lives of many sexually marginalized and diasporic Filipinos. These elsewheres condition our here and our now. They make our being here bearable, livable, and worth imagining new futures for.

New Queer of Color Geographies

At its core, *Diasporic Intimacies* de-territorializes queer of color critique from its normative geographic and topographic locations. It moves beyond the United States to map the confluences of sexuality, gender, nationhood, and race. The contributors of this collection are in direct dialogue with black, Indigenous, and other racialized scholars, activists, and artists who have insisted on the need to resist Canadian multiculturalism's myopic disciplining of difference, inclusion, and tolerance.[5] While reflecting on the impossibility, and thus queerness, of writing blackness into Canadian history, Rinaldo Walcott notes:

> Located between the U.S. and the Caribbean, Canadian blackness is a bubbling brew of desires for elsewhere, disappointment in the nation and the pleasures of exile—even for those who have resided here for many generation. The project of articulating blackness is difficult not because of the small number of us trying to take tentative steps towards writing it, but rather because of the ways in which so many of us are nearly always

> preoccupied with elsewhere and seldom with here. It seems
> then that a tempered arrogance might be a necessary element
> of any grammar that is used to construct a language of writ-
> ing blackness in Canada. A shift in gaze can be an important
> moment. The writing of blackness in Canada, then, might
> begin with a belief that something important happens here. [6]

Walcott's statement foregrounds the potential of racialized, queer, and remaindered lives to act as the necessary fuel for imagining better futures that do not rely on the finite grammars of the present. Blackness is a capacity that enables those who have been historically abjected through the many concatenations of race to will forms of emancipation that have yet to be fully realized. The difficulty of writing race into the Canadian archive, as Walcott continually suggests, is rooted in the reality that for many diasporic people of color, and indeed for many queer people of color, negotiating the difficulties of being here have often required us to imagine elsewheres we have already lived or elsewheres we have yet to travel to.

Even though Walcott's reflections were offered at the turn of the new millennium, queer of color critique continues to be vital in Canada precisely because we continue to encounter contemporary social movements that fight against anti-black racism and settler colonialism, and movements that lay bare the systemic oppression of black and Indigenous bodies through white supremacist modes of governmentality here and abroad. Such a de-territorialization is still necessary, as we witness the global privileging of certain queer communities—often white and upwardly mobile—who are allowed entry into facile notions of acceptable citizenship (flexible and national) through laws that normalize domesticity, inclusion, and tolerance.[7] Such de-territorialization is still crucial as we witness the unequal distribution and extraction of resources between the global north and the global south—a process that relies on the migration and movement of diasporic, often precarious, racialized bodies into spaces where their labor is utilized and violently devalued.[8]

Given the realities that have created the vicissitudes of our present, the time has come for queer Filipinos/as in Canada to take stock of our histories in this place, not only to acknowledge that we are indeed here as queer people of color, but to insist that the conditions that have led to our being here as diasporic subjects stem from transnational attempts to police the lives of those who are marginalized here and elsewhere.

Our futures in Canada are always already bound up with the futures of others in the global south. Yet despite being staged in seemingly bleak circumstances, queer of color imaginaries are composed of utopic acts. Writing and thinking queer Filipino/a history in Canada thus requires that we assertively hold onto the politically vibrant and willfully disobedient histories we have already shared, histories which appear, even momentarily, across multiple mediums of expression, multiple forms of collectivity, and multiple geographic spaces we activate. We must capture the aspirations of the present to enliven possible social change.

Valuing "Messy" Archives and Remaindered Lives

Queer horizons are often contained within incongruent archives, terms, or constructs that resist collection and academic compartmentalization. Queer archives need not rely on educational institutions or museums to exist or to have political use. Rather, these archives are found in many flashpoints, stories, acts, and emotions that constitute quotidian counter-publics and that confound, even as they expand, processes that have attempted to organize their meanings. Martin Manalansan writes that instead of emphasizing seamlessness, queer archives embody the political possibilities imbedded in "mess" as the paradoxical glue that binds queer histories together. [9] "Mess" is the "stuff" of queer archives because it allows, in the most banal sense, orientations, gestures, objects, and attachments that cannot be easily summarized or logically arranged within normalized scripts that delineate family, community, and nationhood.

In both its theoretical and organizational approach, then, *Diasporic Intimacies* attempts to acknowledge the political potentiality of messy archives by placing artistic practices, scholarly research, and community engagement in constant dialogue—within and across specific sections of the book. We enact a queer historiographic project that does not prioritize chronology or unity, but that seeks to embody the politics of putting multiple genres of cultural production (scholarly essays, artistic images, plays, critical reflections, and interviews) alongside each other, without valuing one form over another. Furthermore, we have made the editorial decision to keep all of the authors' preferred gender protocols for discussing ethnicity and national identity. Thus, the use of "Filipino," "Filipino/a," and "Filipinx" appear simultaneously, and in varied fashion, throughout the chapters of this collection. Such a decision rests on the idea that, similar to umbrella terms that have defined various queer communities (LGBTQ for instance), "Filipino" as an index for discussing ethnicity is also subject to change, as scholars and activists point to its limits and future possibilities.

Diasporic Intimacies demonstrates that messy archives destabilize, even as they expose, the disciplinary inequities that continue to shape cultural production and knowledge dissemination around ethnicity and migration in Canada today. Despite its significant critiques of Filipino marginalization, for example, the nascent field of Filipino Canadian studies has yet to examine the intersections of sexuality, migration, and racialization. Such an oversight makes queer analyses the purview of an exceedingly white Canadian queer studies. It also compartmentalizes Filipino studies within an "area studies" framework that imagines queer Filipino Canadian sexualities as always already foreign to Canadian culture and society. More importantly, by acknowledging the reality that queer Filipinos in Canada have pursued community-building and activism for more than two decades, we suggest that the paucity of knowledge around such radical forms of social engagement is not accidental but is in fact systemic. This absence is rooted in symptomatic approaches within dominant Filipino Canadian migration research or community organizing that unwittingly reifies ethno- and homonationalistic ideals of gender, masculinity, citizenship, and cultural acceptance. These tropes are reified when academic fields or community groups meant to improve the lives of Filipinos in Canada reproduce heteronormative notions of gender, labor, leadership, and kinship that then occlude those whose lives do not fit into such norms, and who experience intersectional forms of disempowerment differently.

The experience of transgender Filipinas with deprofessionalization (or the systemic devaluing of past academic and employment credentials upon arrival) offers a good example of such occlusions. Although they experience deprofessionalization like the larger Filipino/a community (which has one of the highest rates of deprofessionalization in Canada), the root causes for such deprofessionalization cannot be entirely subsumed under the current models we have for understanding this vexed process. In the most cited research on this topic for instance, Filipino deprofessionalization is mostly attributed to four key causes: the class origins of migrants before arrival, the labor streams they utilize in order to migrate (such as caregiver and family reunification streams), their credential assessment and access to cognate professions, and workplace attitudes toward race in the workplace.[10]

Yet as many of the transgender Filipinas in my field work point out, their understanding of how and why they have been deprofessionalized extends beyond these neat categories. Their framing of economic disenfranchisement and racism cannot be disconnected from their concerns of "passing" appropriately in their preferred gender. Many trans women also mentioned concerns around a prospective employer's homophobia and transphobia during their interview, which may often cost them the opportunity to seek employment in fields cognate to those they were trained in. Even the actual labor that categorizes Filipinos/as as deprofessionalized often do not include certain type of work that many Filipinos also perform. Sex work for example is a significant occupation that many transgender Filipinas chose. Yet discussions of sex work are absent in current scholarship on deprofessionalization. Instead, discussions often focus on domestic and care work without a frank discussion of sexuality or sex. Aside from its absence in Filipino Canadian research agendas, many community organizations serving migrant populations automatically conflate sex work with victimization and human trafficking. Yet as many of the transgender Filipinas I interviewed suggest, their decision to pursue sex work stems from many complex reasons and desires—rooted not only in Canada but also in their experiences in the Philippines. Dominant perspectives around sex work may thus prevent certain members of the transgender community from participating in, and engaging with, community organizing that would benefit both the organization and the community member.

These examples demand that sexuality be addressed within Filipino/a Canadian studies. By failing to include capacious analyses of how queer communities are disempowered or empowered in differently situated ways, Filipino Canadian studies falls into the trap of normalizing its definitions of such categories as womanhood, masculinity, and victimization around heteronormative concepts and frames. Martin Manalansan gestures to a similar dynamic in "Queer Intersection: Sexuality and Gender in Migration Studies," as he demonstrates how heteronormative investments in global migration research offer limited returns since they often occlude the realities many diasporic Filipinos/as—queer- and nonqueer-identified—face on the ground.[11] By documenting the lived realities of queer Filipinos/as who pursue alternative ideals of family and community, *Diasporic Intimacies* foregrounds nonnormative kinship structures, collectivities, and affinities that survive and thrive as queer people of color animate their multiple meanings.

Key Thematic Concerns

Given its wide and often unruly scope, we have tried to divide this collection thematically into four distinct sections. These sections are not meant to be proscriptive. In fact, the themes, issues, and genres contained in one section are often echoed in another. Instead, each section seeks to trace particular theoretical possibilities within queer Filipino/a Canadian studies, encouraging further conversations, debates, and analyses as the field grows in scope and specificity.

Part 1, "Historical Flashpoints," maps out the political stakes of and strategies for pursuing queer Filipino studies as a historical, community-building, and activist project. These works suggest that in order to fully imagine the political possibilities for queerness to remake our world, we must first locate, re-create, and foreground intimacies, desires, and subjectivities that fall outside of pervasive disciplinary and institutional definitions of community, belonging, and kinship.

Through their contributions, Roland Sintos Coloma and John Paul Catungal offer useful methodological tools for pursuing queer Filipino/a historiography within Canada. They suggest that such a queer Filipino/a historiographic project is not only concerned with cataloging the presence of sexually marginalized individuals within past historical records. A queer historiographic project must also critically insert queerness into archives that may not necessarily have queer content in them, or it must willfully imagine what a queer Filipino/a archive may look like when accounting for solidarity work between and within marginalized groups. In Coloma's contribution, he maps out three strategies for deconstructing queer Filipino history in Canada. In order to account for the past, present, and future of queer Filipino research, Coloma revisits glimpses of LGBTQ Filipino presence in archives ranging from Richard Fung's film *Orientation*, to flyers in the Canadian Lesbian and Gay Archives, to newspaper reports, to published creative writing. In the process, he enacts a recuperative reimagining of these sites.

John Paul Catungal advocates for the proliferation of theoretical analyses attuned to unpacking nonnormative intimacies that may already exist in the work of transnational feminists writing about gender and labor within the live-in caregiver program. Returning to scholarship by Geraldine Pratt, Ethel Tungohan, and Glenda Bonifacio, Catungal calls for the application of what he calls "proto-queer" reading practices, or theoretical frames that subtend even the most familiar archives

by seeing them anew, and by documenting the lives of women historically seen as having a "non-normative, even improper, relationship to
heterosexuality." [12] Continuing such a recuperative reading, Catungal
then hazards a vision of queer Filipino studies that allies with critiques
of settler colonialism in order to influence current strategies for galvanizing Filipino communities in Canada. In so doing, he notes that
we need to complicate the terms that have been the basis for Filipino
Canadian community organizing for quite some time—religion, family,
nationalism, and settlement—since these are often refracted through
colonial and settler colonial genealogies. Taken together, Coloma and
Catungal's contributions are significant not only because they provide
a useful blueprint for theorizing queer histories but because they also
perform a reparative reading of their past scholarship in *Filipinos in
Canada*, one of the most seminal texts in the field today, which, despite
its wide scope, does not have explicitly queer content.[13]

Other works included in this section then complement Coloma's
and Catungal's historical project. These works foreground the valuable
labor of queer *pinay* feminists who, since the 1990s, have galvanized
each other and the larger community around various queer of color
and Indigenous causes. The following chapters are thus comprised of
essay catalogs, documents, images, personal reflections, and interviews
with many exceptional queer and trans Filipinas who, aside from being
friends for more than two decades, have also pursued critical activism
that has radically asserted their presence in both Filipino Canadian
communities and mainstream LGBTQ communities. We feature the
art, drag, community organizing, and personal stories of Melanya Liwanag Aguila, Lisa Valencia-Svensson, PJ Alfariz, Jo SiMalaya Alcampo,
JB Ramos, and many other feminists who started numerous community
groups such as Babaylan, ATBP, Sawa, and Kapwa Collective. These
groups sought to challenge the hetero-patriarchy that exists within
the Filipino Canadian community, as they built solidarity with other
women of color movements. We offer these archives as flashpoints into
the rich and often complex networks of queer of color feminisms that
have existed in Toronto. As illuminating case studies, they offer a corrective to the absence of queer Filipinos/as in contemporary Filipino
Canadian and queer Canadian histories. They also illustrate the power
of feminist *pinay*s to build solidarity around issues of racism, sexism,
and Indigenous rights across and within the city.

Part 2, "Diasporic Art as Queer Intervention," values artistic practice
as a significant site for examining queer and Filipino/a Canadian forms

of expression. This section emphasizes the role of artistic practice and cultural production in how queer Filipinos/as have historically dictated the grounds of their visibility in various mediums of representation. By focusing on the nostalgic, the traumatic, the humorous, and the mundane, the artists and scholars featured in this section model a version of queerness that values art in creating new forms of community and belonging. While diaspora, race, and representation are at the forefront of cultural studies discourses, they paradoxically remain on the periphery of mainstream Western art history and art education. By prioritizing diasporic articulations of Filipino sexuality in art, these contributors open up alternatives to mainstream art history, and in the process produce pedagogic strategies that move beyond territorialized dichotomies of the West and the rest.

In her contribution, Marissa Largo examines the work of Marigold Santos, particularly Santos's use of disarticulation and abstraction, in order to enact what she calls a de-colonial aesthetic that problematizes the ethnographic entrapment Filipina artists often experience in Canadian artistic circles. Such normative forms of visibility often demand that Filipina artists continually essentialize themselves as gendered laborers or migrant subjects in order to be seen or heard. Largo suggests that in Santos's work, she mobilizes an aesthetic that relies on folklore, as well as diasporic understandings of oral history, in order to queer such histories toward "anti-essentialist" critiques of the multicultural state (which often also funds artistic practices).[14]

Expanding on such critiques of visibility, Casey Mecija reflects on the psychic, problematic, and performative ambivalences that her body produces as a performer in the band Ohbijou. Writing about the ways in which her presence as a lesbian Filipina performer has been policed by multicultural narratives of diversity (and marketability), Mecija instead offers a recuperative corrective that reshifts the weight of such bodily presence to mentorship and community-building practices that help queer, young, and migrant Filipinos/as use art as a means to self-belief. On that note, Mecija's piece ends with the song "Balikbayan" or "Returnee," which gestures to the difficulties of finding one's place in a space that cannot fully signify home. By articulating her ambivalence about finding "home" in Canada, Mecija foregrounds the inescapable reality that any project of alliance-building between native communities and diasporic Filipinos/as also entails that Filipinos/as position ourselves as transgenerational arrivants within this settler colonial space. Such a project requires that we complicate our histories beyond a narrative of settlement and integration. Rather, we must contextualize our stakes in claiming a space that is not ours, as individuals marginalized along other axes of oppression.

Moving into other performative landscapes and soundscapes, the contributions by Pantayo, Jodinand Aguillon, and Kim Villagante—artists who work on, hybridize, and retool difference genres of expression (*kulintang* music, dance, poetry, theater, and portraiture)—collectively reflect on the influences of folklore, family, religion, patriarchy, and cosmology on their artistic and activist practice. Through a free-flowing interview and conversation, the members of Pantayo discuss how the genre embodied by *kulintang* music, and the fact that they are composed of *pinay*s (women of Filipino descent, or Filipinas), possibly queer the expectations of "traditional" Filipino representation in Canada. They thus demonstrate the transnational and global routes of queer Indigenous performance. Mindful of the pitfalls that being part of "traditional" and "nationalist" genres entails, especially in Canada, the group instead seeks to subvert such nationalist expectations not only through their musical compositions but in the political choices they have made as a group.

In a similar fashion, Jodinand Aguillon reflects on his history as a choreographer who has moved from Calgary to Toronto, and who has returned to traditional Filipino dance forms not to reproduce them, but to challenge their gendered scripts through deconstruction and play. As Aguillon's personal reflections show, what informs his choreographic practice of HATAW is a desire to reimagine gendered tropes within traditional dance in order to subvert them, twist them, and deploy them against the multicultural logics that often reproduce Filipino ethnicity as an exotic form from "elsewhere" that is untethered to the political concerns of the present.

Finally, through Kim Villagante's interview, the artist reflects on the ways her portraiture, the main style of her practice, has been influenced by the global iterations of mass-mediated culture such as hip-hop and the push and pull of Filipino cultural norms. Refashioning such tropes from the eyes of a feminist Filipina, Villagante gestures to what Christine Balance calls "disobedient" forms of knowing—deploying such disobedient strategies by transposing the urban lanscapes and messy archives she encounters onto faces which become metonyms for alternative forms of *pinay* visibility.[15]

Part 3, "Transnational Imaginaries and the Ruse of Belonging," insists that to queer our understanding of Filipino embodiment in

Canada is to necessarily recite desires, intimacies, and longings that hail from elsewhere and that index a diasporic community's experiences with colonialism, migration, and globalization. With the relocation and dislocation of subjects across the world, diaspora disrupts orders of knowledge that are shaped by gender, race, sexuality, and geography. As Gayatri Gopinath suggests, to understand queerness as diasporic and diaspora as queer is to recuperate "desires, practices, and subjectivities that are rendered impossible or unimaginable within conventional diasporic or nationalist imaginaries."[16] Such a critical approach "may begin to unsettle the ways in which diaspora shores up the gender and sexual ideologies of dominant nationalism on the one hand, and processes of globalization on the other."[17] The works in this section thus expand on the multiple ways in which queer individuals sustain, enliven, and rearticulate diasporic subjectivities in Canada. Whether examining the experiences of aging queer migrants, or exploring the ways in which basketball reifies normative notions of masculinity, or animating how their art and drag draw on nostalgia to create spaces for underrepresented groups, the works in this section foreground the many forms that diaspora, transnationalism, and globality take within Filipino Canadian imaginaries.

Focusing on *bakla* Filipino Canadians in later life, Fritz Pino's ethnographic analysis places the fields of gerontology and queer studies in productive tension. Through the stories of his informants, Pino highlights the theoretical limits of these fields in unpacking the experiences of *bakla* elderly populations in Canada, most of whom carry with them notions of intimacy, health, and wellness that exceed normative scripts attached to other Canadians in later life. For Pino's *bakla* informants, diasporic notions of desire and intimacy affect their relationship to happiness and eventual wellness choices.

Expanding on notions of "health" with regard to appropriate forms of citizenship, May Farrales reads basketball as a site where "healthy" masculinities are performed, and subverted by, Filipinos/as in Canada. Providing a queer reading that particularly rehistoricizes basketball as a diasporic form of nation-building reliant on nostalgia and virility, Farrales forwards a reading of basketball as a sport that foregrounds its political nature, and its complex historicity, when re-performed in a settler colonial space like Canada—with its own pejorative racialization of Filipino/a bodies and masculinity.

Through a series of vignettes, Patrick Salvani emphasizes the role of drag in enabling queer youth of color to find a voice in a place that often does not offer the same routes to visibility for queer people equally. Through a hodgepodge of memories recited in comedic fashion—memories of his grandmother, folkloric tales in the Philippines, memories of food and fast-food joints in Manila—Salvani critiques, with slicing humor, the need for queer Filipino/a performance to undo the various "isms" that queer youth of color often experience most viscerally.

Drawing from similar memories of abjection and hope, Sean Kua, Benjamin Bongolan, and Constantine Cabarios's critical reflections, as well as Julius Poncelet Manapul's interview, reflect on the tensions between peripheral and central subjectivities that undergird queer space. They also remind of us how front-line community work, performance, and art rearticulate a need for queer Filipinos/as to inject themselves into the center, even though such a process can yield ambivalent results. As a whole, these artists and performers trace spectacles of queerness in Canada in order to create counter-narratives to forms of queerness that rely on overwrought, consumerist, and problematic notions of gay pride.

Part 4, "Mourning, Militancy, and Queer Critique," reflects on the role of memory, mourning, and violence in animating queer Filipino critiques in Canada—critiques that while being produced by artists and critics located in Canada nonetheless gesture to queer and trans experiences that occur beyond its borders. Writing about losing friends, family members, and other loved ones due to governmental inaction during the height of the HIV/AIDS crisis in the United States, the critic Douglas Crimp emphatically notes: "For many of us, mourning *becomes* militancy."[18] Mobilizing Crimp's assertions and echoing them in Canada, the works in this section refuse to compartmentalize queer realities in this country from those that are occurring in the Philippines and in other spaces. Through a touching remembrance of one of his film's participants, Augusto Diangson, the artist and scholar Patrick Alcedo conjures Diangson's queer performance and embodiment of camp in order to unpack the many forms of *kabaklaan* that are present in the Philippines and unsettle even as they recite colonial narratives. By recalling Diangson's participation during the *Ati-Atihan* (a local dance festival that hails to precolonial times and that has been hybridized because of colonial histories), Alcedo provides a moving reminder of local queer gestures and affectations that, despite of or precisely because of their facetiousness, dare to poke fun at the most sacrosanct religious and colonial scripts.

Taking such militancy even further, the writings by Gabriela-Ontario, Anakbayan, Lui Queano, and the Congress of Progressive Filipinos (collected in the chapter entitled "Militarism, Violence, and Critiques of the Neoliberal State") directly reflect on the ways in which American militarism and neoliberalism have affected the life expectancies and biopolitical trajectories of the most vulnerable of queer populations. One of the main violent moments they discuss as a critical palimpsest is the death of Jennifer Laude. Jennifer Laude is a transgender Filipina who was found murdered by means of asphyxiation and drowning on October 11, 2014. Laude died in Olonggapo City, which continues to be haunted by the effects of American militarization in the Philippines. She was murdered by Joseph Scott Pemberton, a U.S. Marine stationed in the Philippines through the country's Visiting Forces Agreement with the United States. These contributions highlight how Filipino organizations in Canada link the violence perpetrated on Laude's body to the violence done onto the Philippines, as they call for anti-imperialist futures that also highlight the queer Filipino/a Canadian community's stakes in such a demand.

This section also foregrounds the work of queer Filipino/a community members who mobilized in order to promote HIV/AIDS awareness and education at a time when no information was available about queer Filipinos/as in Canada. In this regard, we feature and publish in full the script of a groundbreaking play entitled *My Grandmother and I*. Written by Lani Montreal, *My Grandmother and I* follows the travails of a family dealing with the death of a gay family member named Dino, who passes away due to an AIDS-related illness. Dino's relatives are in deep denial of his homosexuality and the reasons for his death because of their religious beliefs. As a main anchor in the narrative, however, Dino's grandmother sees his spirit even after his passing, and their interactions and dialogue throughout the play serve as a reflection of Philippine Indigenous spirituality, precolonial traditions, and anticolonial resistance. Considering that it was first staged in 1994, it is remarkable that the play already grapples with multiple political concerns such as Indigenous rights, racism, homophobia, transphobia, militarism, religious conservatism, colonialism, and globalization—all from an intersectional and transnational perspective. *My Grandmother and I* thus represents a unique contribution to Canadian performance history, and we are honored to be able to feature this piece in its entirety.

Ultimately, the contributions in this section problematize such celebratory and homonationalist narratives of inclusion by reminding us painfully of the violence that queer Filipinos—located both within and outside of Canada—have experienced and continue to experience. Whether reflecting on hybridized aesthetics in queer Filipino dance, or on the effects of militarism and uneven economic development across Canada and the Philippines, or on the effects of HIV/AIDS, all these works contribute to understanding queerness from a transnational perspective. These works attempt to grasp the untranslatable; they attempt to limn memories and longings that may not automatically be legible in Canada, but that nonetheless influence how sexually marginalized Filipinos inhabit and interact with this space.

Diasporic Intimacy as a Community Event

This collection was inspired by, and is indebted to, the efforts of many queer Filipino/a community members whose long history of activism and coalition-building practices have, for the most part, been unacknowledged. Before taking shape as an anthology, *Diasporic Intimacies* began as a series of events hosted in Toronto between January 23 and February 15, 2015. Through a full-day conference, a month-long art exhibit entitled "Visualizing the Intimate" (the catalogue of which is included in this book as a chapter), and an artist dialogue, "Diasporic Intimacies" created a much-needed space for scholars, artists, and community members to critically examine the contributions of queer Filipinos/as to Canadian culture and society. The participants covered a range of topics. They discussed various articulations of queer and feminist collectivity, the effects of settlement and migration policy on the community's resilience, the nuances of multicultural notions of diversity and tolerance, the need to document lesbian, trans, and female histories in queer community organizing, the representation of LGBTQ Filipinos in the visual arts, the role that performance plays in understanding queer Filipino sexuality, the way that medical discourses affect HIV/AIDS intervention, transgender capacity-building, notions of aging, and continued advocacy around mental health, to name some of these concerns.

The rich and galvanizing dialogues produced in these events shaped the form and content of this book. As a whole, both versions of *Diasporic Intimacies* seek to create pedagogic strategies for artists, administrators, educators, and community workers interested in creating a more inclusive and contextual approach to engaging with queer Filipino Canadian concerns. On that note, I thus return to the following goals we set out during the conference, since these fuel the historical, political, and social pursuits of this collection:

(1) Interrogate the role of multiple stakeholders—such as art galleries, postsecondary institutions, and community organizations—in providing a capacious and in-depth picture of LGBTQ Filipino representation and cultural practices.

(2) Expand scholarship and critical dialogues about Canadian racialization, by foregrounding how transnational forms of sexual identity influence the articulation of, embodiment of, and the examination of racial and ethnic identity.

(3) Build lasting and sustainable relationships between mainstream LGBTQ communities and those who are often on the periphery of such communities, by diversifying the dialogues, spaces, and concerns between and within these groups.

(4) Develop concrete strategies for inclusion by recommending changes to curriculums in postsecondary institutions (particularly in the fields of art history, curatorial practice, sexuality studies, Asian Canadian studies, and cultural studies) by creating more population-specific approaches to community outreach (in the context of HIV/AIDS prevention and capacity-building around gender expression), and by creating polices that may improve integration and settlement.

(5) Broaden the spaces within which representations of Filipino sexuality have been produced by linking visual and artistic production, front-line community engagement, archival research, and historical projects that raise awareness about the lives of a group of racial and sexual minorities who, even to this day, have not been given sustained and adequate critical attention.

With a sense of promise, we seek to galvanize such support in the pages of this collection as we channel the complex, ambivalent, and challenging goals set out during this inaugural gathering.

Puro Arte in Canada and Beyond

I began this introduction with a gathering of sorts. I thus end with one as well as I gesture to this volume's political potentialities. During the opening reception of "Visualizing the Intimate," a Filipina drag queen wearing an Imeldific hair buffont walked into an art gallery full of Filipino Canadian works and mesmerized the packed venue with a *Tagalog* song. Sofonda Cox, a well-known performer, particularly in the city's gay community, lip-synched "Bituing Walang Ningning" ("Star without Luster"), which conveys the ambivalence of triumph because it comes at the expense of one's moral compass. "Bituing Walang Ningning" is iconic because it was originally sung by Sharon Cuneta, a famous Philippine-based actress. The song comes from a well-known film with the same title released in 1985. This movie follows the travails of two dueling singers, a rivalry that fuels its narrative arc. Dorina Pineda (played by Cuneta) is an impoverished but talented flower vendor who idolizes one of the most famous singers in the country, Lavinia Arguilles (played by queer icon Cherrie Gil). By the end of the film, Dorina outshines Lavinia, becoming even more famous than her muse. "Bituing Walang Ningning" is a staple performance known by many diasporic and queer Filipinos not only because it comes from a film that has biting, witty, and humorous dialogue. The film is also about rising against adversity while not losing your flair, your campiness, and yes, your frivolity. The song is about the ambivalence of success, and about the difficult choice of resisting fame and visibility, especially if both come at a price one is not willing to pay.

Given the symbolic, queer, and diasporic meanings of this song, I was struck by Cox's choice to lip-synch it during a Filipino-themed opening reception. When I asked her why she chose this particular song, she told me that it harkened back to her days in the Philippines; the song reminded her of growing up as a *bakla* child before moving to Canada. She also reveled in the song's being in Tagalog, one of the only times she can lip-synch using her native language. While Sofonda Cox, like the black divas Beyonce, Rihanna, and Nicki Minaj, is noted for her high-octane performances, many in Toronto's gay community do not know her migration history; in fact, few know that she is a diasporic Filipina. I was thus moved by Cox's choice, not only because of its novelty as a performance (she has not performed the song publicly since), but because it offers a particular way of rethinking her role within a mainstream gay community that has willingly embraced her drag because it is anchored in the familiar, and traces its roots to American popular culture. Yet with a song like "Bituing Walang Ningning," Cox not only asserts her Filipino subjectivity, she also wills and hails a different audience—an audience that reciprocates in contingent, nuanced, and complicated ways. As she strutted around the gallery that night wearing an extravagant black ball gown, Cox called on the many first-generation Filipinos who knew the song to sing it with her, and they did (some having a tear or two in their eyes). At the same time, she offered other generations of Filipinos who did not know the song a different kind of spectacle—one that traces its roots to drag performance located in, circulating in, and relevant in the Philippines. In this regard, Cox took those who may not know the song's history or relevance on a journey, a journey that recites her own migration history while asserting the significance of diasporic forms of culture to how we envision our embodiment within this Canadian space. Cox's performance, then, is also an act of knowledge production that values other archives and genealogies of being queer that inevitably seep into, and affect, being queer and Filipino in the diasporic spaces we inhabit.

Writing about Filipino/a performance in the context of American colonialism, Lucy San Pablo Burns notes that "through spectacular acts of performance, through *puro arte*, Filipino bodies instantiate and exceed the totalizing script of colonialism, inviting forms of critical engagement that emphasize more incompleteness of and possibilities of inherited histories."[19] By focusing on moments of *puro arte*, or histrionic forms of embodiment that "have the gall to exist,"[20] Burns encourages us to move beyond overdetermined archives of marginalization and agency. She instead highlights the *processes* that enable the articulation of Filipino/a subjectivity in different and even competing cultural contexts. How might queer Filipino/a performance such as Cox's create a repertoire of histories that mess up multiculturalism's structuring mechanisms? How might queer Filipino/a performance deploy histories we have inherited to unsettle the geopolitical specificities of American colonialism and Canadian settler colonialism? How might our histories as queer diasporic subjects foreground the tense proximities that exist between the experiences of other marginalized communities in Canada?

These questions, and many more, surface in the art, critical scholarship, interviews, and dialogues featured in this book. And rightly so. *Diasporic Intimacies* focuses on processes of subject formation in order to explore under what conditions queer Filipino/a bodies are made legible in Canada, and under what conditions these same bodies conform to or exceed their intended purpose. This collection is less interested in cataloging queer Filipino/a marginalization in order to produce new archives of invisibility or visibility; such a project may end up mimicking logics of state-sanctioned multiculturalism by attempting to locate and foreground new bodies in order to flatten out their contradictions. Rather, it seeks to interrogate how queer Filipino/a imaginaries, interventions, and utopias accrue meaning in a landscape that cannot fully negate nor limit their presence. Queer utopias were made to cross borders. By providing examples of *puro arte* from a range of Filipino Canadian cultural contexts, *Diasporic Intimacies* envisions queer horizons that acknowledge the multiple histories that foreground our relationship to this space—histories that inevitably assert themselves in our present but that need not be the only basis for imagining and creating the future that is yet to unfold before us.

Notes

1. See Fajardo (2011).

2. See Pratt (2004; 2012), Bonifacio (2013), and Tungohan (2013).

3. José Esteban Muñoz, *Cruising Utopia: The Then and There of Queer Futurity* (New York: New York University Press, 2009), 1.

4. Muñoz, *Cruising Utopia*, 1.

5. See Fung (1991), Bannerji (2000), Walcott (2003), Thobani (2007), Sha (2012), and Tuck (2012).

6. Rinaldo Walcott, *Black Like Who? Writing Black Canada* (Toronto: Insomniac Press, 2003), 27.

7. See Duggan (2003), Puar (2007), and Spade (2011).

8. See Ong (1999), Tadiar (2009), and Rodriguez (2010).

9. See Manalansan (2014)

10. See Kelly, Astorga-Garcia, Esguerra, and the Community Alliance for Social Justice Toronto (2012).

11. Martin F. Manalansan, "Queer Intersections: Sexuality and Gender in Migration Studies," *International Migration Review* 40, no. 1 (2006): 237.

12. See Catungal's chapter in this volume.

13. See Coloma, McElhinny, Tungohan, Catungal, and Davidson (2012).

14. See Largo's essay, "Reimagining Filipina Visibility through 'Black Mirror,'" in this volume.

15. See Balance (2016).

16. Gayatri Gopinath, *Impossible Desires: Queer Diasporas and South Asian Public Cultures* (Durham, N.C.: Duke University Press, 2005), 11.

17. Gopinath, *Impossible Desires*, 11.

18. Douglas Crimp, *Melancholia and Moralism: Essays on AIDS and Queer Politics* (Boston: MIT Press, 2004), 137.

19. Lucy Burns, *Puro Arte: Filipinos on the Stages of Empire* (New York: New York University Press, 2012), 3.

20. Burns, *Puro Arte*, 4.

Bibliography

Balance, Christine Bacareza. *Tropical Renditions: Making Musical Scenes in Filipino America*. Durham: Duke University Press, 2016.

Bannerji, Himani. *The Dark Side of the Nation: Essays on Multiculturalism, Nationalism, and Gender*. Toronto: Canadian Scholars, 2000.

Bonifacio, Glenda Tibe. *Pinay on the Prairies: Filipino Women and Transnational Identities*. Vancouver: University of British Columbia Press, 2013.

Burns, Lucy Mae San Pablo. *Puro Arte: Filipinos on the Stages of Empire*. New York: New York University Press, 2012.

Coloma, Roland, Bonnie McElhinny, Ethel Tungohan, John Paul C. Catungal, and Lisa M. Davidson, eds. "Spectres of (In)visibility: Filipino/a Labour, Culture, and Youth in Canada," In *Filipinos in Canada: Disturbing Invisibility*, edited by Roland Sintos Coloma, Bonnie McElhinny, Ethel Tungohan, John Paul C. Catungal, and Lisa M. Davidson, 5–45. Toronto: University of Toronto Press, 2012.

Duggan, Lisa. *The Twilight of Equality? Neoliberalism, Cultural Politics, and the Attack on Democracy*. Boston: Beacon, 2003.

Fajardo, Kale. *Filipino Crosscurrents: Oceanographies of Seafaring, Masculinities, and Globalization*. Minneapolis: University of Minnesota Press, 2011.

Fung, Richard. "Looking for my Penis: The Eroticized Asian in Gay Video Porn." In *How I Look? Queer Film and Video*, edited by Bad Object-Choices, 145–68. Seattle: Bay Press, 1991.

Kelly, Philip, Mila Astorga-Garcia, Enrico F. Esguerra, and the Community Alliance for Social Justice Toronto. "Filipino Immigrants in the Toronto Labor Market: Towards an Understanding of Deprofessionalization." In *Filipinos in Canada: Disturbing Invisibility*, edited by Roland Sintos Coloma, Bonnie McElhinny, Ethel Tungohan, John Paul C. Catungal, and Lisa M. Davidson, 68–88. Toronto: University of Toronto Press, 2012.

Manalansan, Martin F. *Global Divas: Gay Filipinos in the Diaspora*. Durham, N.C.: Duke University Press, 2003.

―――. "The Stuff of Archives: Mess, Migration, and Queer Lives." *Radical History Review* 120 (2014): 94–107

Ong, Aihwa. *Flexible Citizenship: The Cultural Logics of Transnationality.* Durham: Duke University Press, 1999.

Pratt, Geraldine. *Families Apart: Migrant Mothers and the Conflicts of Labor and Love.* Minneapolis: University of Minnesota Press, 2012.

―――. *Working Feminism.* Philadelphia: Temple University Press, 2004

Puar, Jasbir K. *Terrorist Assemblages: Homonationalism in Queer Times.* Durham, N.C.: Duke University Press, 2007.

Rodriguez, Robyn Magalit. *Migrants for Export: How the Philippines Brokers Labor to the World.* Minneapolis: University of Minnesota Press, 2010.

Shah, Nayan. *Stranger Intimacy: Contesting Race, Sexuality, and the Law in the North American West.* Berkeley: University of California Press, 2011.

Spade, Dean. *Normal Life: Administrative Violence, Critical Trans Politics, and the Limits of the Law.* New York: South End, 2011.

Tadiar, Neferti X.M. *Things Fall Away: Philippine Historical Experience and the Makings of Globalization.* Durham: Duke University Press, 2009.

Tuck, Eve. "Decolonization is not a metaphor." *Decolonization: Indigeneity, Education & Society, Vol. 1* (2012): 1–40.

Tungohan, Ethel. "Reconceptualizing Motherhood, Reconceptualizing Resistance: Migrant Domestic Workers, Transnational Hyper-Maternalism and Activism." *International Feminist Journal of Politics* 15 (2013): 39–57.

Thobani, Sunera. *Exalted Subjects: Studies in the Making of Race and Nation in Canada.* Toronto: University of Toronto Press, 2007.

Walcott, Rinaldo. *Black Like Who? Writing Black Canada.* Toronto: Insomniac Press, 2003.

Diasporic Intimacies

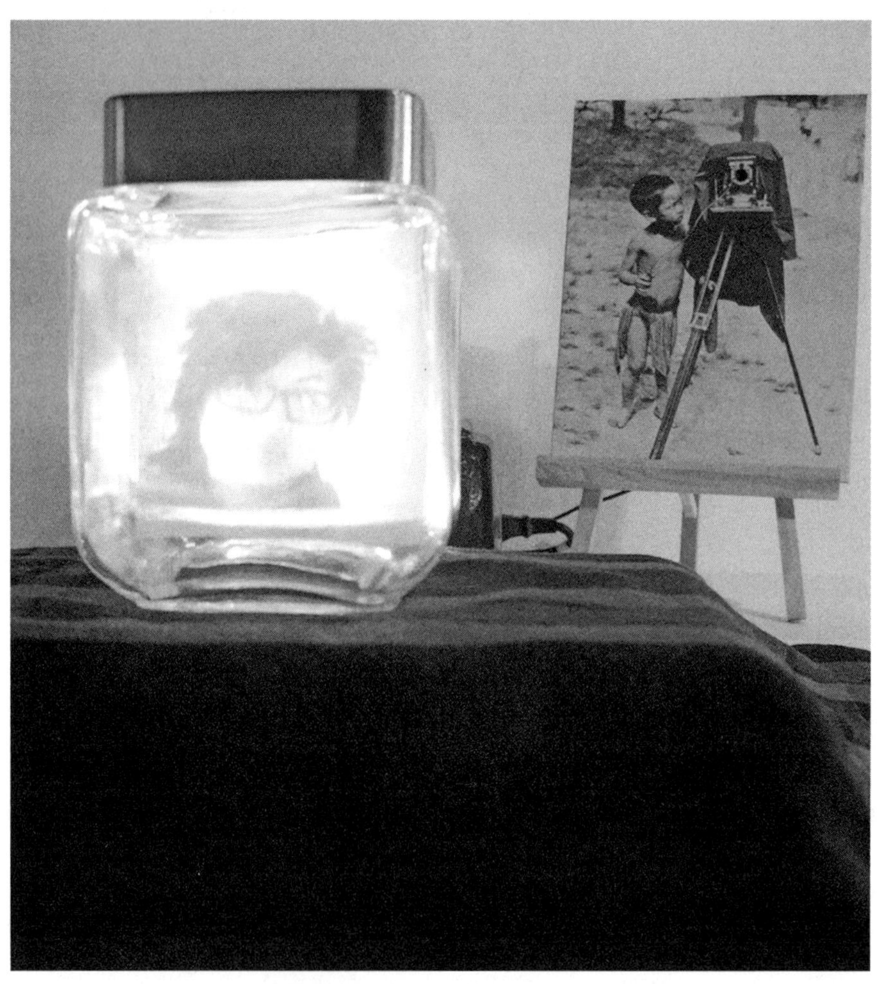

Jo SiMalaya Alcampo, *Paalaala/Remembrance: The Five Stages of Decolonization*, installation, 2009.

Part 1

Historical Flashpoints

This section opens with an image of Toronto-based Jo SiMalaya Alcampo's installation, which grapples with the process of decolonization that the artist has worked through as a queer diasporic Filipina. By combining archival images of Filipinos from the 1904 St. Louis World's Fair (in which Filipinos were presented as "primitive savages" in a reservation for the American public's edification as a way to justify U.S. colonial rule of the Philippines) with a 16mm film loop, sound, and an interactive video projection, Alcampo examines the five stages of decolonization (recovery, mourning, dreaming, commitment, and action) as articulated by the Hawaiian Indigenous scholar Poka Laenui (2009). It can be argued that the entirety of Alcampo's multidisciplinary practice as a community-based organizer, activist, educator, and artist revolves around these five stages.

Similar to Alcampo's work, "Historical Flashpoints" maps out the political stakes of and strategies for pursuing queer Filipino studies as a historical, community-building, and activist project. The essays in this part suggest that in order to fully imagine the political possibilities for queerness to remake our world, we must first locate, re-create, and foreground intimacies, desires, and subjectivities that fall outside of pervasive disciplinary and institutional definitions of community, belonging, and kinship. Other works in this part add to this historical project by foregrounding the valuable labor of queer *pinay* feminists who, since the 1990s, have galvanized each other and the larger community around various queer of color and Indigenous causes. We offer these archives as flashpoints into the rich and often complex networks of queer of color feminisms that have existed in Toronto. As illuminating case studies, they offer a corrective to the absence of queer Filipinos/as in contemporary Filipino Canadian and queer Canadian histories. They also illustrate the power of *pinay* feminists to build solidarity around issues of racism, sexism, and Indigenous rights across and within the city.

In Search of Filipinx Queer Histories in Canada

Roland Sintos Coloma

Where are our histories? Where are the Filipinx and the queers?[1] Where are the histories of Filipinx queers in Canada? As a student of history and cultural studies, I search the past for the lived experiences and embodied perspectives of Filipinx lesbians, gays, bisexuals, and transgender people in Canada in order to understand our histories in the present. I search for our histories—in the plural sense—to avoid replicating and reinforcing "the danger of a single story"[2] that would putatively unveil the reality of Filipinx queers in Canada. Instead I look for different stories to document and convey the unflappable joy and intense pain, the fierce resilience and utter difficulty of being minoritized in Canada in terms of one's race, gender, sexuality, class, dis/ability, language, and citizenship status.

In this chapter, I propose three different ways of searching for Filipinx queer histories in Canada. The first approach focuses on the search for presence, especially in the archives for historical sources and validation. The second approach offers fantasy as a way of giving history to those whose existence in the past is presumed, but whose lives, experiences, and perspectives are not documented, stored, and preserved. The third approach accounts for what is beyond the normative frames of our historical documentation and analysis. These three approaches provide ways to tell truths, give histories, and exceed the norms in queer Filipinx Canadian matters.

For my search, I begin in the archives. The historian Carolyn Steedman states that the term "archive" derives from the Greek word "*arkhe*, as a place where things begin, where power originates, its workings inextricably bound up with the authority of beginnings and starting points."[3] As sites of knowledge and ideological construction, the archives are mainly conceptualized as material repositories for the elites, the victors, those whose histories are memorialized and monumentalized. Archives have been conventionally composed of artifacts, such as official reports, government records, maps, print media, and personal diaries and letters. They have also included new and alternative sources, such as photographs and artwork, performances and memories, fantasies and imaginations, and even feelings and fictionalized accounts. In light of analytical and methodological challenges from social, critical, and "post"-oriented historians that have called into question master narratives, universal foundations, causality, teleology, and authoritative truths, scholars have cast doubt on the archives and the evidentiary and interpretive certainty derived from them.[4]

There is no single, definitive description and meaning for the archive. For the historian-philosopher Michel Foucault, the archive is "the law of what can be said, the system that governs the appearance of statements as unique events . . . [and that] defines at the outset the system of its enunciability . . . [and] the system of its functioning."[5] The historian Antoinette Burton (2006) points out the "limits and possibilities of the archive as a site of knowledge production, an arbiter of truth, and a mechanism for shaping the narratives of history."[6] The anthropologist Ann Laura Stoler argues for an interpretive and methodological move from archive-as-source to archive-as-subject. She considers "archives not as sites of knowledge retrieval but . . . as monuments of states as well as sites of state ethnography."[7] In her engagement with the archive, the literary critic Gayatri Chakravorty Spivak reads against the grain not only to glean the voices of the subaltern, but also to trace the epistemic violence enacted in the past and its manifestation in the present.[8] For the philosopher Jacques Derrida, "the question of the archive is not a question of the past. . . . It is a question of the future, the question of the future itself, the question of a response, of a promise and of a responsibility for tomorrow. The archive: if we want to know what that will have meant, we will only know in times to come."[9]

The critical statements above evidence that the archive is not the sole domain of historians. Scholars from various academic disciplines have discussed the archive as a source of data, as a subject to be investigated, and as a site of epistemic violence. They have provided different ways of reading archival contents, forms, and meanings, and they have tracked the law and system of enunciability of what can be said and not-said as well as the limits and possibilities of the archives. Amidst these multiple, competing, and even contradictory interpretations of the archives, what ought we to do? Should we disregard and abandon the archives for their flaws and bias, for their partiality and incompleteness? Or should we engage the archives, mindful of their constraints and parameters, not only to construct, narrate, and disseminate history, but also to deconstruct it?[10] Towards the latter move of deconstructing archives in my search for Filipinx queer histories in Canada, I look for presence, mobilize fantasy, and explore what's beyond the normative.

Presence as Truth-Telling

My search for Filipinx queer histories in Canada began in 2008 when I moved from the U.S. midwestern state of Ohio to Canada and joined the faculty of the University of Toronto. As a researcher of race, gender, sexuality, and diaspora, my interest in Filipinx queer histories was and continues to be driven by professional and personal motivations in pursuit of community, belonging, resistance, and affirmation. In Toronto, I joined and learned from a critical mass of queer scholars of color who are pushing the boundaries of intellectual, cultural, and political work. This amazing cadre of scholars includes Jennifer Jihye Chun, Ju Hui Judy Han, and Rinaldo Walcott at the University of Toronto; Patrick Alcedo, Jin Hariwatorn, Mona Oikawa, and Amar Wahab at York University; and Robert Diaz and Richard Fung at OCAD University (Ontario College of Art and Design University).[11] It was in Richard Fung's work that I first encountered the "historical presence" of a queer Filipina in Canada.

A renowned video artist and cultural theorist, Fung released *Orientations* in 1986, his first video documentary, to showcase the lives and perspectives of fourteen lesbians and gay men of Asian descent in Toronto.[12] As one of the earliest videos to capture Asian Canadian lesbian and gay images and voices, *Orientations* features a Filipina named Sylvia. A student at the University of Toronto, Sylvia shares her quest for a queer community in the city:

> I didn't even know there was community! I had no idea. I didn't even know. I thought the whole community was St. Charles's Tavern and that didn't look so good. . . . I was having a rough time in school. I finally decided it's sort of now or never. And so one Friday night, I decided I'd go to one of the meetings at school, at U of T [University of Toronto]. The gays and lesbians at U of T, they hold meetings every Friday night.[13]

From the documentary, it was not entirely clear what kind of queer community Sylvia was looking for. The gay bars in the city were male-oriented, and the gay and lesbian student group at the university was predominantly white. She was having "a rough time" and seeking solace in these spaces. Was she searching for a lesbian-centered space, a space for racialized minorities, or a home that would wholly embrace her race, gender, and sexuality as a Filipina lesbian?

For lesbian, gay, bisexual, and transgender Filipinx in Canada, looking for and finding a "home" where they feel accepted is crucial to their survival and well-being. However, home—within the heteronormative Filipinx community or within the white LGBT community—is not always a welcoming and nurturing place for Filipinx queers. In 1996 the group Gay Asians Toronto published an oral history book entitled *Celebrasians: Shared Lives*. In this collection, a Filipino named Engelbert Gayagoy discloses the abuse he experienced at home:

> Both my parents know of my sexuality. My father found out in high school because I was hanging around too many girls. His co-worker's son is on the football team. I wouldn't play sports. . . . My father would always beat me up. . . . My father would always make fun of me, even in front of other people. Like when we had visitors at home. "My son is so gay, he should be a man." . . . If we're all eating, in front of my brother and sister, he would say, "You know, your brother is such a fag."[14]

For Engelbert, being at home with his family resulted in physical and emotional violence perpetrated by his homophobic father. Because of his father's brutality, he reveals, "I didn't know how a man loved. I didn't know how to be loved by a man."[15]

For Nitto Marquez, who immigrated to Canada in 1978, he views growing up being Asian and gay as "a double whammy" due to his interlocking racial and sexual minority subjectivities. In a 1999 interview published in the *Observer* newspaper in Sarnia, Ontario, he says, "Growing up was painful for me because I was always different. . . . People there would either ignore you as if you didn't exist or they looked at you as an exotic sexual plaything." His parents accepted him as being gay, but he did not feel at home in predominantly white gay spaces. In these spaces, he was either ignored for not embodying the idealized white male physique, or exoticized to fulfill the orientalized fantasy of white gay male fetishes. Hence, race, gender, and sexuality function as an intersecting index that variably positions Filipinx queers as being attractive or not attractive under the terms of white gazes and desires. For Nitto, being home in mainstream gay communities means being relegated to "an exotic sexual plaything."

My search for the historical presence of Filipinx queers in Canada functions as a mode of "truth-telling" about our lives and experiences. In his published lectures on *Wrong-Doing, Truth-Telling: The Function of Avowal in Justice*, Michel Foucault (2014) considers truth-telling as "a social practice," as "a weapon in relationships between individuals," and as "a means of modifying relations of power among those who speak."[16] It establishes one's presence in a particular time and place, one's position and perspective on a specific event or phenomenon, and one's relationship with other individuals, groups, and institutions. In Foucault's analysis, truth-telling is linked to wrongdoing and avowal. Although Canada has multicultural policies that aim to support the heritage worldviews, cultures, and languages of immigrants and racialized minorities and has antidiscrimination policies related to race, sex, sexual orientation, and other markers of difference based on human rights law, queers and more specifically queers of color continue to occupy a stigmatized second-class status.[17]

Scattered across various archives and publications are the presences and truth-tellings of Filipinx queers in Canada. My search in Toronto generated the following details. In the Canadian Lesbian and Gay Archives, a 1993 flyer for a "Lesbian Filipina Group"[18] that met monthly in downtown's 519 Church Street Community Centre includes the tagline *"Sama ka na,"* which means "Join us" in the Filipino or Tagalog language. In 1997 the Asian lesbian-gay-bisexual Peer Support Services, which offered Filipino or Tagalog language services, distributed a pamphlet including the phrase *"Lingkod Taguyod Sa Mga Asyanong Makakabaro,"* meaning "Services for Asians like us." In 2000 an international Queer Pinay Meeting was held at the 519 Church Street Centre, which drew participants throughout Canada and the United States. In 2005 the Silayan Community Centre held a "Barong at Saya" dinner and dance event, which was considered a "breakthrough for a fund-raising for the benefit of the Filipino-Canadians' lesbian, gay, bisexual, and transgender (LGBT) group." In that same year, a transgender Filipinx named Lorraine Tagalog, alongside Adel Abdulrahim, "filed a civil action suing the Toronto Police Services Board, a police officer, and a donut shop for 'assault and battery' and 'breach of their Charter rights.'" More recently, the legal rights activist Angie Umbac from the Philippines became Pride Toronto's international grand marshall in 2011. These historical traces of Filipinx queer presence in Canadian archives and publications serve as our mode of truth-telling.[19] They are testimonies of truths about Filipinx queer lives and living conditions. They are evidences of our existence; they are imprints of our realities. They function as avowals in justice that challenge and transform our marginalized positions as racialized and sexual minorities in Canada.

These historical artifacts offer glimpses into the presence of Filipinx queers in Canada. While these glimpses may not cohere into a single comprehensive narrative, they invoke various truths about the lives and realities of Filipinx Canadian queers. The search for historical presence, for images and voices in the past, for visibility is very important. As Richard Fung indicates, "From the earliest articulation of the Asian gay and lesbian movements, a principal concern has been visibility."[20] The same yearning for visibility animated a Toronto-based initiative to establish a scholarly, political, artistic, and community presence for Filipinx in Canada. The first national academic symposium on Filipinx in Canada, entitled "Disturbing Invisibility," was convened at the University of Toronto in 2009, and presentations from that symposium constituted the majority of what became a book of the same title published by the University of Toronto Press.[21] With a focus on my search for Filipinx in mainstream Canadian history, my symposium presentation and book chapter argue that "the sense of abjection, experienced by Filipinos in reading for self-representation in history textbooks, produces an ardent desire to redress their virtual absence. . . . Filipinos as abject beings cannot *not* want to be integrated in historical narrations, for the move from invisibility to visibility heralds their arrival as legitimate subjects of history who belong in the nation-state."[22] The same argument can certainly be made for LGBTQ Filipinx Canadians.

Fantasy as Giving History

In my search for Filipinx queer presence in the Canadian archives, I found historical materials on other Asian Canadian LGBT events and organizations. In 1988 a conference on "Unity Among Asians" was convened by Gay Asians Toronto and Khush, a South Asian gay and lesbian group, with a goal of strengthening North American Asian gay and lesbian communities. Ten years later, an event called "AmalgamAsian" took place at Victoria College in the University of Toronto that aimed to celebrate queer East and Southeast Asian identities. Other events, including Desh Pardesh,[23] and community groups, such as Asian Lesbians of Toronto and Asian Community AIDS Services, helped create an active, engaged, and vibrant Asian Canadian queer scene in Toronto. I wonder how queer Filipinx participated and were involved in these activities and organizations. Where are the queer Filipinx in Asian Canadian and other racialized minority LGBT events and groups?

Within the histories of Filipinx communities in Canada, where are our lesbian, gay, bisexual, and transgender *kababayan* or fellow LGBT Filipinx? When we document and examine the histories of Filipinx who migrated to Canada in the 1950s, '60s, and '70s as nurses, doctors, accountants, engineers, teachers, and factory workers, what were the experiences of those who were LGBT? For those who came in the 1980s and '90s through family sponsorship or temporary foreign worker policies, such as the Live-In Caregiver Program, how were the experiences of Filipinx LGBTs similar to and different from those who had migrated in previous decades? In Toronto community-based organizations, such as the Carlos Bulosan Theatre, Kapisanan Philippine Centre for Arts and Culture, Filipino Centre Toronto, and Philippine Women Centre, how did LGBT Filipinx help establish and develop these institutions?

When I read Filipinx Canadian newspapers and other media outlets, such as *The Philippine Reporter*, which celebrated its 25th anniversary in 2014, I wonder about LGBT Filipinx who are part of community, sociocultural, alumni, and even religious organizations, who are in photographs with families and friends in various events, yet our identities as sexual minorities are not mentioned. LGBT Filipinx in Canada are quite diverse: we are youth and seniors; professionals and blue-collar workers; located in urban, suburban, and rural areas; some are comfortably out, while others are more private about our nonnormative sexual orientations and gender identities; we are single or in relationships; living alone, with families, or with friends; living with HIV and AIDS; involved in Filipinx communities or not; involved in LGBTQ communities or not; recent immigrants and citizens, with visas or undocumented; those who prefer to identify as *bakla* or *tomboy*; and transgender individuals who transition fully or partially. The list can go on.

When queer Filipinx are not explicitly marked or identified in these events, organizations, images, and spaces, yet we presume or know that they were or are there, I suggest that we employ fantasy in the search for Filipinx LGBT histories in Canada. Fantasy occupies the realm of the imagination, the creative, the possible and the impossible, reflecting both conscious and unconscious desires and wishes. Fantasy, especially when we are not present in the archives but exist in the past, becomes a mode of writing ourselves into history. In *The Fantasy of Feminist History*, Joan Scott employs the concept of "fantasy echo" which "enables individuals and groups to give themselves histories. . . . Writing oneself into the story being staged thus becomes a way of writing oneself into history."[24] It is an analytical tool that facilitates the reading of "historical materials in their specificity and particularity. It does not presume to know the substance of identity, the resonance of its appeal, or the transformations it has undergone. It presumes only that where there is evidence of what seems enduring and unchanging identity, there is a history that needs to be explored."[25] Fantasy echo is, therefore, an imagined repetition that forges a continued identity and brings together the past and present.

When we fantasize about the realities, experiences, and lived conditions of Filipinx queers in Canada, especially when we are not documented and present in the archives, yet we know of our existence in the past, I wonder about the epistemological reference points we use to conjure our histories. Do we primarily mobilize our racialized queer understandings in relation to being LGBT in the Philippines, imbued as these are with certain ideas and representations regarding physical appearance, behavior, sexual preferences, job options, and status in life, family, and society? Or do we account for more Western conceptualizations of being LGBT in the context of Canada, embedded in ideas and representations regarding individualism, out-ness, freedom and rights, putatively unshackled from the confines of family, religion, or government? How do we account for the ways in which sexual orientations and gender identities, desires and needs, shift across time and space? In other words, how does being lesbian, gay, bisexual, transgender, queer, being *bakla, tomboy, silahis,* or *bayot*, remain the same or shift in the context of the diaspora?[26]

My search for Filipinx queer histories, therefore, can also be achieved through fantasy that gives history to those who may not be present in the archives, yet exist in the past. Joan Scott's concept of fantasy echo is particularly useful since it offers an imagined repetition or sameness, yet with a difference: "Echoes are delayed returns of sound; they are incomplete reproductions, usually giving back only the final fragments of a phrase. An echo spans large gaps of space and time, but it also creates gaps of meaning and intelligibility. . . . Repetition constitutes alteration. It is thus that echo undermines the notion of enduring sameness that often attaches to identity."[27] In other words, history, through fantasy echo, is simultaneously a projection and an interpretation. It projects similarities, multiple copies, and reproductions of what seems to be the same. Yet the interpretation depends on one's epistemological reference points that enable resonances and distortions to be heard. Filipinx Canadian queer lives and conditions—and subsequently, our histories—are not going to be the same as LGBTs in the Philippines or as mainstream white LGBTs in Canada. However, they offer new frames and possibilities for what it might mean to be queers of color in the diaspora.

Beyond the Normative

Queer of color critique and queer diaspora critique provide important theoretical, empirical, and political contributions and interventions in studies of race, gender, sexuality, class, nation, and diaspora. While this analytical framework has been primarily identified with scholars in the United States, I would like to situate my approach in a particularly Canadian genealogy as I continue my search for Filipinx queer histories in Canada.

In this regard, Richard Fung figures as a critical founder of what might be considered queer of color critique in Canada, with his essay "Looking for My Penis," which is one of the most widely anthologized writings on Asian Canadian queer studies and continues to be intellectually and politically salient. Mona Oikawa and Sharon Fernandez wrote polemical and creative pieces in the 1990s about lesbians of color. Andil Gosine and Amar Wahab have taken diasporic and transnational approaches in tracing the cultural politics of racialized and sexual minorities in Canada and beyond. Critiquing the limits of race/ethnic studies that do not account for questions of sexualities, Rinaldo Walcott writes:

> Black diaspora queers live in a borderless, large world of shared identifications and imagined historical relations produced through a range of fluid cultural artifacts . . . , not to mention sex and its dangerously pleasurable fluids. In fact, black

diaspora queers have been interrupting and arresting the black studies project to produce a bevy of identifications, which confound and complicate local, national, and transnational desires, hopes, and disappointments of the post–Civil Rights and post–Black Power era.[28]

When I was a faculty member at the University of Toronto, I immersed myself in this Canadian-based genealogy and was fortunate to get to know, learn from, and work with leading queer of color theorists and researchers in Canada.

An emerging body of work from faculty members and graduate students of Filipino descent is contributing to the further development and proliferation of queer of color critique in Canada. Robert Diaz has not only brought queer artists, community members, and scholars together for this collection, he is also working on a book project entitled *The Ruse of Visibility: Queer Filipinos/as and Canadian Multiculturalisms* which documents and examines the experiences of transgender, lesbian, and gay Filipinx in Canada. J.P. Catungal completed a Ph.D. thesis in geography at the University of Toronto in 2013 on HIV/AIDS service organizations working with racialized minority communities. A recipient of the prestigious Governor General's Gold Medal, he became a Killam postdoctoral fellow at the University of British Columbia (UBC) and now holds a tenure-track, full-time instructor position in the UBC Institute of Gender, Race, Sexuality, and Social Justice. Doctoral students, such as the University of Toronto's Fritz Luther Pino and Marissa Largo and UBC's May Farrales, are pursuing research on gay elderlies, visual artists, and youth education and sexualities, respectively. Their projects have received funding support, including competitive scholarships from the Social Sciences and Humanities Research Council.

Queer of color critique foregrounds the lived experiences and embodied perspectives of racialized sexual minorities in order to contest discursive, structural, and affective relations and dynamics that marginalize LGBT minorities. It also challenges normative ontologies and epistemologies that produce heterocentric conditions and practices, thereby limiting, if not altogether eliminating, other alternative potentials for difference. My search for Filipinx queer histories takes a beyond-normative direction by considering what has been normalized and considered common sense even in fields that one considers "home"—in this case, Filipinx Canadian studies.

Putting queer of color critique to work while reflecting on the national symposium on Filipinx Canadian studies in 2009 and the subsequent edited volume on *Filipinos in Canada: Disturbing Invisibility* published in 2012, I found myself troubled by and complicit to the hegemonic heteronormativity of Filipinx Canadian intellectual, political, and community work. Although several editors and contributors in the national symposium and edited book identify as queer or part of the LGBT community, including myself, I contend that the heteronormative nuclear family functions as the dominant ontological and epistemic paradigm in Filipinx Canadian studies. In other words, the heteronormative nuclear family serves as the basic unit of analysis and the central organizing principle in this field. For instance, the family supplies the main rationale for labor migration outside of the Philippines (in order to provide financial support and security to the family) and for reunification in Canada (in order to keep the family together and support each other). The family also becomes the justification for an employment migration program that has brought thousands of Filipinx to Canada. The Live-In Caregiver Program (LCP) was established in order to support middle- and upper-class families in Canada as adults balance work and care for their family members, including children and elderly parents. The LCP also makes available the opportunity for Filipinx nannies and domestics to become permanent residents and citizens of Canada and facilitates the migration of spouses and children and the re-consolidation of Filipinx families in the diaspora.

Questions of race, gender, class, labor, citizenship, and transnationalism were critically examined during the national symposium and in the edited book *Disturbing Invisibility*. Yet the power of hegemonic heteronormativity, especially the trope of the family, governed what became intelligible, normal, and commonsensical in our analysis. We unfortunately failed to consider the different experiences of LGBT Filipinx in the migration and integration process, in the labor market and employment options, in family relations and reunifications, and in access to opportunities and resources in the Philippines and in Canada. Hence, we can ask: what other units of analysis or organizing principles might we use to examine and understand Filipinx Canadian lives in our diversity, multiplicity, and intersections? And if we were to keep the family as an analytical trope, how might we reconfigure and recalibrate it in order to account for various relations and arrangements which may be defined beyond blood or marriage? In many ways, the conference and this edited book on *Diasporic Intimacies: Queer Filipinos and Canadian*

Imaginaries, led by Robert Diaz and his co-organizers and coeditors, point to the limits of hegemonic heteronormativity, even in critical projects like Filipinx Canadian studies. They offer significant, necessary, and timely interventions that put at the center queer lives, bodies, realities, and histories.

Centering Filipinx queer matters in historical and contemporary contexts needs to include topics, such as indigeneity, religion, and sex, that were absent in the *Disturbing Invisibility* symposium and edited book. The Toronto-based organizations Kapwa Collective and Ugnayan ng Kabataang Pilipino sa Canada, or Filipino Canadian Youth Alliance (UKPC/FCYA) have taken important leads in generating reflexive discussions and practices not only about indigeneity in the Philippines, but also about settler-Indigenous relations and solidarity in Canada. It is important to note that these Indigenous initiatives are led by queer-identified activists and artists who bring intersectional, comparative, and transnational perspectives to their praxis. Moreover, it is hard to address the connection between Filipino-ness and queer sexualities without dealing with religion and spirituality, even in the diaspora. We need to bear in mind that the Philippines is a predominantly Catholic country, with about 80 percent of its population belonging to the Roman Catholic Church. Although the general population seem to be socially tolerant of LGBT individuals, the government and the Catholic Church in the Philippines have resisted petitions for antidiscrimination laws based on sexual orientation and gender identity, and LGBTs continue to occupy second-class status in their social, economic, and political conditions.[29] How religious beliefs shape the attitudes and behaviors of diasporic Filipinx in Canada, especially in relation to non-normative gender identities and sexual orientations, has not been fully examined.

Lastly, we need to talk about sex. As scholars, activists, artists, and members of Filipinx queer communities, sex—alongside sexual orientations, pleasures and desires, preferences and practices—must be integral in our research, advocacy, productions, and discussions. We must refuse a certain politics of racial/diasporic respectability that constrains and prohibits explicit and public conversations about sex and sexualities. This politics of respectability limits what we say and do not say, what we do and do not do, and how we see and treat each other. It renders taboo much-needed discussions about sexual and reproductive health, about sexually transmitted infections and HIV/AIDS, and about sexual encounters and enjoyment. If so-called respectable mentioning of sex remains within the confines of marriage and procreation, then an overwhelming majority of Filipinx—not just LGBT Filipinx—will be under-informed and even misinformed. Ultimately, the search for beyond the normative serves not only the minoritized group, in this case Filipinx queers, but also the mainstream population that benefits from a more inclusive and transformed sociality.

Conclusion

My search for Filipinx queer histories in Canada is a search for what Michel Foucault calls "limit experiences." These experiences, "instead of being considered central and positively valorized in a society," actually "put into question the very things that were considered ordinarily acceptable."[30] In my search, I have focused on the archives as a primary site for documentary evidence of our lives, experiences, and perspectives. The existing archives offer scattered fragments of our past in the form of pamphlets, posters, video clips, newspaper clippings, and community and organizational publications. While these fragments do not cohere into a structured, comprehensive narrative, they reveal various queer Filipinx presence in Canada. However, not all our activities have been recorded and stored in archives. I presume that queer Filipinx participated in various organizations and events related to race and sexuality. The lack of confirmatory historical sources should not preclude our existence, although it certainly makes writing about it more challenging. To validate our existence regardless of archival materials, I turn to fantasy to creatively imagine our activities and involvement in the past. Fantasy facilitates connections across time and space, and relies on the epistemological references that one employs for these connections.

Whereas the search for presence serves as a mode of telling truths and the use of fantasy as a mode of giving histories, the search for Filipinx queer histories also needs to account for the normative frames that regulate the discursive terrain of our intellectual, political, creative, and community work. For instance, the field of Filipinx Canadian studies is embedded within a hegemonic heteronormative framework, especially in its use of the family as a basic unit of analysis and as an analytical trope. Such normative frames control what can be said or done (as well as what cannot be said or done). Hence, to search beyond the normative challenges us to further disturb the invisibilities in our empirical, creative, and community work.

In our search for Filipinx queer histories in Canada, we need to look for the rich diversity of our lives and experiences, our arrivals and collectivities, our subjectivities and performances. We ought to pay attention to the multiple and intersecting ways in which our race/ethnicity, gender, and sexuality are mediated by and refracted through class, employment, dis/ability, language, religion, migration, and citizenship. While there is no single Filipinx queer story in Canada, our search for our histories—and, essentially, one of the main thrusts of this book—is to chronicle and analyze our hopes and dreams, our narratives of resilience and resistance, and our stakes in our claim of belonging in Canada. It is through the narration of our presences that we both imagine and implant ourselves in the nation.

I end with a poem by Milagros Paredes, then a student at the Ontario Institute for Studies in Education at the University of Toronto, entitled "Coming Home."[31] It was published in 1990 in a special issue on Asian Canadian women in the feminist quarterly *Fireweed*. What is "home" for Filipinx queers in Canada? Why is coming home so important? What might coming home mean, look, and feel like for Filipinx queers in the past, present, and future?

> Coming home to you womon
> is like drinking sweet milk
> from a young coconut
> back home in the late afternoon
>
> With the soft cool sea breeze
> comforting my ocean-sun worn skin
> with the consistent sound of the
> ocean's waves rising and falling
> to kiss the sand
> swelling my body with warm security
> that rocks my soul
>
> Coming home to you womon
> is like wetting my mouth
> with the juices of a young coconut
> on a late afternoon
> by the ocean.

Notes

It has been a pleasure to reconnect with Patrick Alcedo and Robert Diaz in Toronto, especially since we all graduated from the University of California, Riverside, where my intellectual and political consciousness as a queer man of color emerged and developed. Thank you, Robert, for inviting me to return to Toronto, for allowing me to reflect on my search for our histories in Canada, and for our ongoing conversations on race, sexuality, and community.

1. I employ "Filipinx" instead of the conventional term "Filipino" or even "Filipina/o" in order to challenge and disrupt the gendered binaries that mark our lives and subjectivities in the Philippines and the diaspora. "Filipinx" also foregrounds gender-fluidity and transgression that goes beyond normative conceptualizations of identity, embodiment, and performance. It signals the radical possibilities of an/other that refuses facile definitions and compartmentalizations, while simultaneously attending to the colonial, diasporic, and intersectional discourses that constitute it.

2. Chimamanda Adichie, "The Danger of a Single Story," TED Talk, https://www.ted.com/talks/chimamanda_adichie_the_danger_of_a_single_story.

3. Carolyn Steedman, *Dust: The Archive and Cultural History* (New Brunswick, N.J.: Rutgers University Press, 2002), 1.

4. For example, Cook, 2001; Nesmith, 2002; Taylor, 2003.

5. Michel Foucault, *The Archaeology of Knowledge* (1972; New York: Routledge, 2002), 145–46.

6. Antoinette Burton, "Archive Fever, Archive Stories," in *Archive Stories: Facts, Fictions, and the Writing of History*, ed. Antoinette Burton (Durham, N.C.: Duke University Press, 2006), 2.

7. Ann Laura Stoler, "Colonial Archives and the Arts of Governance," *Archival Science* 2 (2002): 90.

8. Gayatri Chakravorty Spivak, "Three Women's Texts and a Critique of Imperialism," *Critical Inquiry* 12 (1985).

9. Jacques Derrida, *Archive Fever: A Freudian Impression* (Chicago: University of Chicago Press, 1998), 36.

10. Alun Munslow, *Deconstructing History* (London: Routledge, 2006).

11. In 2013 Richard Fung received grant funding from the Social Sciences and Humanities Research Council for a project to revisit the interview subjects from his 1986 video *Orientations*. Amar Wahab and I serve as collaborators in the grant. That same year, Takashi Fujitani of the University of Toronto curated "ReOrientations: A Retrospective on the Works of Richard Fung," where I had the opportunity to share in a

roundtable with Rinaldo Walcott and others my nascent ideas on queer of color histories in Canada which informed this essay. I am grateful to Richard, Amar, Tak, and Rinaldo for sharing their wisdom with me regarding the intersections of history, theory, art, and politics.

12. More research needs to be undertaken on Filipinx queer histories in other parts of Canada as well. In 1994, a Filipino gay man started a group for gays and lesbians of color called Diversity in Winnipeg, Manitoba (Warner, 2002: 328). In her book *Pinay on the Prairies* (2013), Glenda Tibe Bonifacio documented and analyzed the experiences of *tomboys* or Filipina lesbians in the provinces of Alberta, Manitoba, and Saskatchewan (123–31). In 2009 Mable Elmore of the New Democratic Party was elected as a member of the Legislative Assembly, representing the Vancouver-Kensington riding in British Columbia. As far as I know, Elmore is the first elected out LGBTQ politician of Filipino descent in Canada. In addition, Pinoy Pride Vancouver was established in 2011, becoming the first LGBTQ Filipinx Canadian group in British Columbia.

13. Richard Fung, *Orientations: Lesbian and Gay Asians*, video, directed by Richard Fung (1986, Toronto).

14. Gay Asians Toronto, *CelebAsians: Shared Lives: An Oral History of Gay Asians* (Toronto, 1996).

15. Gay Asians, *CelebAsians*.

16. Michel Foucault, *Wrong-Doing, Truth-Telling: The Function of Avowal in Justice* (Chicago: University of Chicago Press, 2014), 28.

17. OmiSoore H. Dryden and Suzanne Lenon, *Disrupting Queer Inclusion: Canadian Homonationalisms and the Politics of Belonging* (Vancouver: University of British Columbia Press, 2016).

18. See "Feminist Collectivities, *Tibo* Ethics, and the Call of the Babylan" in this volume.

19. Foucault, *Wrong-Doing, Truth-Telling*.

20. Richard Fung, "Looking for My Penis: The Eroticized Asian in Gay Video Porn," in *How Do I Look? Queer Film and Video*, ed. Bad Object-Choices (Seattle: Bay, 1991), 145–68.

21. Roland Sintos Coloma, "Abject Beings: Filipina/os in Canadian Historical Narrations," in *Filipinos in Canada: Disturbing Invisibility*, ed. Roland Sintos Coloma et al. (Toronto: University of Toronto Press, 2012), 284–304.

22. Coloma, "Abject Beings," 299–300.

23. Sharon Fernandez, "More Than Just an Arts Festival: Communities, Resistance, and the Story of Desh Pardesh," *Canadian Journal of Communication* 31 (2006): 17–34.

24. Joan Scott, *The Fantasy of Feminist History* (Durham, N.C.: Duke University Press, 2011), 51.

25. Scott, *Feminist History*, 67.

26. Martin F. Manalansan, *Global Divas: Filipino Gay Men in the Diaspora* (Durham, N.C.: Duke University Press, 2003).

27. Scott, *Feminist History*, 52.

28. Rinaldo Walcott, "Outside in Black Studies: Reading from a Queer Place in the Diaspora," in *Black Queer Studies: A Critical Anthology*, ed. E. Patrick Johnson and Mae G. Henderson (Durham, N.C.: Duke University Press, 2005), 92.

29. Roland Coloma, "*Ladlad* and Parrhesiastic Pedagogy: Unfurling LGBT Politics and Education in the Global South," *Curriculum Inquiry* 43 (2013): 483–511.

30. Foucault, *Wrong-Doing, Truth-Telling*, 238.

31. Milagros Parades, "Coming Home," *Fireweed: A Feminist Quarterly* 30 (1990): 56.

Bibliography

Adichie, Chimamanda. "The Danger of a Single Story." Video. https://www.ted.com/talks/chimamanda_adichie_the_danger_of_a_single_story.

Burton, Antoinette. "Archive Fever, Archive Stories." In *Archive Stories: Facts, Fictions, and the Writing of History*, edited by Antoinette Burton. Durham, N.C.: Duke University Press, 2006.

Coloma, Roland Sintos. "Abject Beings: Filipina/os in Canadian Historical Narrations." In *Filipinos in Canada: Disturbing Invisibility*, edited by Roland Sintos Coloma, Bonnie McElhinny, Ethel Tungohan, John Paul C. Catungal, and Lisa M. Davidson, 284–304. Toronto: University of Toronto Press, 2012.

———. "*Ladlad* and Parrhesiastic Pedagogy: Unfurling LGBT Politics and Education in the Global South." *Curriculum Inquiry* 43 (2013): 483–511.

Coloma, Roland Sintos, Bonnie McElhinny, Ethel Tungohan, John Paul C. Catungal, and Lisa M. Davidson, eds. *Filipinos in Canada: Disturbing Invisibility*. Toronto: University of Toronto Press, 2012.

Cook, Terry. "Fashionable Nonsense or Professional Rebirth: Postmodernism and the Practice of Archives." *Archivaria* 51 (2001): 14–35.

Derrida, Jacques. *Archive Fever: A Freudian Impression*. Chicago: University of Chicago Press, 1998.

Dryden, OmiSoore H., and Suzanne Lenon, eds. *Disrupting Queer Inclusion: Canadian Homonationalisms and the Politics of Belonging*. Vancouver: University of British Columbia Press, 2016.

Fernandez, Sharon. "More Than Just an Arts Festival: Communities, Resistance, and the Story of Desh Pardesh." *Canadian Journal of Communication* 31 (2006): 17–34.

Foucault, Michel. *The Archaeology of Knowledge*. New York: Routledge, 2002.

———. *Wrong-Doing, Truth-Telling: The Function of Avowal in Justice*. Chicago: University of Chicago Press, 2014.

Fung, Richard, "Looking for My Penis: The Eroticized Asian in Gay Video Porn." In *How Do I Look? Queer Film and Video*, edited by Bad Object-Choices, 145–68. Seattle: Bay, 1991.

———. *Orientations: Lesbian and Gay Asians*. Directed and produced by Fung. Video. 1986.

Gay Asians Toronto. *CelebAsians: Shared Lives: An Oral History of Gay Asians*. Toronto, 1996.

Manalansan, Martin F. *Global Divas: Filipino Gay Men in the Diaspora*. Durham, N.C.: Duke University Press, 2003.

Munslow, Alun. *Deconstructing History*. 2nd ed. London: Routledge, 2006.

Nesmith, Tom. "Seeing Archives: Postmodernism and the Changing Intellectual Place of Archives." *American Archivist* 65 (2002): 24–41.

Paredes, Milagros. "Coming Home." *Fireweed* 30 (1990): 56.

Scott, Joan W. *The Fantasy of Feminist History*. Durham, N.C.: Duke University Press, 2011.

Spivak, Gayatri Chakravorty. "Three Women's Texts and a Critique of Imperialism." *Critical Inquiry* 12 (1985): 235–61.

Steedman, Carolyn. *Dust: The Archive and Cultural History*. New Brunswick, N.J.: Rutgers University Press, 2002.

Stoler, Ann Laura. "Colonial Archives and the Arts of Governance." *Archival Science* 2 (2002): 87–109.

Taylor, Diana. *The Archive and the Repertoire: Performing Cultural Memory in the Americas*. Durham, N.C.: Duke University Press, 2003.

Walcott, Rinaldo. "Outside in Black Studies: Reading from a Queer Place in the Diaspora." In *Black Queer Studies: A Critical Anthology*, edited by E. Patrick Johnson and Mae G. Henderson, 90–105. Durham, N.C.: Duke University Press, 2005.

Warner, Tom. *Never Going Back: A History of Queer Activism in Canada*. Toronto: University of Toronto Press, 2002.

Toward Queer(er) Futures
Proliferating the "Sexual" in Filipinx Canadian Sexuality Studies

John Paul Catungal

Charting Itineraries: A Belated Response and Personal Story

This chapter is, partially, an act of self-reflection on the sexual politics that underpins my previous work. In 2012 my coedited book *Filipinos in Canada: Disturbing Invisibility* was released by the University of Toronto Press. The book came out of the "Spectres of Invisibility: Filipina/o Lives in Canada" conference, which was held at the University of Toronto in 2009. The conference and the book brought together academic and community scholars to discuss the state of Filipinx-Canadian studies and to create space for theorizing Filipinx lives in Canada. My contribution to both the conference and the book was an analysis of media accounts of the killing of four Filipino youths between 2003 and 2008. One of the points I made in the chapter was that sensationalistic accounts of the killing of Filipino youth, with their focus on broken bones and bloody bodies, tend to dislocate youth from the social worlds within which they lived, and that one way that Filipino and allied activists contested this individualization and pathologization was by literally placing these killed Filipino youths in the contexts of their families, schools, and communities. In my chapter, I highlighted the fact that activists actively named the racism of immigration and labor policies, including the forced separation of families, as central to the production of pathologized Filipino youth.

In the conference, Jeffrey Aguinaldo served as the respondent to the set of papers on Filipino youth of which I was part. He reprised this role in the book through a published commentary that closes off the section "Youth Spaces and Subjectivities." His main critique of my work in this commentary reads:

> My question to Catungal is this: Is there room for a queer anal-
> ysis? The "'divided' family" for which he seeks unification reads
> vaguely heterosexual, if only because the immigration policies
> he challenges are typically heteronormative. It seems that a rad-
> ical Filipina/o critique of Canadian immigration policies solely
> for their racist effects leaves standing the heterosexual family
> as the presumed norm. This necessarily ignores other forms of
> familial configurations . . .[1]

I think this is the first time in my life that I've been told to be (even)
more queer. I puzzled over this challenge for some time. Some six years
since the conference, I think I finally understand Aguinaldo's challenge, and this chapter is my own way of thinking about a queer(er)
future for Filipinx-Canadian studies. His incitement to be more queer
is an invitation to think about what kinds of taken-for-granted norms—
about intimacies, desires, social lives, and social forms—are called up
and performed when a category like "family" is invoked. What Aguinaldo is asking for is a strident refusal to take as given the categories of
social life that we invest in in our politics and activism.

The utility of queer theorizing for the purpose of thinking about categories like "family" can be found in its insistence on destabilizing the
social categories that we make use of in our political and academic
work. Cathy Cohen wrote over fifteen years ago:

> If there is any truly radical potential to be found in the idea of
> queerness and the practice of queer politics, it would seem to
> be located in its ability to create a space in opposition to domi-
> nant norms, a space where transformational political work can
> begin.[2]

Cohen's queer politics is not about rescuing from otherness and bringing into normalcy the categories of "lesbian," "gay," "bisexual," or
"trans," but rather unpacking and politicizing the very idea of "normal." Refusing the simple equation of gay with excluded or radical and
of heterosexual with normative or acceptable, she argues very con-
vincingly that some forms of heterosexuality can be queer if they do
not conform to social norms about proper intimacy. She gives, as one
example, the classed and racialized figure of the "welfare queen" whose
form of heterosexual, often single, motherhood has been so passion-
ately demonized in public discourse. In other words, the promise of

queer politics can be found not in identitarianism, but in the necessarily cynical questioning of normalcy. In this way, queer comes to exceed LGBT, even while the former remains an important, if contingent, part of the latter. Instead, queer analysis takes as its object of critique the normalization of certain forms of intimacy, which, in some contexts, includes homonormative and homonationalist forms of gay and lesbian relationships.

Mobilizing and building on this understanding of "queer," this chapter hazards a vision for the intellectual and political future of studies of Filipinx-Canadian sexualities, taking aim particularly at the dangers posed by possible alignments with heteronormative and homonationalist politics. Taking seriously José Esteban Muñoz's injunction that "the future is queerness's domain,"[3] I sketch out some principles that I consider necessary for a queer(er) Filipinx-Canadian studies. Such a project demands an understanding of queerness as performative, as "not simply a being but a doing for and toward the future."[4] I argue that bringing a queer(er) Filipinx-Canadian studies into fruition demands actively orienting ourselves in constant agonism with already available and publicly circulating discourses of politics, embodiment, and knowledge. To do so, we must be cognizant of our genealogical roots and political debts to our forebears in critical, especially feminist, Filipinx-Canadian studies and of our own enrollment and participation in the normalization of particular discourses of race, gender, sexuality, class, and nation.

Recuperative Rereading as Queer Method

In marking the advent of queer Filipinx-Canadian studies, it is tempting to speak of a scholarly "breaking away" from, and even disavowal of, already existing modes of scholarship that do not meet our needs or reflect our politics. This is an approach to the history of knowledge production as a linear evolution, characterized by more or less distinct "waves" of scholarship. I argue that a queer(er) Filipinx-Canadian studies must resist such an approach and remain keenly aware of and acknowledge our debts to so-called older strands of knowledge, particularly those that engage in what I call "proto-queer" critiques. If queer theorizing is the scholarly-political project of questioning the production and politics of normalcy, then our project is to build on already existing critiques of normalcy that are on offer, at the very least, from feminist approaches to Filipinx-Canadian studies.

At this point, it is worth reiterating, following Cohen, that queer politics and theorizing owe a great deal to feminisms, just as queer of color critiques owe much to woman-of-color feminisms.[5] In huge part, this is because of figures who not only straddle both of these fields, but in fact embody them simultaneously. Lesbian and queer women of color including, among others, the Combahee River Collective, Audre Lorde, Cherrie Moraga, and Barbara Smith, demanded the bridging of these projects in a way that arguably refuses the distinctions between them. Similarly, queer Filipinx-Canadian studies is indebted to feminist knowledge productions about Filipinx Canadian lives.[6] Feminist analyses from the community (e.g., the Philippine Women Centre and Migrante) and from the academy (e.g., Abigail Bakan and Daiva Stasiulis, Geraldine Pratt, Glenda Bonifacio, Ethel Tungohan, and many others) offer openings for a queer Filipinx Canadian studies in the interstices and limits of their interventions.

It would be fair to say that most of these scholars have not adequately taken, as the central object of their analysis, the normalization of heterosexuality that, in fact, grounds the processes of gendering that they critique in their work (Bonifacio does have a small section on sexuality). Despite this, I argue that we find in these works what might be called "proto-queer politics": those glimpses of latent anti-normative critique that may not intentionally be called "queer." A recuperative rereading of these works—one that pays close attention to these critiques of sexual normalcy—is a queer scholarly method that deliberately and sometimes generously limns these works for opportunities to bring the sexual and the intimate into the fold of analysis.

A couple of examples might be illustrative of this recuperative method of queer rereading. Space constraints necessitate that these examples are necessarily selective and are not meant to be representative of the entirety of the Filipinx Canadian studies literature as it currently exists. Significantly, both examples examine the experiences of Filipina women who have come to Canada through the Live-In Caregiver Program. I argue that these works can be read productively as offering critiques of sexual normalcy, despite the fact that they do not necessarily proceed from explicitly queer political or theoretical frameworks. Some analytical work on the part of the reader is necessary to recuperate queer possibilities through queer rereadings of these works. This entails reading between the lines, bringing to the foreground issues that may be mentioned but are not necessarily centralized, and highlighting how gender analysis, by effect, opens up scrutiny of the "sexual" and the intimate.

In her works analyzing the social construction of the Filipina domestic worker in Canada, Geraldine Pratt points to the ways that moralizing discourses of "bad mother" and "husband stealer" attach to the bodies of Filipinas through pronouncements by employers, employment agents, government officials, and fellow members of the Filipinx community. These discourses function to construct Filipinas as threats to various normative gendered and sexual orders that Filipinas not only fail to meet, but apparently actively transgress. As racist and sexist social constructions of failed femininity, these discourses reify the "proper" place of women in heterosexual relationships and family forms and fix an idea of proper Filipina-ness in the idealized heteronormatively laden figures of mother and wife.

These figurations of Filipina femininity rely on the social construction of gender norms in the assumed context of heterosexual romance and family. Reading for queerness, it is clear that Pratt's spotlighting of the gendering of the Filipina nanny is also a critique of the nanny's supposedly failed and threatening heterosexuality as a bad mother and husband stealer. In the case of the latter, she is not only constructed as a bad woman but also a bad heterosexual, as she is constructed as a threat to other women's (heterosexual) relationships and happiness. A queer recuperation of this argument exposes the heteronormative foundations of the gendered demonization of the Filipina nanny.

Like Pratt, Ethel Tungohan thinks with the mother as a gendered subject in global Filipinx migration circuits as they touch down in Canada. She examines the ways that Filipinas negotiate normative scripts of proper migrant motherhood. She names both "the private/public dichotomy and nuclear family ideologies" as key to the gendered politics of migrant experiences, noting that female labor migrants with children are caught up in conflicting responsibilities to provide both financial resources, which requires going abroad, and the emotional work of care, which is understood as best done in proximity.[7] Her work argues that, to deal with these conflicts, Filipina labor migrants in Canada engage in practices of hyper-maternalism by taking on the traditionally masculinized role of breadwinner in their transnational families while also engaging in long-distance caregiving and parenting through technology (e.g., Skype). According to one of Tungohan's interviewees, this dual act of caregiving and breadwinning positions her as "both the 'father' and the 'mother.'"[8]

In Tungohan's work, we can dig for some kernels of critique of gender norms under heteropatriarchy. For one, the capacity of the research participant quoted above to understand her embodiment and performance of both fatherhood and motherhood suggests that these subjectivities need not necessarily attach to male and female designated bodies, as the normative heterosexual matrix might assume. Hence, while not self-described as "queer," this critique is, in my mind, readable as a kind of queer performance insofar as it violates the traditional gender division of labor in traditional heterosexual family forms. It thus points to fissures in the rigidity of the nuclear family and its constituent roles. There is, however, a kind of ambivalence in such a queer act. It still relies, discursively, on the "father" and "mother" as necessary figures in familial and parent-child relations. Moreover, while the transnational hyper-maternalism of Tungohan's research participants does upend the idea of the female migrant as a bad mother, it arguably does so by constituting newer idealizations of migrant motherhood against which other migrant women's performances of maternal hetero-femininity might be measured.

As one might have gleaned in my engagement with the above scholarship, part of the work of a queer(er) Filipinx Canadian studies is highlighting the dual latency and importance of sexuality in already existing scholarship. This opens up space for talking about both the existing limitations of current research and possible new directions to which they point. Others have, of course, done similar work in other contexts, which inspires some of the analysis and research directions that I offer here. For example, Brown argues that the popularity of the global care chain concept in analysis of Filipinx labor migration unwittingly fixes the biological mother as the site of care and the source of emotional labor. In such a conceptualization, "the glue that keeps this chain together in a linear fashion is the heterosexualized bodies of both First and Third World women while the fuel for the global dispersal of migratory domestic labor is maternal love."[9] Manalansan further argues that the centrality of the heterosexual married mother in the literature on Filipinx migration circuits produces the perhaps unintended effect of normalizing the nuclear family and heterosexual parenthood:

> The nuclear family is the primary model of the transnational family and . . . heterosexual marriage or heterosexual partnering are [the] only plausible cornerstones of family life, with parenthood gendered in static biological terms and motherhood or maternal love, the province solely of biological (typically married) women with children.[10]

I am in general agreement with Manalansan's arguments, and want to unmap motherhood from biologized hetero-femininity.[11] However, I also want to push the argument further by moving us beyond the heterosexual/non-heterosexual binary. After all, a queer recuperation of Pratt and Tungohan suggests that heterosexual subjects are sometimes *queered* by virtue of their nonnormative, even improper, relationship to idealized heterosexuality. In Pratt's works, the figures of the bad mother and the husband stealer are legible as queer subjects in the same way that Cohen's analysis of the figure of the "welfare queen" renders her heterosexuality queer as it does not map neatly onto normative (classed and racialized) notions of proper heterosexual motherhood. Similarly, Tungohan's fascinating analysis of migrant mothers' messy negotiations of expectations of parental responsibility embraces a performative, as opposed to biologized, understanding of gender and sexuality. This is not to suggest that we need not pay attention to the experiences of lesbian, gay, bisexual, trans (LGBT), and gender-nonconforming Filipinx Canadians. We absolutely must. However, queer(er) approaches to Filipinx Canadian studies must proliferate its objects and subjects of analysis and resist limiting its scope to "LGBT." Doing so reiterates the radical potential of queer politics in terms not of identitarian claims, but of its denaturalization of normalcy.

To be clear, not all works in Filipinx Canadian studies can be read through the lens of "proto-queer politics." It is no accident that Pratt and Tungohan are both explicitly feminist, and thus, unsurprisingly, examine normative ideologies of family and gender roles that have been central issues in much feminist politics and theorizing. That these works contain seeds for proto-queer critique speaks very well to the genealogical and political linkages between feminism and queer theorizing, and indeed arguably to the debts of the latter to the former. This is not to say that feminist analysis is immune from heteronormativity. Indeed, Manalansan points out that "even recent research that purports to sensitively bring gender to the center of migration studies fails to consider how specific normalizing and naturalizing ideas around reproduction, parenting, carework and family formation create discrepant and incomplete understandings of third-world female migrant labor."[12] The work that recuperative queer rereading can do to push these works further is to locate, within them, the seeds of "queer" critique that lay latent, but are nevertheless there for possible further development.

Family, Nation, Indigeneity: Heteronormativities, Homonormativities, Homonationalisms

If queer politics is the project of denaturalizing that which is typically taken to be normal, then a queer(er) Filipinx Canadian studies must be vigilant to our investments in normalcy in activisms and scholarship. Aguinaldo's caution against the unreflexive use of the term "family" is a reminder that we must remain critical of the ways that we create space, if unwittingly, for heteronormativity to suffuse our work. As I noted in the introductory section, "family" is a powerful discourse in part because its warm and fuzzy connotations accrue by virtue of its proximity to heterosexuality. It is thus not surprising that "family" as a category remains central to Filipinx Canadian organizing and activism, particularly given the very real phenomenon of family separation that is, by effect of policy design, a common aspect of Filipinx labor migration to Canada. For instance, the Congress of Progressive Filipino Canadians (CPFC) Declaration, published in 2010 by various Filipino Canadian activist organizations, names "support of families in the process of reunification and/or settlement" as one of several main concerns.

Aguinaldo's critique demands the question: what ideas about family do we refer to when we problematize family separation? This question forces us to contend with the normal family as we understand it, and concomitantly, with the "queer" or abnormal social forms that get constructed as unacceptable. Is it possible to view the separated family as a queer, or non-normal, form of family? As Brown notes, the idea of the separated family as a "problem" emerges partly from an often unspoken investment in the idea of a proper caring mother being one in close proximity to her children and husband. In this spirit, the separated family is rendered abnormal, even in activist circles, because it does not conform to our *spatial* ideas about what family should look like. The opportunity for queer analysis is present here, and it requires that we ask questions about the types of family and ideas about intimacy that we invoke when we problematize family separation. This is not to say that family separation is not a problem, but to ask that we pay attention to our sometimes unspoken investment in particular forms of family.

"Family" is also powerful when it becomes useful for the politics of national recognition.[13] In my ongoing research on Filipinx Canadian performances of diasporic humanitarianism in response to Typhoon Yolanda/Haiyan, I noticed the power of family discourse particularly in media reportage on this "natural" disaster. The story of Romelyn Saneo, a Toronto area caregiver, is one that circulated very publicly after the typhoon.[14] The story celebrates Saneo funding the building of her family home in Bantigue, her hometown, through monthly remittances of about $700. The home that she helped build through transnational financial flows literally ended up saving her family and even other townsfolk, who sought shelter from the ravages of Haiyan/Yolanda in the new, structurally sound, concrete home. Told as a story of a dutiful migrant, mother, wife, and daughter as well as a story of the literal life-saving effects of caregiving work in Canada, the romanticization of the feminized migrant worker in this story is also, at the same time, the romanticization of the heterosexual family and its constituent parts, of the racialized labor regime that Canadian social reproduction requires, and of the labor exportation policy that the Philippine economy and national identity relies on.[15] The romanticization of Saneo's story in the media requires that we pay attention to the articulation between normative ideas of good heterosexuality and femininity and the production of "good" Filipino and Filipino Canadian transnational subjects. A queer(er) Filipinx Canadian studies must thus also attend to the ways that heteronormativity, diaspora, and nationalism are co-constituted, a project whose foundations scholars like Gopinath and Manalansan have laid.

Apart from the heteronormativities and nationalisms that are smuggled into activist and scholarly analysis through the uncritical use of categories like "family," a queer(er) Filipinx Canadian studies must also be cognizant of the effects of homonormativity, homonationalism, and their exclusions on LGBTQ Filipinx Canadians and other queer subjects. Canadian exceptionalism, tinged as it is by nationalist self-congratulation on multiculturalism and gay marriage, is part of the context of the project of a queer(er) Filipinx Canadian studies. As Puar, Haritaworn, Dryden and Lenon, and Diaz remind us, the enrollment of particular queer subjects into the national body politic usually occurs alongside—and indeed through—the often violent demonization of other subjects, including queer ones who are not recognizable as national subjects (e.g., non-monogamous people) or ones understood as threats to queer recognition (e.g., supposedly irredeemably homophobic Muslims). Homonormativities and homonationalisms are thus themselves productive of social exclusions, particularly along lines of race, gender, and class. A queer(er) Filipinx Canadian studies must take seriously these kinds of exclusions and ask in what ways Filipinx

Canadians are enrolled in processes and practices of homonormativity and homonationalism. Given the internal differentiation of queer Filipinx Canadians along lines of gender, class, and sexuality (and other axes of differences), we have different relationships to these processes and practices. A queer(er) Filipinx Canadian studies must thus be keenly attuned to its investments and participation in liberal recognition politics, and must also continually ask which Filipinx Canadians are rendered normal or abnormal in such processes.

In the Canadian context, a politics of homonormativity and homonationalism in which the state is seen as an arbiter of citizen-subjectivity and recognition activates settler colonialism's genuflection to the Canadian state as the highest order, if not the sole source, of political authority.[16] Participation in a Filipinx Canadian politics of formal queer recognition thus demands an interrogation of our complicities in settler colonialism's dispossessions and violations of Indigenous sovereignty in these stolen lands. The focus on "settlement," especially of the "family," that remains central to migrant activisms in the Canadian contexts, as in the CPFC Declaration above, is arguably part of such a participation. A queer(er) Filipinx Canadian studies is one that thinks carefully through the articulations between our politics of sexualities and intimacies and our statuses as visitors, settlers, or trespassers in Indigenous territories. In my experience, this is a sometimes difficult conversation to have, especially with those heavily invested in an unproblematic idea of "settlement" and in the Canadian state as an arbiter of formal recognition. For example, at the National Consultative Forum on LGBTQ that was organized by the Philippine Women's Center of British Columbia in October 2014, my suggestion to subject the idea of "settlement" to discussion was very promptly shut down by a longtime community organizer because it is, apparently, too contentious.

Nevertheless, in some circles, this conversation is already well under way. Some members of the Philippine Studies Series (PSS) at the University of British Columbia, my "home" institution, have been engaging in important conversations about what it means to be Filipinx and to engage in Filipinx Canadian studies in the traditional, ancestral, unceded, and occupied territories of the Musqueam peoples on which the University of British Columbia is located. Sexuality has been an important component of this conversation, with one important initiative worth singling out for discussion. Through the energies and leadership of local community organizers May Farrales, Leah Diana, Sol Diana and Melanie Matining, a series of conversations have grown out of initial ones at PSS about our place as Filipinx Canadians in stolen lands and the ways that both colonialism in the Philippines and settler colonialism in Canada shape our understandings of migrancy, intimacy, and gender. Topics of conversation, spurred on by film screenings, have included, among others, the utility and limits of various traditional Philippine understandings of gender and sexuality and the violent imperialist and settler colonial impositions of Western understandings of gender and sexuality both in Canada and in the Philippines. These conversations have traveled beyond the University of British Columbia campus and have been hosted, through *kamayans, meriendas,* and other food-centered gatherings, in the homes of PSS members and community members.

In some circles, decolonial approaches to Filipinx Canadian gender and sexual politics take the explicit form of returning to gender and sexual subjectivities that are Indigenous to the Philippines, in part to get away from Western notions of LGBT recognition. For example, the U.S.-based Center for Babaylan Studies and the scholar-activists Lenny Strobel and Lily Mendoza offer the queer feminized figure of the *"babaylan"* to Filipinxs in the diaspora for them "to constitute a sense of identity" despite "lack[ing] access to Filipino [*sic*] language, culture and history."[17] Because *babaylan* figures cross gender identities and play important spiritual functions in Indigenous communities, they were targeted by the Spanish colonial government for their violation of Spanish gender, sexual, and religious norms.[18] The *babaylan* is thus seductive for Filipinxs in the diaspora who are looking for Philippine-based ways of doing gender, sexuality, and spirituality. The *babaylan*-centered decolonial politics of the Center for Babaylan Studies has traveled to Canada, partly through the efforts of artists and arts-based organizations based in Canadian cities. It is worth noting, for example, that after being hosted in California the first two times, the Third International Babaylan Conference was hosted in September 2016 by the Kathara Society, a Greater Vancouver theatrical group, and by the Center for Babaylan Studies, in the unceded territories of the Coast Salish people, in Gibsons, British Columbia.

Much more thorough work is needed to examine the racial, sexual, and colonial politics of this turn to Indigenous Philippine-based notions of gender, sexuality, and spirituality in Filipinx Canadian art and organizing. I do, however, want to register two sets of initial concerns, framed as questions. First, to what extent does the turn to *"babaylan"* rely on a pre-contact notion of gender and sexuality and thus on a potentially dangerous romanticization and consumption of a nostalgic past? For whom is such a turn available? Is it available to those without ancestral ties to the culturally and geographically situated iterations of these traditions and knowledges, and if so, what does it mean to adopt Indigenous ways of being that are not one's own? Second, does a claim to Philippine indigeneity by those in the diaspora potentially enable an "I am Indigenous too" discourse of settler innocence that collapses global indigeneities into a level playing field without due regard to the geopolitics of both diaspora and settler colonialism? I ask these questions with discomfort. My qualms emerge from the perspective that a well-meaning gender and sexual politics that relies on problematic racial and colonial politics is possibly appropriative and violent, and thus not an acceptable way forward.[19]

Forging Ahead . . .

Inspired by Muñoz's queer utopian imaginary and his insistence that imagining the future otherwise is a queer refusal of the unacceptable present, I remain optimistic about a queer(er) Filipinx Canadian studies. My hope emerges not from an unfettered vision of a wide-open future, but from an awareness and analysis of the possibilities and limits of the present moment, captured powerfully in Muñoz's idea that "the here and now is simply not enough."[20] As I outlined in this chapter, the project of imagining queer(er) Filipinx Canadian futures entails finding openings and possibilities in the interstices of what already exists. It repurposes and extends what is available and workable, while noting and refusing imaginaries and practices that only serve to reproduce the unacceptable "here and now." It thus also necessitates examining the sometimes unspoken commitments—to family, intimacy, identity, nation—that underpin our current political and academic work, as well as our alignments with problematic heteronormative, homonormative and homonationalist sexual politics, including and especially in their neoliberal and (settler) colonial forms. In laying out these principles, I also seek to imagine more-than-LGBT ways of examining the sexual politics of Filipinx Canadian scholarship and activisms. This is not to displace "LGBT" as a crucial set of political and identitarian formations, but to proliferate the modalities of the sexual that affect how we think about the place of intimacies, relationships, and differences within the broad ambit of a queer(er) Filipinx Canadian studies.

By way of conclusion, I identify two areas of future research that are ripe for exploration. A decidedly non-exhaustive list, these two areas offer ways for us to think through the category "Filipinx Canadian" and its sexual politics without losing sight of its intersections both with the broader category of "Asian Canadian" and with the politics of religion and secularism.

The first future direction concerns the articulations between the categories "Asian" and "Filipinx Canadian" and the possibilities for sexual politics that are enabled by thinking through these categories alongside each other. "Asian" brings together a diversity of regional, national, and ethnic identities into a collectivity that enrolls members into programmatic and governmental rule and that provides a possible strategic forum for solidarities across differences. An important example of the latter is the antiracist, ethno-specific organizing that Filipinx Canadians did in queer communities and HIV/AIDS organizations in the 1980s.[21] Various gay Asian men, including the Filipinx Canadian Nitto Marquez, were central to the formation of the social and support group Gay Asians of Toronto in the 1980s, which subsequently brought into being the Gay Asian AIDS Project and the Asian Community AIDS Services. In addition, the organizing and care work of Filipina bisexuals, lesbians, and queers, as well as trans and gender-nonconforming Filipinxs, in these sexual health and social service spaces remains underrecognized and thus requires further archival and oral history research. Such a task challenges us to unearth community histories of leadership, labor, and love by Filipinx Canadians *in coalition with* other Asians. These examples suggest that a queer(er) Filipinx Canadian studies requires looking for "Filipinx Canadian" sexual politics not only through the category "Filipinx Canadian," but also beyond it. After all, as Mahtani and Roberts point out, "solidarity with other immigrant and racialized groups, in areas where there are overlapping struggles, could add considerable strength in the collective fight for social justice."[22] The strategic breaching of the bounds of this category by those organizing on the ground suggests the need to adopt a methodological openness to examining coalitional forms of sexual politics as one avenue into examining how Filipinx Canadians materialize their sexual politics.

A second area of possible future research concerns the intersections of religious and sexual politics in the lives of Filipinx Canadians. In *Filipinos in Canada* we identified religion as an area ripe for analysis,[23] and this is worth reiterating in the context of Filipinx Canadian sexuality studies. This project is, in some ways, already under way. For example, Glenda Bonifacio begins to look at religion and sexuality in her book *Pinay on the Prairies*, in a section on "Variables of Filipino Identity," which nevertheless still segregates "Religion" and "Sexuality" in separate subsections. The subsection on "Sexuality" does offer glimpses of this intersectionality, however, as when an interviewee thinks through the relationships between religion, liberalism, and sexual politics in this way: "Some Filipinos are Catholic . . . Catholic faith strongly condemns gays, lesbians and transgendered way of life, even in a so-called 'liberal' society [such as Canada]."[24] This point is echoed in some artistic interventions on the intersections of religion, sexuality, and Filipinx Canadianness. For example, the Vancouver-based filmmaker Joella Cabalu explores the familial conflicts and complications that have arisen from her brother Jay's coming out as gay to her religious Filipinx Canadian parents in her short film *Stand Still*. She develops her analysis further in her 2016 feature-length film titled *It Runs in the Family*, which places her brother's sexual identities alongside those of other relatives from Canada, the United States, and the Philippines who also identify as sexual minorities (forthcoming). While a more thorough analysis of Cabalu's two films remains necessary in the future, I mention them here to signal that both films identify the intersection of religion (Catholicism, in this case) and sexuality as a powerful force in the lives of many Filipinx Canadians, in no small part given the colonial forces through which such intersection was and is constituted. This is true for LGBT Filipinx Canadians, to be sure, but in the spirit of a queer(er) Filipinx Canadian studies, it must also be reiterated that Catholicism and Christianity's heteronormativity normalize only certain types of family and, in so doing, also render "queer" other social forms such as divorce and single parenthood. An opportunity thus arises for a queer(er) Filipinx Canadian studies to examine the intersections of religion and sexuality and their colonial genealogies not only for LGBT Filipinx Canadian lives, but also, more capaciously, for the different configurations of intimacies and identifications that constitute and are constituted by Filipinx Canadian sexualities.

In making room for explicitly non-heteronormative ways of thinking through the lives and loves of Filipinx Canadians, this edited collection marks an important development in Filipinx Canadian scholarship. My hope is that the inspiration and energy that emerges from this volume propels us, as community members, organizers, and academics, in a direction that harnesses the radical potential of "queer." Such a direction demands that Filipinx Canadian sexuality studies both include and exceed LGBT Filipinx Canadian studies. It also demands an intersectional analysis that problematizes not only sexual minority identities and problematic intimacies, but also the very social and political conditions that render them abnormal, among them processes of hetero-patriarchy, class differentiation, and (settler) colonial geopolitics, whose collective and intersectional violence plagues not only LGBT Filipinx Canadians, but also many others.

Notes

1. Jeffrey Aguinaldo, "The Social Construction of 'Filipina/o Studies': Youth Spaces and Subjectivities," in *Filipinos in Canada: Disturbing Invisibility*, ed. Roland Sintos Coloma et al. (Toronto: University of Toronto Press, 2012), 409.

2. Cathy Cohen, "Punks, Bulldaggers, and Welfare Queens: The Radical Potential of Queer Politics?" *GLQ* 3, no. 4 (1997): 438.

3. José Esteban Muñoz, *Cruising Utopia: The Then and There of Queer Futurity* (New York: New York University Press, 2009), 1.

4. Muñoz, *Cruising Utopia*, 1.

5. See also Hong and Ferguson, 1984.

6. See *Filipinos in Canada: Disturbing Invisibility*, ed. Roland Sintos Coloma et al. (Toronto: University of Toronto Press, 2012).

7. Ethel Tungohan, "Reconceptualizing Motherhood, Reconceptualizing Resistance: Migrant Domestic Workers, Transnational Hyper-Maternalism and Activism," *International Feminist Journal of Politics* 15, no. 1 (2012): 40.

8. Tungohan, "Reconceptualizing Motherhood," 47.

9. Rachel H. Brown. "Re-Examining the Transnational Nanny: Migrant Carework beyond the Chain," *International Feminist Journal of Politics* 18, no. 2 (2015): 8.

10. Martin F. Manalansan, "Queer Intersections: Sexuality and Gender in Migration Studies," *International Migration Review* 40, no. 1 (2006): 237.

11. Brown, "Re-Examining the Transnational Nanny," 8.

12. Manalansan, "Queer Intersections," 242–43.

13. See Wilkinson, 2013.

14. See CBC News, 2013.

15. See Rodriguez, 2010.

16. See Morgensen, 2011.

17. Melisa S. L. Casumbal-Salazar, "The Indeterminacy of the Philippine Indigenous Subject: Indigeneity, Temporality and Cultural Governance," *Amerasia* 41, no. 1 (2015): 80.

18. See Garcia, 1996.

19. See Yee, 2011; and Morgensen, 2011.

20. Muñoz, *Cruising Utopia*, 365.

21. See Catungal, 2013.

22. Minelle Mahtani and David Roberts, "Contemplating New Spaces in Canadian Studies," in *Filipinos in Canada: Disturbing Invisibility*, ed. Roland Sintos Coloma et al. (Toronto: University of Toronto Press, 2012), 422.

23. Bonnie McElhinny et. al., "Spectres of (In)visibility: Filipina/o Labour, Culture and Youth in Canada," in *Filipinos in Canada: Disturbing Invisibility*, ed. Roland Sintos Coloma et al. (Toronto: University of Toronto Press, 2012), 33–34.

24. Glenda Bonifacio, *Pinay on the Prairies: Filipino Women and Transnational Identities* (Vancouver: University of British Columbia Press, 2013), 128.

Bibliography

Aguinaldo, John. "The Social Construction of 'Filipina/o Studies': Youth Spaces and Subjectivities." In *Filipinos in Canada: Disturbing Invisibility*, edited by Roland Sintos Coloma, Bonnie McElhinny, Ethel Tungohan, John Paul C. Catungal, and Lisa M. Davidson, 402–13. Toronto: University of Toronto Press, 2012.

Bakan, Abigail B., and Daiva Stasiulis. *Not One of the Family: Foreign Domestic Workers in Canada*. Toronto: University of Toronto Press, 1997.

Bonifacio, Glenda Tibe. *Pinay on the Prairies: Filipino Women and Transnational Identities*. Vancouver: University of British Columbia Press, 2013.

Brown, Rachel H. "Re-Examining the Transnational Nanny: Migrant Carework beyond the Chain." *International Feminist Journal of Politics* 18, no. 2 (2015): 210–29.

Cabalu, J., director. *It Runs in the Family* (2016). OUTtv Network.

———, director. *Stand Still* (2012).

Casumbal-Salazar, Melisa S. L. "The Indeterminacy of the Philippine Indigenous Subject: Indigeneity, Temporality and Cultural Governance." *Amerasia* 41 (2015): 74–94.

Catungal, John Paul C. "Ethno-Specific Safe Houses in the Liberal Contact Zone: Race Politics, Place-Making and the Genealogies of the AIDS Sector in Global-Multicultural Toronto." *ACME International Journal of Critical Geographies* 12 (2013): 250–78.

———. "Scales of Violence from the Body to the Globe: Slain Filipino Youth in Canadian Cities." In *Filipinos in Canada: Disturbing Invisibility*, edited by Roland Sintos Coloma, Bonnie McElhinny, Ethel Tungohan, John Paul C. Catungal, and Lisa M. Davidson, 321–40. Toronto: University of Toronto Press, 2012.

CBC News. "GTA Woman's Monthly Support Helped Family Survive Haiyan." *CBC News*, November 21, 2013. http://www.cbc.ca/news/canada/toronto/gta-woman-s-monthly-support-helped-family-survive-haiyan-1.2435578.

Cohen, Cathy. "Punks, Bulldaggers, and Welfare Queens: The Radical Potential of Queer Politics?" *GLQ* 3, no. 4 (1997): 437–65.

Coloma, Roland Sintos, Bonnie McElhinny, Ethel Tungohan, John Paul C. Catungal, and Lisa M. Davidson, eds. *Filipinos in Canada: Disturbing Invisibility*. Toronto: University of Toronto Press, 2012.

Combahee River Collective. "Combahee River Collective Statement." 1983. http://circuitous.org/scraps/combahee.html.

Diaz, Robert. "The Limits of Bakla and Gay: Feminist Readings of My Husband's Lover, Vice Ganda and Charice Pempengco." *Signs* 40 (2015): 721–45.

Dryden, OmiSoore H., and Suzanne Lenon, eds. *Disrupting Queer Inclusion: Canadian Homonationalisms and the Politics of Belonging*. Vancouver: University of British Columbia Press, 2015.

Garcia, J. Neil. *Phillipine Gay Culture: Binabae to Bakla, Silahis to MSM*. Quezon City, Philippines: University of the Philippines Press, 1996.

Gopinath, Gayatri. *Impossible Desires: Queer Diasporas and South Asian Public Cultures*. Durham, N.C.: Duke University Press, 2005.

Haritaworn, Jin. *Queer Lovers and Hateful Others: Regenerating Violent Times and Places*. London: Pluto, 2015.

Hong, Grace Kyungwon, and Roderick A. Ferguson, eds. *Strange Affinities: The Gender and Sexual Politics of Comparative Racialization*. Durham, N.C.: Duke University Press, 2011.

Lorde, Audre. *Sister Outsider*. New York: Ten Speed, 1984.

Mahtani, Minelle, and David Roberts. "Contemplating New Spaces in Canadian Studies." In *Filipinos in Canada: Disturbing Invisibility*, edited by Roland Sintos Coloma, Bonnie McElhinny, Ethel Tungohan, John

Paul C. Catungal, and Lisa M. Davidson, 417–26. Toronto: University of Toronto Press, 2012.

Manalansan, Martin F. *Global Divas: Filipino Gay Men in the Diaspora.* Durham, N.C.: Duke University Press, 2003.

———. "Queer Intersections: Sexuality and Gender in Migration Studies." *International Migration Review* 40 (2006): 224–49.

McElhinny, Bonnie, Lisa M. Davison, John Paul C. Catungal, Ethel Tungohan and Roland Sintos Coloma. "Spectres of (In)visibility: Filipina/o Labour, Culture and Youth in Canada." In *Filipinos in Canada: Disturbing Invisibility*, edited by Roland Sintos Coloma, Bonnie McElhinny, Ethel Tungohan, John Paul C. Catungal, and Lisa M. Davidson, 5–45. Toronto: University of Toronto Press, 2012.

Moraga, Cheríe. "Queer Aztlan." In *The Last Generation*, by Cheríe Moraga, 145–74. Boston: Southend Press, 1993.

Morgensen, Scott. *Spaces between Us: Queer Settler Colonialism and Indigenous Decolonization.* Minneapolis: University of Minnesota Press, 2011.

Muñoz, José Esteban. *Cruising Utopia: The Then and There of Queer Futurity.* New York: New York University Press, 2009.

Pratt, Geraldine. *Families Apart: Migrant Mothers and the Conflicts of Labor and Love.* Minneapolis: University of Minnesota Press, 2012.

———. *Working Feminism.* Philadelphia: Temple University Press, 2004

Puar, Jasbir. *Terrorist Assemblages: Homonationalism in Queer Times.* Durham, N.C.: Duke University Press, 2007.

Rodriguez, Robyn. *Migrants for Export: How the Philippine State Brokers Labor to the World.* Minneapolis: University of Minnesota Press, 2010.

Smith, Barbara, ed. *Home Girls: A Black Feminist Anthology.* New Brunswick, N.J.: Rutgers University Press, 1983.

Tungohan, Ethel. "Reconceptualizing Motherhood, Reconceptualizing Resistance: Migrant Domestic Workers, Transnational Hyper-Maternalism and Activism." *International Feminist Journal of Politics* 15 (2013): 39–57.

Wilkinson, Eleanor. "Learning to Love Again: 'Broken Families,' Citizenship, and the State Promotion of Coupledom." *Geoforum* 49 (2013): 206–13.

Yee, Jessica, ed. *Feminism for Real: Deconstructing the Academic Industrial Complex of Feminism.* Ottawa: Canadian Center for Policy Alternatives, 2011.

Visualizing the Intimate in Filipino Lives

A Catalog Essay

Marissa Largo and Robert Diaz

Curated by Marissa Largo and Robert Diaz, the exhibit "Visualizing the Intimate in Filipino/a Lives" featured the work of eleven emerging Toronto-based artists (Maria Patricia Abuel, Jo SiMalaya Alcampo, Lexy Baluyot, Nikki Cajucom, Martie Hechanova, Marissa Largo, Tim Manalo, Julius Poncelet Manapul, Blessie Maturan, Loisel Wilson Oñate, and Danelle Jane Tran) and the work of artists from two community-based organizations (Kapisanan Philippine Centre for Arts and Culture and the Magkaisa Centre). The exhibit was held from January 23, 2015, until February 15, 2015, as part of a series of events for the "Diasporic Intimacies" conference. "Diasporic Intimacies" brought together artists, community members, and scholars to interrogate the contribution of queer Filipinos/as to Canadian culture and society. By consolidating artists who embody different gendered, classed, and migrant histories, Diaz and Largo sought to destabilize notions of nationhood and national belonging—as these apply not only to Canada but also to the many spaces that diasporic Filipino inhabit. Despite sharing the same ethnic identities, the heterogeneity of the artists' concerns challenge the organizational imperative of Canadian multiculturalism and settler colonialism to discipline ethnic difference through and within multiple iterations of intimacy. "Visualizing the Intimate" thus presented an entangled archive of contemporary art that reflects the polymorphic nature of subject formation in an age of global migration. It features artists who translate haunting personal experiences through innovative materials and techniques.

The "intimate," according to feminist scholar Anne Stoler, indexes relationships grounded in the "familiar and the essential" and relationships "grounded in sex" (Stoler, 2002). Haunted by Stoler's dual definition, "Visualizing the Intimate in Filipino Lives" features the works of emerging Toronto-based artists and the work of artists from community-based organizations as they visualize the personal and political implications of "the intimate" for Filipinos/as in Canada.

In his contribution to the exhibit, Julius Poncelet Manapul examines his diasporic sexual and racial identity against the heteronormative and homonormative standards of Canadian society. He appropriates Western visual culture while juxtaposing its use with Filipino materiality. In the tableau he composed for the exhibition (which is shown below), Manapul reinterprets past works on his crafted *queertopia*—a seemingly perfect abode for him and his queer family—but now, in light of his recent divorce. Articles of unfulfilled promises, such as his marriage license, the crib for his fictional child created from *balikbayan* boxes (containers used by diasporic Filipinos to send goods "back home"), which is flanked by two of his "homonormative mannequins," all point to his intimate and ongoing struggles as a diasporic, queer subject vis-à-vis Western normative ideals.

There is no "happily ever after" as Manapul suggests in his animation *Kissing Utopia Good-Bye* (2012), but only constant recuperative acts as a diasporic, gay Filipino in Canada. Manapul conveys this reality in his playful and multilayered appropriation of Disney imagery and Western gay porn, which signifies for the artist unattainable perfection. His *Queerious Butterflies* (2014) take over the space, performing a transgressive act of embodying a subjectivity that cannot be pinned down by taxonomic classification or colonial imperatives. Instead, these butterflies become the fabric and backdrop by which Manapul fashions an unfurling subjectivity based on his own queer aesthetic. Similarly, the artist's *Queerious Murses* (2015) are fabricated from intricate cutouts that subvert dominant and oppressive queer representations. Embedded and hidden within the ornamentation are Tagalog words that have pejorative provenance, such as *bakla* and *bading* (terms that denote homosexuality, effeminacy, and related performances), or racialized and sexualized slurs, like *rice queen*. Like other diasporic, gay Filipinos, Manapul has reclaimed these terms to reflect his desire to disrupt static and globalized notions of queerness in favor of an emergent subjectivity that is remade through aesthetics. Much like the function

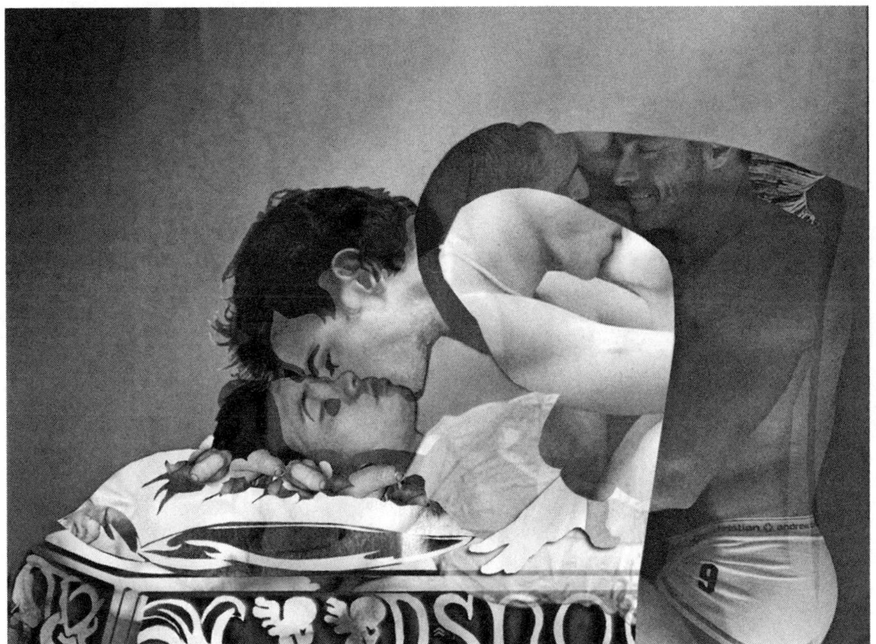

Julius Poncelet Manapul, *Kissing Utopia Good-Bye*, animation, video installation, 2012.

of a designer bag, the murse symbolizes Manapul's efforts to craft a particular identity that externalizes hidden desires for belonging as he moves through the world. Manapul's visual strategy of subverting dominant and normative representations behooves viewers to question their assumptions of race, gender, and sexual identity in light of migration.

Jo SiMalaya Alcampo delves into the materiality of Indigenous Filipino culture and language in her exploration of her diasporic ethnic and sexual identity in *SIYA: Beneath the Barong* (2015). Much like Manapul's reconfigurations of the terms *bakla* and *bading*, Alcampo plays with the fluidity of the term *siya* (which is pronounced as "shah" and means "she," "he," or "they") as a genderless pronoun that exists in the Filipino language. The single-channel video is projected onto a translucent fabric reminiscent of the Filipino Indigenous textile, *piña*—the same material that traditionally constructs the *barong* Tagalog (a formal Filipino men's attire) that Alcampo dons in the video. Alcampo

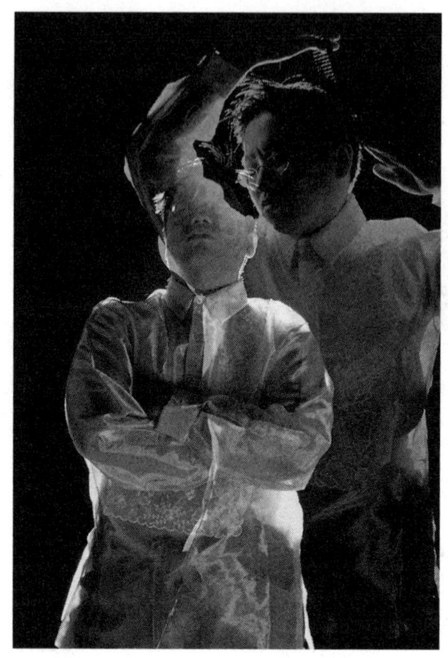

Jo SiMalaya Alcampo, *SIYA: Beneath the Barong*, video installation, 2015.

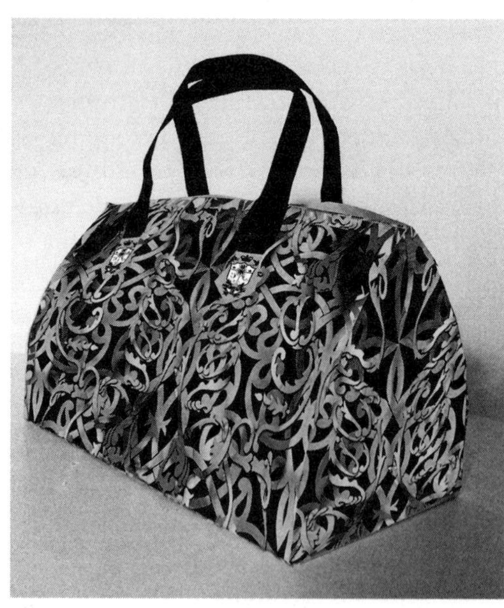

Julius Poncelet Manapul, *Queerious Murse*, digital collage, paper sculpture, 2015.

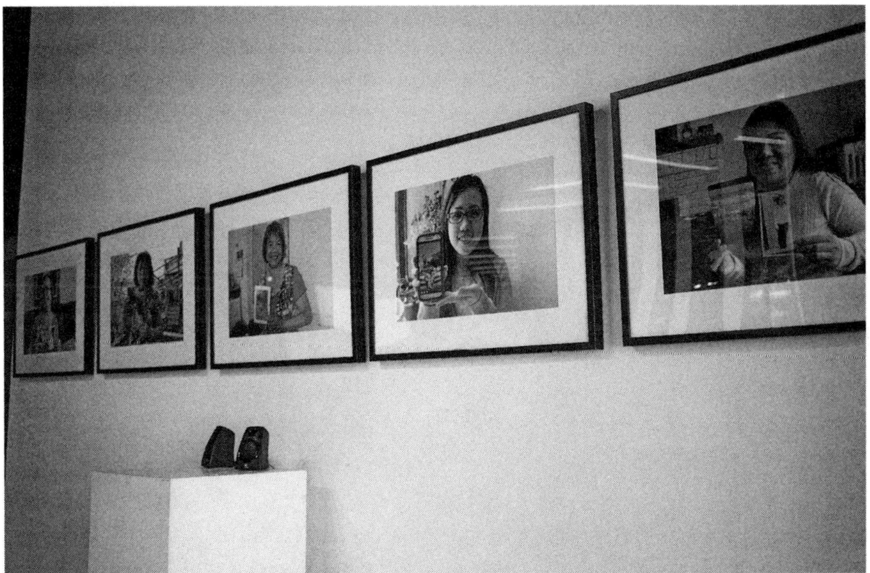

Magkaisa Centre, *The Picture in Picture: Filipino Women across Decades*, digital photography, audio installation, 2014.

performs "macho" poses of an Elvis impersonator while her backlit *barong* reveals the contours of her breast. Alcampo subverts the colonial logics of gender binaries in her performance by whimsically embodying an emergent queer Filipino/a diasporic aesthetic.

Visualizing the intimate comes to terms with the intersections of class and gender in the community-based photo works of the Magkaisa Centre. *The Picture in Picture: Filipino Women across Decades* (2014) series captures the gendered and racialized experiences of Filipinas who have immigrated to Canada from the 1960s to the present. Canada's labor and immigration policies are materially and temporally embodied in the lives of these women whose memories of distant pasts—symbolized in the photographic images they hold—collapse with current realities in the work.

With a similar political thrust, Marissa Largo takes on embodiment in the midst of global migration in the video installation and performance *I Bring Myself* (2012). Largo represents the practice of *pasalubong* (a welcoming gift given upon returning "home") as a performative and

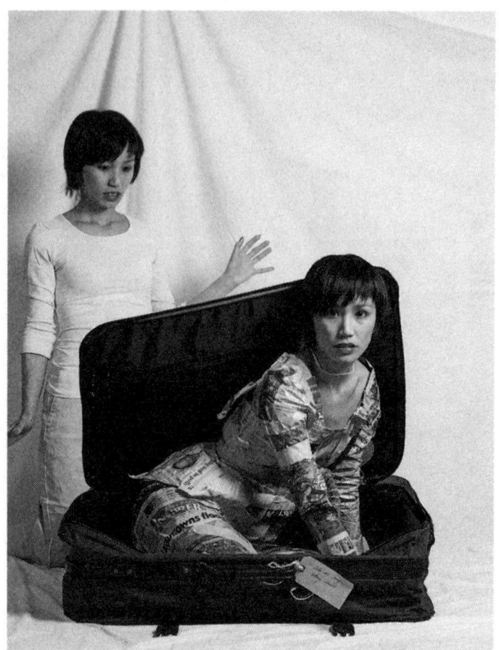

Marissa Largo, *I Bring Myself*, stop-motion
animation, video installation, 2012.

negotiated act of reconfiguring self and home. She visualizes the
intimate by embodying the multiplicity inherent in being a diasporic
Filipina—a part of a body politic of transnational, racialized women.
Read with a political lens, the work alludes to the movement of women
from the Philippines to the global north, which results from unequal
economic power relations. The Filipina in Largo's work is transported
in a suitcase and wrapped in newspaper as if she were a fragile object,
and is a reference to the global objectification of the Filipina. Conscious of how her body is read in Canadian society, Largo interrogates
this problematic by "bringing herself," or in other words, representing
herself as a gendered, racialized subject and actor in her own right.

In another engagement with feminist self-representation, Maria Patricia
Abuel questions conservative gendered expectations with regard to labor,
notions of femininity, and moral behavior to which Filipinas, both in the
Philippines and in the diaspora, are held. Her series of digitally altered
smartphone photos *#selfie* (Babae, Diyos, Trabaho/ Woman, God, Work;

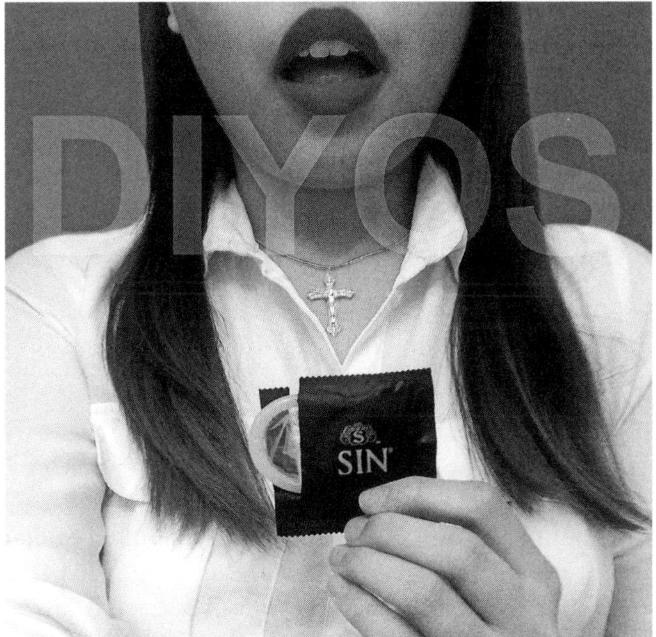

Maria Patricia Abuel, *#selfie*, digitally altered smartphone photographs, 2014.

2014) consists of ironic self-portraits in which she renders herself as the archetypal fair, pious, and sacrificial Filipina. Recognition is often gained by looking into the other's eyes, but in these renderings, Abuel denies the return of the gaze. We can never fully know the women in these photos because they are two-dimensional representations informed by colonial domination, neoliberal agendas, and religious doctrine. Abuel queers the normative and stereotypical expectations of Filipinas in her self-representations and instead puts forward her hybrid subjectivity constructed from multiple and sometimes competing influences.

Nikki Cajucom also looks at the objectification and exoticization of Filipinas in Canada in her photo work *Balut* (2014). *Balut* is a boiled egg containing a duck embryo and is a Filipino delicacy, but in Canada it is often considered a source of repulsion. The artist as a child is born out of a brown egg and into a white hegemony, and like one who dares to eat *balut* in the diaspora, is exoticized and othered. The intimate here is not only the Filipina's body, but also what she chooses to consume.

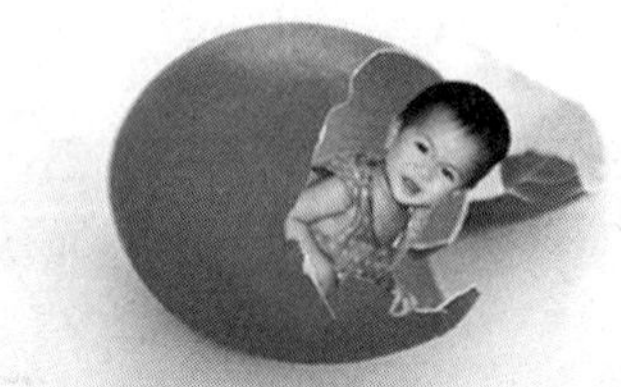

Nikki Cajucom, *Balut*, digital photographic work, 2013.

The consumption and the objectification of Filipina bodies are also the themes of *Filipina Heart/Anywhere But Here* (2014), in which chocolate, a food of desire, is the medium of Blessie Maturan's sculptures of fetishized Filipinas. Maturan recounts several examples of the commodification of Filipino women which she has encountered online on popular dating websites such as Filipino Cupid (formerly Filipina Heart) and on her visit to Angeles City's red light district. The artist's chocolate Filipina bodies are not only objects of desire to be consumed by the global north, but are also bodies that perform labor in exploitative relations which are maintained by sexism and racism.

Tim Manalo's sculptural, multimedia piece *Balut (Night)* (2014) examines food, culture, and diaspora through the lens of a childhood experience. As in Cajucom's piece of the same name, Manalo's work explores the exoticization of cultural difference, but more specifically, through the class-based practice of shaming immigrants for the food they choose to consume. The fabricated yellow backpack evokes childhood, but also carries the double meaning of "pack-up" (the literal translation of the word *balut*) alluding to the migration of his family. Manalo relives the affective consequences of marginalization and the embodied sense of shame imposed by hegemonic powers. Now, with a critical distance, he simultaneously pays homage to the process by which the Filipino delicacy is harvested and to the temporal difference of his ancestors' homeland; the light that emanates from within the bag only lights up when it is night in Canada and daytime in the Philippines.

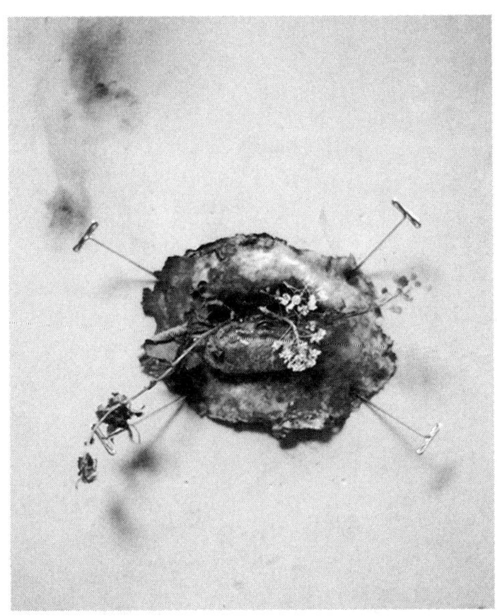

Lexy Baluyot, *Dissection and Decay of Your Flowery Bullshit*, latex, mixed media, 2014.

Lexy Baluyot's fascinating and grotesque sculptures of *Dissection and Decay of Your Flowery Bullshit* (2014) viscerally expresses her disdain for gender-policing comments wielded at her as a child. With her training in prosthetic production, Baluyot's sculptures defy that which is presented as natural, whether it be organic matter and flesh or imposed gender norms, which present intimate intrusions on her queer identity. "I visualized their targeted words, the rationalizations coming from their mouths as an ever-growing stream of flowers and twisting vines, strangling me," Baluyot muses.

In *Out of Place* (2014), with childlike light-heartedness, Danelle Jane Tran photographs her awkward bodily performances and those of her siblings, demonstrating a diasporic consciousness, or in other words, an in-between state in which subjects negotiate two or more cultures and homelands. The expansive backdrop of these photos can be anywhere; the land, water, and sky suggest placelessness and identities that are not necessarily tied to one geography or nation.

In *Urban Vs. Tribal* (2014), Martie Hechanova imagines his emergent queer subjectivity informed by his investigations of the Badjao water tribe of the Philippines and Toronto street style. Through fashion photography, Hechanova blurs the dichotomies of that which is considered traditional and that which is contemporary. Indigenous culture

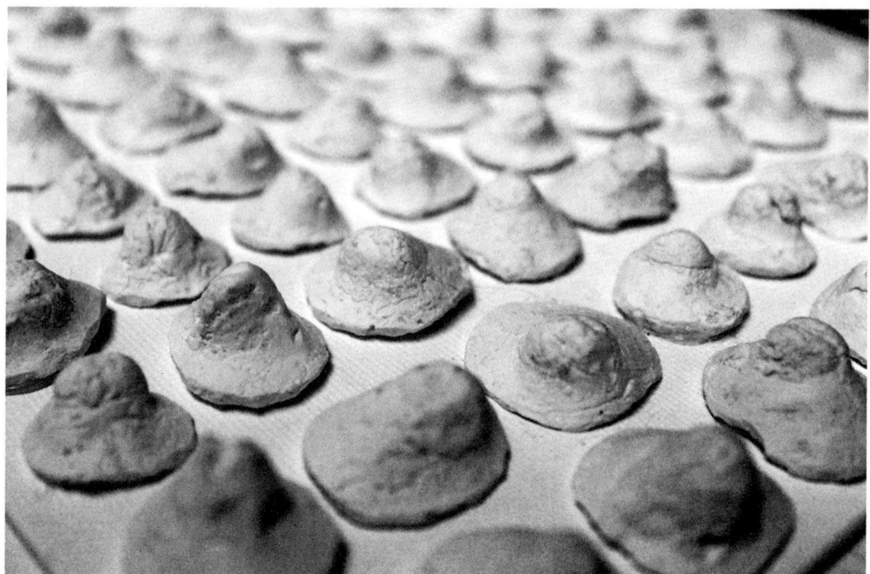

Loisel Wilson Oñate, *A Chest*, plaster-cast nipples, 2014.

is not fixed in a romantic past, but is re-created in a diasporic present and leads viewers to question how precolonial Philippine identity is invoked in the age of global migration and how it may be seen through a queer lens.

Loisel Wilson Oñate's two works expose that which is hidden, shameful, and traumatic. In *A Chest* (2014), plaster-cast nipples are revealed in a repeating pattern and evoke notions of precolonial femininity that does not place shame upon the exposed Filipina body. In *Hear the Intimate* (2014), the artist shares a quiet exchange between her and her *lola* (grandmother) as she recounts a traumatic moment from her past. The disembodied voice of the artist's *lola* is rich with emotion and texture as it conveys the sense of helplessness she first experienced in witnessing the sexual assault of a young female worker at the hands of her employer. Although oceans and decades removed from the initial event, Wilson Oñate's piece is still rife with pain and testifies to the power of the intimate to transcend borders, generations, and language barriers.

Together, these works illuminate the generative possibilities of diasporic intimacy as it is embodied in the lives of Filipinos/as in Canada and represent individual and collective efforts in capturing the personal, political, and affective state of being constituted by multiple "uprootings and regroundings" (Ahmed et al., 2003). These artists signify symbolic interpretations of self, home, family, and community as they are mediated by gender, race, and class—subjectivities that are thrown into flux in the diaspora. Considered together, these artists and their work represent the emerging and dynamic field of Filipino/a contemporary art in Canada.

Bibliography

Ahmed, Sara, Claudia Castaneda, Anne-Marie Fortier, and Mimi Sheller. "Introduction." In *Uprootings/ Regroundings: Questions of Home and Migration*, edited by Sara Ahmed, Claudia Castaneda, Anne-Marie Fortier, and Mimi Sheller, 1–22. Oxford: Bloomsbury Academic, 2003.

Stoler, Ann Laura. *Carnal Knowledge and Imperial Power: Race and the Intimate in Colonial Rule*. Berkeley: University of California Press, 2002.

Feminist Collectivities, *Tibo* Ethics, and the Call of the Babaylan

*Melanya Liwanag Aguila, PJ Alafriz,
Lisa Valencia-Svensson, and
Jo SiMalaya Alcampo*

*In the following interview, some of the founding members of Babaylan
(Melanya Liwanag Aguila, PJ Alafriz, Lisa Valencia-Svensson, and Jo
SiMalaya Alcampo) reflect on their more than two decades of activism,
coalition-building, and friendship. Babaylan was founded in 1993 when
pinay feminists decided to come together in the offices of a Filipino community centre to share their unique experiences as queer Filipinas and to
have, for lack of a better word, fun. As they move between personal stories
of migration, movement, and kinship, these exceptional women also offer
us a glimpse into the vibrant women of color activism that has animated
queer social movements in Toronto since the 1990s. As they discuss their
involvement with, and leadership roles in, various community formations
(from artistic groups like SAWA to social and sports organizations like
Pardz Night, to parades celebrating gay or Filipino pride), the members of
Babaylan also model acts of resistance and belonging rooted in an ethics
of generosity, solidarity, and love.*

RD: What was it like growing up in or migrating to Toronto? How
did this experience affect your sense of place, of belonging, in
Canada?

MA: Before I was born my parents migrated from the Philippines
to Canada in 1967. I was close to my Filipino culture. My first
language was Tagalog; however, when I started school my parents

began speaking to me in English only. My parents were still connected to their roots in Toronto. *Tatay* [dad] was part of a Filipino basketball league. Every weekend we played with other Filipino kids and attended language and cultural dance classes. There was always a big Filipino party to attend. My parents were the first ones in their families to migrate, and some of their siblings followed. Having close family ties in the diaspora helped to strengthen my identity, but within the educational system my experience was sometimes different and not supportive. There was tension and conflict.

PA: From the age of eighteen I've lived away from the Philippines. I was an activist in the Philippines in the Cordillera region. I decided to leave the Philippines because of the violence that we experienced in the movement. I ended up in Hong Kong and lived there for ten years as a domestic worker. In Hong Kong, I would organize beauty pageants in the hotels. The contestants were also migrant workers who were domestic workers, entertainers, and band members. In 1991 I came to Canada through the Foreign Domestic Movement program. I studied midwifery in the Philippines, but I came to Canada as a nanny. I thought Canada was just as big as Hong Kong. I went to Edmonton for six months and then traveled to Toronto. I came to Toronto because I had friends who were also working here. During that time, the employers might not say "Oh you're gay, or lesbian," but being different can cause problems. There's one *amo* [employer] who would tell the *tibo*s [butches], "Oh, I don't want my kids to play with the kids you are taking care of." So I experienced homophobia in the way they treated the kids I was taking care of.

LS: I was born in Toronto, and I'm half Filipino and half Swedish American. I grew up highly disconnected from Filipino culture. I come from a family where, unfortunately, the people who were around me as I was growing up—both the Filipinos and non-Filipinos—didn't see the value of me knowing about the Philippines, and were themselves trying to forget the Philippines, and looked down on it. That is the impact of colonialism. Not that I grew up with very much awareness of my Swedish identity either, but, I think my mother and my *lola* [grandmother] deliberately moved away from the Philippines in their lives. That's why my *lola* never understood my desire to know more. She would say, "Why do you want to go back to the Philippines and learn about your identity, that's a waste of time." And my mother never really wanted to return either. The Philippines represented family for her and that was too painful, so she just pushed it all away. At the same time, it was the 1970's in Toronto. The city was so white. I'm half white, but I looked like a little Chinese kid to most people. I remember being teased for being Chinese even though obviously I am not. That hostility, there was no mistaking it, that subtle energy in how people looked at me, or at my mom. There was an energy there that I picked up, but that I didn't even realize had an effect on me. Yet despite that, the end result of all these factors was that I was actually in denial of the fact that I was not white until I was about 22.

JA: I was born in Pasay City. My family migrated to Ontario when I was five years old. I grew up in Malvern in the heart of Scarborough. I remember the culture shock and racism. For a long time, I refused to speak in school. My teachers told my parents to speak to me in Tagalog at home, but that I should only respond in English. The Colonial Assimilation Project did its best to disassociate me, but thankfully my parents shared traditional Filipino values and cultural practices with us. So my body remembers what the language centers of my brain were trained to forget.

RD: What inspired you to connect to other queer Filipinos then, which seems to be the focus of your activism and community-building since the 1990s?

MA: When I was in high school, I went to an anti-racism camp. It was not just about race, but it also included class, homophobia, and awareness around diversity. The counsellors were queer folks (lesbian and gay), and that's where I met Rose Gutierrez, who was a *Pinay* filmmaker. I ended up volunteering and working with her film production company. I was exposed to women making films and in particular women of color, learning about HIV and women and lesbian parenting. I had a boyfriend at that time and as I was exposed to lesbians of color activism and cultural expression, I transformed and came out (as queer). I think being in such a supportive environment in so many different ways from a career perspective, to making films around the issues of women, to being queer, it was very welcoming and I came out to that. There was another queer *Pinay* activist who was pivotal in my journey. There was an Indigenous

Peoples Filipino youth event that I had attended in my early days. I was very moved and captivated by the facilitator. She was a beautiful woman. She was very strong, articulate, and passionate. I was just in awe and that happened to be Lani T. Montreal. [Note: Lani T. Montreal's play, *My Grandmother and I*, is included in this collection.] Soon after we became strong like sisters and we were side by side in the Philippine Solidarity Group, at workshops, demonstrations, activist projects, plays, and of course the women's dances

PA: I was part of a basketball league in Hong Kong. So when I came to Toronto, we organized a league with seven teams of *tibo* [butch], twelve *tibo*s per team. There were so many *tibo*s, at least 100. They all came through the Live-in Caregiver Program, from places such as Hong Kong and Singapore. This was around 1996. I met many of the *tibo*s at parties. There are those who have also been here for a while wanting to connect with other *tibo*s. So we ended up playing basketball. The league met every weekend. We would post flyers in the St. Jamestown area because many Filipinos go there to send remittances to the Philippines, or buy Filipino food. There were Filipino stores at 260 and 240 Wellesley. The league lasted two years. Many were burned out because, at that time we were mandated to attend English as a Second Language classes in order to complete our permanent residence. We also volunteered in our respective community causes. It was during that time that I connected with Linda Lising, who was a community organizer and a supporter of Babaylan.

JA: Queerness has always been in Filipino culture, whether or not we name it or speak it. In 1992 my mentors, Fely Villasin and Martha Ocampo, introduced me to Melanya, who was illustrating the poster for our play on violence against women in the Filipino community. I found myself fascinated by her artsy overalls, army boots, and wooden jewelry from her recent *balikbayan* journey to the Philippines. When I overheard Fely and Martha say that Mel worked with the lesbian of color community in Toronto . . . I had so many questions! Who were these lesbians? Where was their community? Why was I so drawn to this mysterious person? But I kept silent. I had no role models or positive references for queer folks, only slurs. When I got home, I couldn't even write the word "lesbian" in my journal, I just put dashes where the word should be.

Eventually, I found the courage to attend the LYPS (Lesbian Youth Peer Support) group at the 519 Church Street Community Centre. There were not many people of color, but I met my first queer friends. One day, someone walked into the room I'd never seen before. She strode purposefully into the middle of the circle and dropped a bunch of flyers on the floor. She threw a challenging look at some folks, turned up her shirt collar, and walked out without a word. And that was our friend, Vee [laughs]. The flyer was an invitation to a new "Pinay Lesbian Support Group."

RD: So was this how Babaylan started? It also seems like that since the 1990s, you have been organizing other groups and collectives. Can you speak more about that?

JA: Vee started Babaylan in response to the racism she encountered in the queer community. I joined the following week. After our first meeting at the 519, we walked to St. James Town to get *halo-halo*. It felt like coming home. Afterwards, I met Melanya, and then our two friends who were still in high school at the time also came. Then I met Lisa at a reading of *A Piece of My Heart: A Lesbian of Colour Anthology* and then we started meeting, all of us, in the summer of 1993. We were partying a lot too, we would start on Thursday and just continue until the weekend. There was an event every week. JB, who is the first Filipino drag king, also went to our first Babaylan meeting. She was still wearing her high school uniform. JB was the first student at Mother Theresa's, who refused to wear a kilt. These were the folks who created Babaylan—my first collective. I've chosen to work in collectives since because they demonstrate how grassroots organizing based on shared values can heal communities.

LS: Yes, so in 1993 we were Mel, Jo, JB, Rich, a couple of other people, Vanessa, and also Mel's sibling. We created Babaylan. We would gather at the Philippine Solidarity group office and actually just play. Like literally, play. We would do dance moves, play music, discuss coming-out stories. All of us even remember this one moment when someone brought in these promotional cardboard cellphones, and for half an hour we talked to each other on our "cellphones" (laugh), all of us in the same room, and we ended up discussing important topics with each other.

MA: There were different reasons why people came together for Babaylan. There was a community there, you could feel a sense of belonging. It was also a way to get exposed. We learned Tagalog together because we felt we needed to. We felt the need to find out who we were, about our language and our history and connect to this. This was in the early 1990s. Learning about Tagalog was also learning about colonialism and the history of the *babaylan* as a historical figure. The *babaylan* were feminists, they were leaders, they were powerful, and they were doing things important in society. We wanted to channel into this energy. We became involved in the Philippine activist community. So we were very connected. Through Babaylan we were also exposing our issues and our experience as women and queer people to the larger Filipino community. So members came out to hang out. They stayed. They listened, spoke, and participated and made a difference.

RD: Was there a sense of urgency then, about the issues or causes you were bringing to the forefront? And if so, how did the urgency manifest itself?

MA: Sometimes, we didn't know that we were going to make a difference by being visible. We would crash a particular parade, like a Filipino community parade, or other non-queer or non-women-specific community events and represent and express ourselves. There was a Philippine Independence Day parade, and we brought the queer banners and rainbow flags and we crashed it. We also performed plays, held workshops, and focused on the issues in the Philippines, migrant workers in Canada and our queer experiences. With SAWA, we held an annual Filipino stage at Pride. My very good friend Jowenne Herrera was one of our SAWA members whose artistry, activism, and leadership made us visible. We held a Pinay Gatherings conference in 1999. We housed people, brought them in to speak, held workshops, forums, created partnerships with businesses and partied. Many women of color were organizing cultural events and I was inspired. When we were in the Filipino community, there were queer folks everywhere. Bringing people together and really nurturing that connection feeds your soul. We were creating history, but we were also seeing the results though the people that we were connected with. When you're doing it as a group of queer *pinays*, the connection becomes even stronger.

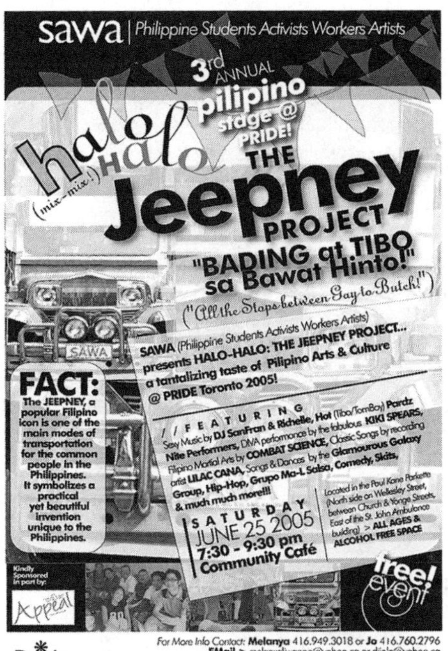

SAWA's advertisement for the Third Pilipino Stage at Pride Toronto, 2005.

PA: I think for me, Babaylan was needed because I didn't have a family, or direct family here. They are in the Cordillera region. So I was basically alone. So I wanted to connect with those who grew up here, so we can also learn from each other. As a new immigrant at the time, it was definitely important for me to know the community. Because I was also working in a different environment, it was a way of going out to meet with different people instead of being confined to one workplace. We organized this organization to learn about each other and be connected to Canadian-based *pinay*s. Sometimes the more traditional community organizations were not so open. When I would go to the traditional Filipino parties, sometimes the older folks would make a comment and say *"di naman kayo lalaki"* (you are not really a man). I needed Babaylan to counter the discrimination that I felt.

LS: I needed Babaylan as well because I don't have much family, I don't have much immediate family. I was devoid of Filipino culture in my life, political or not. So I needed it. I was more political, so I

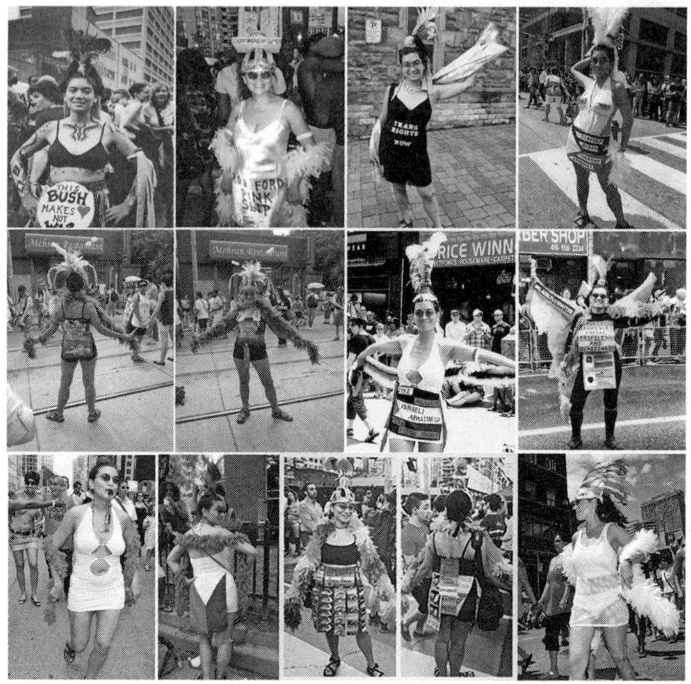

Lisa's socially engaged Pride outfits, 2003–2015.

gravitated to political Filipino groups like PSG and Babaylan, and
also to non-Filipino polical organizations like CKLN Radio, and I
had a part-time job at the local non-profit Adhika Philippine Development Concerns. I was also involved with CAMP SIS and Sistah's
Café. All of that was happening at the same time, in the early and
mid 1990's. I was always motivated by being able to speak out, I
don't like staying quiet on issues. That's why I was so involved at
CKLN, and later made socially engaged outfits for many years for
the Pride Parade and the Dyke March. I feel I was connected to
other people who felt the same way, and so we just naturally did
a lot of things together. We also flirted a lot, and had fun. And all
of that fed my soul. For the past decade, I've poured these same
energies into my documentary film producing. I realize that is my
passion now, so I'm pouring everything I've got into that world.
I'm trying to re-create in my documentary circles the feeling I had
before when I was involved with Babaylan and CKLN and all the

other groups. It's been tough. I've often wished I could just keep all the people and experiences from the 1990's right around me all the time.

JA: I really needed Babaylan. When I came out in Scarborough there was no safe space, I had to hide. When I came out I became estranged from members of my family. So, if your main Filipino cultural contact is your family and you lose that, what does that mean? Babaylan became my other family, a chosen family. We also had activists from the Philippines who mentored us. We participated in political actions in response to the drastic social program cuts by Mike Harris in the 1990s, and we learned about the effects of martial law on our community. We grew up together. We cared for each other through heartbreaks and life's joys. We were friends and we organized together. We taught ourselves Tagalog, we learned Philippine history, and we were also involved in different sectors, like Lisa was with Adhika, I was with Carlos Bulosan, Melanya was with Panday Sining, and the Philippine Solidarity Group. We also started using arts like theater to express ourselves, and writing, and poetry. People would ask us to present at events and we did, but our roots were as a mutual support group.

RD: On that note, it seemed like artistic practice was an essential component of your activism. Can you speak more about that, about the function of artistic practice in your activist work?

MA: My dad migrated as an architectural illustrator. He did perspectives all by hand. I think that's where the drive for me comes from. All the things that I have done always comes from a place of being creative and of being expressive. My career has changed since then, but I was doing a lot of art: visual art, photography, video and performance art. That was the natural place for me to go. The art and films that I made focused on the diasporic experience and trying to find roots while being born in Canada. I made films before and after I was at school (OCAD). At OCAD University I reconnected with a family friend, Jowenne Herrera, and we formed the Philippine Interdisciplinary Students Organization (PISO) because there were no Filipino organizations. We had artists from each discipline—sculpture, painting, communication design, and integrated media. This was in 1998. Then we formed

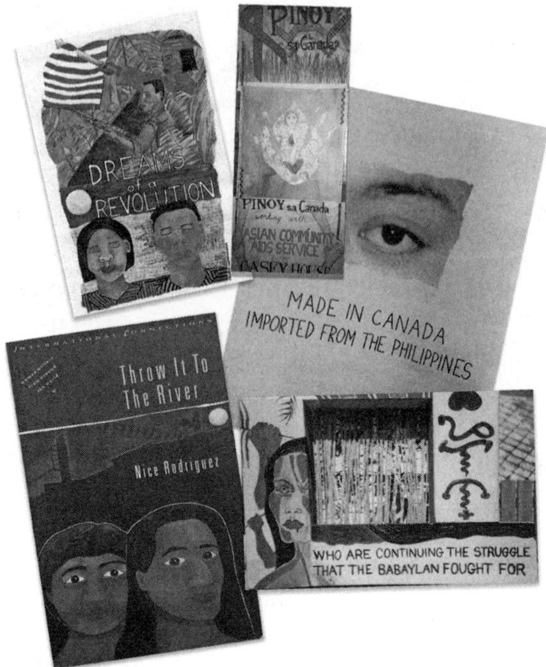

Collage of some of Melanya's artwork.

Students Activists Workers Artists (SAWA) with other community members. Once a month we had a workshop at OCAD, partnering with migrant workers and organizations such as the Carlos Bulosan Cultural Workshop. We also connected with Benguet Ifugao Bontoc Apayao Kalinga (BIBAK) and the Philippine Solidarity Group (PSG) Toronto. We would present our art to people in the community and the doors were open for everybody, not just artists. It was a way to bring artists, community folks, and scholars together. At the end of the year, we made a *bahay kubo* [nipa hut] in the atrium of the school. The artworks that were created from the workshops throughout the year and the art displays from PISO members became the *bahay kubo*. We opened up with a traditional dance by BIBAK and provided Filipino food. There was also a Filipino art show at A Space Gallery and a film screening at Vtape.

JA: I never thought I could be an artist. I applied to OCAD University as a mature student because Melanya went there. She helped

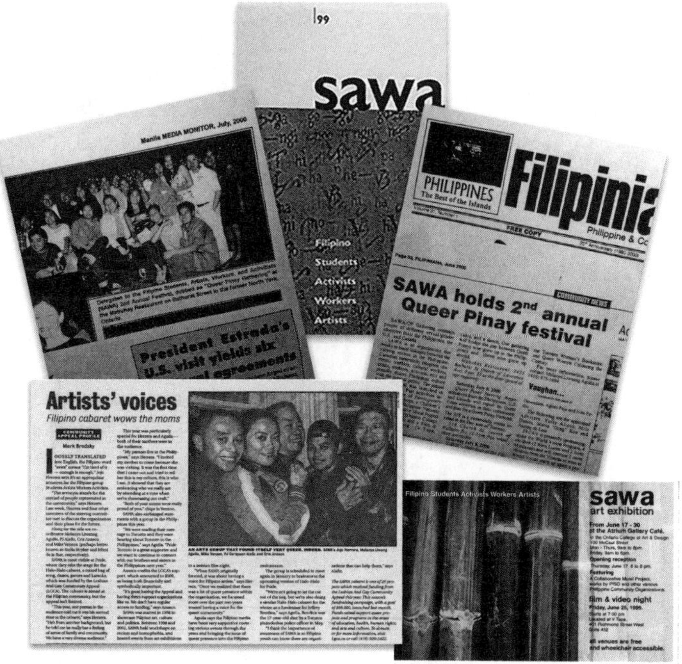

Articles about SAWA in the *Philippine Canadian News.*

me imagine that I could have a place there too. I didn't have any Filipino artist role models around that time, but Melanya would tell me how she made films, and that we could be in them, and that it could be about us and our experiences. Art was a big part of our organizing work. Melanya would make handmade event flyers, and we'd photocopy them at someone's workplace, and then we would go out to events and hand them to people. There was no Facebook then, you actually had to show up and build relationships. We would also go to CKLN, the community radio station, and talk about our events. Babaylan would sing, revolutionary songs on-air like "Babae" by Inang Laya:

> Bakit ba mayrong mga Lisa
> Mga Liliosa at mga Lorena
> Na di natakot makibaka
> At ngayo'y marami nang kasama?
> Mga babae, ang mithiin ay lumaya!

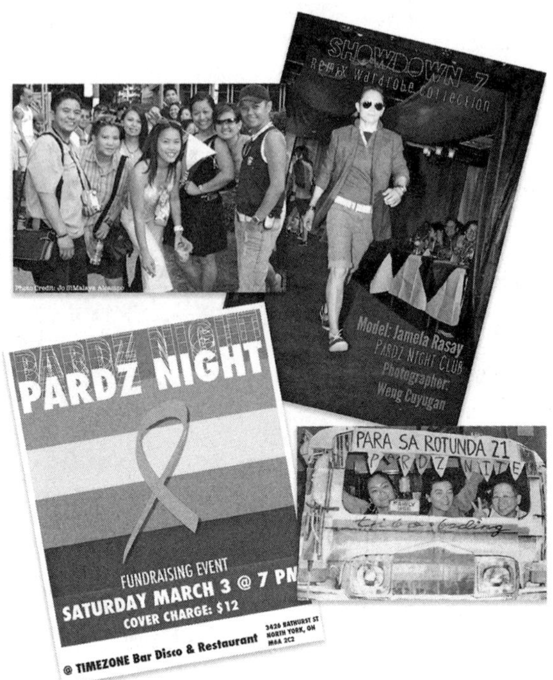

Pardz Night members and events.

Maybe our pronunciation was not perfect, but it was heartfelt!

We would also form dance groups, like what you saw at *Pardz* Night. One time, they had this contest called Mr. Pardz, and JB was one of the contestants. JB chose to talk about political stuff like Babaylan and *tibo* ethics, alternative ways to be *tibo*, that aren't misogynist, or based on toxic masculinity. There wasn't a language for trans identity then or transitioning and embracing the identity of *tibo*. I was proud of JB for opening up a discussion about those issues.

PA: We held one of the first *Pardz* Nights in a community centre. I also gave a party at the Rohampton hotel. It was not a lesbian event at first. It was mixed. It was a fund-raising event for Philippine causes. We saw all these *tibo*s there and saw a community. Then I hung out with everybody and the lesbians who grew up here. I met Cecile, who is a Vietnamese-Filipino, and then Diana in the Filipino community. So we started creating a community. But that's before

Rampa even (the fashion show I organized). That was in 1997, the beginning of *Pardz* Night.

LS: There was a lot of queer Asian activism in other large cities too, in New York, Vancouver, etc. We would collect zines from these other places, like Bamboo Girl created by Sabrina Margarita Alcantara-Tan in 1995, which was a feminist zine that I kept copies of. Of course, performance through my Pride outfits was important for me too. In terms of making of the outfits, there's an absolute strategy in terms of trying to maximize media attention with the outfit, and the humour and cleverness are also key. It works best when you succeed at amusing the audience, because that's where you can hit them with messaging about important social issues at the same time. My outfits were always celebratory and political all at once, even when I wasn't addressing a particular issue with a sign on me. I was always aware that I was a person of color, and that Filipinos standing on the route would be happy when they saw me. From that very first 1993 queer women of color float during Pride, which I was on, I have tried to show the larger queer community that we people of colour are also here. We are queer folks of color in your city and we're walking in your streets right now, right in front of you. If you are part of the white queer community, you will now have to think about us. Everyone will have to think about us now; we are in the middle of Yonge Street [the main street where the Pride parade occurs] and you will have to look at us marching down the street, even for just a few seconds. That's part of the reason I love to march. And it's political because there are queer women of color, like myself, who are not always read as queer, and we are showing the world that we too have political thoughts. A photo of one of my outfits even got published in the *Toronto Star*, which really forced people to pay attention to the issue that outfit was addressing!

RD: I guess, as a final message (given our time constraints), do you have any advice for queer people of color youth, who may want to continue these efforts?

MA: I think the organizations that we were involved in brought us out together because we were friends, activists, and artists, so there was room for all of that—the friendship, the connection, the hanging out. During our time, we also connected with similar groups, such as Kilawin Kolektibo in New York. We were part of the Filipino and women of color communities, we were very immersed. Some of us were also involved with other feminist organizations such as Camp SIS and Sistah's Café, so we worked, socialized, and lived very closely together. When we committed, we had to be present.

PA: For me, I'd say don't be afraid to just do things. Take initiative. We didn't need a grant to have some drag shows or to have some parties. We just needed each other and a cause.

LS: For me, this was all very empowering. Also, I want people to see the importance of cross-solidarity. When we were protesting the staging of Miss Saigon, the Black community was protesting with us as well, so there were Black and Asian people protesting Miss Saigon. And when Black communities were protesting about racism in North York, Asian people would join those protests as well. We have to challenge intersectional oppression, no matter who we are.

JA: It helped to have mentors who nurtured us with loving intent. When I eventually came out, they said, "We already knew, Jo. We were just waiting for you."

The Carlos Bulosan Theatre presented a play that talked about homophobia in the Filipino community. It was called "Not On My Time," it was about generational gaps and stories about family and coming out. My mom went to see it and it helped heal some misunderstandings.

For many of our mentors, their passions were linked to the People Power revolution and to the anti-Marcos dictatorship movement. They came up through that fire. They believed social change was possible and they knew how to organize. I'm grateful that we had that guidance as youth trying to understand who we were, where we come from, and what we want to contribute to the world.

MA: And the love between yourselves as well.

Life Reflections of a Filipino Elvis

JB Ramos

My story spans decades, continents, and different eras of time. It is one of self-discovery, a story of spiritual journey and community. My story starts off, just like many other Filipino immigrants, leaving the Philippines to find a better future, a better life abroad. It was my mother's mom, whom we fondly call "Nanay," who paved the way for our family to come to Canada back in the 1960s. However, it wasn't until the 1970s that my parents made their trek to Canada to start a family. I am the second-born of three children, I have an older brother and a younger sister. I looked up to my brother growing up and wanted to be like him, always excited to get his hand-me-downs. My parents most probably had an idea that I was different in my early years, but never thought too much about it, thinking I would grow out of my boyish nature.

Since my siblings and I were born and raised in Canada, my parents wanted us to be "Canadian." However, I could not help but feel a strong curiosity to want to learn more about where our cultural roots came from. In grade school, my parents enrolled me in Saturday morning "Filipino class." This was where Filipino kids learned how to speak the main dialect of the Filipino language Tagalog, along with traditional cultural dances (such as the *tinikling*), how to play various traditional instruments (e.g., the *banduriya*), the history and various other aspects of what it means to be Filipino (such as the food).

I enjoyed and looked forward to these weekend classes because they gave me a better understanding of where my family came from. Not only that, it was also the beginning of understanding and becoming more aware of my gender and identity. I did not comprehend at that age what or why I felt towards certain girls an "attraction." For all I thought, this was "friendship." But I knew deep within me that it was different. I would envision myself as a boy, and wanted to be able to ask girls to hang out, or give them gifts as boys would to girls to show that they like them. I recall one girl who acknowledged my thoughtfulness;

she said to me "If you were a boy, I would like you." These words reverberated in my soul, much deeper than I could understand at such a young age.

There were endless nights when I would have conversations with God (having been raised Catholic) and ask Him to change me to be a boy, so when I would awake, I could find myself as my "true self." Morning after morning, I would wake up not having my prayers answered and would feel disappointed and angry towards God. It was when puberty hit that I felt completely broken, and my hopes and prayers of being a "boy" were left unanswered and rejected. I cried, cursed, and felt even more angry and confused as my body began to change. It was then that I convinced my parents to let me join a local community center and learn karate. I recalled my dad's stories of his training in the Philippines, and I wanted to be able to do things that he said he could. To be strong, to be able to fight and be fearless.

I wanted to feel a sense of power and strength, despite the confusion and anger I had brewing within me. I was angry, not only at God, but at my parents for making me the wrong gender. I knew from an early age that I wanted more than anything to be like my older brother, a boy.

My parents enrolled me in Okinawan Shorin Ryu karate at the local community center. I studied it from about grade 7 to grade 10. During these four years I competed at local tournaments in sparring and *kata*. This helped me build my confidence and focus my angry energy into something more centered. The movie *The Karate Kid* came out around the time I was studying karate. I found it amazing how a scrawny guy was able to fight and beat so many more intimidating fighters. Those were my early formative years taking karate, and it helped pave the way for my love of martial arts. I was not aware of how much it made an impact on me until years later.

It wasn't until my uncle passed away of AIDS-related complications, on Halloween 1992 (which was ironically his favorite day of the year), that there was a huge turning point, not only in my life, but in my family's as well. It was a realization of having to deal with internalized homophobia and the need for education against sexually transmitted diseases, especially HIV/AIDS. My uncle's passing was emotionally painful for all of us. It forced us to realize how much my family needed to be more open and more understanding. My uncle had been gay, and he was never able to be fully himself with the family. They would constantly ask if he had a girlfriend. Although they probably had an idea of the truth, he was never able to come out and fully be himself. It wasn't until he was on his deathbed that we were made aware of his sexuality, of his other family in the LGBTQ community, and of his love of drag performance as "Kiki Von Klitoris." He was a handsome man, but also a beautiful woman. After his passing, my family slowly started to become more open-minded, and I was able to be more myself and not feel ashamed or hide who I was.

The following year, then, was a year of hope, change, and community-building. This was the year when I became exposed to community events, graduated from high school, and made friends who were *tibo* (a tagalog slang term for "tomboy"). *Tibo* and *pardz*, these were words I had no idea existed until I fatefully became friends with Filipino *tibo*s who had recently migrated from the Philippines. One day, I went to the local mall to get a quick bite from a fast-food chain and there was someone who worked there who befriended me and invited me to hang out with her friends. Although she had just come from the Philippines, this person dressed and acted similarly to me. It was amazing, as I had never met anyone else who was Filipina, boyish, and butch. Little did I know that this friendship would open doors to new ones, and also make me want to understand more of my cultural roots. I had never had friends like these; they were older, and I looked up to them, while they looked out for me. This unspoken understanding and acknowledgment is something I will always cherish close to my heart. I called them "*kuya*," meaning "older brother," while they called me "*bunso*," or "youngest child." We still use these terms of endearment whenever we see each other today. This was the first real sense of community I had felt connected to, a cultural and self-identifying group of people with whom I felt I could wholeheartedly be myself.

My *tibo* friends were a tight-knit group of their own who enjoyed spending time together as a "*barkada*," who valued their family, worked hard, and went to church. We would spend many days of the week "*tumambay*" at each other's homes, from Tuesday nights at a local pub to weekend "food trips and minus-one contests" at each other's homes, and of course, Sunday dim sum or McDonald's breakfasts after church. We spent a lot of time together just enjoying each other's company, food, and conversation. There's a common saying that food brings people together; this was a definite truth I learned. Through our food escapades, I learned to eat chicken feet "*adidas*" and deep fried pork hock "crispy *pata*." They taught me a lot about their experiences growing up back in the Philippines, their relationships, and their challenges in adjusting to life in Canada. They taught me how to be comfortable being myself, and they told me about their experiences with relationships.

I was still in my last year of high school when I first became friends with them. Through them, I realized there was much more out there in the world to experience not only in life, but in relationships as well. I learned about their insecurities in identity and what it meant to be *tibo* to them. I learned about their relationships dating women, straight, married women with children, what it meant to have an "LDR" (long-distance relationship), women with boyfriends, dating more than one woman, multiple women. I learned a lot. They exposed me to things about life and relationships I never knew existed. At this point I was still quite naive, but I was open to learning from them. To them, dating women who would eventually leave them to marry and have children with men was "normal," and they were okay and accepting of this reality. Back then, in the early 1990s, "same sex marriage" did not exist, nor was IVF (in vitro fertilization) a feasible reality. So, to my "*kuyas*," their acceptance of being "temporary" to these women was a reality to them. They just accepted it and enjoyed the time they spent with these women, knowing that all they could be was "temporary." Learning from them the harsh reality of relationships in being with women, I tried to understand where their perspective was on both the *tibo* and woman's side. Never had I met or been attracted to a 100 percent lesbian, as I had never identified myself as one. I knew I was more a boy than anything else, and I knew I was attracted to straight women. Thinking about it now, this makes sense to who I am today.

During this time, while I was busy with my newfound *tibo* community, my mom became quite involved and active in AIDS activism. The death of my uncle, her brother, made her want to give back to the greater community. She volunteered at GAAP (Gay Asian Aids Project), ACT (AIDS Committee of Toronto), and ACAS (Asian Community AIDS Services). Through my mom's community involvement, she helped pave the way for me to learn to be more compassionate, understanding, and open-minded. All the anger, confusion, and frustration I had growing up was not as predominant in my life, as I found that sense of belonging and community I was looking for growing up. It was in the spring of 1993 that my mom mentioned to me and my Scarborough Filipino *tibo* crew that we should go to an event which was being held at a place called "Sistah's Café." It was a women's space located on Queen St. W. We had no idea what we were going to, except that it was supposed to be a Filipino event of some type.

My *tibo kuyas* and I had no idea what we were getting into. The event had a serious undertone, discussing political issues and events happening in the Philippines. They sent me in first to check out the venue, as we had not been to this side of town. So we all sat in the back of the venue and listened. We were not sure of how to react, as none of us had ever been to an event of this sort in our lives at this point. We unknowingly attended the event, assuming it was some sort of "typical" Filipino gathering, one with food, drinks, and music. However, we all sat through the entire event quite confused.

Little did I know that this random evening escapade would pave the way for my journey through community and social involvement which would span a wide range of outlets: workshops, performances, rallies, and gatherings. This one cold Canadian night connected both my worlds, my Western upbringing and my cultural roots. It opened my views and perspective to the fact that there is something more to life than what I had previously thought. On this fateful night I was introduced to another queer *pinay* group, also recently formed, who called themselves Babaylan. They too were older than me, and I felt I had a lot to learn from them. I recall that at the event I needed to use the washroom, so I walked down to the back of the space and met another Westernized *tibo*. The first thing she asked was, "What do you like? Butch or femme?" Immediately, I responded "Femme." I knew at that moment that we would form an inseparable friendship. I stood there, stopped in my tracks, and was taken aback, but I couldn't help but be humored by such a question. After that initial event at Sistah's Café, I went back to my usual routine with my *barkada* from Scarborough. However, I was still trying to absorb and understand what that event and its importance were, as this was so new to me.

Eventually, I found myself being invited to attend informal Tagalog lessons and Philippine history sessions that Babaylan had at a place in the Bloor-Annex area. They were held at PSG (Philippine Solidarity Group). We had our weekly meetings, check-in, telling how our week had been, and then we moved on to the lessons. However, many times we would end up dancing in the parking lot behind the building, as Rich would bring her rental car and blast music out of the windows. Back then, it was still cassette tapes!

Although we had our weekly meetings, for some reason, we were able to spend more than that one day together. We would meet up for coffee, just to talk. I found myself learning a different perspective on things. The Babaylan were either Canadian-born or raised in Canada, whereas my *kuyas* were born and raised in the Philippines and had immigrated here. Although we were all Filipino, we all had different perspectives on life. However, I found a connection to both worlds.

This was the beginning of seeing the world and life in a broader context: of seeing not only the importance of family, but the importance of social activism, education, and community-building. With the friends I made in Babaylan, we participated in various workshops and events, for and with the Filipino and LGBTQ communities. We did workshops in Metrohall, at various social events, and participated in numerous rallies. Through these events, I was exposed to people from different backgrounds and experiences, and I listened and learned a lot about their views and lives. Through Babaylan, we had built connections together and with others. The 1990s were for me a time of growth, self-expression, self-discovery, social activism, and community. One way that we expressed and shared experiences was in the form of performance. I am thankful to have been part of this time in history, never thinking of the impact it would have in the future. Since this was just what we did. I never thought of it as creating change or a social movement. It was how we were, just doing what we all did and enjoyed as a group, a collective. I think this sense of community support was something we all needed during this time. It is very rare to have friendships forged during times of change, to last and flourish for decades. But the connections and friendships made at that time have had a deep-rooted impact in many of our lives, one which many of us still share decades later.

My mom's volunteering in various organizations had exposed me to other community events, which were ones of celebrating life and community. In addition, there was an opportunity to work on a groundbreaking play written by Lani Montreal, who was based in Toronto during this time, called *My Grandmother and I*. My mom landed the role as the mother the second time the play was recast, and I was given a role in part of the dream sequence as one of the traditional dancers. I know that this play helped my mom cope with the loss of my uncle and brought us closer together. Moreover, during this time I had been doing some comic illustrations for a small local newspaper called *Pinoy Sa Canada* (*Filipinos of Canada*). My comic strips focused on issues involving homophobia and education and were a reflection of what I had experienced and was going through.

I met other drag performers, older Filipino gay men and trans women, who loved to perform to songs by Gloria Gaynor, Celine Dion, and so on. The passion and beauty of their inner selves truly came out as soon

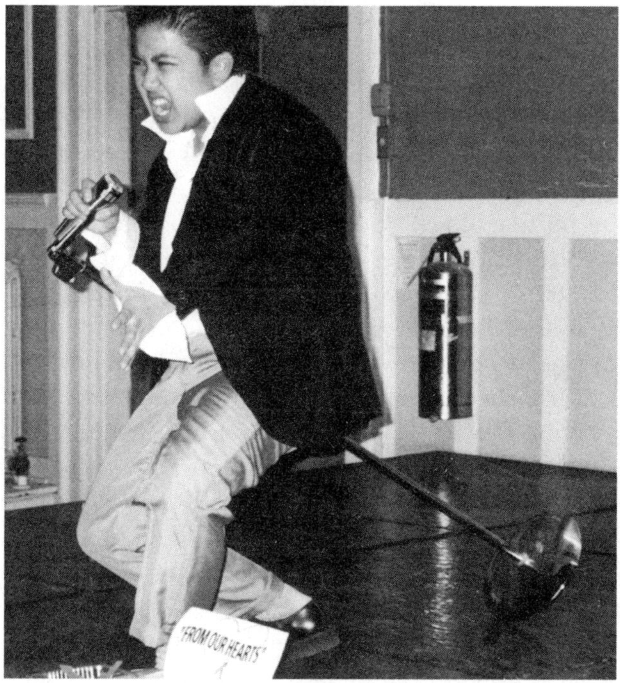

JB Ramos as Elvis.

as they donned their gowns, put on full makeup, and got on stage to perform. These "women" helped bring me out of my shell and pushed me to express myself through performance.

Little did I know that they would eventually coin me the first "Filipino drag king—PinElvis." During this time in my life, I was drawn to 1950s vintage fashion and music. My favorite pop icons were Elvis Presley and James Dean. Although it was decades in the past, this era was one I was drawn to. It could have been my hair, the way I dressed, or the music I listened to back then that gave me that nickname. I had an old retro microphone stand that I would use when I was in a band in high school lying around in the basement, and this microphone stand would become my symbol of self-expression. I would bring it everywhere I went when I performed. There was one song in particular that touched my soul. Possibly because of the experiences I had with women during that time in my life, the song was not sung by Elvis Presley but by Dion and was called "Run Around Sue."

I remember the very first time I was asked to perform, it was at a GAAP/ACAS event, which was held at the 519 Community Centre. Prior to this, I had never performed solo, except for my past martial arts tournaments and competitions. I guess the confidence I had from those competitions did help me in my first "PinElvis" performance. It was very nerve-wracking, but that first time I performed was also liberating. I stepped up on that stage, mic in hand, wearing bright green pants, a white dress shirt, black blazer, and retro black-and-white dress shoes. I recall looking out at the crowd before my song started and thinking to myself, "What am I doing here? Will they like my performance? I can't believe I am actually doing this. Why did I decide to do this?" My heart was racing in my chest, sweat was dripping down my back, and I had a case of extreme nerves. But as soon as I heard the beginning of the song start . . . "Here's my story, it's sad, but true," all the nerves and doubt went away. All my experiences in relationships with women were expressed in this song, and that was all I was feeling. After the song was finished, I felt a sense of nerves again, waiting to see how the crowd would respond. They were fully supportive and seemed to enjoy it, clapping and cheering. It was an overwhelming sense of relief. Throughout the years after, word got around, and this was just the beginning of my various "PinElvis" performances. I have performed at various events, clubs in Toronto, and all the way to New York City.

At this time in my life I was feeling a strong need to figure out who I was and what my purpose here in the world was. Although I enjoyed community, there was also a side of me that thrived on moments of isolation, that needed to be one with myself and go on an inner journey. Although I had great support from my family and friends, I could not figure out what was missing in my life, what the emptiness I felt was, and the strong need to get answers.

At this time in my life, we "Babaylan" were introduced to another sister group from New York City called "Kilawin Kolektibo." They came up to Toronto for a long weekend in May 1994. They attended an event, and my friend Rich and I decided to join them at their luncheon at Mayette's afterward. There was one woman in particular who caught my eye; her name was Christine, or Chris. Little did I know that this fateful meeting, and connection of our souls, would be a major turning point in my life a couple of years later. I was a month shy of my nineteenth birthday and thought I knew everything about life. My special relationship with Chris would only last two years, but it changed me forever.

She was the first Philippines-born *pinay* I was drawn to. Her extreme maturity at twenty-two years of age was very attractive. She lived on her own with roommates in Queens in New York City, studied law, and worked full-time at an office job. Back then, cellphones were only for the well-off. I had a pager. Computers were in the beginning stages of becoming more accessible. Back then, all our communication was through snail mail, phone cards (long-distance calling), and getting paged/beeped. Our friendship developed despite the distance, and we made promises to see each other every few months. We even traveled to Montreal and Quebec City. These were some of the best years of my youth. However, it would soon come crashing down, leaving me utterly devastated and broken. It was the Labor Day long weekend in August 1996. Chris planned to come up to Toronto and introduce me to her only sibling, her brother. They both were driving en route to visit on the last long weekend that summer. She wanted to take the route through Quebec and show her brother this place she really enjoyed. Ironically, this was the place where they got in a tragic accident and Chris lost her life.

I recall feeling uneasy that morning at work, as I was expecting her and her brother to arrive that morning. They never did. That same afternoon, I got a phone call from my mom at work, and she asked me to come straight home. I found this weird, as she had never said that to me before. But it wasn't the words she said, it was the way she said them and the underlying trembling uneasiness I could sense, that made me feel something was not right. When I got home later that evening, my best friend and her partner were parked outside the house. As soon as I saw this, I knew then something bad had happened. I entered the house and they, along with my mom, told me that Chris had gotten into a bad accident. Immediately I ran to my room and started to pack things, wanting to be where she was. I was confused and frustrated, because that's all they told me. Jovi took me for a walk to a park nearby. She knew the truth but couldn't muster the strength to tell me. Shortly after, I saw my mom walking towards us. I knew she was trying to be strong for me, but, she knew she had to tell me the truth. She sat us both down, and with tears in her eyes, she told me that Chris was no longer here and that she had died in the car accident. At that moment I felt my world fall apart and crumble. My heart shattered into a million pieces and complete, utter sadness and darkness surrounded my entire being. Her death and the loss of her left a big wound, one that changed me and threw me into the darkest and lowest point in my life. At such a young age, being only twenty-one years old, I once again found myself hating God and questioning life and my purpose.

The years after this traumatic experience were filled with self-hate and guilt. I blamed myself for Chris's untimely death because I believed it was because she was on her way to see me that she had died. If she hadn't decided to visit, maybe she would still be alive today. I blamed God for taking her away. Shortly after her funeral in New York City I found myself digging deeper into self-destructive behavior. I found temporary comfort in smoking and drinking heavily and engaging in casual relationships. Everything eventually became a blur. During this time I didn't realize I was driving away my closest friends because I hadn't realized that my grief and sorrow were also bringing them down as well. Years passed and life moved on, and somehow I learned to muffle and live with this darkness of loss.

A few years later, we had a Babaylan-Kilawin reunion conference in Toronto, in which all the members came together over a weekend. Who knew that this one weekend would shift my life and give me a renewed sense of purpose? One space where they had us gather was at a local tae kwon do school. Entering the school brought back familiar feelings of what I had enjoyed and found strength doing . . . the martial arts. Being in that space was comforting and sparked something inside me. I felt a renewed need to get back on the "path" that I had strayed away from for many years. I joined the martial arts school a few months later. A couple years into training, we had a guest instructor do a class on Filipino martial arts with the use of rattan sticks. At this point in my life, I had never known or heard about our own martial arts. This was something that sparked a renewed interest in my culture. The fluidity and gracefulness of the way she demonstrated the use and application of the simple-looking sticks left me in utter amazement. It was beautiful but deadly, graceful yet lethal. From that moment on, I knew I found what I had been looking for.

In the early 2000s there was the official inception of the Filipino Martial Arts School, Combat Science: Warrior Arts of Asia, that my mentor founded. She helped me on a different journey in life. She not only taught me about our ancient martial art, but she pushed me to limits I never thought I could surpass. She helped me appreciate and want to learn more about a different aspect of our Philippine culture—its healing and warrior arts. The use of the sticks was just the beginning of years of training and learning not only about the martial art, but about who I was and what I was searching for. With her, and the school, we participated at a variety of events to conduct demonstrations and self-defense workshops. It was amazing being able to share our martial art with the community, since at this time the teaching of the Filipino martial art (FMA) was still fairly new in Canada.

Years passed, and so did my life's focus. My training spurred me on to compete at international competitions in full-contact stick fighting. It was different from the other martial arts I studied in the past, as they were Japanese and Korean-based empty hand martial arts, whereas the FMA was a weapons-based martial art. This "sports aspect" of full-contact stick fighting was quite different from the tournaments I had done in the past. At this point in my martial arts training, I hadn't had to push past the fear of fighting with weapons. There were times when I would cry out of frustration, as I couldn't help but encounter a disconnect between my mind and my body movements.

One thing I enjoyed about the sparring was that once you put on the armor, you were just another fighter. No gender. My mentor taught me to fear no one and not to put up with anyone in and out of the ring. If I let them control me in the ring, it reflects on how I take on challenges in life. This newfound philosophy put a different spin on my thinking. I realized that a lot of my fears and insecurities were in my mind, in what I thought. I competed at numerous international world championship competitions. And it does take a different mindset to dedicate a big part of your life to training and to focus and compete at an international level. For years, I did this and thrived on the physical and mental challenges, to see how far I could push myself and see where it would take me. However, I knew that deep inside there was something else I was pushing and fighting for . . . within me. With my mentor, I traveled the world competing and training, but there was still something I felt I needed to figure out about myself and my life's journey.

Sometime in 2008, I was in a major car accident on the way to Ottawa with some friends. The jeep we were in rolled over and over into a ditch after a freak, unexpected snowstorm. My head hit the windshield, but the impact left no marks or scratches, as if I was left unscathed. My friends were miraculously able to walk away from the wreckage with minor bruises and scratches. When this happened, I felt uneasy and my spirit was unsettled, since it was a traumatic experience. I asked my mentor to give me a *reiki* treatment in hopes of realigning my energy and helping me be more centered again.

That *reiki* treatment is one I will never forget. At the beginning of the session, my mentor said "Someone's here to visit you. Her name starts with the letter C, she's petite . . ." Immediately I felt tears flow from my eyes and a huge release of anguish and sorrow I had been carrying within me for over a decade. I knew it was Christine. My mentor had no idea about that tragedy with Chris, and hearing her come through was an overwhelming emotional release. Chris's message to me was that she had never left me and that I had to move on and not blame myself for what happened to her. I left that *reiki* session in complete awe and exhaustion, trying to grasp the reality of what had happened. After that, I realized there was a reason why I hadn't died in that car accident. I had a greater purpose in this life which had yet to reveal itself.

Years went by, and my life continued to focus on my martial arts training and competing. It wasn't until 2011 that I finally came to terms with what I had been trying to figure out about myself and wanted to change. This was the year I decided to physically become more of the person I felt like within me. This was the year I had chest reconstruction surgery. It was the Family Day long weekend, and I was helping out at a weekend-long martial arts grading. My surgery was scheduled that Monday. After an entire weekend of training, by Monday morning my body was achy from the training, but the rest of me was very eager to get the physical change to reflect the part of me whom I knew had always been there. This decision had been a long time coming for me. I finally felt a sense of freedom.

It's an interesting thing I have learned on this journey of life and being true to yourself. The more you learn to face your fears and accept who you are, the more others will also respect your truth. My transition was never really an issue, as those around me had seen me as who I was on the inside. There isn't a day that I cannot help but be thankful for such amazing support and unconditional love throughout my lifetime.

It wasn't until 2012 that another event would alter and shift my life again. That was the year that I was given the opportunity to move from student to teacher, role model, and leader all at the same time. It was the fall of 2012 when my mentor passed along the school and her knowledge and teachings to me to continue them. I didn't know how to take this revelation, since for about a decade I had followed in her footsteps and assumed I would forever be a student. I never thought a greater sense of responsibility would be given to me. I was overwhelmed and knew little of what it took to run a school, to be a leader, role model, and instructor. Although I had years of marital arts training, it wasn't until this opportunity opened its doors that a different challenge presented itself. At this point, I had no idea which direction I wanted to go with the school. I knew I had to figure out what my vision would be for the future of the school. However, it wasn't until 2014 that I had another life revelation get thrown at me, in the rural Philippine province of Tarlac.

In January 2014 I accompanied my *lola* [grandmother] back home to her small town of San Manuel in Tarlac, just like many elder Filipinos tend to fly back home for the winter and spend their summers in Canada. I knew I had always wanted to see where my family roots lay on both of my parents' sides. Since my previous times of traveling to the Philippines had been just to train with the various Filipino martial arts teachers in and around Manila and compete in Cebu, I had no idea that visiting and going back to my ancestral roots would give me more clarity on my past and present.

During this trip, I learned so much about the old ways and cultural traditions that it was an eye opener. One day during my stay, my *lola* had been asking for the town *abularyo* to come to the house. It was then that she gave me a reading, done with a candle and a bowl of water. The reading stopped me in my tracks and gave me the clarity I was searching for. In a nutshell, it revealed my spiritual path and ancestral connection to a warrior ancestor guiding and protecting me in this lifetime and lifetimes before.

A few weeks after I got back to Toronto, I was still thinking about that revelation and the deeper meaning it gave to my life's purpose, about why I had been given the opportunity to continue carrying on the teachings of the FMA and what it meant. This was the year that opened doors to possibilities of growth and community. I knew I wanted to be able to do more with the school, and reach out to the greater community. It wasn't until the spring, when a longtime dear friend from Babaylan, Jo, reached out to me to see if I was interested in doing self-defense workshops with the live-in caregivers, since there had been a number of violent incidents against live-in caregivers in the news. Little did I know that this was just the beginning of giving back and sharing what the martial arts had given to me.

Unlike many other Filipino martial arts schools, ours has always been known to do work with the various community groups. Opportunities to do workshops with the youth, LGBTQ, and FMA demonstrations and performances and teaching at a yearly martial arts conference soon opened doors for me. I began to see that there was a bigger picture: not just to train, spar, and compete, but to share and give back. There were people out there who could be reached out to, people who might also see the same value of sharing and learning our lethal but beautiful ancient martial art and keep our ancient Filipino culture alive.

Through my life's journey, I have realized that the one constant variable in my life has been that of the martial arts. With it, I found I learned to appreciate my cultural roots and be fearless in being true to myself. It has taught me that strength has no gender. And in that sense, it helped me feel more at home in my own body.

Decades have gone by since that fateful night my life crossed paths with the Babaylan of Toronto, but everything always comes full circle. Many of us still continue our work with the communities through our outreach and skills. Most of all, we have maintained our connection to each other and to our cultural heritage.

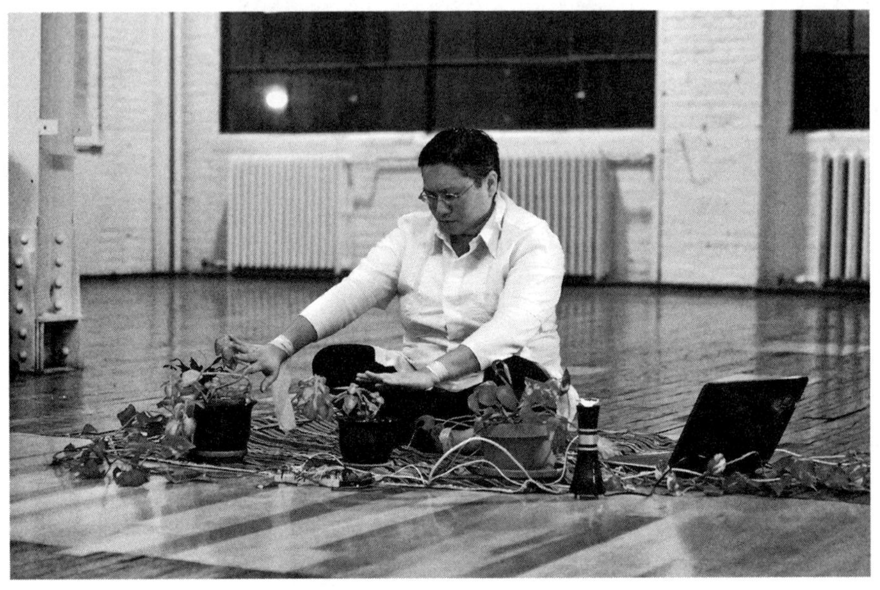

Jo SiMalaya Alcampo performing *Singing Plants Reconnect Memory*, 2011.

Bridging Community and Artistic Practice

Interview with Jo SiMalaya Alcampo

The interdisciplinary practice of Manila-born and Toronto-based Jo SiMalaya Alcampo is informed by her journey to self-knowledge as a queer Filipina artist. While acknowledging her positionality as a settler of color on Indigenous land, Alcampo engages decolonizing work in her many roles as a community-based organizer, activist, educator, and artist. In the following conversation with Marissa Largo, Alcampo traces her formation as a socially engaged community theater artist to her current explorations of Philippine indigeneity and its intersections with spirituality, queerness, racial and gender equity, and collective action.

ML: Can you tell me about your path to becoming an artist? Being a queer Filipina artist, what are some of the unique experiences that have informed the artist that you are today?

JA: In the 1990s, I worked with the feminist theater group, the Company of Sirens. I started with writing plays for their youth section, S.I.S. Theatre in Education. We would create plays collectively around issues like date rape, sexual assault, consent, homophobia, and heterosexism. We would present plays in high schools using Augusto Boal's popular theater principles using audience intervention. So let's say someone is being bullied at school, we'd play out the scene and ask the audience members: How might you support this person as an ally? Or what would you do if you were in their place? Do you want to replace them in the scene and try a different strategy? That was a great way to learn as a youth about how you can take a collective writing process, improvise it, and then put it into a script that would always change. That's what I really liked; the dynamic part of popular theater is the ability to adapt to different audiences. Mainly we toured rural high schools in northern Ontario. I played the person who was coming out and questioning her cultural identity as a diasporic Filipino Canadian youth. After the show, students would come and talk to me, and some would come out, saying, "There has been no one else I have been able to tell this to and there are no supports in my community for this." Those experiences taught me that art has to be responsible and connect folks to community resources and support. That was my first exposure to how social justice can be linked to artistic expression.

After that, Sirens recommended me to audition for a Filipino theater company called Carlos Bulosan Cultural Workshop (CBCW). Now it's called CBT (Carlos Bulosan Theatre). In 1992 I met the cofounders, Fely Villasin and Martha Ocampo. They were part of the Coalition Against the Marcos Dictatorship. CBCW was the cultural arm. They were not directly doing popular theater, but the collective process was similar. We would get together and improvise scenes from our lived experiences and Fely would coalesce that and write it into a script. I'm grateful I experienced community theater where everyone was a volunteer. This was after People Power. There was a sense of hopeful energy. We would read about Philippine history, value-based education, and Sikolohiyang Pilipino [Filipino psychology] in groups and then we would report back to each other what we learned, but we'd do it through theater. We'd act it out. So if you were learning about the value of *makahiya* [being shy or humble], you would talk about the positive and negative aspects in our culture, but by acting it out. But we still had the theory. They would introduce some pretty advanced texts like Constantino and Enriquez. I had no background in Philippine history or culture from texts. My only experience was through my family. They didn't even treat it like it was a big deal! I would sometimes tell them: "You know, I have no idea what we're talking about sometimes. Sometimes you're talking about Philippine revolution and stuff. I'm not sure what it's all about." They said: "That's okay. It's like an immersion."

It was a playful immersion and nonjudgmental because even if you didn't get the theory, what they were trying to do was to link it to something that we could relate to on a personal level. I'll give you an example. When they talked about power, they would explore the Philippine revolution through readings about the Katipunan. They would assign us to reading groups. They put me in a group with these men who, while we were all volunteers, would expect me to be

the one to wash the dishes, clear the table, or even serve them food!
Of course, I didn't feel comfortable with it, but I didn't know how to
articulate that uneasiness and power imbalance.

At the end of the workshop they asked: "Now, does anyone have
any comments about the process?" We learned about the revolution, and we did this great presentation, and the men in the program
would say: "Jo, just speak for the group."

I had no words for emotional labor or patriarchy then, but I had
my own lived experience where I was expected to serve my brother,
father, and uncles. I remembered how my brother was able to have
all this freedom, that I did not . . . I kind of got triggered when I had
this experience with my group. Then when Fely and Martha asked if
anyone had anything to say about the process, I would look around.
The men were all silent. They would ask us again: "Anything?" And
I was like: "I do! I do not like what just happened here! This is how
it made me feel." I was very emotional and I couldn't really articulate it. I just had the emotion. They were like: "Okay, let's talk about
that." [laughs] That was how they unpacked power and privilege as
a group. The artistic work is part of it, but how we worked together
was as important or even more important. I was not aware of that
process until a decade later, when I helped them facilitate similar
workshops. I started to understand that the groups were assigned
very strategically. I asked: "Hey! Is this what you did to me?!" They
said: "Oh yeah!" [laughs].

They were always there for support. They were always check-
ing in. I think their understanding of activism was that it had to be
rooted in something real for the person and that art is not just art
for art's sake.

I didn't know I was going to be an artist interested in activism.
They opened up this possibility for me. I attribute much of who I
am now and how I work collectively to those early experiences. My
mentors understood it was important to nurture young people and
be there to guide them when we had questions.

These lessons stayed with me as I emerged into my own art practice. Folks have since asked me to mentor them. I try to approach
that with mindfulness around what I went through, what I might
change, or what I want to pass on.

ML: You are an artist in your own right, a community-based art
activist, writer, and performer. Your practice, whether it is individual

or collective in whatever medium, seems to be driven by a desire to make connections, between women in the caregiver program, between people and their ancestral land, between the various performances of self. How is art production a process of connecting for you and how is your individual art production different from your collective work?

JA: I think it goes back to connecting. The collective work with CBT was integral in helping me understand that collectivity is very powerful in creating art because you get so many peoples' different perspectives. Because we were all volunteers, it has a different tone to it. It's different when it's volunteer, right? It becomes like family. So that was impressed on me in an early time in my life and I have just continued it. I think out of passion, but also because I think that it is an effective method. It's challenging, like when you are trying to balance out a livelihood as an artist. That's why I do have a separate individual practice as an artist. However, the Kwentong Bayan Collective (where I collaborate with Althea Balmes) was just awarded an Ontario Arts Council Access and Development Grant, which will allow us to grow as artists. So far, our work has all been volunteer with the support of community members, the caregiver groups, and individuals who have helped form our community-based comic book project. It's been challenging to create a comic book without funding. How would it ever be in print? How would you distribute it? So we're now engaging in professional development to learn how to make our work viable, sustainable, and have a wider impact. With Kapwa Collective, we formed because we were just so moved from our visit to the Kapwa Conference, which we attended in 2012 at the University of Baguio, UP (University of the Philippines). The conference was about bridging the academic and Indigenous cultural knowledges. It brought together over 110 ethnolinguistic groups, and many representatives from the Indigenous communities were in attendance. In the first days of the conference, the Indigenous people took the lead and diasporic, non-Indigenous people had to practice listening, which was great! [laughs] Especially, as academics, theorists, or artists, part of our impulse is to want to communicate, talk, process, and share. But it was great to allow attentive listening to happen and have Indigenous people take the lead in the discussions and shape the rest of the conference. A group of us (Jennifer Maramba, Aimee Gomez, Christine Balmes,

Kristen Sison, and myself) traveled to the Philippines together and when we returned to Toronto, we decided that first we needed to support each other, just to process what it meant to have that intense *balikbayan* journey. It was a gift to be able to journey with like-minded folks who would eventually become my *kapwa*.

Next, we wanted to understand our role as settlers on Turtle Island. We have similar questions: What are teachings that have been passed onto us by Elders from this land? How do we identify our own practices from our own ancestral land? How do you connect these teachings as a diasporic person? This ongoing dialogue is reaching a new level because we are now connected with another group called the Centre for Baybaylan Studies. Filipino-American educators, Leny Stobel, Lily Mendoza, and other folks are exploring the intersections of activism, academics, and spirituality. It's becoming fluid and interconnected in a beautiful way. And again, they're volunteers. The work is out of their passion, but they understand the need for sustainability. But there's a movement. I feel it. I feel that the Idle No More movement catalyzed a paradigm shift that's been happening on smaller scales for many years. Questions around indigeneity. Now, the momentum has brought us here.

ML: How do you see your work with *kapwa*—how do you see that lining up with Indigenous movements, artists, and activists here? What are some of the tensions of exploring Filipino indigeneity on Turtle Island when Indigenous here are suppressed?

JA: We just had a retreat yesterday. We talked about sage, tobacco, sweetgrass, and cedar—medicines from this land and the teachings passed onto us by our mentors, Lee Maracle and Laini Lascelles. They've shared knowledge with us and it has been a gift. However, one of the questions that we grapple with is now as a collective, do we continue the practice of smudging taught to us when we are in groups or different events? Is this a practice that we have permission to lead? That's still something that we are in the process of asking. I think for me, what's important is intention, but also understanding the reality that these medicines have been illegal in the past. Indigenous people experience systemic oppression, and some generations were banned from practicing their own medicines in their own ceremonies. I think colonization suppressed Filipino spirituality. We can connect with that. Lee Maracle said in a talk: "Nothing is completely lost. We are disconnected." This is what the Kapwa Collective has been thinking about lately as diasporic Filipinos; how we're disconnected from that Indigenous spiritual practice. Lee Miracle also talks about asking why you are disconnected from a social, cultural, political perspective. Then, how might you reach out, maybe with one gesture, one word? How might you reconnect? It's about doing our own work, I think, while respecting the reality that your access to these traditional practices is in a historical context of Indigenous people being denied their human rights. I think that as settlers, we need to educate ourselves about things like Indigenous sovereignty and host laws, cultural appropriation, and consensual allyship.

When I began my ongoing project with singing plants, I was in my thesis year at OCAD. I told my advisors, "I need to go to the Philippines because I want to explore more about spirituality and how to practice an ethical code of conduct when working with Indigenous culture." My professors said, "Well, who are you going to ask? Who is that one person of authority?" [laughs] Who would be the expert? I said: "I'm not sure, but my instinct is telling me that I need to go to the Philippines." So, I took time off and what helped me was being on the land. Land, water, plants, stones, other beings are very powerful and I think that when we are on this land we need to respect the original stewards, the First Peoples of this land and their relationship to the natural world and other beings. When I went to the Philippines, I met Indigenous people who told me: "You need to spend time on the land and you will receive your answers by being in a ceremony, by being with the plants, by listening— listening deeply—to the land, to the messages that you're getting, to the vibrations, the dreams." It was about experiencing and about getting out of my head. That is what actually helped. I spent time with different communities, listened to the Hudhud chants of the Ifugao people and learned about Indigenous instruments and ethnomathematics. I didn't know how I was going to integrate this knowledge to make art, but I knew that it would have to come from my own hybrid, diasporic perspective in order to be authentic.

My education in art school taught me to do a thorough investigation of your materials. That's when you can realize that this does not come from me. I cannot say that I represent a certain belief, culture, or spiritual practice because it is someone else's. I'm going to find out why this resonates with me and what my connection is from my own personal experience and do that work—to bridge and connect it, but to not represent something that is not mine to represent. When I first started doing art, I often wondered, because I'm Filipino and my parents were from the Philippines, and I was born in the Philippines, does that mean that everything in my culture is free for me to use? Do I have the right to use anything for artistic expression? There's a cultural renaissance building in Toronto with artists remixing Indigenous music, traditional tattooing, visual art, etc. It is a chance to engage in a respectful dialogue about the tensions that arise from this practice and perhaps create an ethical code of conduct for this work.

ML: I think you have articulated it beautifully because it really needs to come from a lived experience and you need to ask those questions. You need to do the work. You went across the world to try to figure it out.

JA: It helped and it was just the beginning.

ML: And you're still asking those questions. It sounds to me like it's an unsettling thing for you. It's something that you continually work on.

JA: It's really great because that unsettling feeling means that it could uncover something that, not just that I need, but that I think can help support the discussion and bring the dialogue to a different place. I feel that's the role of artists: we have to uncover, we share, and we dialogue. I think that will help our community to deepen in our knowledge. If we don't ask those questions, we'll be doing art at a certain place for a long time. I think we have to push our artistic merit and imagine different ways of being.

ML: What can queerness bring to explorations of indigeneity for Filipinos in the diaspora?

JA: Indigeneity and queerness. In my work with the Kapwa Collective, we're creating intersections. For example, when we organized Kapwa on Screen, a film screening at the 519, we featured Indigenous issues and stories by the queer communities. One of the films was *As Told by the Butterflies* directed by Nawruz Paguidopon, who is based in the Philippines. His film is about the LADLAD

Party List, the political party of lesbian, gay, bisexual, and trans-gender people in the Philippines. We learned how COMELEC, the Commission on Elections, told LADLAD: "You cannot run in this election because LBGT people are immoral." LADLAD responded with a great campaign: I AM MORAL. They took "immoral" and they broke it apart: "I am moral." The film follows the LADLAD founder, Danton Remoto, as he visits the Home for the Golden Gays, a safe space for gay senior citizens. The Kapwa Collective decided to program the film because if you have the privilege of sharing art with your community, then why not program queer folks, queer artists, queer discussions along with many other things? We also had work about live-in caregivers and T'nalak Dreamweavers from the T'boli tribe. And it was all integral to the event. It wasn't "special" programming. It was part of the program.

ML: I like that notion that queerness and indigeneity are not simply included, but are integral to your programming. The work of Indige-nous studies and queer studies is about questioning what is deemed acceptable or normative in society, how it's all so messed up, and how to turn these dominant values on their heads. It really becomes the task of creating new frames within how we do our work. That's why we need these intersections of indigeneity and queerness: to see that there are other ways of being in this world that are more peace-ful and more equitable.

JA: Wonderful. To have this book as the first in a series around eth-nic studies and queerness leading the series is incredible.

ML: It sets the tone for some really radical work.

JA: It does. And it's leadership. It's community leadership and ally-ship. And it's going beyond tokenism. Okay, we have an anthology. It's about Filipino Canadian art, for example. Let's have at least one queer artist. It's more than that. I think your process is as important as the work that is going out there.

The Kapwa Collective recently presented *Journey of a Brown Girl* in Toronto. This was a theater performance out of New York created by Jana Lynne Umipig, and their story is collectively writ-ten. They had one story of queerness in it, which is about the late Jennifer Laude. There is a talk back session after the show and they asked for feedback. I noticed that there was no mention of Jennifer Laude's identity as a trans woman. In the first night, they talked about her violent death. There were stories of other women who survived violence or who had been victims of violence in a Filipino context. But they didn't mention that Jennifer was a trans woman or that trans people experience inordinate levels of systemic physical and sexual violence.

ML: So, it's an erasure.

JA: We brought it up respectfully in the Q and A, as an offering, and they listened and included it in the second performance. Just one line helped put it in context and that is the opposite of erasure. It's an acknowledgment. It adds complexity to the issue. In the talk back session, Jana Lynne talked about how it's not her lived experience, being queer or trans. She was very respectful and didn't want to try to put that in the play if it's not her experience.

It made me think, if it's not our lived experience, let's say queerness or indigeneity, how do we move beyond that feeling of not being able to say anything about it, because we don't want to appropriate a voice? I started thinking how, even if it's not our lived experience, we have a lived experience of being in a community and where maybe, you know someone who is queer and even if we don't know anyone who is queer, we are still in a community where there are queer people. And so, given this consideration, what is our story? It's not enough to say "I'm a cis-gender straight person so I can't talk about trans issues." That's not enough. That's like saying, "I'm a white person; I can't talk about racism."

ML: Right. And it goes back to the question of doing the work, reading about it, educating yourself about it, talking with people, understanding where you can build solidarity.

ML: What are your experiences of multiculturalism here in Canada as a queer Filipina artist who is investigating queerness and indigeneity? How does your work push against multicultural ideals, as in inclusivity, tokenism, diversity, tolerance?

JA: I've asked to be on panels in conferences where I'm the only one. Sometimes people think I'm the authoritative voice because

they've checked off a check box. I've been very fortunate with the
people that I've worked with. I feel that in my early years, before I
was working with the Filipino community, when I was doing theater,
we were creating this popular theater that was kind of this idea of
multiculturalism. We were exploring the complexities of class, race,
and gender. And things were like "and this is the gay story" and "this
is the person's story around consent," but there was nothing about a
cultural context or an understanding of what it might mean if someone might say: "Okay, now you need counseling support," but that's
not something we do in our culture. We just don't go to a therapist.

I think I was lucky that after that experience, I joined CBCW
because Martha and Fely worked a lot around violence against
women in the Filipino community. One of our first plays was called
Home Sweet Home and it was about violence within the Filipino
Canadian community. We created workshops everywhere we toured:
Vancouver, Winnipeg, Montreal, and Toronto. We would present
and do workshops with the community organized by the Filipino
Canadian community there. We would use our theater piece as a
bridging of the discussion and then work with the communities
there to talk about their own experiences. For instance, let's say in
a *tibo* relationship, *pardz, mars, butch, fem, tibo or babae* . . . what
does that look like when you're talking about violence in those relationships? How can you talk about violence in a community that is
very small? What if the abuse is coming from other activists? How
can you talk about patriarchy? Even just using that word "patriarchy" in a Filipino context? I was able to start to unpack those things
through the work in the Filipino community.

Also, I've been asked to be on different juries and panels to work
with arts councils and policy-makers. I know that sometimes they
are asking me as an "expert," but I always put into context that I
can only speak from my experience. I'm not going to represent the
Filipino community, but I will bring in my understanding of my
perspective as a queer artist, as a person who grew up in Scarborough and has an understanding of what it means to have different
regions of the city where you have different access to art and these
discussions of multiculturalism or intersectional analysis and how
it's going to be in different ways. Also, working with youth has been
great because I feel like it just clears all the bullshit. [laughs] You
can't be talking in an inaccessible way and you can't be talking in a
single-issue way. It has to be intersectional because youth will call

you on it, which is great. This is beyond the multiculturalism of the 1980s era and the identity politics of the 1980s and 1990s, and now we're into something much more complex.

I grew up in Scarborough during the first Trudeau's time of multiculturalism. We experienced systemic racism. We were an immigrant family and my mom didn't have the chance to go to school because in the Philippines, they had a lot of struggle. My dad is the one who came to Canada. He went to trade school and he sponsored us here. So for many years of our life, he was working and my mom was working in factories in very low-paying jobs, low-skilled labor. If we got sick and she couldn't find a babysitter or we couldn't afford a babysitter, she would stay home with us and get fired. So what she taught me, sometimes if you don't have the education, you're the last hired and first fired. So that socioeconomic understanding of poverty and racism and the challenges of a new immigrant has shaped who I am. Yet, there aren't so many discussions around class, so I feel multiculturalism, from my understanding, came at a time when we first came to Canada, but it was also about class. They wanted an influx of new immigrants in Canada, particularly in Ontario where we lived, but they weren't doing the antiracism work to make it easier for newcomers, which is the same now. But now there's more critical mass to talk about those things. And more artistic work, more nuanced, critical work to talk about caregivers coming in and not being able to practice in the field of their choice and other immigrants. Multiculturalism comes from a specific economic agenda in that time and there hasn't been that discussion around class with art in particular. It's a difficult discussion to talk about. You know, the work that I feel that we both do, engaging newcomer Filipino Canadians, with youth and caregivers. We need to bring those stories into the discourse of artistic production in Canada.

ML: You're right in saying that multiculturalism, as it is dominantly understood, is missing that class analysis.

JA: And class represents itself in many ways. It goes back to what we started with, which is community-based volunteer groups compared to something more hierarchical. When things are funded, there's the funder, there's the manager, there's the mandate, there's the fulfillment of the targets of the funder, there's the report and assessment.

There is also competition for funding, so in order for me to maintain my funding, I have to look at all these other people and how they're doing their branding and their marketing. Now, I'm in competition with them to maintain my funding as opposed to grassroots. My audition with Martha and Fely for CBCW, I created a monologue. I was ready. And they said, "Come on in and have some food!" And the food was great. It was a big part of our meetings, social and getting to know each other. While I was eating, I said: "So, should I audition now?" They said: "Sure, if you want, but this is how we audition. We share together. You get to know us. We get to know you. If you like it, you join. If you don't, it's okay. We're not a professional theater company, but we are very professional in how we treat each other." The plays we put forward were high-caliber plays. The process was very thoughtful and mindful, but everyone was a volunteer. There wasn't that I'm behind a big desk and I'm going to assess and interview you. I'm sure that is your experience in community, grassroots-based organizing as well. They are people who will share meals together.

ML: Absolutely, the meeting doesn't start until after you eat!

JA: There is something about the grassroots that really needs to be valued in art production, in arts education, art educators, as cultural workers, and as individual artists. For me, I'm fortunate enough to work in community in a literacy organization that allows me to pay my rent and have a livelihood. I intend to do my community work for as long as I can and it will probably be volunteer-centered and grassroots. I want to learn how to balance this community work and an art practice that maintains grassroots core values.

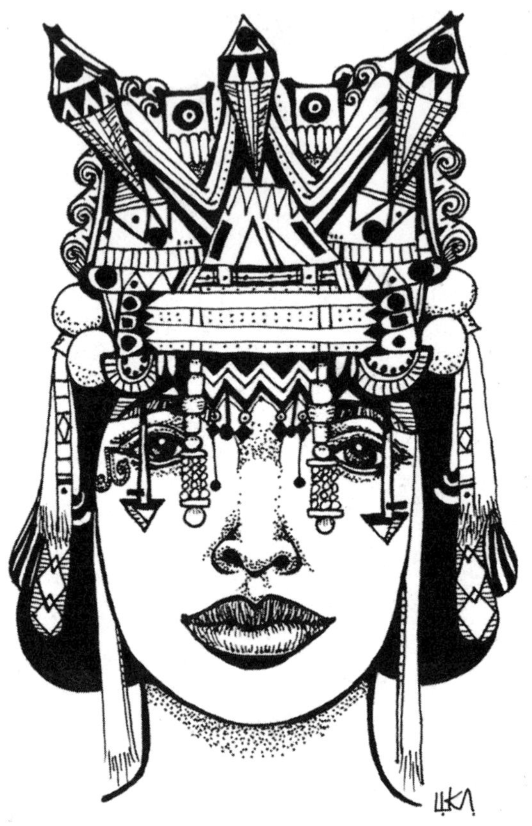

Kim Villagante, *Indigenous Imagination 1 (queen)*, ink drawing, 2014.

Part 2

Diasporic Art as Queer Intervention

Vancouver-based multimedia artist Kim Villigante's illustration opens this section of the book. With her street art aesthetic, Villigante's matriarchal pen drawings signal counter-narratives to male dominated, Eurocentric, and heteronormative orientations in art history. Echoing the politics of these images, the scholars and artists featured in this section foreground diasporic articulations of queerness that complicate "visibility" and "invisibility" as the only legible route for Filipinos/as to exist in Canada as racialized subjects. Such a complication is necessary as multiculturalism colludes with neoliberal capitalism, deploying facile and inadequate notions of inclusion through the valuation of minoritarian lives repackaged as consumable goods, stories, and experiences. By focusing on the diverse affective registers of art and craft, the scholars and artists in this section ultimately reimagine artistic production otherwise, as they unsettle art history's colonial and neocolonial roots. These works embody the potential of artistic practice to serve as a resource for critique, activism, and social change.

Reimagining Filipina Visibility through "Black Mirror"

The Queer Decolonial Diasporic Aesthetic of Marigold Santos

Marissa Largo

Filipinos in Canada oscillate between invisibility and hypervisibility. We are simultaneously made *hypervisible* by the common tropes of the nanny, nurse, or troubled youth, which renders *invisible* other important concerns, contributions, and interventions made by Filipino Canadians.[1] As she complicates the trope of visibility for artists within the black diaspora, the curator and scholar Andrea Fatona reminds us that to be seen or to be made visible does not necessarily entail empowerment.[2] Fatona in fact notes that the opposite in artistic representation may be true—that is, making black subjects invisible as an aesthetic strategy in order to deny objectifying gazes. When minoritized subjects are made visible within official multicultural discourse in Canada, such visibility often continues to legitimize the interests of the nation-state, and reproduce colonial and neoliberal narratives. To be visible is simply not enough, because the lenses through which we are seen are clouded by colonial histories that affect our current neoliberal realities. Simply being visible in various sectors of society such as arts and culture does not guarantee social justice and inclusion.

Problematizing such tropes of visibility, this chapter imagines how a queer, feminist, and diasporic lens can push our understanding of how Filipina-ness, particularly as manifested in the visual arts, complicates and enriches representations that counter limited conceptions of Filipinas in Canada. In going beyond identitarian politics, I explore the analytical possibilities of queer Filipino/a diaspora as a lens in the field of contemporary visual arts using the case of Manila-born,

Calgary- and Montreal-based contemporary visual artist Marigold Santos. Santos immigrated to Canada from the Philippines as a child in 1988. For Santos, her immigration is the "point of departure" for her artistic practice.[3] As a Filipina transnational artist who is engaged in making new representations of Filipina-ness in Canada, her work actively counters normative and restrictive forms of visibility that make room for imaginaries that are de-territorialized from national borders and imperatives.[4]

While the artist does not necessarily self-identify as queer, I want to demonstrate the value in seeing and thinking through Santos's art using a queer theoretical framework that takes into account her diasporic Filipina-ness. I interrogate how a queer feminist diasporic reading of her art can reveal the "impossible subject"—the diasporic Filipina, who through her creative labor presents radically different conceptions of ethnicity, gender, and belonging beyond national frames. Santos deals with themes such as the supernatural, multiplicity, and hybridity and creates complex representations of Filipina diasporic subjectivity that exceed dominant facile imaginaries of what it means to be a Filipina in Canada.

My gesture to the impossible is greatly influenced by the work of Gayatri Gopinath, who weaves together feminist, queer, Asian American, diasporic, and postcolonial critiques in her readings of South Asian diasporic cultural production.[5] She contends that the centrality of queer female diasporic subjectivity is needed to critique the dominant heteronormative and patriarchical frameworks of globalization, nationalism, and diaspora. Gopinath applies a queer reading strategy to key South Asian diasporic texts such as Hindi films, British Asian popular music, Urdu literature, Indo-Canadian films and short stories, and U.S. queer and feminist activism. Her critique of these cultural texts reconfigures conventional understandings of diaspora beyond patrilineality and renders visible queer female subjectivity, which is supplanted under colonial and nationalist logics which posit that the female subject is synonymous with tradition, the nuclear family, and heterosexuality. Gopinath's analytic of *impossibility* allows her to "scrutinize the deep investment of dominant diasporic and nationalist ideologies in producing this particular subject position as impossible and unimaginable."[6] Gopinath demonstrates how the intersection of queer and feminist theories works to challenge and undo heteronormative and androcentric perspectives that permeate postcolonial studies. This analytical and interdisciplinary framework actively addresses the intersecting tensions of racism, colonialism, nationalism, sexism, and heteronormativity. It also provides the political perspective of seeing "other ways of being in the world"[7] which privilege subjects that have been marginalized by dominant discourses of globalization and diaspora.

Within Canada's framework of multiculturalism and its embedded colonial logics, and in the midst of migration and labor programs that render the Filipino/a largely associated with service and care work, Gopinath's notion of impossibility animates cultural production that reimagines Filipino/a subjectivity beyond the colonial and neoliberal scripts. Using the work from Santos's show "Black Mirror," which I visited at DNA Artspace in London, Ontario, in January 2016, as the object of analysis, I argue that such art resists borders, binary logics, gender categorizations, and cultural essentialism and thus is imagining the "impossible" Filipina subject in Canada. In what follows, I adopt a queer feminist diasporic lens in the close reading of her large-scale painting *Re-grounding* (2011), her conceptual reference to the black mirror, and finally to her "shrouded *asuangs*." Within these works, Santos's renderings of disarticulated bodies perform what I would suggest is a decolonial diasporic aesthetic that unsettles the essenialist logics of the colonial nation-state. Furthermore, her conceptual reference to the black mirror, or claude glass, indexes a "queer gesture" that captures a queer diasporic aesthetic practice. In her "shrouded asuangs," a series of ink drawings that playfully explore her preoccupation with the supernatural figure of the *asuang* from Philippine folklore, Santos demonstrates the limits of the trope of visibility for minoritized artists, and how by virtue of their refusal to "face" the viewer, they in fact signify the artist's engagement with feminist self-representation. Taken together, the conceptual use of the black mirror and the shrouded *asuangs* points to a queer and decolonial aesthetic practice that destabilizes dominant imaginaries of Filipina subjectivity in Canada—as always already diasporic.

The Potentialities of a Decolonial Diasporic Aesthetic

The 1980s were a vital time for Marigold Santos; it is when she made the conscious decision to stop speaking Tagalog and exclusively speak English because she "just wanted to be North American." Being North American, or more specifically, Canadian, meant embracing the sights, sounds, colors, and clothes of the time and place:

> Basically, 1980s pop culture on TV and on the radio—that's
> sort of what I learned being Canadian was at that time. So it
> was *Much Music*, watching *The Cosby Show*, watching *Polka
> Dot Door*—all these things that have this kind of color scheme,
> this pattern. That's what it was. Also coming from the Philip-
> pines moving to Canada, you're encountered with different
> weather. It's completely different so you have to wear different
> things, like sweaters, winter coats, and ski pants.[8]

Santos's 1980s pop references are evident in the hyperreal colors of *Re-
grounding* (2011), a stunning work set on a background of bright yellow
phosphorescent paint that radiates as if it were a light source. Although
it is an older work, it dominates one entire wall of the gallery space.
Its pride of place acts as a kind of conceptual "point of departure" for
Santos's new works. It is a larger-than-life depiction of a disarticulated
figure lying tranquilly upon what once was a forest floor, seemingly for
a long while, since the grasses and seedlings have begun to encroach
upon the body. Stumps are what remain of the trees, and like the figure in the painting, are disjointed from their trunk and limbs. We can
only assume that their roots remain intact. The figure is wrapped with
weathered woven textiles, much like the worn wool sweaters that Santos recalls from her first winters in Canada. The flat background can be
just about anywhere; it designates an interstitial space, a neither here
nor there. The sites of the clean lacerations are gilded with gold and
seem to suggest an honoring of these fissures. It is not horrific, like a
scene of a murder, but eerily beautiful and sublime.

Re-grounding demonstrates one of Santos's key visual motifs in her
oeuvre: the *asuang*. According to Philippine folklore, one version of the
asuang, also known as a *manananggal*, is a beautiful woman during
the day, but at night she reveals herself to be a vampiric, shape-shifting
witch who has the ability to separate from her lower body and fly away
to feed on the sick or on the fetuses of expectant mothers. She is a ter-
rifying supernatural being that is an integral part of the Filipino folk
imagination. Like many Filipino children (including myself) who were
told cautionary tales about *asuangs* in order to instill good behavior,
these stories were imparted to Santos by her aunt before immigrating
to Canada. Santos attaches great importance to these stories because
they form the symbolic core of her visual vocabulary to which she continually returns.

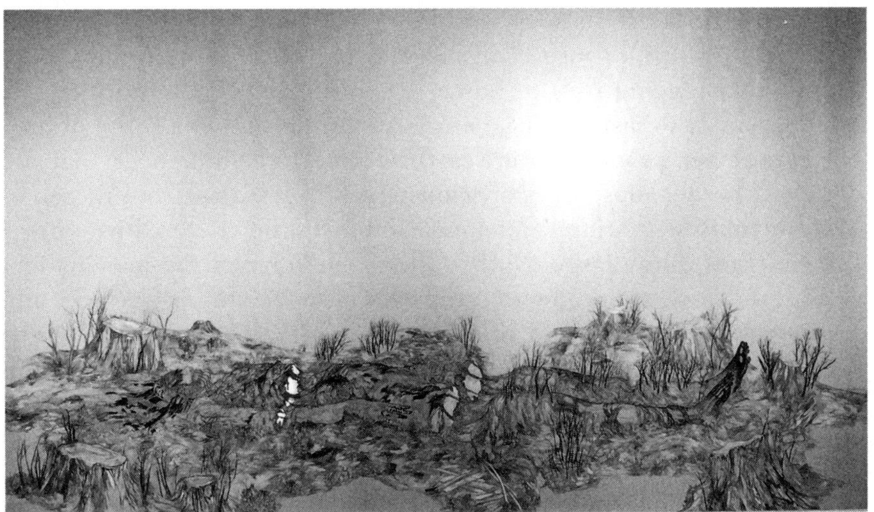

Marigold Santos, *Re-grounding*, watercolor, acrylic, phosphorescent paint, pigment, gold leaf on canvas, 2011.

The severed *asuang* of *Re-grounding* alludes to the multiple and hybrid notions of self that are constructed and reconstructed in the diaspora. This has particular resonance for subjects whose identities are in a constant state of flux due to global movements of "home." Ahmed et al. (2003) challenge dichotomous notions of "migration" and "home," noting that the normative understandings of these concepts are reliant on colonial and imperial constructs such as "nation" and "homeland."[9] The actual experiences of diaspora are largely affective processes in which "home" is something that is not necessarily left behind in migration, but is reconfigured in new spaces. The *asuang* (or *manananggal*) is amorphous and can readily self-disarticulate and recombine, like the diasporic subject who negotiates various cultural attachments and detachments. Not all regroundings are as unilateral as in Santos's shedding of her mother tongue and her adoption of the "Canadian" aesthetics of pop culture and winter clothing. While it appears that Santos's *asuang* in the painting (and arguably Santos herself) is becoming assimilated into the landscape, the figure's severed portions are made impervious to the elements through gilt. Like *kintsugi*, the Japanese art of repairing broken pottery with gold as a way of incorporating the breakage into the history and aesthetic of the object rather than disguising it, the *asuang*'s golden fissures suggest that diasporic loss is also a gain. Some understandings of diasporic aesthetics involve a sense of displacement, which is often marked by trauma and longing for the home[10] (Lemke, 2008). Contrary to this notion, Santos's diasporic aesthetic is not premised on a sense of loss, but rather her production arises from disparate influences that are enriched by her diasporic consciousness. In gesturing toward generative possibilities, Arjun Appadurai comments on the creative energy that emerges from diasporas: they "bring the force of the imagination, as both memory and desire, into the lives of many ordinary people, into mythologies different from the disciplines of myth and ritual of the classic sort."[11] Santos's personal mythologies are constructed through a process of hybridization that she characterizes as "alchemy," referencing the pre-Enlightenment tradition of experimenting with various disparate elements in order to produce gold. Santos's diasporic aesthetic incorporates visual language from her Canadian context, such as woven textures and northern flora, and alchemically combines it with mystical motifs informed by Philippine folklore to develop an aesthetic that is energized by the creative possibilities afforded by her diasporic consciousness. The alchemic composition that is *Re-grounding* reminds us that diaspora is not simply a binary conceptualization of homeland and host land, but is a complex process in which subject formation is informed by multiple uprootings and regroundings.[12] Rather than seeing diaspora as a disjuncture or loss, Santos's art iterates the ways in which diasporic subject formation exceeds the colonial constructs of "nation" and "homeland."

Along with her diasporic aesthetic, I believe that Santos's work also represents a decolonial move which contests the structures and ideology of multiculturalism that subsume minoritized subjects into the colonial frame of national belonging. In her analysis of the works of the Filipino American artist Manual Ocampo, Sarita See (2009) argues that the disarticulation of Filipino bodies in his work is a response to the erasure of Filipino/a subjects within the U.S. empire. Not only does "disarticulate" refer to the dismemberment in Ocampos's often-gruesome images, but it has the dual meaning of "disrupt the logic of."[13] Similarly, Santos's disarticulated *asuang* demonstrates the evisceration of stable ethnic identities that Canadian multiculturalism necessitates. In the Canadian context, while multiculturalism is touted around the world as the ideal model to foster a harmonious citizenry, many scholars critique it as the legitimization of white settler society and colonial domination, which others racialized and Indigenous peoples while claiming to benevolently tolerate difference.[14] Using the logic of "we" and "they," Himani Bannerji asserts that the nation mobilizes the ideology of multiculturalism to organize its disparate polity through processes of racialization and establishes conditions for exclusion.[15] Sunera Thobani extends this critique by proposing that national subjects of European descent are "exalted" over immigrants of color, Indigenous peoples, and refugees in Canada.[16] Moreover, Anglo- and Franco-Canadian cultures are enshrined as the hegemonic center in what Rinaldo Walcott defines as the state's naturalized "ethnonationalism."[17] Multiculturalism requires fixed categories such as "racial minorities" in order to absorb ethnic difference into Canada's colonial construct, which positions people of color on the periphery of national belonging.[18] In addition, the nation disciplines racial difference by policing citizenship through immigration and multiculturalism policies, making racialized subjects "not-quite-citizens."[19]

Like black diasporic cultural producers in Walcott's research, Santos offers a politics of ethnicities that contest national belonging. National belonging and notions of "home" are linked to the political choices that subjects make in their day-to-day lives and are contingent on how individuals position themselves in relation to their location and history. The disarticulated *asuang* embodies a contested national belonging because she is simultaneously capable of uprooting and regrounding herself. Her *asuang* refuses to be assimilated into the country, refuses national belonging, and instead supernaturally supersedes it. In addition, it is not by accident that Santos's *asuang* is gender-fluid. Walcott further argues that one's positionality, which includes race, gender, sexuality, class, and other political categories, informs the multitude of black ethnicities within the diaspora. In a nation-state that seeks to preclude racialized and diasporic subjects from full national belonging, a politicized understanding of ethnicity also requires gender and sexuality as central concerns in order to resist colonial imperatives. This nuanced understanding of subject formation is evident in Santos's decolonial diasporic aesthetic, which envisions her positionality as extending beyond essentialist and nationalist definitions of racial and gendered minority. Her *asuang* disarticulates herself and the logic of the nation-state. Such imaginative works push against the very borders of the nation within which Santos works and in doing so, unsettle its logic.

In another decolonial move, Santos recovers and reinvents Indigenous knowledge through her mobilization of the *asuang* in her art. In

Santos's earlier work, as in the original precolonial version, her *asuangs* were genderless. In her latest work they are androgynous, female, and/ or gender-fluid. They are queer magical figures who represent a surplus of identifications that defy the colonial logics of ethnicity, gender, and nation. In the essay "The Viscera-Sucker and the Politics of Gender," Herminia Meñez maintains that the *asuang* initially had no gender for the non-Hispanized animists in various regions of the Philippines. The attribution of the female gender to the *asuang*, Meñez believes, is the result of a "colonial encounter" between sixteenth- and nineteenth-century Spanish missionaries and the *babaylans*, the female shamans who had powerful roles in pre-Christian Indigenous societies. Meñez believes that contemporary narratives of the *asuang* represent "inversions" that functioned to subvert feminine power.[20] The prophetess, who was especially resistant to foreign invaders, had equal status with the male warrior-chief because of her heroism in battle and access to magical powers. Other *babaylans* were knowledgeable in medicine and midwifery. According to Meñez, the life-giving attributes of the *baylan* are inverted in the viscera-sucker who is linked to death. This inversion is emphasized by the fact that when the *asuang* self-segments, she leaves her reproductive organs behind to prey on the sick and unborn.[21] Not unlike a Western vampire, Catholic symbols can incapacitate the *asuang*: holy water, a crucifix, and the priest's cincture (belt) to prevent her from self-segmenting and taking flight.[22] What were once revered and powerful women in precolonial societies became demonized harbingers of death with the spread of the Catholicism and the Spanish colonial project in the Philippines.

The recuperation of the mythology of the *asuang* unsettles colonial inversions and reimagines an empowering gender-fluid figure that is capable of navigating the many tensions of diaspora. Such recuperation through art can be understood through "decolonial aesthetics," which, according to David Garneau, "can be a way for the marginalized, refused, and repressed to return."[23] Decolonial aesthetics consist of raw and unbeautiful work that defies colonial traditions and invite Indigenous and non-Indigenous alike to question the current colonial state. Garneau, citing the manifesto of the Transnational Decolonial Institute, observes that decolonial aesthetics provoke affective responses in order to embody and honor "those ways of living, thinking, and sensing that were violently devalued or demonized."[24] The physical fragmentation and gender-fluidity of Santos's *asuangs* destabilizes fixed ethnic and gender categories, but also represents the reconfiguration of suppressed and demonized Indigenous knowledge, both strategies working together to form a decolonial diasporic aesthetic.

Decolonial diasporic aesthetics are responsive to the subordination of racial, sexual, and cultural difference within the framework of national and neoliberal ideologies. They are not simply the recuperation of pre-colonial culture, but an active process of creation that works within and pushes against the limiting imaginaries of the colonial settler nation. Decolonial diasporic aesthetics involve queering Western aesthetic values and privilege the repressed, hybrid, multiple, entangled, and subjectivities in excess of national imperatives and configurations. The visual reconfiguration of suppressed Indigenous knowledge is combined with motifs derived from Western and pop culture to reimagine Filipina visibility. Through these avant-garde strategies, Santos's decolonial diasporic aesthetic embodies an emergence of a potent Filipina diasporic subjectivity.

The Queer Gesture of "Black Mirror"

Santos named her latest show, "Black Mirror," after the seventeenth-century drawing tool used to create picturesque landscapes. Also known as the claude glass (after the French Baroque landscape painter Claude Lorrain, who became synonymous with the aesthetic), the black mirror is a small, darkened, reflective surface. The artist turns his back *away* from the subject to be rendered and observes it through the black mirror. Due to its convex shape, the mirror brings more of the landscape into the focal plane. Not unlike some popular Instagram filters, the resulting reflection has a simplified color and tonal range and produces a soft, painterly effect, which the artist then translates onto the canvas.

The use of a black mirror is an act of defamiliarization or *making strange*.[25] When an artist uses a black mirror, he forgoes direct observation in favor of a mediated and selective process. This process effectively *denaturalizes*, or in other words, queers, the subject. According to the performance studies scholar José Muñoz, queer aesthetics "attempt to call the natural into question."[26] If queer aesthetics denaturalize that which is accepted as natural, then Santos's symbolic invocation of the black mirror signifies a desire to see the current state of the world in a transformative manner. Santos does not accept the present at face value, but instead finds her own truth within it, as she so eloquently writes in her artist statement:

> With their backs turned to their physical subject, the black mir-
> ror would reveal colours and light compounded, with noise and
> extraneous detail avoided. What was of importance and signif-
> icance was portrayed. Invented truths were created. This truth
> becomes their new vocabulary, a visual language in which to
> create their narrative and personal myth.[27]

I suggest that this "new vocabulary" or this new way of seeing can
be understood as a queer gesture. The practice of looking away from
that which is desired denaturalizes the way we preceive the world and
defamiliarizes what is seen by refusing "straight" visibility in order
to imagine futures that are unburdened by the colonial and hetero-
patriarchical gazes. Muñoz (1999) explains that queer gestures are
openings for minoritarian subjects (queers, people of color, and other
marginalized subjects) who have historically been denied opportunities
to engage in representation beyond the stereotypical, to place oneself
within history.[28] Santos queers the meaning of the black mirror, from a
European landscape painting tool to a cultural process that allows her
to imagine a different way of being in the world that accounts for her
multiple positionalities. This process is similar to Muñoz's theory of
disidentification, which

> scrambles and reconstructs the encoded message of a cultural
> text in a fashion that both exposes the encoded message's uni-
> versalizing and exclusionary machinations and recircuits its
> workings to account for, include, and empower minority identi-
> ties and identifications. Thus, disidentification is a step further
> than cracking open the code of the majority; it proceeds to use
> this code as raw material for representing a disempowered pol-
> itics or positionality that has been rendered unthinkable by the
> dominant culture.[29]

One might imagine an exhibition full of dreamy pastoral scenes, but
instead it is full of curious depictions of supernatural figures that refuse
easy identification. Santos's invocation of the black mirror is a disidentification; she is not depicting picturesque scenes typical of European
landscape "masters," but referring to her affective process as a diasporic subject who continues to grapple with the movement of "home."
The back and forth of the constant migrating home and practice—first,
her movements between the Philippines and Canada, and secondly, the

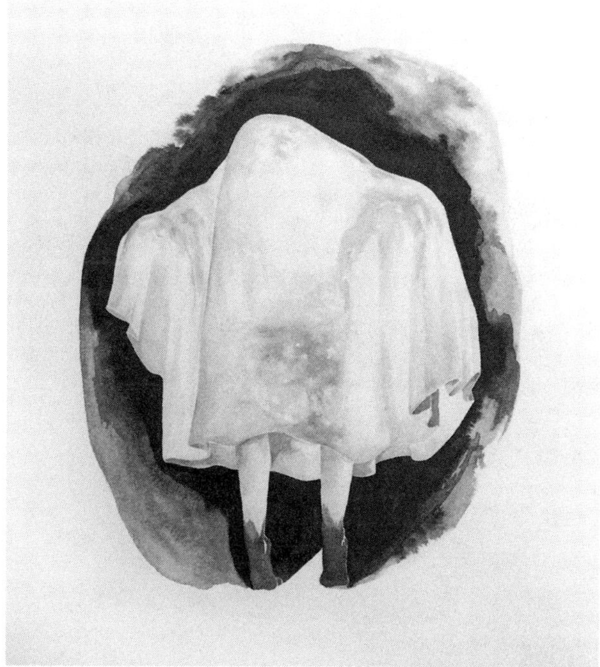

Marigold Santos, *shroud (toes across the floor)*,
10 × 11.25 inches, ink on paper, 2015.

push-pull movements between Montreal, the location of her studio and teaching practice and Calgary, her official residence—is analogous to the back-and-forth gesture of using a black mirror.

The "Black Mirror" show included seven monochrome ink renderings and one oil painting of *asuangs* covered by shrouds. The smaller ink renderings show the *asuangs* in little vingnettes where they are crouching, standing, or engaging in what appears to be light-hearted child's play. Santos recounts the playful practice of children hiding under blankets as a form of armor or protection from unknown forces. The seemingly futile notion that one is invincible against dark supernatural powers by covering oneself with a blanket is a belief that is self-empowering. Believing is a choice: "It's not about hiding because they are afraid, but it's about a choice—a willful choice."[30]

Here, I return to the queer feminist diasporic lens and contend that the shrouded *asuangs* perform queer gestures of feminist self-representation

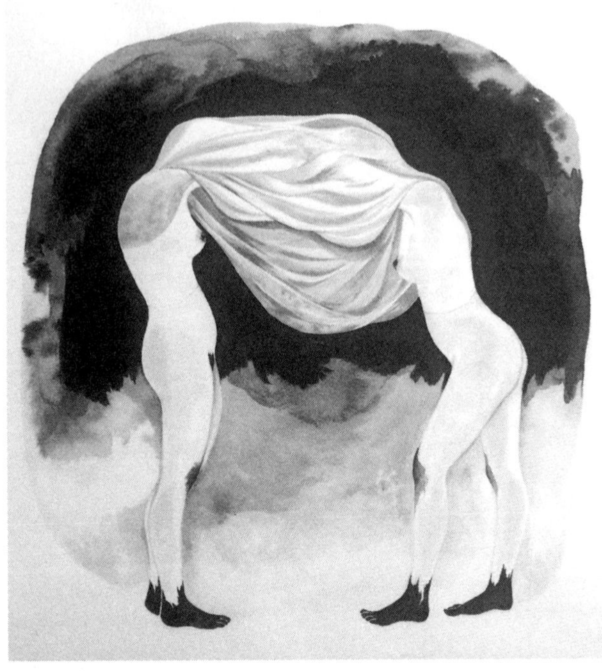

Marigold Santos, *shroud (overhead)*, 10 × 13 inches,
ink on paper, 2015.

that complicate the trope of visibility precisely because they choose
not to be seen. Santos communicates the conceptual basis for the
works through a description of a disidentificatory gesture: "It's definitely looking and having my back turned, looking and having my back
turned. That's where the shrouds come in. The shroud pieces are really
about a figure that's being covered by choice."[31] While their faces are
concealed, the figures of *shroud (overhead)* (2015) have their bodies
revealed. Faint lines across their torsos remind us of their supernatural abilities of self-disarticulation. In popular Filipino storylines, the
asuang is often a nonconforming female who is shunned by her community. As such, the *asuang* is symbolic excess, a woman who can
harness the power of nature and is thus fearsome and resides outside
of the social order. However, Santos's shrouded *asuangs* seem to revel
inside the social order of domesticity and counter the fearsome versions who reside outside of it. They are depicted in intimate scenes that
evoke memories of children in imaginative play and female figures in
various stages of revealing or concealing their bodies. They appear to

be female, but Santos maintains that the *asuangs* have unfixed gender identities:

> I wanted them to be women, but women that could also be androgynous, too. So the ones that you could absolutely see that are gendered, are women, but the ones that are obviously without breasts can also stand to be whatever. They are gender-neutral. And that's what I kind of think about asuangs. They don't necessarily have gender.[32]

The limits and possibility of Filipina visibility are embodied in Santos's *asuangs* who disidentify with gender, notions of home, and domesticity. Their gender-fluidity and location in the domestic realm demonstrate an impossible Filipina subjectivity that is illegible in the Canadian nation-state. While the shrouded *asuangs* engage in playful performances, Filipina women perform gendered labor within the confines of the home. While the *asuangs* choose not to return the viewer's gaze, Filipina domestic workers often cannot choose the terms of their visibility and their labor remains invisible, for the most part. These impossible queer figures that reside within the domestic realm stretch the dominant imaginary of what Filipina subjectivity could be or should be; that is, residing outside of colonial, neoliberal, and hetero-patriarchal frames.

In the oil painting *blanket asuang (big sister)* (2015), an *asuang*'s head is covered by a crocheted blanket adorned with flowers—a product of women's handiwork. The unraveling reminds us of the tenuous limits of visibility as "knowable" and "recognizable." The blanket is a porous barrier separating the states of being seen and unseen. For the racialized and gendered subject, to be seen does not guarantee power. Being able to choose the terms of one's visibility entails a practice of power. This is often a choice that is unavailable to minoritarian subjects in Canada who are simply made legible by the labor they produce and by fixed identifications as dictated by the nation-state. Santos elaborates on the ability to choose to not be visible as a feminist practice of power:

> I'm playing with the fact that it's choice, but it's a choice that is a response to your surroundings. I am making this statement. I am making this choice because I can clearly know that there are other situations where I can't make this choice. There is a reason

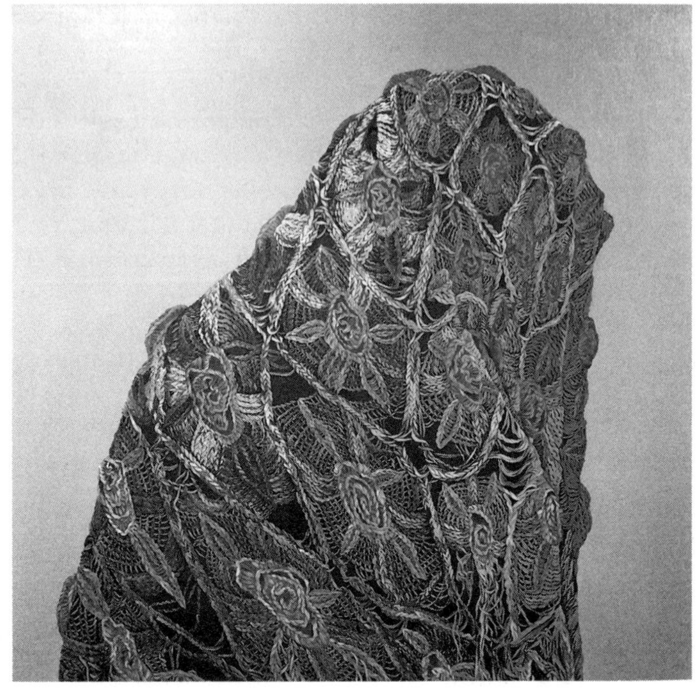

Marigold Santos, *blanket asuang (big sister)*, 30 × 30 inches, oil on panel, 2015.

why you are making a stand because you're countering something else or you're making a statement because you observe something or you're responding to something else. For me, that's where the *asuang* came from. She's an inversion or a reconfiguration of something that was demonized and power was taken away from this figure in society. I would want to empower that.[33]

Like the demonized prophetess, diasporic Filipina subjectivity is subjected to colonial and hetero-patriarchal optics. The shroud denies these optics and instead asserts visibility under her prerogative. The work of the artist here reinvests power in this figure, not simply by recovering the *asuang*'s original significance, but by queering it so that she represents diasporic Filipina-ness in all of its richness, ambiguities, and complexity.

This reading represents an intervention that counters tropes of the Filipina in Canada that are predicated on neoliberal and multiculturalist logics. The *asuang* and Santos herself are impossible subjects within these logics. As a contemporary Filipina Canadian visual artist, Santos is engaged in creative labor that does not reproduce dominant narratives of domesticity or care, but rather, radically contrasts them. Instead, Santos is a multifarious subject who exceeds colonial scripts of femininity and domesticity, both dominant in the Philippines and in Canada, and the expectations of a minoritized cultural producer to perform visibility for mainstream consumption. Such queering of logics in Canada is a process of world-making. Santos, through her queer shrouded *asuangs*, embodies feminist self-representation that allows for a freedom of being that undermines binary conceptions of gender and multiculturalist logics of prescribing to a fixed ethnic identity:

> I feel like I can't escape it sometimes because I am a woman and I use my own body all the time. So inevitably it is going to work its way into my work. I cannot not have a female presence also. It's very important for me to have genderless images, but it is also really important for me to talk about feminism, to talk about myself as a woman. It's not like I'm erasing gender identity, it's just that that is what is part of what multiplicity is. It's very important in conversations today to talk about that and it's something that I think about all the time too. Having multiple identities and not necessarily having to choose. Being able to have the power of multifariousness. I think there's power in that.[34]

Aesthetics as World-Making

In his analysis of Felix Gonsalez-Torres's *Untitled (Orpheus Twice)*, which consists of two large mirrors placed beside each other, Muñoz contemplates the meditative and imaginative work that takes place when one gazes into a reflective surface: "This looking at a mirror is thus an act that works like the symbolic passport; it speaks of a critical imagination that begins with self-analysis and a vaster social critique of how the world could be and indeed should be."[35] Like Santos's queer gesture of the black mirror that simultaneously makes strange and brings close, gazing into the mirror's denaturalized reflection is both a creative and disruptive act of world-making, or in other words, the creation of a world in which diasporic identity formation is unhinged from dominant racist, heterosexist, and patriarchical ideologies. Aesthetic practices like Santos's that are queer, decolonial, feminist, and diasporic work to generate just futures for minoritarian subjects. Using a queer feminist diasporic lens, Santos's art shows us the creative possibilities of imagining multifarious Filipina subjectivity that is unhindered by colonial and hetero-patriarchal matrices. Her use of supernatural imagery, such as alchemy and Philippine mythology, *denaturalizes* the world as we see it, and hence queers it. At the center of her decolonial diasporic aesthetic is the reinvention of the *asuang*. This figure is not just recovered from its Indigenous roots, but her meaning is transposed into the context of a settler nation-state. Rather than being settled into the nation, it unsettles notions of belonging to it. The *asuang*'s disarticulation speaks to the unfixed and multiple nature of cultural hybridity that exceeds dominant configurations of ethnicity, gender, and nation. Such imagery signifies an excess that cannot be contained by colonial logics, including multiculturalism, as it transcends the frame of the nation.

Santos's dis-identificatory move, such as the queering of the seventeenth-century European landscape tool to conceptually elucidate her diasporic affect, subverts heteropatrilineal grand narratives in Western art history. In addition, the gender-fluidity of her shrouded *asuangs* and their refusal to be seen queer the trope of visibility. For minoritized subjects, to be seen does not necessarily achieve empowerment. The shrouded *asuang*'s refusal to be seen demonstrates an act of feminist self-representation that wields power through choice. Unlike Filipina domestic workers who cannot choose the terms of their visibility within the Canadian imaginary, these *asuangs* are electing invisibility. This counters the paradoxical state of Filipinas in Canada who are hypervisible as care workers in domestic spaces, but whose labor goes unseen behind the walls of privates residences. In light of these tropes, Santos as a practicing contemporary visual artist is an impossible Filipina subject in a society which misrecognizes the subjectivities and contributions of minoritized others. Santos's work and the artist herself surpass superficial representations of diasporic Filipina identity in the Canadian imaginary.

The artist's critical brilliance lies in the fact that her representations are undeniable forms of Filipina-ness, but are simultaneously anti-essentialist. Through artistic reimagining, she is able to create representations that refute national definitions of ethnicity and deny heterosexual imaginaries of diasporic subjectivity. The queer *asuang* embodies and performs a refusal to conform to neat identitarian categories prescribed by dominant ideologies. Her queer decolonial diasporic aesthetic is precisely what makes Santos's work reimagine new forms of Filipina visibility in all its complexity and power and offers liberating possibilities of being in a dominantly normative world.

Notes

1. Roland Coloma et al., eds., *Filipinos in Canada: Disturbing Invisibility* (Toronto: University of Toronto Press, 2012), 5.

2. Andrea Fatona, "In the Presence of Absence: Invisibility, Black Canadian History, and Melinda Mollineaux's Pinhole Photography" *Canadian Journal of Communication* 31 (1): 235.

3. Marigold Santos, personal interview, November 2, 2013.

4. In Marigold Santos's case, having a higher degree of visibility in the Canadian art scene is certainly beneficial to how Filipinos/as are perceived in Canada and how we imagine possibilities for our communities and ourselves.

5. See Gayatri Gopinath, *Impossible Desires: Queer Diasporas and South Asian Public Cultures* (Durham, N.C.: Duke University Press, 2005).

6. Gopinath, *Impossible Desires*, 16.

7. Gopinath, *Impossible Desires*, 47.

8. Marigold Santos, personal interview, November 2, 2013.

9. Sara Ahmed et al., eds., *Uprootings/Regroundings: Questions of Home and Migration* (Oxford: Berg, 2003), 7.

10. Sieglinde Lemke, "Diaspora Aesthetics: Exploring the African Diaspora in the Works of Aaron Douglas, Jacob Lawrence, and Jean-Michel Basquiat," in *Annotating Arts Histories: Exiles, Diasporas, and Strangers*, ed. Kobena Mercer (Cambridge, Mass.: MIT Press, 2008), 122–44.

11. Arjun Appadurai, *Modernity at Large: Cultural Dimensions of Globalization* (Minneapolis: University of Minnesota Press, 1996), 6.

12. See Ahmed et al., *Uprootings/Regroundings*.

13. Sarita See, *The Decolonized Eye: Filipino American Art and Performance* (Minneapolis: University of Minnesota Press, 2009), xviii.

14. See Bannerji (2000) and Thobani (2007).

15. See Bannerji (2000).

16. Sunera Thobani, *Exalted Subjects: Studies in the Making of Race and Nation in Canada* (Toronto: University of Toronto Press, 2007), 6.

17. Rinaldo Walcott, "Rhetorics of Blackness, Rhetorics of Belonging: The Politics of Representation in Black Canadian Expressive Culture," *Canadian Review of American Studies* 29 (1999): 8.

18. Walcott, "Rhetorics of Blackness," 15.

19. Walcott, "Rhetorics of Blackness," 6.

20. Herminia Meñez, *Explorations in Philippine Folklore* (Manila: Ateneo de Manila University Press, 1996), 88.

21. Meñez, *Explorations*, 89.

22. Meñez, *Explorations*, 90.

23. David Garneau, "Extra-Rational Aesthetic Action and Cultural Decolonization," *FUSE Magazine*, September 2013, 16.

24. Garneau, "Extra-Rational Aesthetic Action," 16.

25. See Mecija's chapter, "Good-bye Ohbijou," in this volume.

26. José Estaban Muñoz, *Cruising Utopia: The Then and There of Queer Futurity* (New York: New York University Press, 2009), 138.

27. Marigold Santos, "Artist Statement," Black Mirror.

28. Muñoz, *Cruising Utopia*, 1.

29. Muñoz, *Cruising Utopia*, 31.

30. Marigold Santos, personal interview, January 8, 2016.

31. Marigold Santos, personal interview, January 8, 2016.

32. Marigold Santos, personal interview, January 8, 2016.

33. Marigold Santos, personal interview, January 8, 2016.

34. Marigold Santos, personal interview, January 8, 2016.

35. José Esteban Muñoz, *Disidentifications: Queers of Color and the Performance of Politics* (Minneapolis: University of Minnesota Press, 1999), 143.

Bibliography

Ahmed, Sara, Claudia Castaneda, Anne-Marie Fortier, and Mimi Sheller. "Introduction." In *Uprootings/Regroundings: Questions of Home and Migration*, edited by Sara Ahmed, Claudia Castaneda, Anne-Marie Fortier, and Mimi Sheller, 1–22. Oxford: Berg, 2003.

Appadurai, Arjun. *Modernity at Large: Cultural Dimensions of Globalization*. Minneapolis: University of Minnesota Press, 1996.

Bannerji, Himani. *The Dark Side of the Nation: Essays on Multiculturalism, Nationalism and Gender*. Toronto: Canadian Scholars, 2000.

Fatona, Andrea. "In the Presence of Absence: Invisibility, Black Canadian History, and Melinda Mollineaux's Pinhole Photography." *Canadian Journal of Communication* 31, no. 1 (2006): 227–38.

Garneau, David. "Extra-Rational Aesthetic Action and Cultural Decolonization." *FUSE Magazine*, September 2013, 14–23.

Gopinath, Gayatri. *Impossible Desires: Queer Diasporas and South Asian Public Cultures*. Durham, N.C.: Duke University Press, 2005.

Lemke, Sieglinde. "Diaspora Aesthetics: Exploring the African Diaspora in the Works of Aaron Douglas, Jacob Lawrence, and Jean-Michel Basquiat." In *Annotating Arts Histories: Exiles, Diasporas, and Strangers*, edited by Kobena Mercer, 122–44. Cambridge, Mass.: MIT Press, 2008.

McElhinny, Bonnie, Lisa Davidson, John Paul Catungal, Ethel Tungohan, and Roland Coloma. "Spectres of (in)Visibility: Filipina/o Labor, Culture, and Youth in Canada." In *Filipinos in Canada: Disturbing Invisibility*, edited by Roland Sintos Coloma, Bonnie McElhinny, Ethel Tungohan, John Paul C. Catungal, and Lisa M. Davidson, 5–45. Toronto: University of Toronto Press, 2012.

Meñez, Herminia. *Explorations in Philippine Folklore*. Quezon City: Ateneo de Manila University Press, 1996.

Muñoz, José Esteban. *Cruising Utopia: The Then and There of Queer Futurity*. New York: New York University Press, 2009.

———. *Disidentifications: Queers of Color and the Performance of Politics*. Minneapolis: University of Minnesota Press, 1999.

Santos, Marigold. "Artist Statement." http://marigoldsantos.com/MARIGOLD_SANTOS/STATEMENT.html.

See, Sarita Echavez. *The Decolonized Eye: Filipino American Art and Performance*. Minneapolis: University of Minnesota Press, 2009.

Thobani, Sunera. *Exalted Subjects: Studies in the Making of Race and Nation in Canada*. Toronto: University of Toronto Press, 2007.

Walcott, Rinaldo. "Field Notes: Artists, Academics Dialogue the Past and Future of Diaspora Literary Expression." *Callaloo* 32, no. 2 (2009): 624–27. doi: 10.1353/cal.0.0415.

———. "Rhetorics of Blackness, Rhetorics of Belonging: The Politics of Representation in Black Canadian Expressive Culture." *Canadian Review of American Studies* 29, no. 2 (1999): 1–24. doi: 10.3138/CRAS-029-02-01.

Good-bye Ohbijou

Notes on Music, Queer Affect, and the Impossibilities of Satisfying Multicultural Ideals in Canada

Casey Mecija

Aesthetic representation enacts our being in the world. It expresses
disavowed affects of relationality: loss, conflict, and pleasure
    —Georgis, 2013, p. 77

During the years 2004 through 2013 I defined myself, in part, as front
woman for the band Ohbijou, a seven-piece orchestral pop band that for
a time was recognized as a fixture of the Canadian music scene. Often
described as "pop darlings" and representatives of Canada's "multicultural art scene," Ohbijou felt burdened with the task of responding to
what others demanded of us. After some commercial and critical success, extensive touring, and hundreds of live shows, our band decided
to go on hiatus. My relationship to this band and to our reception is
one of ambivalence. Good feelings about our accomplishments are
tinged with complicated responses to what critics articulated was dis-
tinctive about our music, and larger audiences' reception of our band
due to my race, gender, and sexuality. I continue to make music and art
post Ohbijou, but my time in this band was formative in the lessons it
taught me about how Filipina/o and queer culture is represented, consumed, and reworked in artistic and aesthetic practice.

Through an engagement with details of my autobiography, I will
argue that my music and its performance on Canadian stages present
an aesthetic intervention made both inside and outside the insistences
of cultural authenticity and the burden of representation. By examining

119

the affective excesses of my music, performance, and encounters with audiences, this chapter considers, more broadly, how Filipino/a diasporic experiences are complexly enunciated to create new social meanings that "listen against" the demands of Canadian multiculturalism. Although my auto-ethnographic approach to this chapter limits objective critique, for me, this is not a deficit but a formative interruption to the notion that critique can occur as disembodied practice. I employ Christina Balance's method of "disobedient listening" to undermine dominant discourses that confine the Filipino/a performing body to stable understandings of what Filipino/a music should sound like or how it should be performed. I also turn to Dina Georgis's work on queer affect because it considers what is in excess of conventional representation and historiography. Georgis describes queer affect as the emotions and sensations that are attached to unconscious knowledge. Georgis's theory of queer affect opens up an aesthetic space with which to theorize the psychic liminalities and contradictions of Filipino/a subjectivity in music and performance. Near the end of this chapter I transcribe the lyrics for one of Ohbijou's songs, "Balikbayan," which is written for and about the Filipino/a diaspora in Canada. I am intent on excavating the enigmatic agency that is in excess of my memorized words or choreographed movements to argue that performance creates a reparative space with which to interact with the world in ways that are both cognitive and unconscious.

In this chapter, I employ a capacious definition of "queer," using it to describe aesthetic experience that pushes against our associations with "ordinary" encounters. I align my research with scholars who have argued that positioning queerness as a methodology outside of LGBTQ identity politics plays at the limits of knowledge production and reconceptualizes diaspora in terms of affiliation and social relation (Diaz, 2016; Eng, 2010; Gopinath, 2005; Manalansan, 2003). Within this framework I think through my role as a diasporic performer as a presence that playfully "queers" representations of Filipino/a acceptability and belonging. I explicate on what is ultimately "queer" about a Filipino/a woman playing pop music in Canada while remaining attentive to how my "roots" and "routes" enigmatically come together and fall apart in this performance (Hall and Gay, 1996: 6). I inquire into how my body has been inscribed as a performer and thus am questioning the affective costs of being read through romanticized lenses in a Canadian multicultural landscape. The psychic negotiations of performance and diasporic experience are uniquely addressed by queer and affective descriptions of the fissures of unknowability that undo my-self.

Robert Diaz (2016) positions queerness as "a tactic for animating aesthetic practices and performances of world-making" (p. 345). I would like to suggest that my presence on the stage exposes the "messy" convergences between diasporic experience and the overwrought demands of Canadian multiculturalism in order to imagine something new, to conceptualize a queer world-making. Alongside Diaz, I center queerness as a method that allows for new iterations of difference that problematize how Filipinos/as have been historically racialized within a Canadian context. Representing pieces of my autobiography is a difficult project, but one that hopes to highlight what kind of human is being fashioned by the Canadian multicultural state and what other social formations and subjectivities can be imagined outside of state regulation. I now turn to a memory from my childhood to help situate how my desires as a child can be mapped onto my artistic practice as an adult.

The Specter of the Bottomless Bottom: Queer Aesthetic Experience

As a ten-year-old child, I spent most of my summer days in the backyard, digging a hole to Asia. I lay on the grass surrounded by a mound of dirt, the clay still moist from my digging efforts. My little body was halfway in the hole in an attempt to reach as far as the length of my arm would allow. I struggled to sweep the bottom of the earth with my shovel and kept digging despite knowing the impossibility of my project; I kept reaching despite the ground becoming too deep to touch. This phenomenological excavation propelled me to dream an impossible geography, the psychic contours of my persistence shaped by hope and possibility. This was a queer aesthetic experience. If queerness is something we may never touch but is instead an ideality (Muñoz, 2009: 1), I was compelled to reach for a *bottomless bottom* by the potentiality of the destination, of the horizon, knowing full well I would never get there. This childhood memory forges a queer temporality that creates space for "contradictory modes of embodiment and forms of expression" (Diaz, 2016: 345). My experiences as a child help frame my desires as an adult to suggest that aesthetic encounters like music or my childhood play accrue meaning through unpredictable affiliations.

As a field of research and inquiry, cultural studies has argued for the consideration of different forms of aesthetic experience and interrogates how we attach value to those encounters (Diaz, 2016; Georgis,

2014; Moten, 2003; Muñoz, 2009). This turn to aesthetics helps to creatively elaborate on the historical and social circumstances of exclusion, hope, and optimism. In my dig to Asia, I was improvising a return; "[an] improvisation that proceeds from somewhere on the other side of an unasked question" (Moten, 2003: 756). In *The History of the Psycho-Analytic Movement* (1966), Sigmund Freud theorized that the subject's desire to repress that which is difficult to know and to feel is never fully successful. Repressed material will resurface and be symbolized in uncanny, enigmatic, but also sometimes pointedly obvious ways. As a second-generation Filipino/a born in Canada, my relation to being Filipino/a and the geography of the Philippines manifests in unpredictable forms. How I affiliate myself with a country I was not born in but am racially marked as having kinship with can be confusing. Music and performance have provided me with moments of reprieve from the discursive regimes of racial authenticity. However, performing a self beyond the somatic logics that uphold white supremacy is a difficult task. How can the quotidian and the improvised (such as digging a hole or singing a song) hold conscious and unconscious acts of disobedience? What meanings can be gleaned from my performances with Ohbijou outside of capital logics? What is corruptive about my presence as a musician playing music in Canada?

Multiculturalism and Disobedient Listening

During Ohbijou's tenure and afterward, as a solo musician, I continue to be frustrated by the ways in which my Asianness is often conflated with notions of an "inclusive" Canadian multiculturalism. Encounters with scholars who, from within the academy, are theorizing the ways that discourses of multiculturalism land on and make meaning of racialized bodies in Canada, has helped me to reflect on the ways that I have been both hailed and excluded as a "Canadian musician"(Cruz, 2016; Diaz, 2016; Hall, 2003; Razack, 2002; Walcott, 2011). Rinaldo Walcott performs an important reading of multiculturalism in which he is interested in how racialized bodies are demarcated as "multicultural." He writes:

> This approach has largely focused on representation at the level
> of race and ethnicity, often as marked in bodies, and has most
> often produced homogenized groups in which internal differences are given little space for expression. (Walcott, 2011)

Sherene Razack (2002) also produces work on the project of Canadian nation-building which elucidates the institutionalized structures of power that deem bodies as "multicultural." The national narrative of Canada is built on the mythology that Europeans peacefully settled an uninhabited land (ibid.). Concomitant with European colonialism was the organization of bodies into racialized hierarchies that continue to persist socially and institutionally. The project of multiculturalism has come to define and name those bodies who do not cleanly fit into the colonial project. Filipino/a Canadian studies has worked to explain multiculturalism as a racializing logic, but as Robert Diaz (2016) argues, the field "has been limited by a continued reliance on heteronormative ideations of family, kinship, religion, civil responsibility, and gendered citizenship" (p. 329). Reading the music and performances of Ohbijou within and against the field of Canadian Filipino/a studies helps to queer its methods and theories. My experiences in Ohbijou offer an aesthetic site with which to theorize the queer contours of the rhetoric of the Canadian multiculturalism.

One way in which the rhetoric of multiculturalism imbues itself in music creation and performance is through Canada's funding structure. Canadian musicians like myself often rely on state and/or private funding to make and distribute their art. In order to appeal to these funding bodies, such as the Canadian Council of the Arts and many other institutional and private sources of funding, I must appeal to the "multicultural" nature of the Canadian nation, but not seek to transform it into something beyond that. Sherene Razack highlights how institutional policies of multiculturalism have concrete impacts on how government funding is allocated:

> It is of enormous consequence who fits under the multicultural category and who doesn't. It's not a category you want to be in because usually 5% of the budget (as in the case of Canada Council) will go to multicultural groups and the rest will go to the unnamed "normal" citizens. (Razack, 2011)

Walcott and Razack posit that the failures of the federal multicultural act and provincial multicultural policies necessitate public institutions to forefront multiculturalism as paradigmatic to their activities. Walcott (2011) asserts that these multicultural policies legitimize the institutions that implement them without addressing the "deeper structures of their orientation."

There have been many textual moments where Ohbijou was sutured to notions of multiculturalism. The media often referred to Ohbijou as "multicultural." In an article written in *The Grid TO: Toronto's Weekly City Magazine*, Ohbijou is described as "the poster kids for this city's latest indie-rock scene by combining hyper-local connections and multicultural experiences for a uniquely Torontonian sound" (Charlesworth, 2011). In an article written for a college weekly, the author describes us as "multicultural in both influence and membership" (Cora Perry, 2009). We have also been introduced on the radio as the "multi-culti" band. This association is a polite way of saying that not all of us are white, which is the usual configuration of bands in Canada. Attendant to this proclamation is often a conflation between our bodies and the sound of our music: our music becomes a multicultural sound, or is referred to as "world music," which is a slippage of reading raced bodies. Christine Balance (2016) refers to such ascriptions of race as *"inference and interpretation"* (p. 45). She deduces that racial visibility, or in this particular case, Filipino/a legibility, is assumed to heed multiculturalism's "call to identify and market objects and performances as authentically belonging to and indicative of a single culture" (ibid.). Toronto media outlets like *The Grid TO* refused to make sense of the distinct cultural makeup of our band members and the concomitant multiplicity of our experiences.

Sounding Asian and the Burden of Representation

An ambivalence surfaced when moments of pride in Ohbijou's corpus of work and its reception collided with well-intentioned but racist consumptions of our music. We were lucky to be invited to play a show in a beautiful botanical garden in Brussels, Belgium. After playing our music set to an attentive audience, I was confronted by two young white Belgians:

> "You played a really great set tonight."
> "Thank you so much, we really appreciate you being here."
> "We could really hear the Asian influence in your music."

I was surprised and confused by this response. How did our performance "sound" and communicate Asianness? We were an orchestral pop band that played pop songs inspired by the indie rock that was popular at the time of our youth. In the 2005 novel *What We All Long For* Dionne Brand writes: "People stand and sit with the magnetic film of their life wrapped around them. They think they're safe, but they know they're not. Any minute you can crash into someone else's life" (Brand, 2005: 4). Brand gestures toward social and affective forces that animate our lives' trajectories and explores how our subjectivities intersect. Here, she captures why it is necessary to think with transnational trajectories, as we seek to understand our encounters with strangers. How have constructions of otherness confined my work as a musician to a single narrative? Edward Said (2000) eloquently writes: "Most people are principally aware of one culture, one setting, one home" (p. 186). My body, in this moment, was outside the boundaries of "home." An ascription of otherness sustains racial hierarchies within the context of colonialism. The strangers who hailed me into conversation that evening understood that I played Asian-influenced music because my body was read as Asian, not because of the sound, or the melody or the instruments. My Asian body was collapsed into a particular sound and mode of expression. I was left with the lingering questions: How do I respond to racist interpretations of my artistic craft that foreclose the wholeness of my being? Why, relatedly, was I hesitant to name this experience as racist?

Richard Fung (1995) describes feeling a "burden of representation" from non-Asian and Asian audiences who desire an authentic account of an "other" experience. Fung critiques expectations of Asian authenticity as an unfair demand to witness a performance that is most often derived through economies of stereotypes. Fung explains that there are many ways to arrive at a complex understanding of Asian subjectivity. In "The Trouble with 'Asians'" (1995), he describes how generalizations of Asianness can work to force Asian cultures into an "amalgam not unlike the mishmash of Hollywood orientalism" (p. 126). This schema of Asianness conflates the experiences of Asians living in the diaspora with those living in Asian countries. Fung reminds me that the historical trajectories that bring us into contemporary social relations in Canada are too messy to force into rigid regimes of race, gender, class, and sexuality. Importantly, he describes how the ways in which we come to call upon our racialized subjectivities depends on the audience that we are addressing. Thus, depending on the venue and audience, and the amount of security or safety that surround me, I speak and perform myself differently.

The iterations of myself which are performed on stage sometimes reduce and sometimes inflame my queer Asianness. There is political significance in how and when I identify myself as queer; it becomes a contentious proclamation when expectations of who I am are hailed from normative powers. As a performer, I often feel I am being squeezed into a homogenized narrative—one which does not account for the multitude of ways that I express and feel my gender, race, and sexuality. Like Richard Fung, I am intent on distancing myself from a socially constructed, homogeneous identity that swallows up or represses the complications of my experience that can't be domesticated in a single story. Expectations of Asian authenticity urge me to ask: what assumptions are being made about my Asian body and its sonic, kinetic, and affective performance?

Attendant to the lack of representation of Asian people in Canadian and American popular music, dominant hegemonies have controlled the social production of the Asian image as perpetually foreign (Pyke and Johnson, 2003). Though my gender may complicate stereotypical representations of Asian femininity, I wonder how my consistent hailing as a "quiet" and "nice" front woman is wrapped up with these stereotypes. The visual logics that position Filipina-ness as feminized and subservient are disrupted by my queerness and gender and "disobey the rules of visibility politics" (Balance, 2016: 47). I do not neatly fit into expectations of the nation. I am not white, nor conventionally feminine, nor do I perform a genre of music that is often associated with racialized performers.

Robert Diaz (2016) argues that multiculturalism and the concomitant tropes associated with Filipina experience cannot bring to bear the unsettling presence of Filipino/a bodies that play at the limits of normative representations. He also positions aesthetic practice as a method of resistance that displaces these racializing and gendered impulses. He argues:

> Filipino/a Canadian artists have thus paradoxically reanimated the body and its erotic potentialities in order to critique the colonizing and racializing practices of the multicultural and settler colonial state. These artists have fragmented, disarticulated, and occluded the body's normative aesthetic form. They have refused to acquiesce to demands for anthropological authenticity that police how and to what extent signifiers of Filipinoness exist within mainstream representational practices. (Diaz, 332)

Being a queer, Filipina performer in Canada is an act of disobedience. Despite being hailed as a "multicultural" artist, my body on stage intervenes in normative presentations of music and performance. I utilize performance as a site to play with notions of subjectivity that "disobediently listen" (Balance, 2016) to competing ideas of Filipino/a appropriateness and the civilizing efforts of state-sponsored multiculturalism. My queerness and gender make new meanings and elicit unpredictable proximities to how Filipino/a bodies have been historically read and consumed by empire. Balance (2016) argues for a method of "disobedient listening" that "disavows a belief in the promises of assimilation by keeping one's ears open to hidden and distant places not of this world" (p. 5). Ohbijou, in many ways, "disobediently listened" to the nation; in our presence one could confront an interruption to expectations of race, gender and sexuality.

Christine Balance (2016) suggests that the artist is in a position of "rendering" the world. These renditions are often disobedient to stable notions of racial authenticity. She argues that aesthetic "renditions betray those desires for an origin or original" (p. 16). My racialized presence in Canada is met by demands for cultural authenticity; a multicultural rendition of nation that at once gestures to another "homeland" and reifies a national narrative of white supremacy. However, these demands aren't so easily satisfied. My presence onstage aestheticized a rarely represented bodily experience for audiences that had the option of recognizing the incommensurability of Filipino/a diasporic experience and Canada's expectations of racialized appropriateness. My body on stage enacted a queer response to the impulses of "Canadian exceptionalism's reliance on fraught notions of identitarian presence and visibility—notions which always return to ahistorical versions of plurality" (Diaz, 2016: 332). How do music and performance encourage my race, gender, and sexuality to surface in ways that don't so easily cooperate with the common scripts of Filipino/aness in Canada?

A discussion of genre helps to highlight how we might listen differently to the racialized asymmetries that underwrite the nation. Ohbijou was often labeled as a band that played indie rock or orchestral pop music. These are genres that aren't usually associated with racialized performers. In Ohbijou's case, the incongruity of genre and presumed performer broadens the scope of what meanings can be gleaned from my presence on stage. The sound of our music hailed comparisons and was even described as imitative of the Canadian orchestral rock band Arcade Fire. Beyond the shadows of this association (which only work to affirm Arcade Fire's whiteness as the source of originality), mimicry appears as a familiar Western trope that my performances put pressure on and rubbed against. I deem my appearance on Canadian stages "queer" because of Canada's implicit and normative emphasis on whiteness and the related sounds commonly understood as representative of the nation. My use of "queer" is not only a reference to my sexuality but to the process of making "strange." I want to imagine queerness beyond the bounds of identity, a *bottomless bottom* that cannot be fixed or stabilized but is always calling into question social and imaginary landscapes of belonging. Queerness, as conceptualized here, is a dynamic between a people and a space that can be identified as something outside of and beyond LGBTQ identities. Hannah Dyer (2014) situates queerness "as a means to reference the capacity for creative living . . . a definition of queerness that denotes something new, beyond what has been imagined" (p. 15). Drawing on Dyer, "queer" can be understood as a transformative force, helping describe a more capacious aesthetic possibility for the racialized subject playing music. My presence reroutes the hold of whiteness on the genres of orchestral pop and indie rock and creates the conditions for examining the limits of categorizing aesthetic forms.

I am compelled to think of queerness as transformative, along with being collaborative and coalition-building. My individual experience is situated alongside a history of Filipina artists who exist within a push and pull between racism and the determination to create specters of possibility. Layering affective processes of racialization into the framing of queer as a rub against the normal helps to understand my unique positionality as a musician in Canada. Filipino/a diasporic experience is made from what Stuart Hall calls the "unstable points" of identification; the constant reproduction and transformation of identity (Hall, 2003: 238).

Queer Affect and Imagining Filipino/a Futures

At this moment, encouraged by a community of queer and feminist artists, particularly other Filipinos in Toronto, I am seeking a way out of the confines of an economy of stereotypes that circulate around my body and ask: How does racialized and queered subjectivity impact one's imagined future? It is a relief to realize the many ways of being Filipino/a and the many ways of feeling queer—it is something that cannot be contained because it is always shifting in conscious and unconscious expressions. Dina Georgis (2013) contends that aesthetic production provides emotional elaborations of disavowed affect. We distance ourselves, she suggests, from the vicissitudes of pain and suffering connected to racial difference and diasporic experience. Georgis argues that aesthetic production "provides a playground wherein love, pleasure, aggression, and the vulnerabilities therein are enacted to do the work of comprehending what has not fully assimilated into consciousness (p. 13). Ohbijou provided me with the space to creatively symbolize my desire and subjectivity through music and performance. My singing and movements on stage give expression to queer affect and wrestle with the affective space of diaspora as that which is in-between, never wholly invited into the nation and never completely outside. My queer presence on stage mimics the unpredictable contours of Filipino subject formation within the context of Canadian empire.

Inspired by my experiences coordinating the Clutch program run out of the Kapisanan Philippine Centre for Arts and Culture—an arts program which explores identity for young Filipina women—I have been motivated to seek out my own relationship to queerness as part of my Filipino/a heritage. Youth arts programs for diasporic subjects, specifically Clutch, may be described as a queer undertaking where participants are encouraged to create artistic responses to what it means to be Filipino/a in Canada. I thank Kapisanan and this program and its participants for allowing me the opportunity to feel welcomed within a community of Asian artists who resist normalized multicultural treatments of their work. The young Filipinos/as in this program have been some of my greatest teachers and have encouraged me to ask important questions about my own family's diasporic experience.

Inspired by my experiences with the Clutch program, I began to trace out my own familial history. I desired a better understanding of my family and the struggles they encountered when emigrating from the Philippines, concerned with how I might use familial narratives to spur songwriting and performances. I spent time asking my parents questions about how they came to live in Canada. I discovered that my mother arrived in Toronto on December 22, 1975. Her first impressions were that it was cold and that she longed for the tropical weather she grew up with in the Philippines. Like many other Filipina women in the 1970s, my mother had come to Canada to be a nurse. She was motivated by the possibilities of a better future for her family outside of the poverty of the Philippines. The results of my research and return to familial narratives was a song written with Ohbijou called "Balikbayan" (2011). This song marks the first time that I found the strength to speak directly to my Filipina-ness, and the psychosocial injury which is migration. Paul du Gay and Stuart Hall's (1996) suggestion that a search for identity should not be a "return to roots but a coming-to-terms with our routes" clarifies the psychic negotiations which this song and its performance have incurred for me (p. 6).

"Balikbayan" (which borrows its name from a Tagalog term for both goods and bodies which move across Filipino/a diasporic routes) is one of the last songs recorded under the moniker Ohbijou and is a revealing point of departure. Almost released with a title that more people could easily pronounce (under pressure from our record label to make it more radio-friendly), "Balikbayan" has worked to hail a community of Filipinos/as who were previously unaware of our shared identifications. The comments from audience members after we have played this song point out the importance of unveiling shared racial identification with audiences: "Oh, *Balikbayan*," you must be Filipino too!" Another listener told me that "Balikbayan" was the soundtrack to his return to family in Kenya over the summer because the lyrical content reminded him of his difficult journey. The writing and performance of "Balikbayan" has taught me that music which wrestles with the wounds of leaving a homeland and the sorrows and nostalgic remakings of home elsewhere help to heal diasporic damages. These are the song's lyrics:

"Balikbayan" (2011)

Here on these hours,
the sun hangs over,
the parallel, a spell,
we feel the myth, the distance like a metal case.

My family, the limbs of which, spread
the body of this land.
I'll pour my blood, on this place
to keep you safe, keep you safe.

We'll send it home, *balikbayan*. We'll send it home, *balikbayan*.

The heavy freight, it carried
the weight, of a better life.
You separate, your kids get old,
the air gets cold, we feel alone.

> Our country, this in between
> the hours hang, we're still not paid.
> We'll fold our clothes, and write our notes—
> send them home, send them home.
>
> We'll send it home, *balikbayan*.
> We'll send it home, *balikbayan*.

Despite Ohbijou's hiatus, I continue to use music as craft, as pedagogical address, and as therapeutic practice in order to respond to colonial histories and the movement of racialized bodies amidst a landscape of Canadian multiculturalism. The affective pulls and repulsions which have circulated between my performing body and my audience, when I am on stage, provide theoretical fodder for explorations into what "Canadian" popular music can and cannot grapple with. Sara Ahmed's (2004) reflections on the political uses of emotions which derive from encounters between bodies, particularly between white and raced bodies, explain some of what happens when I get up on a stage and sing to an audience My body is a text onto which sentiments of exclusion are written, but I must also grapple with the good-natured invitations into the Canadian nation which are extended in the reception of my music. I have not meant to simplistically ignore good press or the "successes" we have had as a band, but to suggest that most forms of Canadian multiculturalism offer invitations for participation in the nation-state which demand of me performances of authenticity which I do not feel comfortable producing. Indeed, to try to appease these demands is always already to fail. Further, I have meditated on the impossibility of my body satisfying normative performances of femininity and sexuality. I have hoped to suggest that my, this, queer brown body is excessive of the limits of polite multiculturalism and have extrapolated on the political potential of reinscribing what has been abjected.

I will continue to use music, visual art, and film as craft and as therapeutic practice in order to respond to colonial histories and the movement of racialized bodies amidst a landscape of Canadian multiculturalism. The recognition that I will never, despite arduous and devoted research, locate the source or definition of my queer Filipina-ness has led me toward queer theory for its insistence that queerness is a site of perpetual instability and contingency. This chapter's quest was to meditate on how my racial difference and presence onstage negotiate with the incoherence of Filipino/a and queer subjectivity. Frantz

Fanon (1952) pleaded, "O my body, make me a man that always questions" (p. 206). Perhaps in order to create a more just world we need to imagine our bodies not as part an answer or a remedy, but as part of an interminable inquiry about queer diasporic experience.

Bibliography

Ahmed, Sara. *The Cultural Politics of Emotion*. New York: Routledge, 2004.

Balance, Christine Bacareza. *Tropical Renditions: Making Musical Scenes in Filipino America*. Durham, N.C.: Duke University Press, 2016.

Brand, Dionne. *What We Long For*. Toronto: Vintage Canada, 2005.

Charlesworth, J. "Bellwoods Social Scene." September 28, 2011. http://www.thegridto.com/culture/music/bellwoods-social-scene/.

Cora Perry, Rose. "A True Canadian Band *Ohbijou* Hits Home." The Interrobang, October 12, 2009. http://www.fsu.ca/interrobang_article.php?storyID=4719§ionID=3&issueID=123.

Cruz, Denise. "Global Mess and Glamour: Behind the Spectacle of Transnational Fashion." *Journal of Asian American Studies* 19, no. 2 (2016): 143–67.

Diaz, Robert. "Queer Unsettlements: Filipinos in Canada's World Pride." *Journal of Asian American Studies* 19, no. 3 (2016): 327–50.

Dyer, Hannah. "Becoming Otherwise: The Queer Aesthetics of Childhood." Ph.D. dissertation, University of Toronto, 2014.

Eng, David L. *The Feeling of Kinship: Queer Liberalism and the Racialization of Intimacy*. Durham, N.C.: Duke University Press, 2010.

Fanon, Frantz. *Black Skins, White Masks*. Paris: Éditions du Seuil, 1952.

Freud, Sigmund. *On the History of the Psycho-Analytic Movement*. Edited by J Strachey. New York: W. W. Norton, 1996; first published 1914.

Fung, Richard. "The Trouble with 'Asians.'" In *Negotiating Lesbian and Gay Subjects*, edited by Monica Dorenkamp and Richard Henke, 123–30. New York: Routledge, 1995.

Georgis, Dina. *The Better Story: Queer Affects from the Middle East*. Albany: SUNY Press, 2013.

Gopinath, Gayatri. *Impossible Desires: Queer Diasporas and South Asian Public Cultures*. Durham, N.C.: Duke University Press, 2005.

Hall, Stuart. "Cultural Identity and Diaspora." In *Theorizing Diaspora: A Reader*, edited by Jana Evans Braziel and Anita Mannur, 233–46. Malden, Mass.: Blackwell, 2003.

Hall, Stuart, and Paul du Gay. *Questions of Cultural Identity*. London: Sage, 1996.

Manalansan, Martin F. *Global Divas: Filipino Gay Men in the Diaspora*. Durham, N.C.: Duke University Press, 2003.

Moten, Fred. *In the Break: The Aesthetics of the Black Radical Tradition*. Minneapolis: University of Minnesota Press, 2003.

Muñoz, José Esteban. *Cruising Utopia: The Then and There of Queer Futurity*. New York: New York University Press, 2009.

Pyke, Karen D., and Denise L. Johnson. "Asian American Women and Racialized Femininities: 'Doing' Gender across Cultural Worlds." *Gender & Society* 17, no. 1 (2003): 33–53.

Razack, Sherene H. *Race, Space, and the Law: Unmapping a White Settler Society*. Toronto: Between the Lines, 2002.

Sherene Razack in conversation with Zoë Druick. Interview by Z. Druick. June 15, 2004. "Between the Lines." http://www.btlbooks.com/othertext info.php?index=479.

Said, Edward W. *Reflections on Exile and Other Essays*. Cambridge, Mass.: Harvard University Press, 2000.

Walcott, Rinaldo. "What's Art Good For? Critical Diversity, Social Justice, and the Future of Art and Culture in Canada." Lecture presented at Strategic Development Meeting on Equity, Edmonton, Alberta, June 2011.

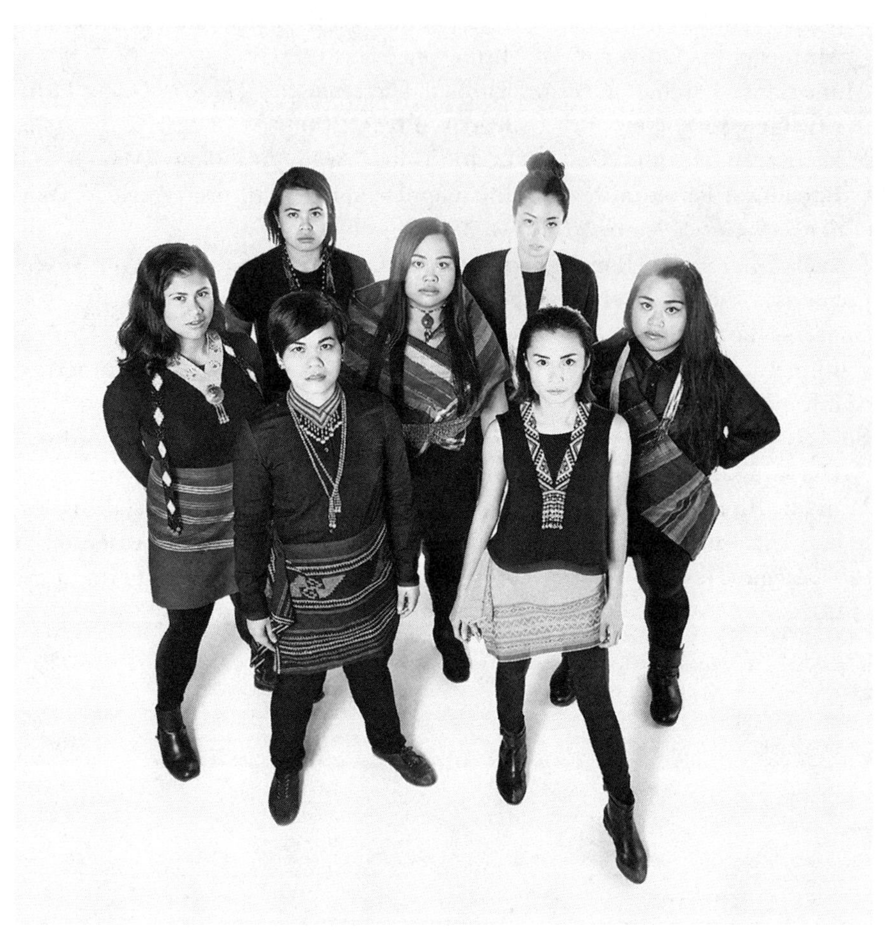

Members of the all-women *kulintang* ensemble Pantayo. Photo by Philip DaSilva.

Sonic Collectivities and the
Musical Routes of Pantayo

*Christine Balmes, Eirene Cloma,
Michelle Cruz, Joanna Delos Reyes,
Kat Estacio, Katrina Estacio,
and Marianne Grace Rellin*

In the following interview, the members of the all-pinay kulintang ensemble Pantayo reflect on the stakes and risks of claiming and hybridizing Philippine-based artistic genres and traditional music, particularly as women. As they negotiate what playing kulintang means for them, these women also assert the need to problematize how and to what extent we can claim solidarity or collectivity with each other—especially when Filipino/a histories are not in fact monolithic, but diverge in complex, even contradictory ways.

>**ROBERT:** How has Pantayo, as a collective, been an important way to thrive, survive, and create belonging in Toronto, as women, as queer women, as Filipinas?

>**KAT E:** Forming Pantayo was necessary for us to explore and be confident about our individual identities. Moving to Canada in my late teens, I found myself pretty lost navigating my new home as a young Filipino immigrant. I've tried to find belonging with other Filipinos by joining different social and cultural groups in Toronto. In Pantayo, though, I found people who are on a journey parallel to mine, who share similar and complementary artistic practice and aspirations, who, at the end of the day, really just want to create *kulintang* music that moves us.
>
>As a collective made up of diasporic and settler Filipino Canadian women, we've cultivated an environment that's conducive to

creating, growing, and being critical with each other. I think that's why we're responding to these questions in this way; each person can voice their own opinion, while still being part of a collective voice. In Pantayo, we have a collective identity, one that I think also informed our individual identities. Pantayo is a safe space for me to foster a process of continuous evaluation, to look within, to ruffle through ideas and issues, and make critical connections to the tacit cultural knowledge I've known all my life.

KATRINA E: Belonging also came as a result of us wanting to learn about *kulintang* together. We make a conscious effort to be together and process things together and it enriches all of us. We talk about issues that intersect with our music, even though it can be challenging because the language is not the most accessible.

CB: I think about belonging in relation to our audience: people who watch us, who have expressed that they want to learn *kulintang* music with us, and those who have said that our music has inspired them. When we play, audiences see our brown Filipina bodies and our knobbed instruments. Seeing these elements together in performance is representation: for folks who are like us, or those who are familiar with our culture. Self-identifying as queer is another way that we create belonging with our audience. When we talk about our identity, it is a way for our audience to connect with us. If our music touches a non-Filipino audience, our presence is an invitation to ask questions and find out more.

On the one hand we can be aware and careful of being tokenized, but another way to think about it is that by staying true to who we are and by talking about our identity, we're telling people that they can belong in any space: they don't have to assimilate, and they can achieve some kind of success just being themselves. And that's powerful even if a particular space or listenership does not necessarily identify 100 percent with all the intersections of our identities as queer diasporic Filipino women.

JDR: When I was younger, I went to local indie shows and it was really weird because I didn't see people on stage that were visibly like me. Now with Pantayo, I'm in a position of navigating the indie music scene—and almost infiltrating it. We've been given platforms like the Wavelength Festival, Long Winter, and X Avant at the Music

Gallery to play music shows as queer brown women. That's really neat. Experiencing all these with Pantayo is what gives me a sense of belonging, because I get to represent in a mainly white male-dominated scene with people who are like me.

MR: Being a part of Pantayo allowed me to connect deeply to my Filipino identity. Growing up in the Philippines, I was surrounded by the pervasive influence of Western culture; there was almost a sense of shame in owning and mining your identity. If I hadn't moved to Toronto and found Pantayo, I don't think I would be aware of how colonized I was. Pantayo opened my eyes to the decolonization process and has helped me feel empowered by my identity. I'm so grateful that I found my community in this group of women.

MC: When we all got together as a group, we already had a solid idea of who we are as people. I don't want to say that we didn't grow from that—we obviously have. But our identities as individuals and as a collective just continue to become more solid as we move forward. We were in community with each other before we became Pantayo, and we're so lucky to find belongingness with each other.

RD: How has Pantayo been a way to "queer" or problematize the types of music, performances, and collectives expected of women?

CB: It's important to remember that traditionally, *kulintang* was something considered as a woman's instrument. Other instruments in the ensemble were considered to be male instruments, such as the *agong*. In the Philippines today, all the instruments in the ensemble are played by both men and women. I think in North America—for people who are only familiar with seeing men play the instrument—that information might be lost. When I went to listen to the ethnomusicologist Bernard Ellorin talk at the University of Michigan in 2016, he said that the reason why most *kulintang* players in North America are male is because there is a religious ban on traveling for Muslim women. So all these people like the late Danongan "Danny" Kalanduyan and Joe Usopay Cadar—who are both men and are recognized in North America as the *kulintang* masters—they were the ones who brought *kulintang* music here because this ban was not imposed on them. They had the privilege to freely cross borders. There are power structures that influence and dictate the way we access and perceive this kind of music.

KAT E: Knowing that background on how *kulintang* music made its way to North America makes me look at how Pantayo plays *kulintang*, and how we're creating different conversations on what we can do with *kulintang* music. I find that we tend to add pop-inspired rhythms and arrangement, and this is what I think makes our sound a bit different. We were also able to push the boundaries of what *kulintang* music can sound like through a video game soundtrack project we recently worked on with the Toronto-based band Yamantaka // Sonic Titan. I think this is also one way that Pantayo queers the expectation of what *kulintang* music is and can be.

EC: We play our own instruments and arrange our songs. In my observation of bands that are woman-fronted and songs featuring women, in most instances, a man is producing the song or making the executive decision of how the piece will be composed, arranged, and packaged. In having agency and autonomy from conception to outcome, we queer these expectations of women in music.

KATRINA E: When I tell people that I play in a band, usually one of their first questions is, "Do you sing?" Many assumptions are made about women in music, especially their technical abilities: women are singer-songwriters with an acoustic guitar, not shredders, drummers, or electronic musicians. It's not unusual to find yourself in a conversation that turns condescending. It's empowering that Pantayo exists, is different, and queers stereotypes of women in music: I don't have to sing.

KAT E: Music performance is not just about a four-piece rock outfit in a bar or venue with a stage. Playing *kulintang* in mainstream concert venues around Toronto for non-Filipinos challenges that norm. Whenever we send our stage plot to event organizers and sound technicians, I always have to explain that the *kulintang* is "like a xylophone" because that's the closest thing that they might understand. Looking back on the performances that we've had, I noticed that we also haven't actively put our music out so we could get bookings. I don't know if that's a good thing or a bad thing, but we have been so lucky that we never felt the need to package our music in a way that's more digestible or appealing to people other than us. Even though our approach in music-making is now shifting, we still have to answer for ourselves in the music that we create. We live in a pretty interesting time and what we offer is something that's different, something that is celebrated by and is increasingly becoming a priority of promoters who want to program diverse and inclusive shows/festivals.

MC: We didn't have to try extra hard and put up a front on who we are as musicians and as a collective. We already had an idea, again, of who we are and we still continue to grow and expand from that. It's about how genuine we are, not just as a group but also in the artistic direction we take, and how we pursue it. We don't try to whitewash ourselves so we can get into these [events and shows]. We continue to do what we do, we don't try to impress other [artists or groups]. Being in Pantayo is the healthiest way of being in a collective. We're pretty lucky to have each other, and we've found security within our own selves and as a group.

RD: On that note, why is Pantayo all-women? How does that queer or unsettle normative expectations of women's labor, performance, and embodiment?

KAT E: I think it's important to create spaces where women can experiment and thrive, especially in a male-dominated music industry. The North American *kulintang* community has Danny Kalanduyan, Kulintronica, Datu, as well as *kulintang* ensemble musicians that accompany Filipino folk dance troupes. With Pantayo being an all-women *kulintang* ensemble, we are able to contribute to this conversation with the intention of including the voices of women. As a group that is visibly all-women, Pantayo queers the expectations of *kulintang* music (and music in general) as an activity performed only by men. We have an active role in producing diasporic Filipino content in Toronto and in Canada.

CB: There are other women who have brought *kulintang* to North America like the New York-based contemporary composer and percussionist Susie Ibarra. She had this project called Electric Kulintang with a Cuban-American beatmaker and they created a genre called Filipino trip-hop using *kulintang*. Recently she created a documentary with director Joel Quizon called "The Cotabato Sessions" that focused on Danny Kalanduyan's family's performing art practice. Titania Buchholdt has done a lot of work bringing and disseminating instruments in the West Coast. My first teacher in *kulintang* was Dr. Felicidad Prudente, who was a visiting professor of ethnomusicology when I was an undergraduate student at the University of Michigan.

KATRINA E: The music teachers at the school where I initially learned *kulintang* were women. Dulce De Vera and Ethel Miranda from the Music Department at Assumption Antipolo (an all-girls school) taught *kulintang* to grade school and high school students, respectively. Later on I found out that they had a student group/club called Salintura, where they learn, play, and perform Philippine music and instruments.

KAT E: Until recently, I found out that most of the sheet music pieces that Pantayo has access to are the works of Professor Aga Mayo Butocan from the University of the Philippines. She has taught a lot of students via the Department of Ethnomusicology, and has done album recordings. The Los Angeles-based Kollective Binhi has women members in their collective. They create Indigenous Filipino-inspired clothing and jewelry, and also play *kulintang*. Gingee is another musician/producer from Los Angeles who incorporates *kulintang* with her DJ sets. She fuses electronic music with global bass, world music, and hip-hop. There's also Anahata, a band based in Manila. Their *kulintang* player is a woman, and in their music, they combine *kulintang* with Afro-Cuban percussion, cello, piano, and vocals. We always try to see what other Filipino women in music are doing to remind ourselves that there are others like us in the diaspora.

JDR: If you look at the Filipino diaspora, women's labor is stereotypically tied to being nurses and caregivers in the health care industry. We have so much respect for these women, because they are the pillars of our community. Presenting Pantayo as an all-women group who work in arts and culture merely adds to the dialogue of what Filipino women are doing in the diaspora. Given the ways that colonial/imperialist values impact gender stratification in diasporic Filipino communities and families, it is even more important to have creative spaces for Filipino women to be seen.

EC: Pantayo is all-women and notably holds space for women with diverse expressions of gender and sexuality. I appreciate how there is no expectation to perform and present ourselves in a hyper-feminine way. I encounter this expectation in micro and macro ways in many other Filipino spaces and communities. It gets exhausting to navigate the heteronormativity, classism, and cis-sexism. In Pantayo, I feel seen in my body, my essence, and my truth.

JDR: Also, why do all-men groups never get questioned, "Why are you all men?"

CB: Exactly. It's normative. All-men groups never have to declare that they are all men in that group because that's almost what people expect. People never have to question that privilege and never have to wonder why the members are all one gender.

MR: Or when there are women in a group, they fill the background roles—as accessories—to men playing the music.

CB: Women have a lot to contribute to the music scene. But when it's the men who are leading groups, sometimes they are the ones who make the decision about how it should be. It's not an equal playing field: not all voices get heard. I think that Pantayo as a collective of women, and the fact that we learned about *kulintang* music, its history, and how it's played as a collective created a different dynamic within the group that's more respectful of each other and where we are in terms of skill and process. It's like that African proverb: If you want to go fast, go alone; if you want to go far, go together.

In women collectives, there's also a lot more community outlook into the way that the work is being done. We always carry with us this concern regarding how our work reflects on us as Filipinos and to the Filipino community. How do we represent the different parts of our community that we carry in us? Personally, we all have our connections to groups like Anakbayan, Kapisanan Centre for Arts and Culture, Scarborough Arts, settlement work—all these things that we are also informed by all our connections that we have outside of just being Pantayo. We can't help but carry that into our work as Pantayo and reflect it.

MR: We also make an effort to share the practice with and include the community in our process; music-making is not always an isolated endeavor for us. We invite peers who are new to *kulintang* to learn the instruments with us and perform with us at gigs regardless of their skill level. When we played at the Black Lives Matter protest in Toronto in 2016, we invited the community to make noise with us using our instruments. We also regularly collaborate with other bands and other artists in spoken word, dance, and martial arts. I like the idea that we are able to create inclusive spaces and bring people together through music.

EC: Women in the community consider what and how much labor everyone's doing. The decision-making process is also different.

RD: So, why music, and what does creating this type of music do for you personally and politically?

MC: It's a great platform to be an advocate for the issues that matter to us as a group. By playing *kulintang*, we bring attention to the instruments and the culture that the music came from. When Pantayo performed at X Avant X Festival at the Music Gallery in 2015, we were able to use our time on stage to speak about Lumad (Indigenous peoples) killings in the Philippines.

KAT E: Playing with Pantayo and learning about *kulintang* music is the medium for me to be able to learn more about Filipino culture, and my identity. Music is also the avenue in which I am able to articulate the learnings that I now know after this process.

Like what Marianne said earlier, Pantayo was also the reason why I was open to decolonizing myself. I now understand that as people who aren't Maguindanaon or T'boli, we come from a place of privilege and that we must remain cognizant that we are consuming a culture that is not inherently ours. Just because we are Filipinos who are performing Filipino content, it doesn't mean we are not appropriating. We always mention in our bio that our music is inspired by the Maguindanaon and T'boli *kulintang* traditions because it is our way of making sure our audience knows that we are not the originators of this music. We give credit where it is due as a form of respect to the continuous work that people from those tribes are doing, as well as the works that the academics have done in order to disseminate this information. Furthermore, acknowledging the tribes that we are borrowing from also makes a point that we are not taking up the space that is meant for the voices of Indigenous peoples; rather, we are saying that we are creating something that is just inspired by their culture.

If I was asked this question maybe five years ago, pre-Pantayo Kat wouldn't have been able to articulate all these things, or at least pinpoint that these are issues that are directly related to our music-making and our identity as a collective. It is through music, specifically, *kulintang* music, that I am able to learn about issues that are now so integral to how I see the world and how I relate with other people. In Pantayo, I have an avenue to talk about these issues, and embody the learnings in our music. Moreover, I don't think I'd be able to grasp all these if I read about it from an academic journal article, for example.

CB: Arts is just more accessible than academia. And I think the fact that we're all-women, queer, playing *kulintang* music is already a statement. People just need to break it down, interpret it in their own way, similar to reading a scholarly article: you have to interpret it and try to understand it. But I think we're already theorizing something just by being together and continuing to do our work.

MR: I do think that our music poses a challenge to our audiences, though, partly because the music that we create resists categorization. It reflects our plethora of musical influences (sometimes, all explored in one song) and mirrors our always-shifting and layered identities.

If you look back at all the interviews, reviews, and articles about us, the discussions have always been around our identities and how it influences our music, the history of the instruments, and/or the politics surrounding *kulintang* music. I don't think any writer has attempted to explain our music in technical terms and/or has categorized our music as part of a specific genre, and I think that that is empowering and freeing as a musician. It gives us permission to be more experimental. Echoing what Kat has said, we do not feel the need to "package" our music to easily appeal to broader audiences. The music that we create cannot easily be commodified and/or consumed passively. Creating and listening to diasporic *kulintang* music always involves a negotiation of complex identities.

RD: How has Pantayo, as a collective or individually, culled from or taken from our diasporic past to think about our present in Canada?

KAT E: I think that is part of the reason why I like the whole idea of us having a record. It's a way for us to document the work that we are creating that is very specific to our experience as a group of Filipino women in Toronto, and to the time we created it. It's very specific to "the now." In the future, if and when people revisit it, they will hear what we were doing in this particular space and time. What we do now could affect the future of *kulintang* music, the future of how women are perceived in music, how Filipinos are doing cultural work through music, etc. I was reading up on Afrofuturism, about how it can be used "as a lens to better understand our lives and their possibilities beyond our present circumstances." I like how we can also explore these ideas in our work as a means of decolonizing.

CB: In developing our first full-length album, we consciously and collectively agreed upon intentionally changing and modifying *kulintang* song structures in order to contribute to its evolution.

Many of the things that characterize our band now are due to being located in Canada while playing a musical tradition that is still relatively inaccessible outside of the Philippines and in certain parts of the United States. Working with *kulintang* music has limited us in many ways, but it has also provided us with a lot of freedoms in many others. Limiting because we made a conscious decision as a collective to educate ourselves first on the *kulintang* tradition that has been around for a long time and continues to be evolved by Indigenous musicians. Limiting because instruments and knowledge are not easy to acquire. Luckily, it is a tradition that has been written about extensively by different ethnomusicologists and scholars in the Philippines and abroad. I think we understand that part of being relevant, part of having power is that we get to be part of that conversation about who we are. And for me, it's a privilege to be able to do that work, so I think we're pretty lucky that we have a lot of people around us who are interested in identity.

Playing *kulintang* is freeing because it allows us to have a voice in the community. I think it's a good time to be a queer musician of color in Toronto today because we are surrounded by musicians who are queer and/or people of color who are using their voices to talk about social justice and identity issues.

EC: Christine, I appreciate how you highlight that *kulintang* can allow us to understand the Philippines' relationships with its neighbors and to locate it within a Southeast Asian cultural context. And we begin to become readers and writers of a narrative of the Philippines that is an alternative to its representation of only a colonial/postcolonial space. The Philippines, just like any other place, has its own internal dynamics, its own relationships with its neighbors and so forth. A lot of diasporic Filipinos, typically with a second-generation gaze, see Filipino identity and culture in a very binary way: before or after the Spanish colonization. I remember going to a community event and a presenter stated, "We are all Indigenous." A statement like this sounds like essentialized definitions of Filipino-ness, erasing thousands of years of history and cultural mixing in the region. As a second-generation Filipino, I'm learning to be mindful of my gaze: how I perceive Filipino culture and other Filipino bodies.

KATRINA E: Even the name of calling ourselves Filipinos is imposed on us. And Philippines? Who is this "Philip"? I have no connection with this "Philip."

CB: So you're saying we can't be ahistorical about how we treat our identity. We can't just be like I'm Indigenous to this part of the Philippines or my parents are Indigenous to this part of the Philippines because we're no longer connected to those roots.

EC: Or not acknowledging the rich history and cross-cultural interaction that came before the Spanish. *Kulintang* carries historical relationships between countries: we see this in gamelan from Indonesia. Talking about where Indigenous instruments come from and uncovering the history is a way to recognize that the Philippines is not a homogenous nation. When we acknowledge that the origins of our instruments and music are from the southern Philippines, it challenges people's perceptions of Filipinos as only Tagalog-speaking and Christian.

KATRINA E: Everyone is not Manileño. Within the Philippines, there exists many ethnographic groups with different languages and distinct cultures: Cebuanos, Ilocanos, etc. People think Filipinos are all the same, but we're not.

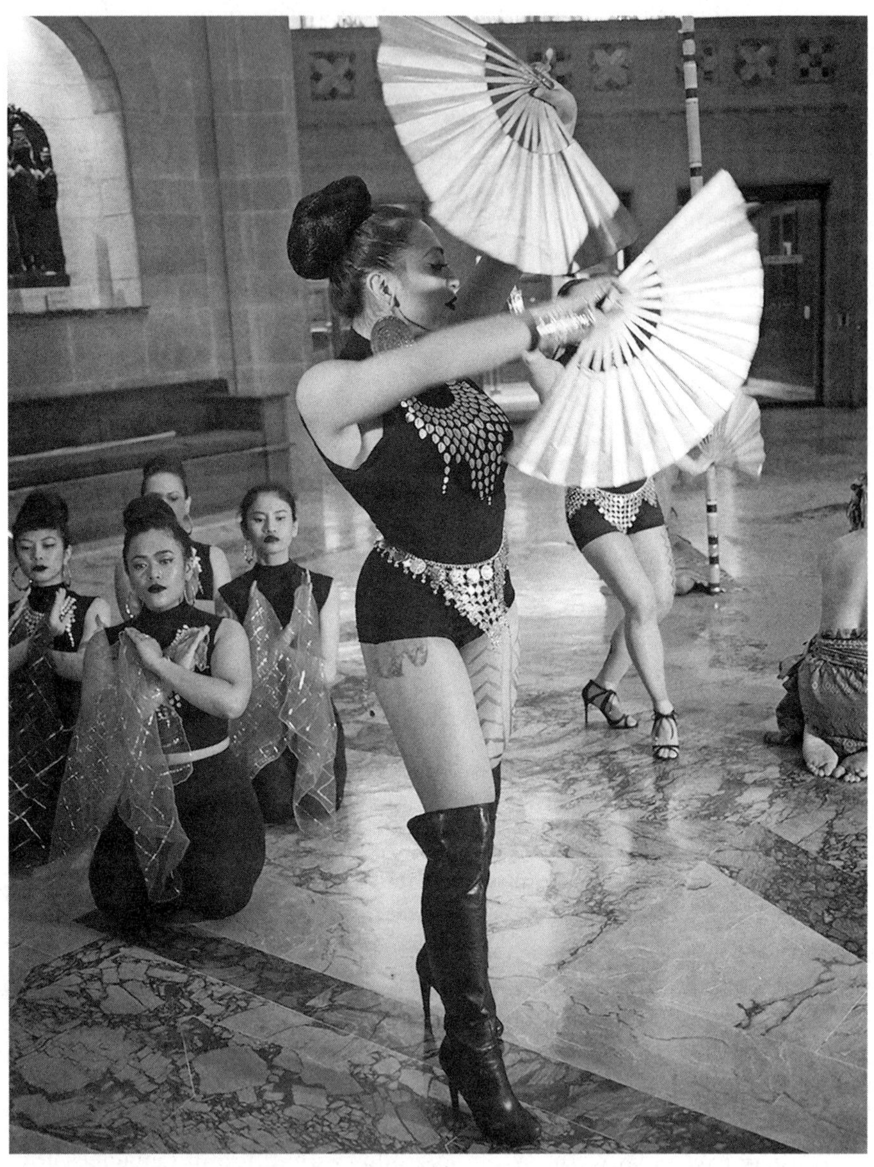

HATAW performs at the Royal Ontario Museum, Toronto, 2016.

HATAW

Queer Choreography and the Routes
of Diasporic Filipino-ness

Jodinand Aguillon

What follows is in an excerpt from a presentation that Jodinand Aguillon delivered at Kularts in San Francisco on May 14, 2016. Aguillon was the keynote speaker for "Dialogue on Philippine Dance + Culture in the Diaspora." In his speech, he charts the multiple sites of inspiration that influenced his passion for choreography and dance—sites that range from Hollywood movies to queer pop icons to hybridized forms of folk dance. As he discusses his movements between and within Edmonton and Toronto, Aguillon also provides a map—both geographic and metaphorical—of the archival flashpoints that manifest in the types of embodiment that queer diasporic artists choose to rearticulate as they pursue their creative and artistic pursuits.

I'd like to start by thanking the coeditors for giving me this platform to share my story among people whose work I've admired and respected from afar. I'm truly humbled to be speaking on a subject that's so incredibly important to me—ME. The year was 2004. I was about to receive an award of recognition. As the youngest person to be appointed artistic director of the Philippine Barangay Performing Arts Society, I felt like a pretty big deal.

We were winning every competition we entered. Chinese fan dancing and Ukrainian kicks had nothing on us. We had just come back from our first North American ambassadorial tour through Vancouver, San Francisco, Disneyland, and Las Vegas. I was at the helm of three tour buses filled with more than sixty dancers ranging in age from five to twenty-two—along with their parents. I felt invincible. My eyes were fixated on the next goal at hand: my dream of moving to California to become a backup dancer for Britney Spears.

It's my pleasure to share with you how growing up with accessible, popular media like MTV and the internet played important roles in the development of HATAW. I've been a big fan of pop culture since as far back as I could remember. Some parents would make their children play the piano when relatives came over. We couldn't afford a piano and even if we could, I did not have the discipline to learn it. Instead, I would stand at the center of the room and perform a song and dance routine to Madonna's hit "Like a Virgin." From an early age, it was clear to my family that I was somewhat *gifted*. Growing up in Sherwood Park, Alberta, all my friends were white. I lived your typical "the only Filipino kid in a very small town" story. I excelled in my studies and got all the lead roles in every school musical. Like many Filipinos, who were introduced to Filipino folk dance through Hawaiian dance—as studies show, for every Filipino folk dance troupe that is formed, two more Hawaiian dance groups pop up—my initial motivation to learn more about Filipino folk dance was because I wanted to learn moves like *The Running Man* and *Roger Rabbit*.

In 1993, I remember one of my *titas* taking me to the Alberta Provincial Museum to watch a production entitled *Pilipinas* performed by the Philippine Barangay Children's Dance Troupe. I sat there sort of bored while watching Filipino kids my age doing traditional folk dance. I couldn't help but think that this wasn't anything like *Sister Act 2*.

But then after the intermission, a familiar tune that I had heard on the radio began to play. The same dancers I had written off as losers stepped out, dressed in cool 1990s streetwear, and performed a hip-hop dance routine to TLC's song "What About Your Friends." Suddenly, these Filipino kids were "cool." Being Filipino was "cool." Soon after seeing that show, I auditioned for the Barangay troupe, and for the next twelve years I would devote my weekends, alongside my new crew of Filipino friends, to learning and eventually teaching folk and modern dances. To be honest, I was never really the *best* dancer, but I was pretty good-looking so I usually got solos or performed front and center.

In 1995 Janet Jackson released her music video for the song "Runaway." The styling and choreography brought together influences from different cultures around the world and made it look so sexy. I spent a good chunk of puberty memorizing all her music videos and wishing I was a better dancer. I knew I needed to expand my repertoire and learn different forms of dance. Dance classes were too expensive, so instead,

I learned how to salsa and ballroom dance by escorting every Filipina debutante I knew in Edmonton. Marko Doyle, cofounder of Vinok, "Canada's United Nations of Dance," introduced me to other forms of traditional worldance.

When I traveled back to the Philippines I was able to attend workshops with ABS-CBN and Douglas Nierras of Powerdance—a contemporary dance company. As the members of Barangay grew older, a few of us formed a small hip-hop crew called Freeflo. We'd perform at community events, nightclubs, and opened for acts like Snoop Dogg, Ashanti, and yes, even Sean Desmond. Which brings me back to the late 1990s and early 2000s, when this thing called the internet happened and quickly became an accessible resource and learning tool. In between updating my Geocities site and my Asian Avenue account, I curiously downloaded an album by a band called Pinikpikan.

Their sound was familiar and yet completely foreign at the same time. Folk music from the future. You didn't hear this kind of music from the radio and you sure as hell couldn't order it through Columbia House. Even to this day, it was unlike anything I had ever legally downloaded from the internet.

I found myself inspired by something not so popular. It moved me. While I continued to consume media for the masses, I still wanted to create new ways to feel represented. Pinikpikan inspired the direction I wanted to take Barangay: *folk fusion*. A hybrid of traditional and new, popular and niche. And somehow it worked. This was an idea that came to fruition back in 2004 when I had apparently reached the peak of my artistic dance life in Edmonton. I accepted that award I mentioned earlier and shortly after quietly resigned as artistic director. Actually, off the record, there was so much drama and so many *titas* saying: "Give my daughter a solo." I was like: "Uhh . . . I'm like twenty years old and I just wanna dance. K BYE!"

So I stopped. Everything Filipino and folk dance just stopped. I took a break and threw myself full force into other things like corporate retail and partying. I don't really remember much. But eventually I moved to Toronto. A new beginning. Sadly, Electric Circus was no longer a thing, but I joined an all-male Tahitian dance group—Otea Tane—and had the honor of touring with North America's longest-standing Filipino folk dance troupe, Fiesta Filipina. And through my involvement with spaces like the Kapisanan Philippine Centre for Arts and Culture and the Carlos Bulosan Theatre, I was fortunate to have been given opportunities to choreograph small numbers for a few theater productions.

About a year ago, on a whim, after witnessing the speakers of Next Day Better (a creative speaker series for diasporic communities) and after reuniting and reminiscing with old dance friends in Edmonton about the good old days and how much they missed dancing, it became clear to me just how fortunate I was to be part of such an incredibly talented community here in Toronto. How I could walk into a space like Kapisanan, where freaks like me were the majority, and how fortunate I was to have access to fellow artists beyond just a computer screen. Real people in real time.

I suddenly got that same *kilig* feeling I got when I first heard Pinikpikan. Inspired to make things happen, I immediately told my best friend—Facebook—and posted a call-out looking for dancers. Within a few weeks HATAW somehow magically, cosmically happened. Sporting borrowed *malongs* from our sisters' Kapwa Collective and Pantayo, paired with $6 crop tops from Ardenes, we put our best foot forward and proudly united as HATAW. Our debut performance was at last year's Kultura Filipino Arts and Culture Festival—featuring my favorite song by Pinikpikan—"Kalipay."

And now here we are. Much like dance, a good joke, or a great idea, timing is everything. I believe that our time is now. While we further develop as a collective, we look forward to a handful of challenges. HATAW remains unfunded and is fueled by the dedication of our talented volunteer artists, choreographers, and our community partner, the Kapisanan Philippine Centre for Arts and Culture.

In closing, HATAW isn't about changing tradition or reinventing a culture. We draw inspiration from our known Filipino heritage, evolve through our lived experiences, and perform in ways that move and inspire us today. We do this through collective stories and collaboration and connecting talent to community—folks like you and me. Telling our stories through our movement. After all, the art of reinterpreting, remixing, and revisiting is indeed in our blood.

Between the Earth and Sky
Interview with Kim Villagante

Artist Statement

My name is Kim Villagante. My stage name is Kimmortal. I am a multi-dimensional artist: a visual artist, rap poet, singer-songwriter, and actor. My story as a queer Filipina Canadian inevitably reveals itself in the work I create. Within my visual arts practice, I have been honing my craft in doodling, or what is more formally known as line drawing.

A lot of my drawings are of faces. Faces have been my main subject since I was young. Many of the faces I draw today differ from the faces I would doodle as an elementary school-aged student who attended a predominantly white middle/upper-class private Christian school. The faces I would adorn had blonde hair, blue eyes, and pointy noses. As a young girl, I would pinch my nose in front of mirrors, praying that the bridge of my nose would elevate, and I would stand on my tiptoes imagining I was taller.

Rewind back in time to before I was born. My father was a portrait artist in the Philippines; he owned and ran a successful business with many staff. For ten years, after immigrating to Canada, he continued with this business, traveling to different locations in and near Vancouver, setting up his portrait stand. I remember as a young child hearing his brushstrokes from the kitchen studio and watching him peer through a large magnifying glass to replicate the small details on the photographs. As a toddler, I would sit on his lap and watch these faces come to life. My dad stopped his portrait business and became the custodian at my school, which allowed us to get a tuition discount. My classmates made jokes about his job at the school. Immersing myself in the arts through dance (I taught choreography to my friends), theater, and visual art was a way of transcending the social and economic differences, the restrictions of religious schooling, the silencing I felt, and it was a way to connect to the outside world.

151

In my last few years of high school, I began to research hip-hop culture and discovered graffiti through images I found online of graffiti murals in the subways of New York City. My sketchbook filled with pencil portraits of legendary hip-hop artists such as Tupac, Notorious B.I.G., and Aaliyah. I was entranced with hip-hop culture and identified with its gritty and raw essence that told the stories of struggle among African Americans growing up in urban ghettos. At that time, I did not recognize that the leaders in hip-hop culture to which I was drawn were people of color. The faces I drew began to change as a result.

Fast forward to graduation. I applied and was accepted into the bachelor of arts program in visual arts and art history at the University of British Columbia. Throughout university, I juggled different jobs as an art teacher, teaching private lessons and leading weekly art classes at an elementary school. My road into performing my poetry and music was nurtured at local shows around Vancouver and open mic shows put on by students of color organizations. Many of the performers I met at these shows were artists of color who expressed their struggles through singing and poetry, talking about liberation, their experiences as people of color, and healing through art and music. I was drawn to the power of words, and at these shows I met many others who identified as queer, feminist, and who were also involved in the community's activist organizations. Many of our conversations encompassed decolonization and redefining the boundaries of love, which began to be reflected in my poetry and art. It was also during this time that I came out as queer.

My faces have grown with me; every line and curve of my pen is influenced by my journey. The noses I draw are rounder, the curves are fearless, the hair is black, and the eyes are wise. My shapes are not afraid to be fragmented pieces, like tangents reflecting unfinished sentences and lingering questions I have around my identity and my history. My current "Indigenous imagination" series reflects a yearning to visualize my tribal roots that I will never fully know as a member of this Filipino diaspora. Where memory is peppered with the blockages of pain and trauma due to the realities of colonization, I resort to my artistic mediums to imagine my family's past, what will never be spoken about. I wonder about the matriarchs, the queens, the woman warriors. Even if it is not accurate, I trust that perhaps the ancestors can give me glimpses through my linework. I can continue the bloodline passed down to me through my father, who discontinued his artwork in the name of survival. Through my many art history classes in university, I

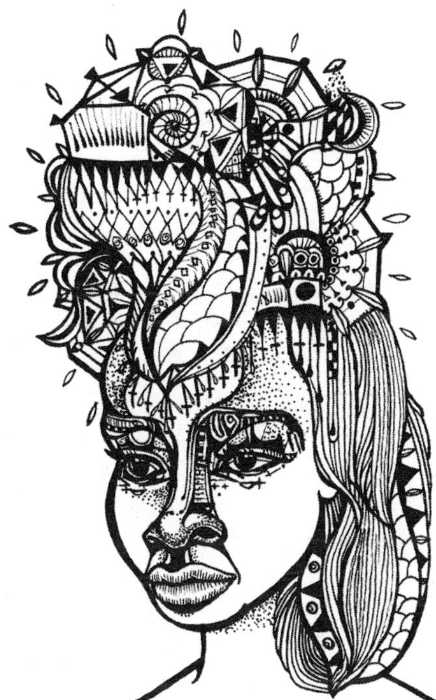

Kim Villagante, *Indigenous Imagination 2 (girl)*, 2014.

studied the paintings and sculptures created via the white male gaze. I take pride in being a queer woman of color drawing women and gender-nonconforming people of color. Through my art, I'm interested in the notion of writing myself into the present and the future, for representation, for survival, and like a graffiti tag, for making my mark on this planet.

MARISSA LARGO: In your artist statement, you recount how the arts have always provided you with a way to "transcend social and economic differences." Your art practice also has a strong justice-seeking thrust, as you connect much of your production to your anti-oppression activism. How is your multifaceted art practice a form of, not only imagining, but also making a new world?

KV: I am obsessed with creating my own universe and being surrounded by my own creations. Sometimes I listen to my songs over and over again, and much of the art on my walls is my own. On the outside this matches the definition of a narcissistic artist, but perhaps my preference connects to my desire to see myself reflected in a society where my community's creativity and labor are either completely absent or not given enough space for deeper articulation. Through the arts I am able to sculpt a new home, fill the air with my own sonic sound waves and visual stimuli, carve out windows in the walls, sit with my hard questions, dig for answers, invite people in and keep some out, and basically take up space. Through my art and music, locating and picking out consistent threads is an indicator to me that I have a language that is my very own. This gives me pride. When people hear this language and understand, I am able to have a conversation, there can be connection. Here is where community is created. This is a part of creating a new world.

I believe representation, being visible and having a voice in the media, is important to the communities I belong to, and so this comes through in my art as well as my community work. Much of my energy goes into organizing events, and I'm learning how to better articulate how my art practice also involves community work, or would be nothing without the community that informs and gives me energy to persist at it. As an artist who is a queer woman of color, finding other artists who I can relate with and audiences I can connect to has not been easy via locally established mainstream/popular events that systemically underrepresent the communities I belong to. As a result, I've learned to collaborate with others to create our own platforms that spotlight and celebrate queer Indigenous, black, and people of color artists. One example is "She," an event that happens alongside International's Women's Day that showcases black, Indigenous, mixed race, and self-identified women of color artists. Being able to dictate the flow of a show, give a platform for other artists, and bring your communities together is a way of collectively creating a new world. I've seen musicians feel safe enough to enter deeper portals in their performances because of the intentions of the event that acknowledges the intersections of our identity.

ML: In one realization of Flerida Peña's play *Sister Mary's a Dyke?!* you play the lead character of Abby, a Catholic schoolgirl whose emerging queerness is foregrounded by the church's oppression of women and non-normative sexual identity. As a queer Filipina, what were the parallels and tensions for you as you performed and embodied Abby?

KV: Like Abby, I also attended a private school, though not Catholic but Christian, for the majority of my elementary and high school years. I had a sheltered upbringing throughout my school years, which allowed me to tap into Abby's naivete. As a twenty-six-year-old artist, it was initially difficult for me to go through such intense changes when playing Abby, especially since many of the shifts she went through occurred in my early twenties. Abby goes through a huge transformation: from experiencing her first lesbian relationship, to becoming a radical feminist political activist, to ultimately leading her classmates to attack church patriarchy at the tender age of fourteen. My solution to these challenges was to pocket particular experiences from my own life that I could draw upon to more authentically embody Abby during key moments. One scene has Abby coming in from her history class where she is still digesting the fact that women do not have the honor of becoming ordained in the Catholic Church. In an emotional conversation with Jesus, Abby expresses how unfair it is that her "kind and intelligent" teacher cannot be a church leader just because she's a woman. In this scene, I drew from my own experience watching both my mother and my sister struggle to make ends meet as well as demand respect working in jobs they were overqualified for, and I also thought of the stories and struggles of Filipina migrant workers I've worked with via the Philippine Women's Center. All these thoughts brought on my anger and tears in that particular scene.

One of the challenges for me as an actor was being able to imagine outside of whiteness when imagining the character of Abby and Abby's world. There was much in the script that referred to Abby's thoughts around sexuality and gender, which allowed me space to ponder as an actor, but I couldn't locate her thoughts around race or being Filipino. Perhaps my difficulty lay in the fact that I have never seen a play or media piece where the main character was Filipino. Also, my own high school experience probably informed my acting since I was one of four Filipino students in a majority white and Asian student population.

Whiteness took precedence in my imagination of Abby's world. I imagined other characters I mentioned within the script as being white, from my teachers, to my love interests, to the pope and archbishops. Yet what surprised me was how the audience interpreted my world very differently. At one point, I do a British accent to impersonate a head nun in my school, who I envisioned as a white

nun, but after the show, a playwright friend of mine asked me if I
was playing a Jamaican woman's accent. Another Filipino friend
of mine said she couldn't help but think of herself when she was
in Catholic school when she saw me performing. The set designer
of the play drew a picture of my love interest that became my prop
throughout the run of the shows. Interestingly, the picture she drew
depicted an Asian girl with short black hair and almond eyes, yet my
imagination of Abby's love interest was a white girl. It wasn't until
after the play that I realized how the lens from which I imagined
Abby's world was colored white, and even more how it was difficult
for me to see through this lens.

In high school I didn't understand what it meant to be Asian
Canadian, or the diversity of what it looked like to be Filipino
Canadian. I knew I didn't fit into the heteronormative, the ideal
femininity that the Filipina girls I knew seemed to be comfortable
with. Hip-hop was a culture I could identify with more than my Filipino culture, because I saw brown girls like me bending the rules,
including gender norms.

One theater director, Diane Roberts, who I had the honor of
being directed by via another theater production, *Sal Capone: The
Lamentable Tragedy Of,* talks about her experience in theater school
as a young Jamaican-Canadian student. Her theater teacher had
the class engage in a daily warm-up activity where students were
directed by a white theater instructor to erase their identities and
ultimately put on a white mask before entering into their characters.
I'm reminded of how much leaders in the theater scene can dictate
how much of a role race, sexuality, and gender can play on the stage.
I didn't feel comfortable or encouraged to explore what it meant to
be Filipino in the role as queer Abby, and my theater director and
leaders in the rehearsals process were mainly white. They understood what it meant to be queer, but the complexity of it for me as a
queer and Filipina felt different in my body. Working from my own
experience going to a majority white high school, as well as a lack of
representation in Canadian media of Filipino characters, as well as
a feeling that there was more attention focused on her gender and
sexuality than on her race, I struggled to understand what it meant
to be a queer and Filipino Abby.

ML: Throughout Western art history, portraiture was reserved for
the powerful and privileged, which were more often than not white

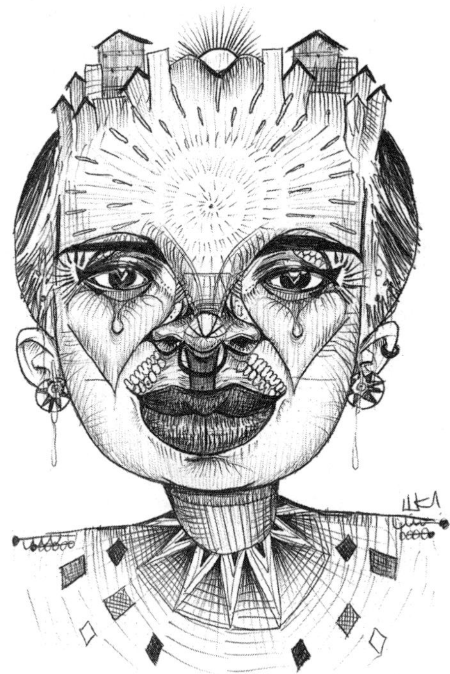

Kim Villagante, *Indigenous Imagination 3 (home)*, 2014.

males. Your portraits are counter-canonical in every way: graffiti-style renderings of queer of color matriarchs and women warriors. What is the significance of your materials, style, and motifs as an artist and social activist?

KV: Through my practice, I can make a mark on the pervasive whiteness, maleness, and straightness in Western art history. I draw my black lines on blank white paper or on canvases that have been coated in layers of white paint. Art styles that change or expand our perception of reality such as outsider art, spiritual/intuitive art, and surrealist art have always been work that I've been drawn to. I am drawn to street art graffiti's ties to being a political art form of resistance and assertion for marginalized communities. I mainly draw women and hope to challenge traditional representations of femininity. By sitting in the artist seat, I can subvert the male gaze so prominent throughout art history. Most of the women and gender-nonconforming faces I draw do not smile, and the shapes that spill out from their heads reveal the patterns we have made of the world around us as well as the complexity of our inner universes.

The symbols and shapes in my art have been something I've always drawn, but after viewing the work of Filipino tribal tattooists from centuries ago and recognizing similar line work and patterns in my own line drawings, I felt more connected to a long tradition of Filipino artists that have come before me.

Understanding the importance of healing in the context of our identities as queer, racialized, and postcolonial subjects is integral to my work as an artist and community activist. For me, healing and self-love means finding time to create. In my arts-based workshops, I encourage stream-of-consciousness writing and drawing sessions where I encourage participants to spontaneously create without judgment. My intention here is to release what is happening on the inside. My process counters the reliance on mathematical accuracy, measurement, perfect symmetry, and realism and relies instead on my intuition. I do not plan a piece before I paint or draw; I allow the women I paint to inform the motion of my hand before I mark a page. There have been times when I've pushed to control an artwork and found my work overcrowded.

It makes me very happy when other women of color tell me they see themselves reflected in my work, because I understand it is important for me as well as my community to be seen, and honored in the external world.

ML: As a queer Filipina, you use the performing and visual arts as a way of "writing" yourself "into the present and the future"? What is the value of doing this work for queer Filipinos/as in Canada?

KV: The value of doing this work for queer Filipinos and Filipinas lies in understanding the multiplicity of our experiences here in Canada. I am but one voice among histories of Filipino settlers here in Canada, and so perhaps one of the aims is to keep articulating these complexities. I would like to be a part of sparking critical conversations and have been honored to be included as a voice in these matters. I know what it feels like to feel alienated even among people who share the same identification labels as me: not feeling Filipino enough among other Filipinos, feeling too queer among my family, hiding parts or pushing out parts of myself, all to feel a sense of belonging . . . Writing myself into the present and future means understanding that my story matters amid this institutionalized multiculturalism that wants to homogenize our experiences, dampen our relationship to our ancestry, ignore the complexities of what it means to be queer Filipino "Canadians," and consume us like a dish in a buffet aisle labeled "ethnic." Our work in academia, the arts, and beyond are important remnants of a growing pool of knowledge that can be accessed for future generations.

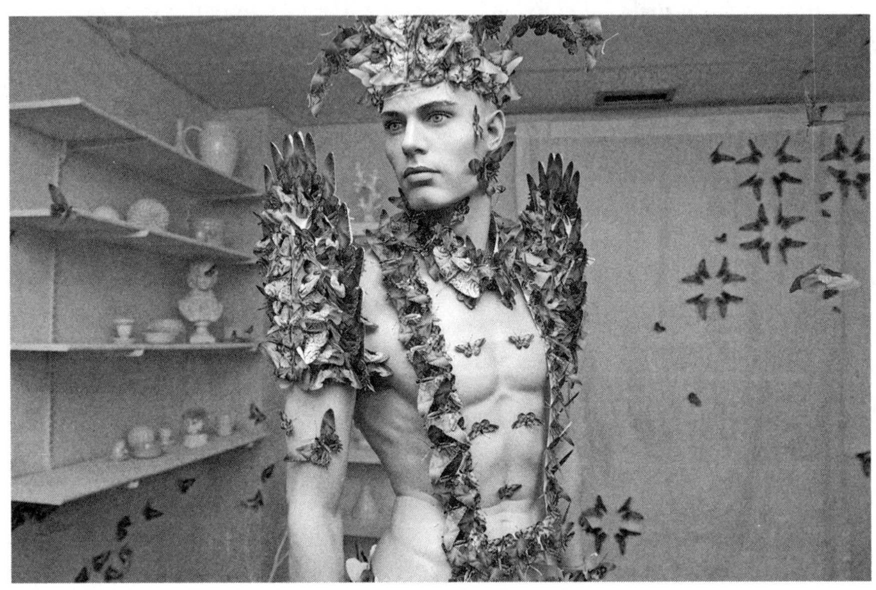

Julius Poncelet Manapul, *Queerious Hybrid*, installation at Open Gallery, OCAD University, February 2015.

Part 3

Transnational Imaginaries and the Ruse of Belonging

Julius Poncelet Manapul's installations of *Queerious Hybrids* serve as the coalescing image for the thematic concerns of this part. Challenging the heteronormative, and now homonormative values of Canadian society, Manila-born, Toronto-based Manapul uses a diverse archive in his multidisciplinary practice that ranges from *balikbayan* boxes to personal documents such as his marriage license and divorce papers, gay pornography, and Philippine Indigenous butterflies and birds. Through ornamentalization, the artist playfully recuperates homophobic and racist slurs into curvilinear designs that adorn intricate paper cuts and designer "murses" (men's purses)—a subversive process which defies globalized notions of gay identity. Utopian world-making is an important preoccupation for Manapul; his creation of an idealized domestic realm constructed of *balikbayan* boxes centered around his fictional child, Christian James, gestures toward a hopeful queer futurity that is still impossible in the present.

In the same vein, the works featured in this section insist that to queer our understanding of Filipino embodiment in Canada is to necessarily recite desires, intimacies, and longings that hail from elsewhere and that index a diasporic community's experiences with colonialism, migration, and globalization. With the constant movement of goods and bodies across the world, diaspora disrupts orders of knowledge that often serve to discipline or anchor hegemonic notions of gender, race, sexuality, and geography. The artists and scholars featured in this section thus expand on the multiple ways in which queer individuals sustain, enliven, and rearticulate diasporic subjectivities in Canada—without automatically succumbing to what we call the ruse or fallacy of "belonging" as the only goal for creating a semblance of home in the elsewheres we inhabit.

Older Filipino Gay Men in Canada

Bridging Queer Theory and Gerontology in Filipinx Canadian Studies

Fritz Luther Pino

Historically, the field of gerontology has predominantly focused on the experiences of older white men as the main objects of inquiry.[1] However, over the past twenty years, the field has also made efforts to diversify its research subjects in order to take into account intra-cohort differences in the elderly population in North America, and to move beyond a focus on the particulars of retirement.[2] In this turn to diverse subjects, critical gerontologists, particularly those informed by feminist lenses, have mobilized an intersectional approach that consequently makes visible the experiences of historically neglected groups, such as women, racialized immigrants, sexual minorities or LGBTQ seniors, and seniors with disabilities.[3] Such an intersectional approach has been useful in identifying how particular markers of difference—such as race, gender, and class—have shaped experiences of aging.[4] To date, the dominant or popular use of intersectional approaches in both quantitative and qualitative gerontological study continues to map the markers of difference that are compounded by and create what we conceive as the aging subject.[5]

In light of these theoretical shifts and developments, however, what remains clear even within intersectional gerontological approaches is a continued reliance on subjects located within, and often conceived through, an attachment to one nation-state. Such a limitation renders invisible the experiences of aging subjects who are diasporic, and who establish notions of belonging that span multiple geographic locations and multiple notions of intimacy. In particular, such a limitation also fails to examine the taken-for-granted, yet dominant discourses and practices within nation-states that constrain the quality of life of older racialized sexual minorities who are affected by and in many ways index transnational and global circuits, terrains, and movements.

Mindful of gerontology's theoretical, political, and geographic limitations, this chapter places the field in dialogue with queer analytical approaches in order to elucidate and attend to the experiences of Filipino sexual minorities who are aging in the diaspora. Working within an intersectional model that places diasporic identity at the center of its critical and theoretical inquiry, I examine how gerontology and queer studies can enrich each other's political parameters, despite having critiqued each other's limits in the past.[6]

This chapter highlights how older Filipino gay men in Toronto, Ontario, bring out the theoretical emphases of queer theory and gerontology through their lived experiences as older racialized and diasporic queers. Since 2012 I have immersed myself in the day-to-day lives of older Filipino gay men in Toronto. I performed both formal and informal interviews by participating in and interacting with my participants through everyday conversations. I argue that older Filipino gay men, who often see Canada through the lens of racialized and diasporic sexual minorities in the country, challenge normative discourses and narratives around the confluences of aging, queerness, sexuality, and gender.

My fieldwork suggests that for older Filipino gay men in Canada, narratives of sexuality and aging go beyond the need to navigate Canadian institutional, medical, and political apparatuses. Many older Filipino gay men I encountered noted a relationship to being in Canada that simultaneously gestured to different notions of desire, belonging, and physical maintenance. Specifically, their experiences also subtend dominant discourses around aging that often circulated, and which supported very limited notions of relationships, habitation, and community. Instead, my informants enact desires that have different material, political, and social implications, when compared to their non-racialized counterparts.

The Desires of Mama Riva

Born in 1927, Mama Riva[7] came to Canada in 1972 as an independent immigrant. He moved to Canada when a foreign-owned logging company in the Philippines downsized. Like many Filipinos in Toronto, Mama Riva worked in several different jobs that were not commensurate with his Philippine academic credentials and lengthy professional experience in the homeland, where he often occupied leadership roles in local companies. At the time of our interview, Mama Riva was eighty-eight years old and lived alone in a subsidized studio unit in downtown Toronto.

During our conversation, Mama Riva shared with me his sentiments of living in Canada as an older Filipino gay man. He notes:

> Here in Canada, I cannot find a sexual partner because most gay men here hook up with another gay man. In the Philippines, I don't do that. We, the *bakla* [queer man] don't do gay-to-gay relationship. That's why I'm sad here in Canada.

Mama Riva does not seem to be satisfied with his life in Canada, especially when finding a sexual partner in the country. He observes that in Canada, the normative sexual partner of gay men is also gay-identified. He refuses to be with a gay-identified man as his sexual partner because that is not what he has been used to in the Philippines. As a queer man born and raised in the Philippines, he identifies as *bakla*. *Bakla* is a Filipino term for a queer man that also applies to nonnormative gender and sexual identities and practices.[8] In terms of sexual relationships, the *bakla*'s normative partner choice is not another *bakla*, but rather a heterosexual man or, in common tropes, a *"lalake,"* someone who identifies as straight and performs traditional masculine roles and tasks.[9]

To make the relationship work, it is expected that the *bakla* has to provide the *lalake* with either money or some other form of material object (e.g., gifts). This is part of the norms and traditions of their sexual relationship. According to some of my informants, given that the *bakla* are not "true or real women,"[10] who are the normative sexual partner choice of the *lalake*, they have to engage in material or financial provisioning so as to be taken as a sexual partner by the *lalake*. Therefore, a relationship with the straight man always involves financial/material exchange.

Mama Riva continued to report that even when a *bakla* in Canada tries to offer money to a straight man to become his lover, the straight Canadian man would refuse because of his fear of being considered as a homosexual, or a prostitute. He then claimed that the only time he could be with a *lalake* was when he goes to strip clubs and spends time with male hustlers. He narrated how different the situation in Canada is from the Philippines. As he reported, in the Philippines, regular straight men or *lalake* (those who don't work as escorts or in strip clubs), when offered gifts or money, can be a *bakla*'s sexual partner or lover.

Mama Riva explained the possibility of *bakla-lalake* relationships in the Philippines and the impossibility of *bakla*-straight man relationships in Canada from a class or socioeconomic perspective. According to him, in Canada, straight men do not need the money of the *bakla* because they have their own means of livelihood; hence, they have their own income or financial capacity. However, the class situation in the Philippines is different. Because of the substandard economic situation in the Philippines compared to Canada, regular straight men in the Philippines pursue intimacies with a *bakla* because of the normative expectation that a *bakla* would offer money. Hence, the situation becomes an economic opportunity for the *lalake*.

Mama Riva is sad in Canada, though, because he could not apply or enact his sexual desires and practices based on the *bakla* scripts. At his current stage as an older *bakla*, accessing a *lalake* even with male hustlers or in strip clubs is no longer convenient for him. He pointed out that cost matters in such an economic transaction. As a retiree, Mama Riva relies on the government for financial support. Therefore, the sadness that he feels at being in Canada is a result of how the sociopolitical space (i.e., Canada) limits the cultural scripts of his sexual intimacy that he embodies and embraces.

Consequently, Mama Riva claimed that it is more convenient for older *baklas* to access a *lalake* in the Philippines than in Canada. They don't necessarily go to strip clubs and pick up male escorts, given the normative queer dynamics in the Philippines where a regular *lalake*, other than a male escort or hustler, could hook up with a *bakla*. Moreover, it is cheaper in the Philippines than in Canada. Canadian dollars have stronger value when spent in the Philippines than in Canada. To date, one Canadian dollar is equivalent to 30–35 Philippine pesos. As he and some of my informants who have traveled to the Philippines reported, "It is better in the Philippines since the Canadian dollar can go far!" Mama Riva emphasized: "Oh, I just spend 200–300 pesos with them, but of course, I have to buy the drinks," and he laughed. He continues: "Whereas in Canada, you spend in dollars."

However, Mama Riva knew that his experience of sexual intimacy with the *lalake*, even if it is based in the Philippines, is not for the long term. Instead, he considers it temporary. While the relationship is dependent on the economic capacity of the *bakla*, he expects that the relationship would not last for various reasons, such as the *lalake*'s decision to focus on having a woman as his only sexual partner; the aging of the *lalake*, since an older *bakla* does not prefer an older *lalake* (one who is of his age); and even transnational distance (i.e., when an older *bakla* needs to go back to Canada and cannot maintain the financial provision at a long distance).

For Mama Riva, since his sexual relationship with the *lalake* is temporary, he continues to make an effort or search for a new opportunity to establish a new sexual relationship once his current one has ended. For him, the temporariness of the *bakla* sexual intimacy in later life even motivates him to continue to pursue or search for an opportunity to experience it. Therefore, the temporariness lies in the ways in which a relationship is expected not to last, but has to be built with a new one again, so long as the *bakla* is financially capable to desire a *lalake*.

Mama Riva reveals how older Filipino gay men navigate and experience sexual intimacy in later life. He demonstrates that the sexual intimacy of the older *bakla* is not a straightforward process, but rather is labor-intensive: sexual intimacy not only always entails costs and financial resources, it also entails movement in that he continually has to actively search for it. He added that even in the Philippines, he needed to connect with his *bakla* friends to access a *lalake* so as to be discreet because his family and community would reprimand him. As he reported, the actions of an older gay man who is sexually engaged with another man deviate from the normative discourse of a *lolo*, or grandfather, who is read as a wise, proper, well-respected figure in the Filipino community by virtue of his lifelong experiences and hetero-patriarchal image. Hence, Mama Riva considered that sexual intimacy is not always readily available, that he has to continue to exert effort to be able to experience it.

While Mama Riva critiques the homonormative discourse of queer intimacy in which intimacy can only be imagined by engaging in same-sex relationships, the temporary nature of the *bakla* sexual relations enabled Mama Riva to also resist the discourse of coupledom which has been embedded within heteronormative and domestic logics. The discourse of coupledom has been thought of as a route to happiness, given that an evidenced-based study shows couples have higher levels of life satisfaction than their single or unattached counterparts.[11] The discourse of coupledom even shapes gay relationships because it is deemed a situation or position that lessens sadness and brings out happiness. The happiness is produced by having a permanent and steady partner who is able to provide care and support—the kinds of things that seem relevant and needed for an elderly individual. However, coupledom has become a dominant discourse that creates an only possible "happiness" route for queer subjects.[12] Hence, the associated feelings of happiness enable the discourse of coupledom to work. The happiness route conceals other routes and other possibilities of being a racialized and an aging diasporic queer, such as being sad, being single, or being in a non-monogamous relationship. Mama Riva's sexual desires and practices point to a different possibility of being queer beyond normative sexual relationships.

The *bakla* script and practices may also have limits. In this context, one limit is that the sexual desires of the *bakla* could be hegemonic because they foreclose other possible intimacy scripts, relationships, and connections with other forms of beings, objects, and desires.[13] The qualifications of what it means to be a *lalake* for the *bakla* may produce forms of normativity in which other possible qualifications for a desirable or potential sexual partner are put aside. Mama Riva is haunted by the script of the *bakla* around sexual partner choice because it has impacted his ability to establish intimacy outside of that choice. As I continue to discuss in the subsequent sections, there are material and bodily implications of the older *bakla*'s sexual desires and practices.

Queer Diasporic Intersectionality and Gerontology

Mama Riva's experiences, then, hail from queer scripts that render him illegible within the normative discourse of queer sexual desires and practices, within gerontological studies, and within stories of aging in a global northern context. The very few studies that have been done on racialized sexual minority aging have pointed out how the intersections of minority identities in terms of age, race, sexuality, and gender become sites of marginalization and inequalities in old age.[14] In Mama Riva's narrative, his experience of marginalization is not necessarily based on his embodied racialized and sexual identity alone. He articulates later life longings outside of Canadian queer norms since he approaches intimacy through a diasporic queer script of the *bakla*.

Clearly, then, as the narrative of Mama Riva suggests, if gerontology wants to be fully engaged in the lives of older minorities, it has to foreground a transnational intersectional lens. This lens is a critical approach of intersectionality that continues to question the dominant discourses and narratives of the state that have made nonnormative older minorities illegible. Mama Riva's experiences cannot be read exclusively within the cultural dynamics of queer sexuality and aging in Canada, but rather within the interaction and intersection of discourses, scripts, and ideas on aging, sexuality, and queerness from Canada and from the Philippines. Consequently, then, the diasporic subject position of Mama Riva challenges the normative practice of institutionalized kinship demanded by, and often operationalized through, the state.

Drawing from transnational feminisms, postcolonial theory, and queer studies, a *queer diasporic intersectionality lens* is concerned with the "movement of people, capital, ideas, and knowledges across national borders and the ways in which these movements impact identities, relationships, homes and communities, as well as experiences of marginalization and oppression."[15] Its genealogy involves queer of color scholarship, where the concept of the queer diaspora is used to expand the critique of whiteness in LGBT and sexuality studies by interrogating the impact of globalization, transnationalism, migration, nation-state formations, citizenship, and imperial capitalism on the lives of queer immigrants of color.[16]

Indeed, as mobilized in this book, queer does not refer only to LGBTQ subjects but also to "some forms of heterosexuality that do not necessarily conform to social norms of proper intimacy," since "queer" is after all a critique of normalcy. However, in this context, queer includes both queer bodies commonly held as sexual minorities such as lesbians, gays, bisexuals, and transsexuals and their range of practices and desires that are dissident and non-heteronormative.[17] Meanwhile, diasporic subjects are those who have moved out from their homeland either voluntarily or through involuntarily migrations, and while living in a new land, they have maintained intimate connections and affiliations with their homeland.[18] Both *queer and diaspora* are disavowed or marginal subjects of the nation: "queers" are a deficient copy of the heterosexual within heteronormative logics, and "diasporas" imply an outsider or an inauthentic subject of the nation due to his or her diasporic affiliations and origin.[19]

A queer diasporic reading of aging enables the field of gerontology to become more attentive to nonnormative aging practices, desires, and subjectivities that have always been part of the everyday lives of aging diasporic and racialized sexual minorities. Specifically, as the narrative of Mama Riva reveals, a queer diasporic intersectionality lens enables us to politicize the concept of aging and make it even more attentive to questions of nation-state formations founded by the dominant norms and systems of heteronormativity and of whiteness that institutionalized desires and intimacy; these heteronormative norms and systems thrashed out and policed those desires and practices that seemed to be a disrespect and a threat to normative family formations, reproduction, intergenerational relations, and domesticity. In other words, *queer diasporic intersectionality lens* reveals the limits of both mainstream and deemed marginalized spaces.

Travel to the Philippines

While the conflicting queer scripts that most older Filipino gay men faced have impacted their notions of intimacy and have contributed to their feelings of sadness, the experience has also materially impacted how they approach the toll of aging on their physical bodies. For example, travel, which is often seen as a pleasurable endeavor that retirees undertake as a means to "enjoy" their life in old age,[20] is given new meaning through the stories of my participants. Most of my participants regularly travel to the Philippines from Canada as a means to find the *lalake* they are searching for. One informant exclaimed, "If you want a *lalake*, go to the Philippines!" Another one also stated, "That desire for a *lalake*, that could only work in the Philippines."

Indeed, for older Filipino gay men that I have conversed with, the Philippines is imagined as the space where they can enact their *bakla* scripts of intimacy, thereby allowing them to feel a sense of belonging. It is noteworthy, as the case of Mama Riva suggests, that such queer longing for belonging and intimacy has been prompted by the feelings of sadness in dealing with conflicting queer scripts. Consequently, then, sadness enabled older Filipino gay men to move, to travel, or to return to the Philippines to experience belonging and a diasporic understanding of intimacy.

Mama Riva returns to the Philippines twice a year, while his friend Shalah goes to the Philippines once a year but would stay in the country for about five months. Mama Riva then suggests with a laugh that he and Shalah "meet in my little town where we can see our men." Shalah came to Canada in 1970 when he was thirty. He was seventy-five years old when I met him. Like Mama Riva, he lives alone in a subsidized studio apartment.

When discussing his regular returns to the Philippines, Shalah stated that he has to be conscious of his health because he had a history of a terminal illness. He has to make sure that he had saved up some money in case he needs to spend it on medications during his travels. For Shalah, his awareness or consciousness of the limitations of his aging body allows him to think more wisely of his travels. Meanwhile, when I visited Mama Riva in his studio apartment three months before his next trip, his invitation that we have dinner also contained an important disclaimer:

> My darling, sorry I do not have rice because that increases my cholesterol and sugar. I only have bread and these healthy salad and fish. You know, I'm traveling to the Philippines soon, I don't want to get sick. I'll be eating different kinds of food there.

Clearly, as they discuss the significance of a return to their pursuit of alternative intimacies, they also reveal that such a return has physical and economic consequences—as their aging bodies needs to adjust to the regular wear and tear involved in traveling, and as they incur heavier financial costs for such frequent traveling. For them, returning to the Philippines necessitates that they maintain good physical health and that they are able to save up for the heavy financial costs of these trips.

However, while returning to one's country of birth is possible for Mama Riva and Shalah, such an option is not necessarily possible for some older Filipino gay men. One participant who goes by the name of Farah claimed that some older Filipino gay men he knew of, including him, do not have the opportunity to travel back to the Philippines due to financial constraints. According to Farah, he only had gone back to the Philippines once, in 1992, for a relative's wedding because "it's expensive to travel to the Philippines." Farah was sixty-four years old when I met him in 2014. He was completing a certificate on beauty and aesthetics at a private college using the government grant that he received. This grant is intended for low-income citizens who wanted to pursue a "second career" program. Furthermore, Farah commented:

> Those who don't have the money, of course, they can't travel. Plus, some of them have health issues. So, they would just stay here in Toronto and wait for that moment when a *lalake* would come to them.

Farah's observation clearly points to the associated costs of return and traveling and the fact that some older Filipino gay men do not have the economic capacity to participate in the said migration return. The economic condition is in line with a community study on the poverty of Filipino seniors in the greater Toronto area. The study revealed that limited financial means are one of the sobering realities of Filipinos in old age.[21] Specifically, the study indicates that 70 percent of Filipino seniors live in poverty because a majority of them rely on government support. The reality is connected to their experiences with de-professionalization and de-skilling during their working years.[22] These past experiences affect their financial situation upon their reaching old age. These financial constraints also impact their health situation, as Filipino seniors spend more on out-of-pocket expenses (such as medications and other health care needs) compared to their non-racialized counterparts.

Of particular significance, Farah observed that those who cannot return engage in the act of waiting; if not, in the act of longing for home and belonging. I contend that the act of waiting is a form of negotiating sadness. If sadness enables return, then sadness continues to be the emotional state of those who waited and did not participate in the said return. Sadness can be contained in the act of waiting, since it allows Farah and those who stayed put to imagine a possible queer intimacy that has yet to come. Waiting and staying put, while exposing the limits of travel and return, allows for a queer longing to take place. This queer longing is a bodily experience because it involves the thinking and feeling functions of the body.

Hence, the narratives of the return of older Filipino gay men to the Philippines is indeed a bodily experience because those who can return and those who cannot return are in some ways engaged in bodily work: those who can return need to be equipped with financial resources and attend to their physical health condition; while those who cannot return engage in waiting, longing, and yearning, and may somehow face the financial costs of what it takes to access a *lalake* in Canada.

A Gerontological Lens for Queer Theory(izing)

Hence, it is for this reason that older Filipino gay men draw out the conceptual emphasis of gerontology and the concept of aging. For older Filipino gay men, the physical and the biological changes of their bodies should be considered when engaging in their queer diasporic experiences. This is in line with what gerontologists have emphasized when illustrating the social, structural, and political conditions of aging; its biological and physical impact should not be overlooked as well.[23] Older Filipino gay men did not only reveal the limits of the normative queer scripts and discourses, but also how such scripts and discourse impact their aged bodies. For example, Mama Riva and Shalah demonstrate how the transnational search for the *lalake* has had some impact on their aged bodies.

While queer theory has been engaging on the phenomenology of the queer body,[24] putting age in the analysis expands queer theory by recognizing the ways in which age or aging experiences impact queer sexual desires, mobility, and aspiration. The concept of aging allows queer theory to be more specific in terms of its analytic engagement of the body beyond race, sexuality, gender, and class. In the diasporic space in which my participants are situated, age both enables and limits their desire for a particular sense of intimacy and transnational life. Mama Riva, Shalah, and Farah, for example, have responded to the conflicting scripts of queer intimacy by taking into consideration the material consequences of aging. Their acts of return or not returning are particular responses to sadness, which is the affect of the conflicting queer scripts of *bakla* and gay, and indeed has bodily ramifications.

Hence, this attention of queer theory to the figure of the aged subject strengthens the task of queer theory in terms of exposing the limits of the dominant narratives and discourses of queer migration and transnational experiences. Stories of queer diasporic migration have centered on active and younger queer bodies. Their experiences are analyzed in terms of their active engagement in the labor market, domestic life, popular culture, and social movements that shape their sense of diasporic intimacy. However, as the narratives of older Filipino gay men suggest, the sense of diasporic intimacy is not only about the intersections of race, class, gender, and sexuality, or even about participation in state institutions, but is also about age and these men's nonnormative practices in later life. Age enables or limits queer transnational life, including that of migration return. This evidences the porosity of migration borders for those who are active, able-bodied, and younger queer subjects. In other words, migration does not only privilege those bodies in the dominant racial, sexual, gender, and class positions—the traditional analytics of queer diasporic theorizing, but also those in particular age groups—the active, younger, or middle-age groups. Ultimately, then, the aging condition of older Filipino gay men reminds us of the significance of aging—its biophysical limitations—and how it impact queer desires. Aging, then, serves as a new site for a queer analysis.

Queer Diaspora and Aging: Implications for Filipino Canadian Studies

In this chapter, I argued that through the queer diasporic experiences of older Filipino gay men, I was able to bridge queer theory and gerontology. My participants assert particular scripts and desires that demand closer scrutiny. In this regard, I explored how their lived experiences of aging were impacted by their subject position as racialized and diasporic sexual minorities in Canada. By drawing the critical emphases of both gerontology (i.e., the concept of aging) and queer theory (i.e., the queer diasporic intersectionality approach), I suggest that we are better able to produce an approach that attends to their aging bodies and queer diasporic subject position. By bridging queer theory and gerontology, the sociopolitical, historical, and cultural realities of older Filipino gay men in the diaspora are put into the center of the analysis to provide an alternative form of understanding the lives of older sexual minorities.

Returning to Mama Riva and Shalah's narratives, we see how an archive of older Filipino gay men contributes to our understanding of what it means to live as transnational migrants. Here, I document the lived experiences of older racialized queer migrants, where travel and return to the homeland become one of their everyday realities. This travel and movement towards a home was driven by the ways in which their spaces of settlement could not fully create conditions for a satisfactory quality of life in old age. Indeed, their travel and movement are propelled by sadness, and at the same time, by a sense of hope for a better reality if one is to travel back to a home. Retrospectively, I decided to conduct this work in order to foreground the experiences of racialized sexual minorities who are aging in the diaspora, since their experiences are indeed left out in gerontology, queer theory, and ethnic studies. They are instead eclipsed by the dominant norms and discourses in research and knowledge production that reproduce normative meanings of belonging. While there has been substantial evidence of the struggles, marginalization, and displacement of LGBTQ elderly populations (Brotman, Ryan, and Cormier, 2003; Woody, 2014), older

Filipino gay men offer a compelling case study because they question the meanings of what it means to belong to a "home" and to normative institutions of nation-states. They indeed question the state itself, including those scripts and practices of being gay or queer, old or aging, and racialized or "ethnic." These trenchant critiques of state discourses challenge dominant stories of transnational migration that often rely on normative, and even state-sanctioned practices, desires, affects, and kinship structures. Consequently, then, by allowing us to see their later life years, they invite us to imagine broadly what it means to live as historically marginalized subjects.

Moreover, the lives of older Filipino gay men beg a question: what does it mean to purchase sexual intimacy in later life? As the participants have revealed, sexual relationships of older Filipino gay men with straight-identified men is impossible if there is no financial or material resource involved. In short, the relationship would only become possible when the *bakla* has the socioeconomic resources that serve as a ticket to the straight men's world. That is to say, if there is no such medium of exchange, then sexual intimacy with the *lalake* could not be experienced. While I do not aim to fully address the question I pose above because that needs an ample space to articulate, I ask the question so as not to dismiss the significant issues on sexual economy, especially on sex work and its implications for later life intimacies and sexualities. Debates on the legalization and continuous policing of sex workers, the positions and stand of social justice movements and advocates, and the participation of nonnormative gender and sexual identities in the sexual economy have crucial material and bodily implications and impacts on the participants given their sexual practices.

Finally, in this chapter, I highlight the minoritized positions, intimacies, affects, desires, and enactments of older Filipino gay men in order to expose not only the limits of normalcy through an interdisciplinary analysis, but also to recuperate queer subjects' contribution to transformative politics. The violence of global imperialism, neoliberalism, white supremacy, and hetero-patriarchy have not only left trauma on queer bodies, but also have invited queer folks to be more complicit in hegemonic systems. Queer subjects themselves participate in such hegemonic discourses and practices of the nation, hoping that these would lead to a good life.[25] The situation has indeed concealed the political potential existing and embedded in their subject positions. Their anti-normative practices and desires could offer new modes of living, desiring, and relating that continuously acknowledges histories of unequal power relations and violence. To foreground nonnormative sexualities is not an essentialist gesture. Rather, I hope to strategically reinvigorate the potentialities of being "queer" and/or *"bakla"* for a more ethical and socially just relation with the world.

Notes

1. Caroll Estes, "Critical Feminist Perspectives, Aging, and Social Policy," in *Aging, Globalization, and Inequality: The New Critical Gerontology*, ed. Jan Baars et al. (Amityville, N.Y.: Baywood, 2006), chapter 5.

2. Dale Dannefer, "Reciprocal Co-Optation: The Relationship of Critical Theory and Social Gerontology," in *Aging, Globalization, and Inequality: The New Critical Gerontology*, ed. Jan Baars et al. (Amityville, N.Y.: Baywood, 2006), chapter 6.

3. See, for example, Toni M. Calasanti, "Theorizing Age Relations," in *The Need for Theory: Critical Approaches to Gerontology*, ed. Simon Biggs, Ariela Lowenstein, and Jon Hendricks (New York: Baywood, 2003), 199–218; Ann Cronin and Andrew King, "Power, Inequality and Identification: Exploring Diversity and Intersectionality amongst Older LGB Adults," *Sociology* 44, no. 5 (2010): 876–92; Wendy Hulko, "Intersectionality in the Context of Later Life Experiences of Dementia," in *Health Inequalities in Canada: Intersectional Frameworks and Practices*, ed. Olena Hankivsky et al. (Vancouver: University of British Columbia Press, 2012), 199–217.

4. See Toni M. Calasanti and Kathleen. F. Slevin, eds., *Gender, Social Inequalities, and Aging* (California: Altamira, 2001); and Toni M. Calasanti and Kathleen. F. Slevin, eds., *Age Matters: Realigning Feminist Thinking* (New York: Routledge, 2006).

5. Sharon Koehn, Sheila Neysmith, Karen Kobayashi, and Hamish Khamisa, "Revealing the Shape of Knowledge Using an Intersectionality Lens: Results of a Scoping Review on the Health and Healthcare of Ethno-Cultural Minority Older Adults," *Ageing & Society* 33 (2012): 437–64.

6. On the one hand, gerontology critiques queer theory for being ageist because of the dominance of youth-oriented scholarship (see Herdt and de Vries, 2004) and for its highly critical tone that overlooks the material and physiological impact of the aging body (see Brown, 2009; Twigg, 2012). On the other hand, queer theory critiques gerontology for being homophobic and heterosexist since it fails to take into account aging non-heterosexual lives (see Heaphy, 2007, 2009). I contend that this disconnection should not remain as it is. While these disciplinary divides are due to differences

in methodological, theoretical, and political thoughts, discourses, and knowledges that govern each of the fields, there is still room for a productive conversation that allows these fields to work together to engage in more robust social justice work. Both fields consider intersectionality as an approach that explores issues related to marginalization and inequalities. Both fields also embrace intersectionality as a lens that renders visible the lives and experiences of minority subjects.

7. The names of informants and identifying information have been changed for confidentiality.

8. Robert Diaz, "The Limits of Bakla and Gay: Feminist Readings of My Husband's Lover, Vice Ganda, and Charice Pempengco," *Signs: Journal of Women in Culture and Society* 40, no. 3 (2015): 721–45.

9. Ronald Baytan, "'Bading Na Bading': Evolving Identities in Philippine Cinema," in *AsiapacifiQUEER: Rethinking Genders and Sexualities*, ed. Fran Martin, Peter A. Jackson, Mark McLellan, and Audrey Yue (Urbana: University of Illinois Press, 2008), 181–95.

10. See Martin F. Manalansan, *Global Divas: Filipino Gay Men in the Diaspora* (Durham, N.C.: Duke University Press, 2003).

11. Stevie C. Yap, Ivana Anusic, and Richard E. Lucas, "Does Personality Moderate Reaction and Adaptation to Major Life Events? Evidence from the British Household Panel Survey," *Journal of Research in Personality* 46 (2012): 477–88.

12. See Sara Ahmed, *The Promise of Happiness* (Durham, N.C.: Duke University Press, 2010); Michael Cobb, *Single: Arguments for the Uncoupled (Sexual Cultures)* (New York: New York University Press, 2012).

13. Robert Diaz, "The Limits of Bakla and Gay: Feminist Readings of My Husband's Lover, Vice Ganda, and Charice Pempengco," *Signs: Journal of Women in Culture and Society* 40, no. 3 (2015): 721–45.

14. Juan Battle, Jessie Daniels, Antonio (Jay) Pastrana Jr., and Carlene Buchanan Turner, "Never Too Old to Feel Good: Happiness and Health among a National Sample of Older Black Gay Men," *Spectrum: A Journal on Black Men* 2, no. 1 (2013): 1–18; Ruth Hall and Michelle Fine, "The Stories We Tell: The Lives and Friendship of Two Older Black Lesbians," *Psychology of Women Quarterly* 29 (2005): 177–87; Imani Woody, "Aging Out: A Qualitative Exploration of Ageism and Heterosexism among Aging African American Lesbians and Gay Men," *Journal of Homosexuality* 61 (2014): 145–65.

15. Gita Mehrotra, "Toward a Continuum of Intersectionality Theorizing for Feminist Social Work Scholarship," *Affilia: Journal of Women and Social Work* 25, no. 4 (2010): 417–30.

16. David L. Eng, Judith Halberstam, and José Esteban Muñoz, "What's Queer about Queer Studies Now?" *Social Text* 23, no. 3–4 (2005): 84–85.

17. See David L. Eng and Alice Y. Hom, *Q & A: Queer in Asian America* (Philadelphia: Temple University Press, 1998); Gayatri Gopinath, *Impossible Desires: Queer Diasporas and South Asian Public Cultures* (Durham, N.C.: Duke University Press, 2005).

18. See Rhacel S. Parreñas and Lok C. D. Siu, eds., *Asian Diasporas: New Formations, New Conceptions* (Stanford, Calif.: Stanford University Press, 2007).

19. See note 23.

20. Here, I refer to the dominant representations of older adults in the film *The Best Exotic Marigold Hotel*, released in 2011. Directed by John Madden, it featured a group of British retirees who travel to India and find the "exotic" hotel as the space where they have transformed their selves and are able to flourish, with new beginnings of life, love, and kinship. This representation of seniors eclipses the lived experiences of older Filipino gay men whose transnational movement and mobility and search for intimacy is not always pleasurable, but taxing, if not a failure.

21. Roland Sintos Coloma and Fritz Luther Pino, "'There's Hardly Anything Left': Poverty and the Economic Insecurity of Elderly Filipinos in Toronto," *Canadian Ethnic Studies* 48, no. 2 (2016): 71–97.

22. Philip Kelly, Mila Astorga-Garcia, E. F. Esguerra, and the Community Alliance for Social Justice, Toronto, "Filipino Immigrants in the Toronto Labour Market: Towards an Understanding of Deprofessionalization," in *Filipinos in Canada: Disturbing Invisibility*, ed. Roland Sintos Coloma et al. (Toronto: University of Toronto Press, 2012), 68–88.

23. Toni M. Calasanti, "Theorizing Age Relations," in *The Need for Theory: Critical Approaches to Gerontology* ed. Simon Biggs, Ariela Lowenstein, and Jon Hendricks (New York: Baywood, 2003), 199–218; Stephen Katz, "Busy Bodies: Activity, Aging, and the Management of Everyday Life," *Journal of Aging Studies* 4, no. 2 (2000): 135–52; Chris Phillipson, "Aging and Globalization: Issues for Critical Gerontology and Political Economy," in *Aging, Globalization, and Inequality: The New Critical Gerontology*, ed. J. Baars et al. (Amityville, N.Y.: Baywood, 2006), 81–101.

24. See Sara Ahmed, *Queer Phenomenology: Orientations, Objects, and Others* (Durham, N.C.: Duke University Press, 2006).

25. See Ahmed, *The Promise of Happiness*; Jasbir Puar, *Terrorist Assemblages: Homonationalism in Queer Times* (Durham, N.C.: Duke University Press, 2007).

Bibliography

Ahmed, Sara. *The Promise of Happiness*. Durham, N.C.: Duke University Press, 2010.

———. *Queer Phenomenology: Orientations, Objects, and Others*. Durham, N.C.: Duke University Press, 2006.

Battle, Juan, Jessie Daniels, Antonio (Jay) Pastrana Jr., and Carlene Buchanan Turner. "Never Too Old to Feel Good: Happiness and Health among a National Sample of Older Black Gay Men." *Spectrum: A Journal on Black Men* 2, no. 1 (2013): 1–18.

Baytan, Ronald. "'Bading Na Bading': Evolving Identities in Philippine Cinema." In *AsiapacifiQUEER: Rethinking Genders and Sexualities*, edited by Fran Martin, Peter A. Jackson, Mark McLellan and Audrey Yue, 181–95. Urbana: University of Illinois Press, 2008.

Brotman, Shari, Bill Ryan, and Robert Cormier. "The Health and Social Service Needs of Gay and Lesbian Elders and Their Families in Canada." *The Gerontologist* 43, no. 2 (2003): 192–202.

Brown, Maria T. "LGBT Aging and Rhetorical Silence." *Sexuality Research and Social Policy* 6, no. 4 (2009): 65–78.

Calasanti, Toni M. "Theorizing Age Relations." In *The Need for Theory: Critical Approaches to Gerontology*, edited by Simon Biggs, Ariela Lowenstein, and Jon Hendricks, 199–218. New York: Baywood, 2003.

Calasanti, Toni M., and Kathleen. F. Slevin, eds. *Age Matters: Realigning Feminist Thinking*. New York: Routledge, 2006.

———. *Gender, Social Inequalities, and Aging*. California: Altamira, 2001.

Cobb, Michael. *Single: Arguments for the Uncoupled (Sexual Cultures)*. New York: New York University Press, 2012.

Coloma, Roland Sintos, Bonnie McElhinny, Ethel Tungohan, John Paul C. Catungal, and Lisa M. Davidson, eds. *Filipinos in Canada: Disturbing Invisibility*. Toronto: University of Toronto Press, 2012.

Coloma, Roland Sintos, and Fritz Luther Pino. "'There's Hardly Anything Left': Poverty and the Economic Insecurity of Elderly Filipinos in Toronto.' *Canadian Ethnic Studies* 48, no. 2 (2016): 71–97.

Cronin, Ann, and Andrew King. "Power, Inequality, and Identification: Exploring Diversity and Intersectionality amongst Older LGB Adults." *Sociology* 44, no. 5 (2010): 876–92.

Dannefer, D. "Reciprocal Co-Optation: The Relationship of Critical Theory and Social Gerontology." In *Aging, Globalization, and Inequality: The New Critical Gerontology*, edited by J. Baars, D. Dannefer, C. Phillipson, and A. Walker, 81–101. Amityville, N.Y.: Baywood, 2006.

Diaz, Robert. "The Limits of Bakla and Gay: Feminist Readings of My Husbands's Lover, Vice Ganda, and Charice Pempengco." *Signs: Journal of Women in Culture and Society* 40, no. 3 (2015): 721–45.

Eng, David L., Judith Halberstam, and José Esteban Muñoz. "What's Queer about Queer Studies Now?" *Social Text* 23, no. 3–4 (2005): 84–85.

Eng, David L., and Alice Y. Hom. *Q & A: Queer in Asian America*. Philadelphia: Temple University Press, 1998.

Estes, Caroll."Critical Feminist Perspectives, Aging, and Social Policy." In *Aging, Globalization, and Inequality: The New Critical Gerontology*, edited by Jan Baars, Dale Dannefer, Chris Phillipson, and Alan Walker, chapter 5. Amityville, N.Y.: Baywood, 2006.

Gopinath, Gayatri. *Impossible Desires: Queer Diasporas and South Asian Public Cultures*. Durham, N.C.: Duke University Press, 2005.

Hall, Ruth, and Michelle Fine. "The Stories We Tell: The Lives and Friendship of Two Older Black Lesbians." *Psychology of Women Quarterly* 29 (2005): 177–87.

Heaphy, Brian. "Sexualities, Gender and Ageing Resources and Social Change." *Current Sociology* 55, no. 2 (2007): 193–210.

———. "The Storied, Complex Lives of Older GLBT Adults." *Journal of GLBT Family Studies* 5 (2009): 119–38.

Herdt, Gilbert, and Brian de Vries, eds. *Gay and Lesbian Aging: Research and Future Directions*. New York: Springer, 2004.

Hulko, Wendy. "Intersectionality in the Context of Later Life Experiences of Dementia." In *Health Inequalities in Canada: Intersectional Frameworks and Practices*, edited by Olena Hankivsky, Sarah de Leeuw, Jo-Anne Lee, Bilkis Vissandjée, and Nazilla Khanlou, 199–217. Vancouver: University of British Columbia Press, 2012.

Katz, Stephen. "Busy Bodies: Activity, Aging, and the Management of Everyday Life." *Journal of Aging Studies* 4, no. 2 (2000): 135–52.

Kelly, Philip, Mila Astorga-Garcia, Enrico F. Esguerra, and the Community Alliance for Social Justice, Toronto. "Filipino Immigrants in the Toronto Labour Market: Towards an Understanding of Deprofessionalization." In *Filipinos in Canada: Disturbing Invisibility*, edited by Roland Sintos Coloma, Bonnie McElhinny, Ethel Tungohan, John Paul C. Catungal, and Lisa M. Davidson, 68–88. Toronto: University of Toronto Press, 2012.

Koehn, Sharon, Sheila Neysmith, Karen Kobayashi, and Hamish Khamisa. "Revealing the Shape of Knowledge Using an Intersectionality Lens: Results of a Scoping Review on the Health and Healthcare of Ethnocultural Minority Older Adults." *Ageing & Society* 33 (2012): 437–64.

Manalansan, Martin F. *Global Divas: Filipino Gay Men in the Diaspora.* Durham, N.C.: Duke University Press, 2003.

Mehrotra, Gita. "Toward a Continuum of Intersectionality Theorizing for Feminist Social Work Scholarship." *Affilia: Journal of Women and Social Work* 25, no. 4 (2010): 417–30.

Parreñas, Rhacel, and Lok C. D. Siu, eds. *Asian Diasporas: New Formations, New Conceptions.* Stanford, Calif.: Stanford University Press, 2007.

Phillipson, Chris. "Aging and Globalization: Issues for Critical Gerontology and Political Economy." In *Aging, Globalization, and Inequality: The New Critical Gerontology,* edited by Jan Baars, Dale Dannefer, Chris Phillipson, and Alan Walker, 81–101. Amityville, N.Y.: Baywood, 2006.

Puar, Jasbir. *Terrorist Assemblages: Homonationalism in Queer Times.* Durham, N.C.: Duke University Press, 2007.

Twigg, Julia. "Adjusting the Cut: Fashion, the Body and Age on the UK High Street." *Ageing and Society* 32 (2012): 1030–54.

Woody, Imani. "Aging Out: A Qualitative Exploration of Ageism and Heterosexism among Aging African American Lesbians and Gay Men." *Journal of Homosexuality* 61 (2014): 145–65.

Yap, Stevie C., Ivana Anusic, and Richard E. Lucas. "Does Personality Moderate Reaction and Adaptation to Major Life Events? Evidence from the British Household Panel Survey." *Journal of Research in Personality* 46 (2012): 477–88.

Colonial, Settler Colonial Tactics and Filipino Canadian Heteronormativities at Play on the Basketball Court

May Farrales

During the 2016 election cycle, both the Philippine and international media were abuzz when popular boxing hero and Philippine congressman Manny Pacquiao made public his opinions on same-sex marriage in his bid for a seat in the Philippine senatorial election race. Pacquiao told the media: "It's common sense, do you see animals mating with the same sex? Animals are better because they can distinguish male from female. If men mate with men and women mate with women, they are worse than animals."[1] The eight-time boxing world champion and national hero's comments drew reactions that rippled through the Philippines and the world. The international sporting brand Nike quickly dropped its endorsement of Pacquiao, Philippine politicians and organizations took their turns weighing in on the storm his statements created, and debates in the public spaces of social media and in the intimate relations of homes moved across the country and globally.

While much can be said about the ways that Pacquiao's statements conflate animality with homosexuality, and "common sense" with the supposed naturalness of heteronormative couples, for the purposes of this chapter, I am primarily interested in the dynamic and vexed relationship between gendered sexuality and normative notions of nation that swirl around the core of the controversy. After all, Pacquiao is celebrated as a national hero. His narrative follows a particular rags-to-riches storyline—beginning with his humble beginnings as a boxer from the Philippines' southern rural region literally and figuratively fighting his way to international stardom and notoriety. His playful encounters with Western media and audiences gained him a reputation as an underdog success story representing the fighting spirit of the Philippine nation. His fierce nationalism captured in songs that he sings himself like "Laban Nating Lahat Ito" ("This Fight Is All of Ours") gained him a reputation as a man who loves and fights for his people and nation. In other words, Pacquiao's heteronormative masculinity fuses with dominant notions of nation and nationalism.

The figure of Pacquiao, as boxing legend and national hero, lends itself to think about the gendered and sexualized nature of nation-building and nationalist narratives, and the role of sports in reproducing such narratives. More specifically, Pacquiao as a hetero-patriarchal figure of a nation opens opportunities to think about the nature and purpose of sport as a space of gender and sexual performances and performativity. As scholars such as R. W. Connell (2005) have pointed out, competitive sports where men's bodies are in motion produce spaces wherein exemplary masculinities are tested, made, and remade.[2] The homosocial regimes producing masculinities in this forum range from the bodily acts of learning the sport to the institutions of sport. Brendan Hokowhitu (2004) links Indigenous masculine physicality, sport, and colonial nation-building in his examination of how Maori masculine physicality was and continues to be channeled differently in the settler colonial context of New Zealand.[3] From bodies that needed to be tamed in the name of "civilizing the native," to bodies whose physicality could be harnessed for hard labor in the name of nation-building, to the spectacle of the simultaneously untamed and tamed physical masculinity that the Maori male body provides for the national consumption of sport, Hokowhitu demonstrates how colonial techniques produce masculinities.

In this chapter, I work with and extend upon such scholarly interventions on normative masculinities and sport and draw connections between colonial projects and processes and the disciplining and management of racially inflected gendered sexualities. Since basketball is an important site for subject- and community-formation in the Philippines,[4] I follow the sport as a performative site in the lives and formations of Filipinos in Canada. More specifically, I explore Filipino gendered sexualities in Canada, at play on and around basketball courts, by asking the questions: How might basketball demand particular gendered sexualities from Filipinos? And how might these gender and sexual performances be traced to the colonial display of virile bodies and properness? I draw on ethnographic observations at Filipino basketball leagues and interviews with basketball players and league organizers on the traditional and unceded territories of the Musqueam, Skxwú7mesh, and Tsleil-Waututh peoples (also known as Greater Vancouver). From these observations and interviews, I pay particular attention to what racial and gendered sexualities come to be.

I offer a queer reading of Filipino racialized gendered sexualities that is attentive to the hetero-patriarchal processes that work through and on bodies. Following the lead of queer of color and Indigenous scholars who emphasize the need to tease out how white hetero-patriarchal logics work as a system of power that recenters whiteness and normativity, I focus in on how basketball might be working as a site in which hetero-patriarchal systems rooted in colonial legacies from the Philippines and settler colonial processes in Canada are routed through. I follow two lines of inquiry. First, I examine how basketball functions and is imagined as a life-saver to produce virile masculine subjects. Second, I think about how the communal sport provides life lessons on proper gendered sexualities. I demonstrate that colonial techniques deployed in the Philippines continue to exercise influence in the present and in the Canadian context, but that these techniques of gender and sexual disciplining also take on different forms in the context of settler colonial relations that structure Canada. In other words, I am concerned with how the process and practices of heteronormativity change with geography in the process of migration. In arguing that colonialisms work on and through bodies at play on the basketball court, I suggest ways in which basketball as a site created and conditioned by overlapping systems of power also works as a space that can both reinscribe normativity, but also can offer possibilities for alternative ways of being in relation to one another.

Basketball as Life-Saver: Making Healthy Masculinities

In a CBC special report entitled "Basketball and Montreal's Filipino Community," the article explains the beginnings of a citywide Filipino basketball league in the 1980s. It describes the "tumultuous times" from which the league emerged—tumultuous because "rival gangs" of Filipino male youth totting "jungle bolos" were spreading through

the city's most concentrated Filipino neighborhood.[5] The league organizer tells the reporters that through basketball they aimed to "help
newly-arrived immigrants adapt to their new surroundings." This media
piece is structured to suggest that the league organizer had helped to
ease the tumultuous tensions. It notes that the organizer has become
an important link between the police and Filipinos, and community
members quoted in the multimedia story claim that the basketball
league has helped to heal what were violent divisions among Filipino
youth.

This notion of, and more generally the idea of health at various
scales, is a common narrative among Filipino men who gather at the
basketball court. The narrative of health moves from mentions of one's
bodily health to the community's overall well-being in rapid strokes.
This story of conditioning lends itself to delve into the workings of colonialism in both the Philippines and Canada, especially if participation
in basketball is understood in terms of physical and moral fitness for
its life-saving potential. For a number of the Filipino cis-males I interviewed, basketball was spoken of as a sort of life-saver. Consider the
thoughts of Bayani, a twenty-year-old son of a former live-in caregiver:

> I remember in grade 7 we were doing this [anti-drug] pro-
> gram . . . at the same time that kids were doing drugs. When I
> was growing up, basketball actually helped me stay away from
> that kind of stuff . . . So basketball is bigger than anyone else
> thinks for me because I was surrounded with people who did
> that stuff at such a young age.

For Bayani, being involved in his local basketball program helped him
stay away from drugs, and it gave him an opportunity to surround himself with peers not involved in drugs. Bayani speaks to how basketball
metaphorically, and perhaps even literally, saved his life. Other participants spoke of basketball as a life-saver in more visceral ways.

Consider forty-year-old Kevin's reasons for playing basketball in a
Filipino league:

> I like it because it's high-paced, it's competitive—they're also
> competitive in other sports, but you know, I like basketball most
> and I know I get cardio better—better circulation. See, I'm
> a nurse so I understand that running, jogging, basketball are
> good for your heart, blood circulation and stuff like that. That's

one of the reasons why I stay in basketball. I think that's my first love . . .

Notions of healthy masculinity run through this call to health and the ways in which basketball promotes health and perhaps even "saved their lives." Alongside and within the rhetoric and narrative that basketball makes for good boys or citizen-subjects through the disciplining of their time and behaviors, these men speak specifically to how basketball fosters an ideal of a healthy or virile masculinity. How can we make sense of this aspiration for healthy bodies?

In the Philippines, producing morally and physically fit bodies became a primary concern for U.S. colonialists' work to manage a newly conquered population. Warwick Anderson notes of the American colonial project in the Philippines: "The Filipino emerged in this medio-moral vision as an immature, contaminating type, but also as a potentially reformable one if subject to the right techniques of the body" (2006: 5).[6] In other words, as part of the U.S. civilizing project in its tropical Southeast Asian colony, notions of Western hygiene and health were collapsed with ideas of virtue and moral fitness. The Filipino body and population came to be one that could be rescued from its "dirty" tropical surroundings and inherent degeneracy if subject to proper techniques. But as Anderson is careful to point out, this rescue of the Filipino was and is never complete. The colonial project categorizes bodies along racial logics where the white male heteronormative subject reigns supreme, and hence racialized bodies like that of the Filipino are necessarily always and already outside of, yet needed, for white rightness. Despite the perpetual partiality of correcting the "immature and contaminating" Filipino, Anderson explains that, as part of its civilizing mission, it was useful for U.S. colonialism to organize its health and hygiene programs in the Philippines along this trajectory of possible transformation.

The potential to transform contaminating and immoral bodies can help us make sense of how Filipino masculinities at play are contoured by the life-saving potential of basketball to produce healthy bodies. As Lou Antolihao (2012) describes in his analysis of how basketball superseded the sport of baseball in the Philippines in popularity and scope at the end of the twentieth century, the popularity and prominence of any sport in national esteem is part of a nation-building project.[7] Basketball was introduced to the Philippines in strategic ways through YMCA programs in 1905. The sport gained popular momentum via the network of universities and colleges that U.S. colonialism established as part of its efforts to usurp Spanish colonial educational influence with a U.S.-style education system and ways of knowing (Antolihao, 2012).[8] With Anderson, who speaks to how colonial programs worked to promote hygiene and health, and Antolihao, who speaks to how colonial physical educational programs worked to promote modernity in the Philippines, the significance of basketball as a colonial technique to align bodies along the trajectory of health and modernity is clearly delineated.

However, while helping to contextualize how Filipino men who play basketball aspire to physically and morally fit bodies, there is a further geography that needs to be taken into account. While the techniques deployed by U.S. colonialism to correct the dirty and degenerate bodies and moral makeup of the Filipino through sport shed light on how basketball is imagined as a "life-saver," how might we think about this paradigm within techniques of settler colonialism deployed in Canada? In this context, settler colonial techniques, as Patrick Wolfe (2006) puts it, are designed to "eliminate the native."[9] Through the logic of territoriality, Wolfe argues that at the center of this type of colonial project was, and continues to be, the conquest of land through the violent dispossession of Indigenous peoples. Queer and feminist Indigenous and settler colonial scholars have pointed out that this project of dispossession goes hand in hand with the policing and disciplining of genders and sexualities to conform with white hetero-patriarchal norms targeting Indigenous women and ancestral forms of kinship in violent ways (see Justice, Rifkin, and Schneider, 2010).[10] Driskill et al. (2011), for example, argue that settler colonialism conditions normative sexualities in countries like Canada.[11] Sarah Hunt and Cindy Holmes (2015) insist that as part of the project to eliminate Indigenous people, the imposition of binary systems of gender on Indigenous systems of gender serves the purpose of narrowly aligning Indigenous status and rights along heterosexual lines, with the material effect of leading to, as they put it, "fewer and fewer Native people over time."[12] Given that this is the type of colonial project in which the Filipino in Canada is situated, it is necessary to think more carefully about how colonial techniques that inform the heteronormative masculinities at play on basketball courts in Vancouver change over space. To do this, I turn to thinking about how notions of health and moral fitness are evoked as lessons in how to be proper citizen-subjects who embody gender and sexual appropriateness in a settler colonial state.

Basketball as Life Lessons in Healthy Heteronormative Masculinities

For Jason, a son of a former live-in domestic worker who is now in his thirties, staying active and being involved in community is a lesson he wants to pass down:

> I just enjoy playing basketball. It's just something about it. Now I'm just trying to keep moving because I have a three-year-old son, I want him to still see me playing when he's growing up. So I bring him to all my games and he likes it! . . . I want to play with him; keep moving, because I never had that with my dad . . . . And I see here in Canada, I see parents, dad, and son, they do things more together. I wanna do that with my son.

Jason thus sees basketball as a life lesson—something intimate that is meant to be passed down from generation to generation. Boni, who migrated to Canada as a teenager and played on his public high school team, elaborates on very particular life lessons that basketball offers:

> For me, basketball is not just basketball—it's a life experience. When you're playing basketball, you have to make quick decisions. In the future, you realize that sometimes that will happen, and you have to make the right and proper decision. When my coach told me that, I was like "Oh wow, that's something else," and then pretty much he got me engaged, he taught me, he helped to build me as a person.

The ability for basketball to make good boys or citizen-subjects undergirds Jason and Boni's thoughts on what they have learned and what they want to teach through participation in the sport. In other words, part of learning how to play basketball is learning how to be proper men. For Jason, this means being a good father and role model to his young son; for Boni, this means applying the lessons of discipline to make the "proper decision" in his life. The proper or ideal Filipino man is envisioned to be, as one participant put it, a man who has "principles, they have conviction, and they are responsible—responsible in every aspect of their life, as a father, as a person, as a fellow citizen."

Heterosexuality and the heteronormative (im)migrant family are assumed in these articulations of life lessons in appropriateness.

The idea of a healthy heteronormative Filipino masculinity is more pronounced in conversation with anxieties over Filipino women playing basketball. Gayle, a woman in her twenties, plays regularly in drop-in gyms and in a mixed league with her husband. While her husband supports her playing the game, she has not met the same encouragement outside of her family and their peers:

> **BONI:** Well, I hear Filipinos here tell her to stop playing basketball or stop running around because—
>
> **GAYLE:** Yah, because "You're married now."
>
> **BONI:** "You're married now and you won't be able to conceive." That's what they're saying.

What becomes apparent here is the simultaneous gender and sexual disciplining at the moment when Gayle's body becomes a site for sexual reproduction within the notion of a heteronormative family. When I asked her husband what he thought of that, he said that he was unsure how to take the advice because he did not know if their warnings were well-founded. The play of women and girls is tolerated only to a certain extent. It was acceptable for Gayle to play basketball before her marriage, but after getting married this acceptance changed because her role as a wife and future mother took precedence. This anxiety over women playing basketball permeated my discussions with different league organizers who want to host games for girls' basketball teams. While enthusiastic about the possibility of organizing games and tournaments for elementary-age and high school-age girls, they become more cautious when I ask if they would ever consider organizing activities for women in their twenties or older. In Kevin and Carl's minds, the demand for girls' basketball is ripe in the community. After all, Kevin explains, "girls have the right to play just as much as boys." This outright enthusiasm for school-age girls and youth playing basketball, however, is not matched for women beyond their teenage years. In other words, bodies that are rendered as sites of heteronormative reproduction are regulated and disciplined in different ways. Undergirding these techniques of gender and sexual disciplining is the naturalization of heteronormativity.

Learning to Be Proper Masculine Subjects in a Settler Colonial State

As Kale Fajardo (2011) has shown in his exploration of the fluidity of Filipino masculinities, there is a dominant masculine narrative of heroism in the Philippine nationalist script that advances a hyper-masculine and macho version of the Filipino cis-male.[13] As the *haligi ng tahanan* (the pillar of the home), the Filipino man provides for his family in material ways, and is imagined as the backbone of the nation. Rhacel Parreñas (2005) argues that these gender and sexual expectations sharpen with international labor migration because the men who usually stay in the Philippines exaggerate their disciplinary role while mothers work abroad.[14] While Parreñas thinks of how gender norms are accentuated by labor migration for those left behind in migration, I am concerned with how these gender norms and hetero-patriarchal expectations travel as Filipino men live and work abroad. While their views that basketball helps them become better fathers and responsible male subjects echo with the cultural logic imbued in the refrain *haligi ng tahanan*, those with whom I spoke frame the life lessons of basketball in spatial terms that locates the power of these lessons within proper heteronormative masculinities in Canada. Basketball as a life lesson providing a road map towards individual industriousness and self-discipline in Canada is constructed not as a continuation of masculine roles in the Philippines, but in relation to and against characterizations of hyper-masculinity and unruly styles of play in the Philippines. Consider Kevin's thoughts on this:

> For the most part the ones who have stayed a longer time here in Canada, they play more organized basketball. They're more skilled . . . Because here they follow the rule, here I think there's more discipline here . . . Because someone will tell them "You can't play like that here." . . . They're told "Ah, you're in Canada—you're in America, you cannot do what you can get away with in the Philippines."

As Kevin, Boni, and Jason made clear, basketball provides an opportunity to teach boys lessons necessary to make them physically and morally fit men. They further explain how one can tell if a player has just arrived from the Philippines since he is "more physical and plays a less disciplined" brand of basketball. Take, for example, Bayani's assessment of the differences in play:

> I know most of my friends grew up in the Philippines, . . . they play basketball over there, they got to experience . . . how their barrio plays against other barrios and it gets competitive that way. . . . Kids coming from the Philippines, they have a different way of playing basketball. They're so much more rough. Over there, they're very into aggressiveness, and they'll hurt you—that's what I find because I've experienced it. I've noticed that some of my friends that came from there, they're very into injuring you.

After some time, however, the player learns through formal and informal structures that basketball played in Vancouver is less about the physicality and more about the finesse and team play. This was the perspective of a number of men I interviewed. Jason explained that this change in play is also based on the fact that the players sell their labor, which requires that their bodies are healthy for physical labor. He spoke of a league in Abbotsford where Filipinos who are temporary foreign workers play. According to Jason, they are less physical and violent in that league because the workers cannot get hurt or they may jeopardize their employability, and hence their immigration status in Canada. Again, basketball provides an opportunity to teach boys lessons necessary to make them morally fit men—a lesson that one can only learn outside of the Philippines and, more importantly for this chapter, one they can only learn in Canada.

Within these life lessons set in a geographical binary of "here" versus "there," colonial contours come into play in two interrelated ways. On one level, the Western teleological and spatialized binaries that undergird colonial narratives of the "modernized and civilized" West versus the "backward and wild" other are taken up and reproduced by Filipino men in Canada. This framing of the Philippines echoes Geraldine Pratt's (2004) assessment of how the Philippines is cast in dominant liberal logics that pervade Canadian imaginaries.[15] The Canadian state, nanny agencies, and families often minimize the abuses that live-in caregivers undergo in Canada through their imagined geographies of non-Western places in general, and the backwardness, violence, and primitivism of the Philippines specifically. Philip Kelly (2015) also points to the ways in which Filipinos in Canada imagine the Philippines as "inferior" as a result of the combined forces of the norm of whiteness in Canada and the Philippines' history as a subject of colonial powers.[16] The ways in which the men speak of the unruly styles of basketball played in the Philippines versus the more disciplined brand of basketball they claim boys and men learn in Canada slips into this binary-based narrative. Colonial-style techniques are applied to expurgate the wild tendencies associated with the Philippines in order to produce morally fit men in the process of migrating, or as the league organizer in Montreal put it, "adapting to their new surroundings." The production of morally fit men in their new surroundings in Canada speaks to colonial techniques of heteronormativity in a second way.

I also situate the making of appropriate heteronormative masculinities in the settler colonial and capitalist nation building processes vis-à-vis the concept of what it means to be a proper citizen-subject of Canada. Sunera Thobani's (2007) theory of exaltation hones in on how in dominant Canadian relations the white settler colonialist sits at its apex as the ultimate citizen-subject. She argues that exaltation, as a technique of power, functions to propagate the white settler colonial subject as the "stable, conscious, unified, and enduring figure, whose actions are shaped primarily by reason" (7). Thobani works through this idea of exaltation to explain how securing the white settler colonial subject at the apex of relations necessitates the simultaneous denigration and dehumanization of Indigenous people. She also works through the prism of exaltation to apprehend the immigration of the "non-western" immigrant whose labor is necessary for capitalist development in Canada. She argues that exaltation differentiates certain subjects, marking the white settler as one who dwells in the world as the exalted subject, while the non-European immigrant is cast as a perpetual outsider of the national subject, and the Indigenous person is marked for elimination. In this making of race and nation, Thobani concludes that "the racial configurations of subject formation within settler societies are thus triangulated: the national remains at the centre of the state's (stated) commitment to enhance well being; the immigrant receives a tenuous and conditional inclusion; and the Aboriginal continues to be marked for loss of sovereignty" (ibid., 18). By aspiring to masculine moral fitness—a fitness that presumes heteronormativity—it can be said that, as racialized immigrants, Filipinos are aspiring to gain more than a "tenuous and conditional inclusion" in the nation through their gendered and sexual performances." Thus the techniques of settler colonialism, organized around the fundamental logic of dispossessing

Indigenous peoples and their lands, reshape dominant gender and sexual paradigms associated with the colonial project in the Philippines when Filipinos migrate to Canada.

In this chapter, I have discussed how Filipino masculine sexualities at play on basketball courts in Canadian cities open up opportunities to think about the work that different brands of colonialism do over time and space. I posit that Filipino masculine sexualities come to be in negotiation with colonial hetero-patriarchal and racial logics. These colonial hetero-patriarchal and racial logics move between the Philippines and Canada. Dominant gender and sexual paradigms formed in the Philippines' colonial encounters with the West take on different meanings and shapes in Canada's own settler colonial and capitalist brand of normative discourses around citizenship. More specifically, how the Filipino men who play basketball in Canada talk about the possibility of redeeming and reforming themselves into healthy men through the sport and the possibility of becoming morally fit, heteronormative family men in spatial terms speaks to how the impossible colonial desire of the "civilized native" is taken up and reformulated in Canada. In the Philippines, basketball was introduced by American colonialism in its efforts to civilize and modernize the Filipino native. In Canada, Filipinos continue to play the sport with aspirations to teach and learn lessons on how to be proper citizen-subjects of the Canadian settler colonial state.

While I focused my discussion on these colonial processes, I do not want to leave the sole impression that there is nothing queer about Filipino men playing basketball in Canada. Indeed, there are queer moments, challenges to the ideas of nation, and rejections of dominant racial logics that I witnessed taking place on and around the basketball courts I visited. These stories lie beyond the scope of this chapter but form its underbelly. As Indigenous feminist scholars such as Audra Simpson (2014) teach us, colonialism is a pervasive but also incomplete project—one available to disruptions and rejection.[17] It is therefore important that as Filipinos/as in Canada interested in the project and politics of queering, we are also mindful of the colonial projects that our gender and sexual politics are enrolled and complicit in. More to the point, we should be asking ourselves what is decolonial or disruptive about our efforts to gain more than, as Thobani (2007) put it, "tenuous and conditional inclusion" in a nation based on settler colonial foundations.

Notes

1. See Pacquiao's interview here: http://www.theguardian.com/sport/2016/feb/16/manny-pacquiao-gay-people-worse-than-animals.

2. Raewyn Connell, *Masculinities* (Berkeley: University of California Press, 2005).

3. Brendan Hokowhitu, "Tackling Māori Masculinity: A Colonial Genealogy of Savagery and Sport," *The Contemporary Pacific* 16, no. 2 (2004): 259–84.

4. Lou Antolihao, "Rooting for the Underdog: Spectatorship and Subalternity in Philippine Basketball," *Philippine Studies* 58, no. 4 (2010): 449–80; Rafe Bartholomew, *Pacific Rims: Beermen Ballin' in Flip-Flops and the Philippines' Unlikely Love Affair with Basketball* (New York: Penguin, 2010).

5. Jesse Feith and Angela MacKenzie, "'In Our Blood': Basketball and Montreal's Filipino Community," *CBC News Montreal*, April 16, 2014, http://www.cbc.ca/news/canada/montreal/in-our-blood-basketball-and-montreal-s-filipino-community-1.2612499.

6. Warwick Anderson, *Colonial Pathologies: American Tropical Medicine, Race, and Hygiene in the Philippines* (Durham, N.C.: Duke University Press, 2006).

7. Lou Antolihao, "From Baseball Colony to Basketball Republic: Post-Colonial Transition and the Making of a National Sport in the Philippines," *Sport in Society* 15, no. 10 (2012): 1396–1412.

8. Antolihao, "From Baseball Colony to Basketball Republic," 1412.

9. Patrick Wolfe, "Settler Colonialism and the Elimination of the Native," *Journal of Genocide Research* 8, no. 4 (2006): 387–409.

10. Daniel Heath Justice, Mark Rifkin, and Bethany Schneider, "Introduction: Special Issue on Sexuality, Nationality, Indigeneity," *GLQ: A Journal of Lesbian and Gay Studies* 16, no. 1–2 (2010): 5–39.

11. Qwo-Li Driskill, Chris Finley, Brian Joseph Gilley, and Scott Lauria Morgensen, eds., *Queer Indigenous Studies: Critical Interventions in Theory, Politics, and Literature* (Tucson: University of Arizona Press, 2011).

12. Sarah Hunt and Cindy Holmes, "Everyday Decolonization: Living a Decolonizing Queer Politics," *Journal of Lesbian Studies* 19, no. 2 (2015): 154–72.

13. Kale B. Fajardo, *Filipino Crosscurrents: Oceanographies of Seafaring, Masculinities, and Globalization* (Minneapolis: University of Minnesota Press, 2011).

14. Rhacel Parreñas, *Children of Global Migration: Transnational Families and Gendered Woes* (Stanford, Calif.: Stanford University Press, 2005).

15. Geraldine Pratt, *Working Feminism* (Philadelphia, Pa.: Temple University Press, 2004).

16. Philip F. Kelly, "Transnationalism, Emotion, and Second-Generation Social Mobility in the Filipino-Canadian Diaspora," *Singapore Journal of Tropical Geography* 36, no. 3 (2015): 280–99.

17. Audra Simpson, *Mohawk Interruptus: Political Life across the Borders of Settler States* (Durham, N.C.: Duke University Press, 2014).

Bibliography

Anderson, Warwick. *Colonial Pathologies: American Tropical Medicine, Race, and Hygiene in the Philippines.* Durham, N.C.: Duke University Press, 2006.

Antolihao, Lou. "From Baseball Colony to Basketball Republic: Post-Colonial Transition and the Making of a National Sport in the Philippines." *Sport in Society* 15, no. 10 (2012): 1396–1412.

———. "Rooting for the Underdog: Spectatorship and Subalternity in Philippine Basketball." *Philippine Studies* 58, no. 4 (2010): 449–80.

Bartholomew, Rafe. *Pacific Rims: Beermen Ballin' in Flip-Flops and the Philippines' Unlikely Love Affair with Basketball.* New York: Penguin, 2010.

Connell, Raewyn. *Masculinities.* Berkeley: University of California Press, 2005.

Driskill, Qwo-Li, Chris Finley, Brian Joseph Gilley, and Scott Lauria Morgensen, eds. *Queer Indigenous Studies: Critical Interventions in Theory, Politics, and Literature.* Tucson: University of Arizona Press, 2011.

Fajardo, Kale B. *Filipino Crosscurrents: Oceanographies of Seafaring, Masculinities, and Globalization.* Minneapolis: University of Minnesota Press, 2011.

Feith, Jesse, and Angela MacKenzie. "'In Our Blood': Basketball and Montreal's Filipino Community." *CBC News Montreal,* April 16, 2014. http://www.cbc.ca/news/canada/montreal/in-our-blood-basketball-and-montreal-s-filipino-community-1.2612499.

Heath Justice, Daniel, Mark Rifkin, and Bethany Schneider. "Introduction: Special Issue on Sexuality, Nationality, Indigeneity." *GLQ: A Journal of Lesbian and Gay Studies* 16, no. 1–2 (2010): 5–39.

Hokowhitu, Brendan. "Tackling Māori Masculinity: A Colonial Genealogy of Savagery and Sport." *The Contemporary Pacific* 16, no. 2 (2004): 259–84.

Hunt, Sarah, and Cindy Holmes. "Everyday Decolonization: Living a Decolonizing Queer Politics." *Journal of Lesbian Studies* 19, no. 2 (2015): 154–72.

Kelly, Philip F. "Transnationalism, Emotion, and Second-Generation Social Mobility in the Filipino-Canadian Diaspora." *Singapore Journal of Tropical Geography* 36, no. 3 (2015): 280–99.

Parreñas, Rhacel. *Children of Global Migration: Transnational Families and Gendered Woes*. Stanford, Calif.: Stanford University Press, 2005.

Pratt, Geraldine. *Working Feminism*. Philadelphia, Pa.: Temple University Press, 2004.

Simpson, Audra. *Mohawk Interruptus: Political Life across the Borders of Settler States*. Durham, N.C.: Duke University Press, 2014.

Thobani, Sunera. *Exalted Subjects: Studies in the Making of Race and Nation in Canada*. Toronto: University of Toronto Press, 2007.

Wazny, Adam. "Winnipeg the City of Dominance: Filipino Basketball Teams Feared at North American Tournaments." *Winnipeg Free Press*, March 2, 2012. Retrieved from http://www.ugnayan.com/ca/Manitoba/Winnipeg/article/1EKN.

Wolfe, Patrick. "Settler Colonialism and the Elimination of the Native." *Journal of Genocide Research* 8, no. 4 (2006): 387–409.

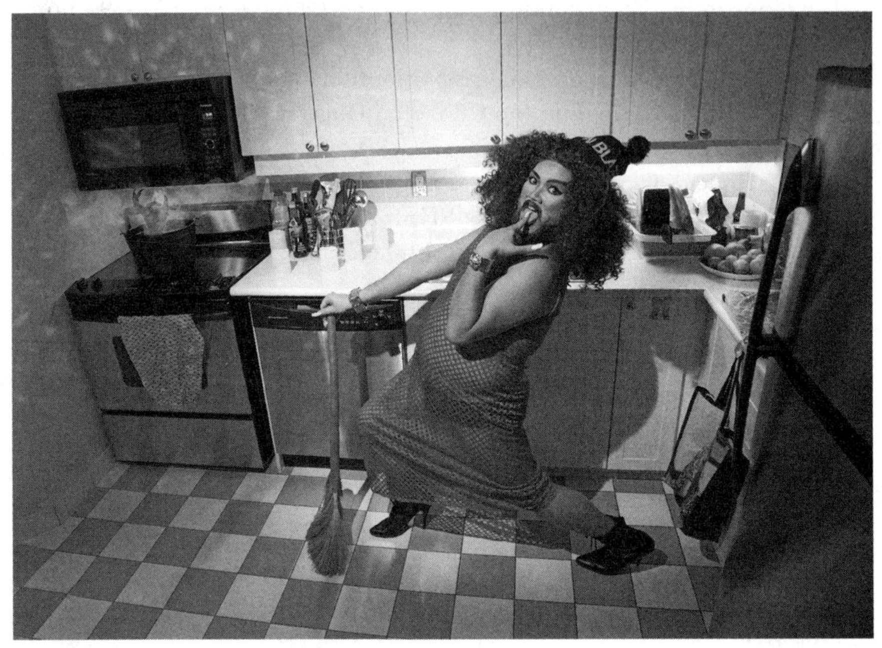

Patrick Salvani performing at the Rhubarb Festival. Photo by Akriti Jain.

Dragging Filipinx
A Series of Performative Vignettes

Patrick Salvani

Vignette I. Drag, Horror, and Community Work

I am not your average gender queer pansexual hairy Asian Filipinx panda queen who parties like a white girl and tells scary stories. I am the Fathermom to many drag superstars; my art engages audiences in the complexities, nuances, and sometimes explicitness of being queer, trans, and gender-nonconforming Filipinos here in Canada; and I work towards building community and creating lasting families.

As Filipinos in the diaspora, and people of color in Canada, our histories are not taught. Our voices are not regularly centered, let alone appropriately valued monetarily for our work. We forget to dream and are forced to grasp on tightly to constructed narratives around identity, gender, and politics rather than fully understanding and honoring our histories and advancing them. In Canada, it's not easy finding our way back home. By re/discovering our histories, honoring families both blood and chosen, exploring food and art, I can construct a path that leads me there, while also dreaming and screwing things up along the way to keep life interesting.

I gew up in the Philippines in a place where sometimes there's no electricity at night. Fear became familial and scary stories felt comforting. My grandma loved telling me scary stories and my mom loved watching horror movies with me. When my grandma died, and I moved across the country away from my family, I was comforted by writing horror stories (and cooking lots of Filipino food). Horror stories provide an alternative way of understanding and relating to loss, family, migration, politics, and community. I want the nonbelievers to understand the beauty and power in horror stories as a representation of community, politics, and a way to invigorate change.

I know how complicated it is to only be seen and consumed in pieces—hiding our bodies, our stories, our feelings in order for others to feel whole. My art exposes my queer Filipinx rice belly-ness, and that cannot be made more digestible. We are all complex, layered, and want to be seen as whole. That is freedom. That is why I make art, and that is why I write horror stories and why I co-created the Drag Musical.

The Drag Musical began in 2009 as a solidarity initiative of the Asian Arts Freedom School (AAFS). I was facilitating the writing cycle along with Yaya Yao, and through our outreach efforts we saw a shift in participant demographics—from university-educated second-generation children of the diaspora to immigrants who don't have English as their first language. We also saw an increase of queer, trans, and gender-nonconforming Filipinos coming to the space, with sometimes thirty participants attending weekly. In order to create more accessible programming, a lot of our "writing" activities included theater, movement, meditations, illustrations, and dance. So, we were in essence the worst writing facilitators ever and the first Drag Musical Directors to come.

The program is a twelve-week paid performance and writing-intensive program for LGBTQ youth of color. Each participant gets home-cooked Filipino meals, free everything, and a drag and movement mentor to help them for the final showcase. The program welcomes people we don't know, people who we fight for into our communities and families. Six Drag Musicals later, it is the largest and longest-standing queer and trans people of color show in Toronto. Though the final showcase is what people witness, the program is more about people who have been systematically silenced working together to take the stage for the first time.

The Drag Musical further prioritizes the need to combat the systemic violence against black and Indigenous peoples here in Turtle Island, as well as globally. Being a queer Filipino artist in Canada, I understand the need to make this foreign land feel like home. Central to my work is the belief that it is imperative for us to center the voices of queer, trans, and gender-nonconforming people—all while searching for the stories that will set us free from our inheritances of cultural and gendered violence. Our freedom is dependent on how we all fight and find freedom together.

Vignette 2. *Pasalubong*: A Horror Story That Honors the Complexity of My *Lola* and the Undying Love from My "Family"

My grandmother once told me, "When the *kumakatok* come, there is *walang pag-asa*—No hope."

I stand in front of my past—my parents, my baby sister, distant relatives, old friends and recognizable strangers. They all stare up at me as they wait for me to start. The warmth of the lights only makes me think of how tight my pants are and how my tucked-in shirt makes my stomach pop out. I hate it here. I pull the mic closer to my trembling lips. "I miss you so much Grandma," I stutter as I let my tears flow.

The sound reverberates throughout the church.

I pause, trying to regain my composure. My eyes fixate on three tall white candles burning beside the podium. I watch as wax drips along the candlesticks and pools around the base.

I want to tell everyone about how I grew up listening to my grandma's stories in the Philippines: about her washing clothes where the caribou drank water; how her mother taught her how to make candles for All Saints Day, frightening stories of *bruhas, aswang, multo*, and superstitions; and how she conceived my father with some asshole during the Second World War while thinking she wouldn't survive. I want to tell them that every time she held my hand . . . I knew I was safe. Instead all I could mutter was "Grandma, I learned so much from you about family. Though I could tell you always longed to be home. If you can hear me . . . you were home. I was home when I was with you."

Knock Knock knock!

I grumble "What the fuck?" and roll from side to side in bed.

It's my first night back in Toronto from Calgary—back from the funeral, back from being with my family. I was back, alone and scared.

Knock knock knock!

A loud gust of wind blows against the blinds and my eyes snap open.

Knock Knock Knock!

I feel a chill seep into my room as my muscles tighten and instinctively my body starts to curl into a ball under my sheets.

I wait silently and without moving. After half an hour of complete stillness, my fear turns into tiredness and my tiredness turns into uneasy dreams of my grandma. . . .

I'm surrounded by narrow walls lit dimly by candles on the ground. It's quiet and eerie. I feel a sense of familiarity as I look down to see my hands holding tight to the handlebars of a wheelchair where my grandmother sits, her head resting on her chest. Every step I take is slow and with intention. I'm at my grandma's nursing home. The screams and bellows of other seniors and the sound of scurrying nurses are only faint echoes within the dark emptiness.

My grandma stares ahead as her voice finds life, "I heard them knock last night! When the *kumakatok* come, there is *walang pag-asa*. Someone in our family will die and there is nothing you can do."

My throat clenches tightly.

Unexpectedly, my grandmother raises her small and fragile hand towards mine. I suddenly find my hand cradled in hers. She grasps my fingers and lifts her head. "The *kumakatok* are here."

Ring ring ring!

I wake up half-consciously, place my phone against my ear, and blurt out, "*Walang pag-asa!*"

"What? You okay, buddy?" A familiar voice beckons.

I mumble, "Huh?"

"You okay? Remember we made plans, we're welcoming you back. We'll be there in an hour to pick you up."

I shake off my lingering dream, "Yah yah, I remember. Can't wait!"

As I get dressed in my room, the memories, the knocking and fear for both my sister and parent's safety weave into a routine of me pacing, calling, pacing, calling, pacing, calling. No answer.

Where is my family?

My friends Saafi, Kareem, and Mooky arrive an hour later to pick me up. I open the door as they all hug me tightly. I don't care that my hair is a mess with sweat dripping down my forehead because at that moment it feels good to be held in their arms. Before I can say anything my friend Saafi whispers in my ear, "Sometimes the only good place to be is . . . to not think at all. We're gonna enjoy today. Period." She pulls me closer. "Seriously, bitch. Let's get drunk!!"

Her words sink in, so I decide not to trouble my friends with my Filipino superstitions. I quickly zip up my backpack, trying to conceal a gift for my friends.

"What's that?" Saafi asks, trying to peek inside.

I chuckle. "It's a give-you-life kind of gift. It's called *pasalubong*. You'll see."

As we bike to Trinity Bellwoods, I call my family at every traffic crossing. Still no answer. I casually tell my friends to ease their curiosity, "I just have to check in, you know."

We find a spot in the park framed by tall luscious cedar trees surrounded by hipsters, lovers, and wanderers. Kareem sits next to Saafi. He tells us a story with his usual pitchy enthusiasm about the guy he's dating and their tumultuous love affair. I can't help but say, "Looks like you guys are in love."

Kareem waves his hands dramatically and covers his ears.

Our conversations go from random hookups, bad pickup lines, and fuck-the-police stories to dreams and parties. We laugh, cuddle, and cry as our bodies absorb the heat of the sun. It feels like I am back in the Philippines. It feels like home. At moments I catch Mooky peering at me and quickly averting his eyes away. He awkwardly sits beside me not saying a word.

I grin."What?"

"What? Nothing," he replies with a nervous giggle. We all stop for a moment and just smile at one another. I close my eyes toward the sky and let the light fill me with so much warmth that I don't want it to stop.

"Oh yeah, I have a gift for you all," I say excitedly. I unzip my bag and pull out the gift wrapped in banana leaves. I start unraveling it. "This is what Filipinos call *pasalubong*, a gift for family when they welcome you home. This belonged to my grandma . . ." I pause as I hear Saafi clearing her throat. Kareem lovingly reaches for my hand. "I miss my grandma, I miss my parents, I miss sharing our memories of the Philippines like we were back there again."

I see Saafi bite her lower lip as she holds back words. She clears her throat again. Mooky stares at the ground while anxiously picking at the grass. I see his eyes twitch.

"Filipinos always ask me when's the last time I've been back home. And when I'm with you guys, I am home. This is home. I feel safe here."

I spread open the banana leaves to reveal three rose-colored candles.

"In the Philippines my grandma would sit by a huge tin bowl filled with melted wax. The bowl was almost half her size." I spread open my arms, outlining the vastness of the bowl. "She would pour the wax over the strings which were attached to a large ring made of bamboo. Before the wax set, she would straighten the strings by pulling down on them tightly. My grandma would repeat this for hours to get the perfect-sized candle."

I pass a candle to each of my friends.

"She made these in the Philippines and this is my gift, my *pasalubong* to you all, to my family."

I take a deep breath in anticipation of their reactions.

Suddenly, Saafi begins to cough uncontrollably. She clamps her hands against her mouth. Blood sprays from her lips and splatters on my shirt. She looks into her palm. We look at her. Chunks of fleshy blood-soaked guck rest in her hands. Saafi's body begins convulsing. "Oh my God," Kareem gasps. He tugs at his ear frantically and shakes his head in disbelief.

"Oh my God. Oh my God."

My heart begins to race and my stomach starts to turn.

The fear in Saafi's eyes disappears as her eyes roll back into her head. Mooky reaches for her, trying to calm the ferocity of her shaking body.

"Oh my God!" Kareem starts screaming as he abruptly jumps back from the group. "Oh my God, help me! Help me!!!"

I turn to see Kareem grabbing his ears while blood forcibly seeps through his fingers. My momentary wonder switches into complete terror as Kareem's knees buckle and his lifeless body collapses onto me.

I hold him as his blood starts to drip down my arm.

I look towards Saafi and see her body is completely still.

"No, no, no, no, no," I plead.

The peaceful murmur of the park evolves into shrieks of panic. Dogs bark, lovers hold each other tightly as they scurry away, children torturously wail and cry, and the wanderers start to trample each other in hysteria.

My body sits frozen.

Mooky grabs my shoulders and stares into my eyes "What the fuck is going on?!" His voice is trembling.

"I'm so scared, please!"

My eyes lock onto his bloodshot eyes as red tears begin to flow down his cheeks. One by one I analyze each drop falling from his chin down to the ground, forming a growing puddle of blood at my feet.

I am no longer in control of my body or my soul; I sit in a catatonic state as the blood of my friends continues to drown me. My body sways, mimicking the leaves rustling in the wind, while my lips begin to murmur repeatedly, "*Walang pag-asa. Walang pag-asa. Walang pag-asa.*"

The last thing I hear before my entire world becomes silent . . . is the incessant ringing of my cell phone.

One week later, I sit alone in the church watching the sobbing families of my friends hold each other as they follow the three coffins out to the cemetery. I hate this. I begin kicking the church pew in frustration. I pull out my phone from my pocket, hoping to distract myself from my own sadness.

One new message.

I slowly bring the phone to my ear and listen. It's my mom. "Did you forget we went to Banff?" She laughs. "Also, Dad found a note for you in Grandma's things. Hopefully, it will comfort you. Your grandma wrote, '*Mahal kita*, I love you so much. Remember, life is a gift and so is death.' Okay *anak*, gotta go, call us back. Oh, and hope your family in Toronto enjoyed their *pasalubong* from Grandma."

The End.

Vignette 3. *Sarap*: Manananggal Creation Play

More many Filipinos in Canada, it can feel like food is our only way back home. We forget our language, leave our traditions behind, and disconnect from our spirituality. For those people that don't have that . . . um . . . acquired taste, they'll never understand that with just one bite of the right dish, you can taste the stories from back home—each ingredient and way of cooking providing its own lesson. These stories tell of our homeland, our bodies, our longing, and our monsters.

Like a Queenie who is regal, eloquent, and a little slutty and with a whole lot of baggage, the Host enters the dining hall where his/her dinner guests are waiting. The Host lip-synchs the lyrics to Lesley Gore's "You Don't Own Me."

Nookie: Yes yes yes. Good to see you again. Where'd you get those glasses? Your makeup is superb. I don't think we've ever met, what's your name? You're cute. I'm so glad you're all here. (*Nookie sensually caresses his/her large belly in a circular motion*) Dinner is gonna be very filling.

I need to cook one more dish. You don't mind do you? I made this dish the other night for the family I work for. That family had too much money to ever cook for themselves. On the other hand, I grew up with a mom who was just a horrible cook. She was the youngest of twelve children growing up in the Philippines and that meant she was always too young to cook for anyone, let alone for the entire family.

My grandfather loved making large meals. All the men in the family loved to cook. My grandfather would love feeding us these special sausages called *longannisa*. "That pig!" He pointed out the beast to slaughter. You could say he picked the one that's lived a good life.

My grandfather would sit (*miming each motion, slowly and with intention*) molding the ground pork, then squeezing it into these whitish goat intestinal casings. Roll it in his hands and then, TWIST. No sausage was ever the same size. And because of that goat casing, the spices and the juices could mix throughout.

Have you ever tasted Filipino sausages? The sweetness, the spiciness, the juiciness—You would never forget it because it tastes soooo (*Nookie deep throats his/her middle finger*) good.

Ok, let's finish this dish. It's called *adobo*. It might sound Spanish, but let me guarantee you that this dish is truly Filipino.

My uncle taught me this recipe. "Come here boy, err, girl, man, just come here! I'm going to show you something." My uncle took care of me when my mother left for Canada. He was always drinking and at night when he thought I was asleep, he would sit beside his bottle of whiskey crying that he couldn't find a job.

We begin with marinated meat in soy sauce. My uncle would tell me, "Don't stay out in the sun, you don't want to be as dark as that soy sauce bottle." Now add a pinch of peppercorns—just a pinch. When I was growing up I was told to pinch my nose (*Pinching the bridge of his/ her nose*) so I could look like one of those English movie stars. "I'll be back." Or someone like that.

See how SIMPLE this recipe is! Turn the heat up to high and let it boil. Do not forget the water.

My grandfather would add cups upon cups of water to every dish he made. *Sinigang (pouring water into the pot), nilaga, arroz caldo* . . . corned beef soup . . . lettuce soup. He added water to everything so there would be enough food to feed all the children. My mom said she got used to always being hungry. She wanted to be just like her older sisters. But my grandparents forced her to do business administration.

Lower the heat and let it simmer.

I have a problem keeping time. I think it's in my blood. My mom would tell me on the phone that once she works these 2 years, 104 weeks, 3,900 hours we would be reunited. Her boss wouldn't claim all the hours she worked because they wanted to save on taxes. So she told me it would be just a little longer. And that she loves it here in Canada and she loves me. Even when that boss fired her because he said she was "trouble," she got another job with another family that she really loved and where she wouldn't get fired for not answering the knocks on her bedroom door at night. She worked more than double those 2 years, 104 weeks, 3,900 hours, but the Canadian government was "busy." I didn't understand it at that time, but eight years would pass and I would never see my mother again.

My uncle told me, "When your feet are planted far away from your heart, you're basically cut into two and no one can survive."

I would survive for her, though.

Now, where's my timer? Tick Tick Tick Oh, I just love that sound.

I don't want the dish to burn and I never want to forget!

My last memory of my mother was when she was tucking me into bed the night before she left—her eyes red and swollen. I told her that night, "I want to be rich! I want to buy us a house and eat unseasoned baked chicken with you in Canada." My mom caressed my forehead. "When you're older, my beautiful baby girl, my *anak*, and the moon is full, go to the water and immerse yourself there overnight." See, I was born with a beard and a giant rice belly—I came out just like this. Hello, I'm born, kind of thing.

My mom thought I was a magical healer, a woman rich with wisdom—a *babaylan*. But *babaylan*s weren't the rich I wanted to be.

So when I turned seventeen, I moved out of my uncle's cement home. I crossed borders to be in these foreign waters. And when the moon was full, I walked deep into them. There, I saw eyes staring back at me. He told me his name was Licalibutan, the Creator, the Destroyer. Then suddenly, the wind blew ferociously as it roared my true destiny.

The character lip-synchs and dances to lyrics to Pussycat Dolls' 'When I Grow Up.'"

Nookie: Well, my destiny wasn't exactly like that. Do you smell that? It's bay leaves. It's an herb that thinks it's a spice. Smells good, doesn't it?! Enjoy it while it lasts, because we need to add vinegar. The vinegar preserves the food, especially in the scorching heat of the Philippines, and adds that touch of savory and some sweetness to every dish.

The last family my mother worked for, they were so sweet to her because they always said, "thank you" and paid her for the hours she worked . . . Hmm. But they got their kids into a day care and my mom got a job at a gas station. Her last phone call to me she said, "This land is where we will fulfill our destiny." I cooked this dish from, err, for the family I worked for. I made it special for them.

When I started working there, I was told the food I cooked was too gross, too spicy, too saucy, too unhealthy, too much rice. Is that fish? Are you cooking Spam? Can you turn on the kitchen fan?

Their two children always laughed at me, pulling at my hair and calling me "fat." They wanted "normal" food like kale chips and chili cheese fries; tasty food like those dishes where lemon is the only seasoning and toasted brown bread with no crust.

Oh my, Tik Tik Tik

I can't forget to stir *(Angrily stirring)*. So I don't work there anymore. I got FED up with it.

The kids came home late one night from a swim meet. I had *adobo* waiting for them. "Man you're lucky we're hungry, becuz this smells like vinegar. Gross." As I watched them eat their words, and chew ferociously on the meat. I glared, "Stop calling me Man. Only my family can call me that. You can call me *Manananggal*."

As they laughed in my face, telling me to leave their spoiled asses alone, they asked, "Where's mommy and daddy? They're supposed to take us to Grandpa's house." "Your family is HERE with you *(looking deep within the pot)*. Do you know my mother worked for your grandfather when your dad was a little kid? My mother was trouble, while your family lived a good life."

(Picking up the serving spoon and licking it)

Mmmm. *Sarap.* Let this be a lesson for you all: when you fuck with the help, remember. survival is a beast and vinegar can make ANY MEAT taste good. BAHAHAHAHA!

The character lip-synchs You Don't Own Me.

ROARRRRRRR

Nookie: Young and Free-Range Meat!

Hope you're hungry because dinner is served.

Taking Up Space Is Revolutionary

Sean Kua

I gain visibility as a queer Filipinx artist by taking up as much space as I can, especially in straight white cis spaces. I constantly talk about my Filipinx identity, I talk about the food my family makes for family barbecues or Pasko, I watch their faces scrunch up in confusion and curiosity when I talk about how my mom seasons her food; I proudly share my traditions and bravely speak Tagalog in non-Filipinx settings. When I perform I make sure my Filipinx identity is acknowledged because I don't often see many Filipinx bodies on stage, or at least any-one claiming it. When I declare my Filipinx identity in a sea of white bodies, or speak fondly of my upbringing in a Filipino household, I feel I'm accomplishing mini-revolutions and every time I take up room in white spaces I feel like I'm committing acts of self-love. I have spent such a long time denying my culture, denying my Asianness, claiming to be half-white as a way to escape my culture.

When you grow up in Canada in the 1990s, it's rare to see Filipinx faces in the media, let alone Asian people, and even in 2015 I still don't see very many Filipinx bodies in the media. I grew up in Scarborough and had a ton of Filipinx classmates in school, many of whom were like me, half Filipino, half Chinese, but I was always embarrassed about myself. I didn't want people knowing I was Filipinx, or Chinese, I didn't want them laughing at my culture, or my food, or asking me why my clothes always smelled like I had just come from a buffet. At first it was a way to protect my culture. I didn't want to hear my classmates making racist jokes about my family, but then it became a daily ritual to deny everything that I was, am, altogether which eventually led to a good, long, complicated fifteen years about my ethnicity. Somewhere along the line I learned I was a quarter white, making me half Filipino, a quarter Chinese, and a quarter white, so then I tried passing myself off as a dark-skinned white person, or at least more white than Filipino. Ultimately, I couldn't escape my identity, obviously, my last name is very clearly Asian, my skin is caramel in the summer and it takes several months for my tan to fade. But when you're six years old and kids are pointing out that you have rice and spam for lunch and how weird it is, you become a little self-conscious and start begging your mom to pack you Lunchables instead. A lot of my Filipinx classmates went through the same ordeal, but on the odd day one of us had brought in last night's leftovers as lunch we reveled in each other's food, "Oh my god, you have *sinigang* for lunch? I had that last week!'" "Your parents cook spaghetti with hot dog, too?" "My *lola* makes the best *pancit!*" Aside from school lunches, I remember being embarrassed when talking about my culture. In high school my friends were such assholes about it, they'd laugh at my mom's accent, mock my lunches (Lunchables became a little too expensive to buy every week, so my mom started packing me leftovers instead to save money, and my high school's cafeteria served hot plastic passed off as grilled cheese sandwiches), and whenever I brought them over to my house I would hide the *tabo* in my bathroom to avoid an awkward conversation; in short, I didn't really talk about my culture. I'd always cringe when someone would say my full name when passing me in the halls; it felt like they knew who I really was. Every time my last name was spoken aloud that voice inside my head would go off, "Uh oh, they know who you really are," and it made me feel uncomfortable.

When I was nineteen I was beginning to accept my Filipinx identity. I started seeing a few Filipinx on TV, I was appreciating the rich history behind every cuisine, I started learning about the history of the Philippines. One of my cousins was working as a sous chef in one of the most prestigious kitchens in Toronto and had dreams of opening up a restaurant in hopes of making Filipino cuisine more mainstream. At this time I was in my first year of college, I was in a class full of white people and I had a classmate, a white girl, who, on several occasions, called me "whitewashed" and "white at heart." When I argued with her, insisting that I was Filipinx, she replied that deep down I was white and I knew it. Her justification for this was I didn't speak the language and my food wasn't stinky enough. Something about it hurt me. I spent a long time ignoring my culture and my identity, or trying to claim I had more white blood than Filipino, or convincing myself that if I used enough papaya soap and sun block I could be as pale as the celebrities in the Philippines; but there was something behind my classmate's voice. The way she said it was almost like she hated my skin color and I was only learning to love it. Maybe I was getting bored of people's old jokes about Filipino nannies, maybe I was feeling toxic after all these years of denial, maybe it was the lack of Filipinx role models I saw on TV, or maybe it was the number of white people I was exposed to that I truly knew I didn't want to be like them. So I began exploring my Filipinx identity through my artistry. I was writing more songs about racism, internalized self-descrimination, being caramel and queer. When I started playing open mics and small shows I saw the crowd, I saw who they applauded on stage, but most importantly I saw who wasn't on stage—people of color, specifically Filipinx's. Side note: I studied classical voice at the Royal Conservatory of Music and I remember very rarely seeing Filipinx opera singers. My voice teacher, Denise, who's a five-foot, five-inch woman of color, told me that opera is a very, very white industry, and if I pursued a career in opera I would be in the smallest percentage of Filipinx opera singers. This fact drove me to hone my craft so that one day I could sing on an opera stage and make my Filipino fam jam proud. I didn't pursue opera; instead, I chose to continue writing songs and performing them around the city. I still don't see many Filipinx's on stage; don't get me wrong, we exist and we take up all the space we can, but there isn't a ton of us performing. When I see other Filipinx's performing I revel in their artistry, much like my Filipinx classmates did whenever one of us brought in our Filipino *baon* to school. If I could make a career as a musician, if I could be successful enough that I gain recognition globally, I want every queer Filipinx at home to see me. And if I could send my six-year-old self a message, I'd say, it's so important, whether you are an academic, a journalist, a musician, a dancer, a poet, a lawyer, a doctor, a nurse, a teacher, a caregiver, an entrepreneur, whatever your little heart dreams of, or wherever you are right now, that you know you are worth it. Your dreams are beautiful, you will spark a revolution every time you proudly declare your Filipinx self. Never let anyone bleach your melanin, erase your history, we've had centuries of oppression that have already taken so much of us. Insert your gorgeous gold skin into every white nook and cranny, let them absorb your radiance; remember your ancestors and take up as much space as you need. No one else will give you space if you continue to deny your identity.

Queer Diasporas on the Front Line

Interviews with Benjamin Bongolan and Constantine Cabarios

In this chapter, two front-line community workers in Toronto share their experiences of providing support to LGBTQ newcomer youth, caregivers, and Filipino gay men who have been affected by HIV/AIDS. As queer Filipinos themselves, Benjamin Bongolan and Constantine Cabarios respond to questions that draw out the underlying tensions of their race and gendered identities in a predominantly "white" profession in the Canadian context. They discuss the stigmas encountered within diasporic Filipino communities around queerness, and the heterogeneity of the queer Filipino community in Toronto and its diverse needs. Further, both Bongolan and Cabarios highlight the importance of creating safe spaces and increasing the accessibility of services, while working towards establishing policy changes that benefit the margins of the margins of the various communities they serve.

Benjamin Bongolan, *newcomer family settlement services coordinator at The 519 (a nonprofit LGBTQ community in Toronto)*

How does your queerness and Filipino/a-ness influence your front-line community work?

My lived experience as a Filipino and as an LGBTQ-identified person help inform my everyday work as a public servant supporting LGBTQ newcomers, newcomer youth, caregivers, and refugees. My personal understanding of Filipino and queer culture help ensure that the programs and services I offer are reflective and responsive to the needs of the communities I serve. When I first began my career in settlement, I knew immediately that working with my own community meant going into churches and other faith-based community settings. Interestingly enough, faith-based communities are where I first formed my own personal group of queer Filipino friends. At this time,

I worked at a youth organization in North York in 2010. I was successful in engaging newcomer Filipino youth at local Filipino churches and in various high schools in northwest Toronto. Having spent many years with the Filipino Students Association of Toronto at the University of Toronto, I was able to tap into my personal network of friends, colleagues, and contemporaries and this contributed greatly to my success in the settlement services sector. When I entered the more specialized field of LGBTQ newcomer settlement, my lived experiences with homophobia, coming out, and personal LGBTQ experience in Canada further enhanced and complemented my training in newcomer settlement services. Ultimately, my queerness and Filipino-ness inspired me to constantly consider intersecting equity issues, analyze systemic barriers, and contribute to the well-being of people, particularly those from ethno-racial groups and individuals who identify as LGBTQ.

The opportunities I've had to embrace my sexual orientation and cultural identity did not occur as an act of personal will; instead, I've been greatly influenced by studying and working in the city of Toronto since I was eighteen. These formative years provided me with great exposure to the communities and cultures that I didn't always have access to while living and growing up in Mississauga.

From your perspective and experience over the years, how has the queer Filipino/a community changed in terms of visibility and presence?

From my personal experiences in Toronto, I can attest that opportunities to access queer Filipino-specific spaces have been minimal. There is very limited targeted outreach conducted to seek out queer Filipinos and engage them in meaningful LGBTQ programming. Correspondingly, when there are opportunities available for queer Filipinos in queer Filipino-specific spaces, challenges arise with regard to the types of programming that are offered, and whether that space is focused more for newcomers, youth, adults, seniors, academics, or artists. There is no singular "LGBTQ Filipino Event" that can fully encompass all of the needs of the queer Filipino community in Canada.

What are some improvements that can be made to better serve queer Filipinos in Canada (in terms of service provision, policy, or in the community in general)?

Thorough and effective LGBTQ Filipino programming would consist of offering a full suite of services spanning newcomer settlement, housing, trans, family, employment, social recreation, culture and media arts, and education and training opportunities. The challenge lies in creating these queer Filipino-specific opportunities and seeking out funders (ministries, corporations, or foundations) to provide permanent financial support for these services. From my experience with community outreach, I learned that your visibility and consistency are vital to your success in engaging with a specific demographic. When I first began outreaching to newcomer youth, I noticed that in the specific neighborhood I was working in (Weston Mount Dennis and Eglinton Avenue West), this specific demographic spent most of their time in the local Tim Hortons and McDonald's, and thus I made myself present in places where these youth congregated. The same principles apply when seeking out LGBTQ Filipinos; you must strive to be present where they may be present, be creative with where you outreach, and recognize that the LGBTQ Filipino experience certainly extends beyond the Church and Wellesley Village. The principle of self-determination is essential when developing programming for queer Filipinos; one must recognize that queer Filipinos are experts on themselves, and they should have the ability to have control the decisions and outcomes in their lives; thus it's imperative that queer Filipinos be included in the program development process.

Constantine Cabarios, *registered social worker and mental health counselor for the AIDS Committee of Toronto, providing clinical counseling to a diverse group of gay, queer, and bisexual men.*

How does your queerness and Filipino/a-ness influence your front-line community work?

The queer Filipino community, from my perspective, has adapted to the societal, economic, and political changes in Canada according to the dominant ideologies at the time. As with most immigrant communities who have settled in major Canadian cities, queer Filipinos/as after "coming out" have either chosen to remain close/connected to their family supports, have been distanced/ostracized by their kin, or have remained "in the closet." This adaptation I believe is not unique to the Filipino/a experience. However, what sets us apart from the Canadian experience is the strong sense of family, spirituality, hard work, respect for authority and wisdom, and "quiet" perseverance that has allowed the Filipino/a queer community to flourish alongside and within the mainstream LGBTQ communities in Canada.

My queerness and Filipino identity have definitely had a strong influence on how I practice my community work. Since I grew up here in Canada and have resided here for most of my life since 1975 (I am now forty-nine years old), my queerness was shaped by the predominantly white LGBTQ perspective due to my interactions with members of the mainstream gay community. During my formative "coming-out" process, there were only a couple of gay Filipinos that I could look up to for guidance within my circles, and the other "role models" were either white or from other cultures. Hence, my queerness was shaped by a global point of view with a regard to multiculturalism within a pluralistic, Canadian society.

The coming-out process for me as a gay Filipino man was different in that I had to find a balance between respecting my strong Filipino family values while incorporating the more liberal, Canadian queer sensibility. As a result, I did not have to follow the Western way of coming out and making a dramatic declaration of being a *"bakla"* in front of my family, my friends and community; rather, I chose to gradually acclimatize those that needed to know, and inform them about who I was when the moment called for it. This process, I believe, has defined how I practice my community work as a social worker within the HIV sector providing clinical counseling for gay, queer, bisexual, and trans-identified men.

Given that social work is a predominantly female and white profession, my multiple and intersecting identities (i.e., racialized, privileged, and queer person of color) come into play in how I interact with and provide services to diverse individuals, groups, communities, and others in the sector that I work in. I feel that my competence, experience, education, skill level, and credibility may be under scrutiny because Filipinos are not as well represented in this sector compared to other health care professions (e.g., nursing, personal support worker, home care support, and other related fields). I have always maintained my unique Filipino perspective on queer identity regardless of who the service user may be, and as a result this has brought in a dynamic global connectivity/approach in how I interact with people.

I have come to realize that due to our diverse, historically colonial past, which is entrenched in religious, cultural, socioeconomic, and political influences, I am able to connect with many if not all of the service users I have come in contact with due to my intersecting identities. I believe that my queerness and Filipino-ness are an advantage in how I practice as a social worker because of my adaptability to different work environments, resilience, work ethic, respect for process, humility, quiet perseverance, and strong sense of culture and heritage. It is these universal qualities that people connect with, and that is what it takes to be able to do "good" community work.

From your perspective and experience over the years, how has the queer Filipino/a community changed in terms of visibility and presence?

As stated earlier, Filipinos/as have adapted to the norms of Canadian culture while retaining their uniqueness within a pluralistic and multicultural society when the first wave of immigrants (i.e., mainly educated health care aids and technicians) arrived during the 1970s and later when the second wave (i.e., mostly female domestic workers and nannies) came in the following decades. With the permanent settlement of these immigrants, the queer Filipino/a presence and visibility also grew and adapted to the Canadian ebb and flow of queer politics, identity, and ideology.

I have been a silent witness to the historical accounts of the gay bathhouse raids in the 1980s and the HIV/AIDS epidemic which devastated the gay community in subsequent years. It is because of this that I carry the same burden of "survivor guilt" as some of my clients who until today continue to struggle with grief and loss. Those who have fought for the rights and privileges that the broader queer communities are enjoying today include the newcomers who now have the freedom to marry as equals under the law. Throughout my involvement within the HIV sector, I have been fortunate enough to have met incredible and brave Filipino gay men who, through no fault of their own, either succumbed to the ravages of the disease or continue to live on and act as role models for other Filipinos who may have been infected or affected by HIV today. In some cases their visibility and presence came to the forefront because of the diagnosis and through circumstances beyond their control, and their "coming-out" process was accelerated.

With the advent of same-sex marriage around 2006 and more recently transgender rights, there is more awareness of the larger LGBTQ presence and there is more acceptance in Canada. As result, the queer Filipino/a community has mirrored these changes in their participation in the political process and community advocacy work. This is evident in some of the emerging literature coming out of the social media platforms and artistic communities, which is building confidence in the activist movement and mobilizing the next generation to freely express themselves in mediums that are alternative, groundbreaking, and a fusion of both Filipino and Canadian qualities and values.

What are some improvements that can be made to better serve queer Filipinos in Canada (in terms of service provision, policy, or in the community in general)?

I believe that as a service provider, there needs to be more awareness and education in the community. Filipino media, both traditional and social media platforms, should include all voices, and especially our LGBTQ communities. Throughout my years of involvement in social service agencies like the Silayan Filipino Community Centre and Asian Community AIDS Services, I have been able to assist in developing organizational policies and programming and contribute to research projects which hopefully will advance the presence and visibility of the queer Filipino/a voice in concert with the broader Asian communities.

According to a Toronto census analysis in 1996, Filipinos are the second-largest ethnic population in the Greater Toronto Area (GTA). There should now be a concerted effort for better service provision, adaptive immigration policies, and culturally relevant services specifically targeted to outreach to Filipinos, or at the very least address their emerging, unique, and perhaps unidentified needs—notwithstanding our queer brothers and sisters. For example, as a clinical counselor, I have only provided service to one Filipino gay client in the last four years of my employment. The client was referred to me by another agency that happened to know of a Tagalog-speaking counselor at a "large AIDS service organization." What would have happened if the worker was not aware of other Filipino counselors? Where would this Filipino client have gone if he was looking for a qualified Tagalog-speaking counselor? Given the growing size of the Filipino population in the GTA, one would assume that there may be more queer Filipinos who may need counseling due to issues related to mental health, HIV/AIDS, or sexual identity. Perhaps Filipinos/as do not see themselves accessing services provided by other Filipinos/as, and they prefer to seek the services of non-Filipinos/as, or they are more adaptive or resilient in their coping?

I feel that an awareness of the common issues (e.g., political discourse/involvement) that all Canadians share regardless of their cultural and ethno-racial background should be incorporated in the daily fabric or conversations of the Filipino communities so that they are more engaged with the broader Canadian communities. However, our

Filipino cultural values will never and should not change when it comes to the importance of family and kinship; and in this regard, some of the attitudes and stigmas around common issues such as mental illness, HIV/AIDS, and homophobia should be in line with how Canadian society has approached and progressed with providing appropriate services to the LGBTQ communities. I believe our ability to adapt to our changing environment is a key strength in our survival as a community and that the more visible we are in representing our uniqueness within the mainstream and broader Canadian context, the more we will be able to create the necessary and appropriate programming of services and policy changes within the communities we belong to.

Queertopia Is a Country That Does Not Exist

Artist Statement and Interview with Julius Poncelet Manapul

**The Unattainable Queertopian Fantasy:
Growing Up Queer as the Outsider**

My installations and performances explore the idea of the postmodern gods in today's society and how we place icons of models, celebrities, and the homonormative on altars to be adorned. The idea of power and perfection that our culture embraces, and which is manifest in our new "postmodern gods" in the age of our "new idol culture," is questioned in my work. The effects of religion and postcolonialism on queer identity are paramount in understanding the nature of the queer community and the repression it creates. It is through the re-creation and execution of new religion and culture that I focus on hybrid manufactured gods, altars, and shrines of homoerotic representation. This only exists in my alternate reality that I have created since childhood, where I still wish to wake up to a new fantasy where religious beliefs, cultural differences, and queer bodies can belong. I consume these images, digest the materials, and regurgitate them to create new hybrid forms.

It is my childhood experiences and adolescent years of discovering my sexuality and masculinity and how they were accepted and rejected in social norms that heavily informs my work. I cut to create these drawn images. I explore gay magazines and pornographies for my collages and installations, transforming the images into heavenly altars and shrines of homonormative questionings. In the act of cutting, I create religious and regal patterns from the male forms, revealing and concealing the male body at the same time.

The only way to escape the confinement of religious and social norms as a boy was to focus on an alternate reality. I remember trading my action figures for my sister's Barbies and using my mother's shoebox to cover a toy remote-control truck I got for Christmas, transforming this male norms object into a float parade for the Barbies to ride on. At an early age I learned to alter and transform my reality into my imaginary world to fit my needs against what the religious conventions and social norms expected of me. As I grew older, fashion magazines and sexuality captured my attention. These four things: religion, the refashioning of gender-prescribed roles, Westernized versus Indigenous fashion, and sexuality have had a big influence in my life and are recurring themes in my work.

As much as ideas of gender roles and sexuality have influenced my work, so have experiences of racism and historical colonization. When I immigrated to Canada from the Philippines at the age of nine in 1990 I felt alienated and mocked for the way I looked, my poor command of the English language, and my cultural habits; my way of being was tested and seen as primitive to the Western concepts. I was not supposed to eat rice with my hands or squat on the floor when I'm not in the mood to sit in a chair; I needed to be tamed as the Spaniards did the natives in the Philippines. Again, I was faced with a set of boundaries and rules of behavior. Growing up in Canada as an adolescent exploring the queer communities for the first time, I experienced a great deal of racism and a sense that I was the "other," and years later when I visited the Philippines again in 2004 I became the other as well, due to the changes the Western culture had inspired in me. Feeling like I did not belong to neither of two countries, I have embodied this hybrid form of new alternate culture without land. This is a feeling of racial melancholia as told by David L. Eng in his book *The Feeling of Kinship,* where he explores the lack of belonging, the feeling of being sad with the loss of one's heritage, yet not knowing what was lost at the same time. This ask the questions: where do I fit in? and how can I belong other than "whitewashing" myself for survival and opportunity? The other awakening question is, why do I need to fit in to a category of always knowing and being the norm at a certain place rather than unknowing and outside the norm? My artwork now asks the question, who is exotified within the constructed fantasy between utopian difference and belonging? I wanted to construct my own utopian fantasy of belonging that may not exist in the tangible concept of reality but does exist in the mind, memory, dreams, the experience of otherness, and the feeling of kinship that exists with all the people going through racial melancholia.

My crafted hybrid work stems from my childhood and young adult experiences of struggle that I had to face through unattainable fantasy. They represent an alternative world where I can belong without any restrictions. A new breed of what is held up as the "sacred and the profane" at the same time, unbound by conventions and control. This new utopian hybrid manufactured fantasy can only exist in the mind or as an idea. We all have different perceptions, taste, and values as much as we assimilate to the norm, so our idea of utopia can never manifest due to constraining obstacles of differences that we place on each other. The theorist Giorgio Agamben simultaneously envisions the contemporary as the darkness and the light creating the in-between. To see darkness is to know the presence of light and to see light is to know the presence of darkness; it is this middle ground and the in-between that creates the present. My interest lies in this thin line of knowing and unknowing, the thin line of the horizon, being in the present and the unattainable utopian future we can never touch. Dare to create the thoughts of the alternative from the conventions of religion, gender, race, fairy tales, capital power, commodity, homonormative, and everything in between. What I have found as a diasporic queer Filipino was fear and isolation to cloister myself in my own shadows. It is to live among others which awakens my own existence; it is this act of gathering and mental gathering that is a big challenge in life. It is also another way that I can get closer to the unattainable queertopian fantasy before one disappears and walks alone towards death of the imaginaries.

Growing up in the Philippines as a gay boy gave me another perspective on queer identity outside the North American norm. My experience as a gay Filipino finding my place in religion, queer culture, and queer identity is deeply personal. The harsh reality for many queers of color is that sometimes our messages are lost and taken from us. Our rights to speak out and stand out are merely imagined worlds that we must construct.

I cut gay magazines and gay porn, both digital and print, to create drawn images. The act of cutting out cultural aesthetics, ornamentations, insects, and primitive patterns allows me to comment on power and privilege in the daily lives of both queer and heteronormative communities. By cutting patterns from the white male masculine form, my work reveals and conceals the male body at the same time, suggestively playing with colonial tropes of the wild, primitive colonizer of transformation and conformity of my childhood experience. Creating a space of my own, I have crafted homonormative gods, demons, and queens, which begs the questions, what is sacred? What do we worship or hold up as perfect? What is masculine? Who decides? And who has the power?

My earlier art borrows iconography from structures of oppression in my personal and cultural history and my pieces constructed from gay pornography. These creations invert the power dynamics present in my personal experiences of religion, immigration, sexuality, and gender. In the show "Cabinet of Queeriosities" curated by Marissa Largo for Toronto World Pride 2014 at a pop-up gallery, I looked to the cultural aspect of the cabinet of curiosity and the crafted aesthetics in parallel to queer identities. Repeated images and patterns were used throughout my art practice.

My work is deeply personal. In it I explore the hybrid nature of Filipino culture and my queer identity. With the aid of collected personal documentations and pictures, merged with publicly available prints and digital images that have penetrated our perceptions of cultures and sexuality, I explore my ideas of identity and, in new hybrid forms, I create temporal personal utopian domestic spaces. From competing viewpoints, I create hybrid forms. This exchange between the audience and the producer, the private dimension and the public dimension, is as much part of the exchange in my work as the tangible staged constructions.

The utopian space that I create only exists in my dreams and imaginaries and will never manifest in reality. Everybody's utopian image is just as selective and diverse as their taste, knowledge, experience, and upbringing. All this lends to different readings that become familiar or unrecognizable to every individual audience exposed to any crafted image or space, either public or private. It is these subjective readings, interpretations, and constructions that make our individual utopia so unattainable; it can never manifest itself in the realm of reality. Thus for now it will have to remain within the realm of the other side of the looking glass, where happy endings remain a fantasy and a childhood memory that can only be remembered in imaginary curious space.

As seen from the show "Through the Looking Glass: Inside My Domestic Portrait" curated by Laura McPhie at UTAC Gallery, the University of Toronto Art Centre, 2013.

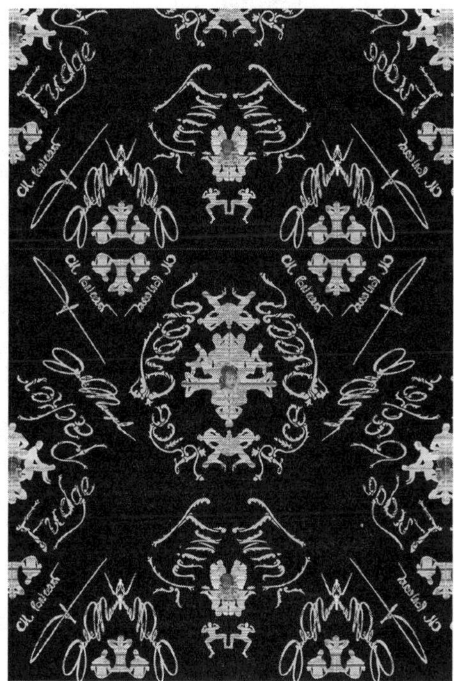

Julius Poncelet Manapul,
Queertopian Marriage Wallpaper,
digital collage, 2013.

MARISSA LARGO: The center of your installation for *Visualizing the Intimate* was a crib crafted from *balikbayan* boxes for your fictional child Christian James. The empty crib gestures to your impossible presence as a queer diasporic Filipino man within a nation that imagines your subjectivity outside the heteronormative, domestic realm. What does the impossible child mean for you?

JPM: This impossible child represents my own experience with the unattainable structures and confines of heteronormativity within the ideal family structures of the mother, father, and biological child. The child also represents the unattainable structures and confines of homonormativity viewed as the perfect middle-class white or whitewashed queer male with an adopted child, or any child that can never be biologically both parents. These expectations of family structures limit my own queer diasporic identity to rebuild my own understanding and readjust my own reality to conform to these structures given to us. This *balikbayan* box represents these diasporic exchanges between two cultures and the idea of my own

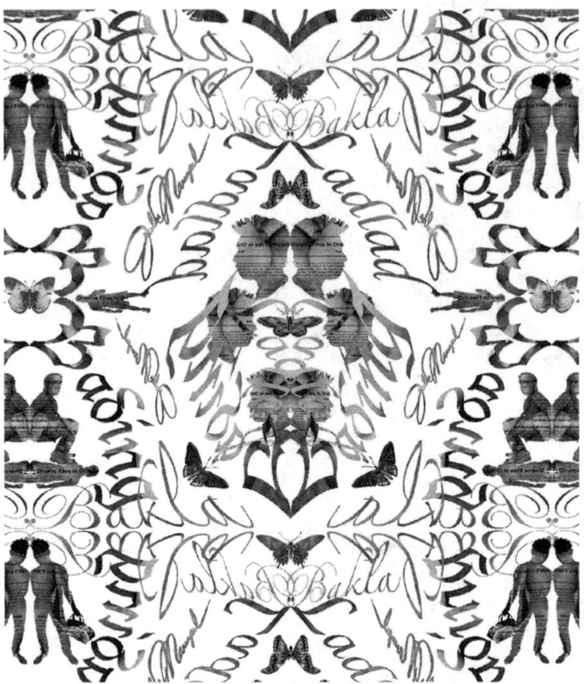

Julius Poncelet Manapul, *Queertopian Divorce Wallpaper*, 2015.

rebirth and transformation to new and different understandings, re-creating a new child that can never exist within the unattainable queertopia.

ML: In our work for "Cabinet of Queeriosities" for WorldPride Toronto 2014, we very much worked within and against globalized notions of queerness that are capitalized by celebratory pride movements. How do these tensions with dominant notions of queerness continue to materialize in your current work?

JPM: Since the main materials that I use in my work are images of queer male identities within the circulated realm of all media such as gay porn, gay magazines, gay advertising, and so on, the available images that I use represent a certain view of the queer community which is the predominant homonormative representation. It is important that I use these materials that are given to me to comment on the lack of visibility of my own cultural queer identity, thus again limiting us through the typical rice queen's dreams, the potato queen's nightmare, and the feminization and exoticization of queer Asians living in the midst of Western queer culture, as David L. Eng explored in his book *Racial Castration*. I need to be more aware of where I fit in all this, making my work more intimate and personal using my own personal images and personal documentations as part of my medium that I weave through these homonormative materials.

ML: The backdrop of your queertopia was once your marriage license wallpaper. It is now your divorce wallpaper. How do you reconcile utopic imaginaries with unfulfilled realities in your art?

JPM: These utopic imaginaries, or as I call them "queertopian imaginaries," are the unattainable expectations we entrap ourselves into, and to reconcile with these is to accept that there are certain possibilities that are not predominantly represented within our cultures. If artist who are queers of color refuse to talk about these pressing issues as queer Filipinos, I will continue to make work that I can find my own identity in and re-represent these pedagogies where I cannot find myself in.

ML: Your ornamental aesthetic as seen in the intricate curvilinear designs of your *Murses* [see photo, page 72]disguises racist and homophobic slurs within. What does this act of subversion in your art mean for you as a queer Filipino?

JPM: These racist and homophobic texts are rendered purely aesthetic as part of the *Murses* patterns which remove their meanings in exchange to pure visual. It is an act of reclaiming these texts that have burdened my past experience and reusing them to become the *Murse* that is commoditized within the realm of race, sexuality, and gender. These male purses can be sold to us in ideas and representations, but not the tangible paper objects themselves, which are unusable.

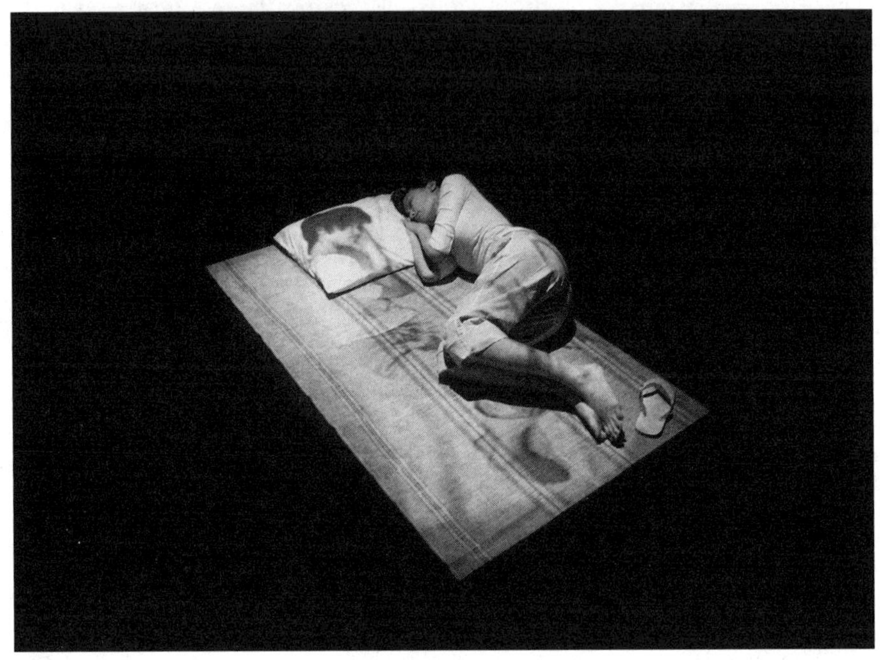

Marissa Largo, *Jet Lag*, video installation, performance, 2009.

Part 4

Mourning, Militancy, and Queer Critique

In the multimedia performance piece *Jet Lag*, Marissa Largo interrogates her embodied experiences of diaspora, racialization, and gender through the re-creation of a childhood memory of a visit to the Philippines. Like the pieces in this part, *Jet Lag* points to how the effects and affects of multiple temporalities weigh heavily on the body and psyche. *Jet Lag* points to the multiple temporalities inhabited by queer diasporic Filipinos and suggests that dreams or fantasies allow us to image alternative, more just realities. This echoes Roland Coloma's assertion that "fantasy occupies the realm of the imagination, the creative, the possible and the impossible, reflecting both conscious and unconscious desires and wishes" (see Coloma's chapter in this volume).

The contributions in this part problematize such celebratory and homonationalist narratives of inclusion into the nation-state by reminding us, at times even painfully, of the violence that queer Filipinos—located both within and outside of Canada—have experienced and continue to experience. Whether reflecting on hybridized aesthetics in queer Filipino dance, or the effects of militarism and uneven economic development across Canada and the Philippines, or the effects of HIV/AIDS, all these works contribute to understanding queerness from a transnational perspective. These works attempt to grasp the untranslatable; they attempt to gesture to memories and longings that may not automatically be legible in Canada, but that nonetheless influence how sexually marginalized Filipinos inhabit and interact with this space.

Dancing Queer to Be Intimate with the Roman Catholic Church, or Remembering Augusto Diangson

Patrick Alcedo

Continuing the ethnographic work I started in "Sacred Camp: Transgendering Faith in Philippine Festival" (2007), this visual essay argues that the paradoxes in *panaad* or devotional promise, sacred camp, and carnivalesque provided the late Augusto Diangson with ways in which to "claim membership in the Roman Catholic community of Kalibo, Aklan, central Philippines while also negotiating the Church's institution of heterosexuality" ("Sacred Camp," 107). Similar to that earlier piece, this essay maintains that stories of mischief about the exploits of the Santo Niño (Holy Child Jesus) outside the cathedral—for example, of him leaving the altar at night to play with kids in the plaza or the town square—and his gender ambiguity as a prepubescent boy further allowed Augusto to dance as a Folies Bergére chorus girl during the annual Ati-atihan festival.

Celebrated every January, Ati-atihan is a festival that simultaneously honors the putative ancestors of the Filipinos, the dark-skinned Atis (Negritos), and the Santo Niño, arguably the most beloved religious figure among Catholic Filipinos. Ati-atihan attracts Catholic devotees to go to Kalibo, for they believe that the Santo Niño showers blessings and accepts forgiveness during the festival. A devout Catholic, Augusto believed that it was the Santo Niño who saved him from a near-fatal appendectomy and blood poisoning. He promised the Santo Niño that he would dance for him for three straight days during the festival to publicly express his gratitude.

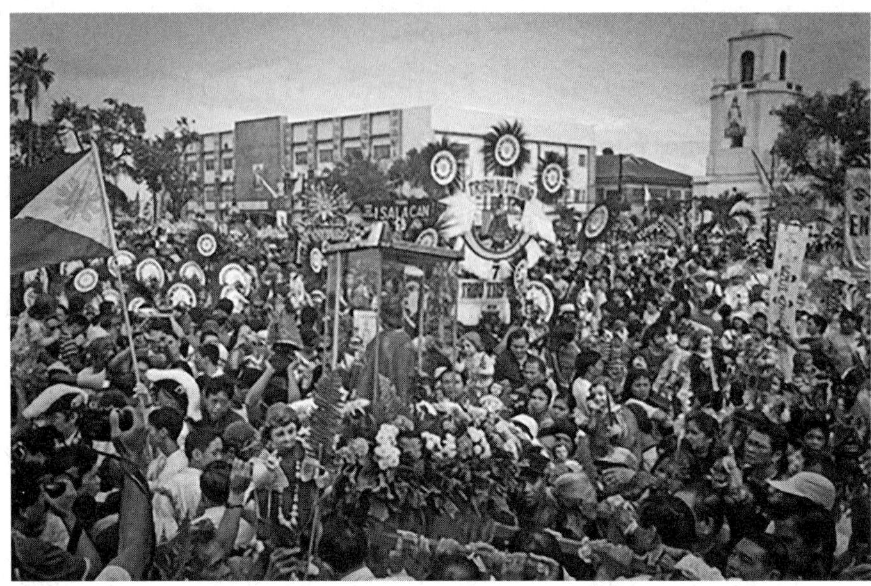

Ati-atihan Festival in Kalibo, Aklan Festival. Photo by Nana Buxani.

Augusto identified himself in his native Aklanon language as an *agi*, a man of the "third sex," as he explained in English. As a self-identified gay individual myself, I have always had a sense of intimacy with Augusto, who I fondly called Tay Augus, Daddy Augus. Growing up in Kalibo, my siblings and I took ballet classes with him during summer months; he shaped our earliest understanding of what it meant to perform for the public, to be on stage "with a heart," as he would constantly remind us during our dance recitals. As I explain in "Sacred Camp," to be called a *bakla* (a Tagalog word) in Aklan could be derogatory, as its semantics are not as fluid as the Aklanon *agi*. *Agi* encompasses the gamut of being gay, homosexual, queer, third sex, for its semantics are playful. *Agi* acts like a floating signifier and embodies campiness, as in the Aklanon banter: "*Nag-inagi ka eon man.*" "There you are *agiing* again." "There you are with your dramas once more." It is in the fluidity of *agi* that Augusto decided to navigate both his quotidian and his festival life.

While in my earlier article, I paid attention to Augusto's transformation into a Folies Bergére chorus girl—his putting on makeup, donning a headdress, and wearing a sequined bustier and thong—here I focus on his actual dancing, that moment when he went out of his house to dance in the streets of Kalibo in drag. Such travesty—ubiquitous in the

Ati-atihan: of priests in mufti, of newlywed men dancing as pregnant women, of men and women in *mummuu*-like garbs to blur gender identities, and others—I understand through the optic of the carnivalesque.

When I asked Augusto a year later what drew him to the figure of the Folies Bergére chorus girl, and why of all the possibilities of mimicry he chose to embody that image for his *panaad*, he said, *"Dahil manami guid a nga mayad do andang costume, ag andang choreography ag saut."* "Because their costumes were extremely beautiful, and their choreography and dance were so well-put together." Augusto fondly recalled the first Folies Bergére performance he saw, a group of high-kicking Caucasian-looking women in stiletto, in the late 1970s in Manila at the Cultural Center of the Philippines, which was built by Imelda Marcos to announce that the Philippines was capable of providing a nurturing and appreciative oasis for world-class performances. But it was the "Ice Folies," a cast of international figure-skating champions, that left a deeper impression on him. This group corporealized for Augusto the foreign image and the kind of dancing body he was imitating from the magazine his niece had sent him from Chicago almost a decade earlier. Their performance embodied the extravaganza he wanted sewn into his *panaad*; it would deepen the rest of his Santo Niño devotion and continually change in an excessive fashion the face of the Ati-atihan festival.

Augusto saw these Caucasian-looking figure skaters at the Araneta Coliseum, which in the early 1960s was considered to be the world's biggest covered coliseum. This performance space has always been the venue for Binibining Pilipinas, the "Miss Philippines Beauty Pageant," the grand prizewinner of which represents the Philippines in the "Miss Universe" contest, and first runner-up in "Miss World." In 1975, the coliseum gained additional international visibility when it hosted the unforgettable "Thrilla in Manila." The still much talked-about event in the boxing world pitted Muhammad Ali and Joe Frazier against each other.

Augusto clearly remembered the teams of white lithe bodies, dancing mostly to adagio music, that were floating on the immense oval rink to please the Filipino public. He was in awe to find that the coliseum in a tropical country—right in the middle of the urban center Cubao and a known space for other events, such as high-priced gambling in a cockfighting derby—suddenly had its performance space filled with ice. Just like Ali and Frazier were never the same after that unforgettable match, Augusto left that coliseum no longer the same person. He was firmer in his resolve to stay as a Folies Bergére chorus girl throughout his Ati-atihan life.

Roughly two decades after that phenomenon, in 2000, his sacred promise remained intact. He used a white tiara as a necklace, wrapped it around the base of his headdress, teasingly covered his vulgar thong with a drooping tutu, fitted precious and semiprecious jewels into his fingers, and street danced for three straight days. His body in fulfillment of his *panaad* braved the scorching sun, its reverberating heat, and the thick humid air that enveloped the entire town when night fell. Augusto became like those Folies Bergére chorus girls on ice, but not quite. He was different, much more glamorous and extremely passionate, dignified in the silver tiara—a surfeit of style and intense feelings that together motored his loyalty to the Folies Bergére chorus girl image, and the repetitiousness of his *panaad* that exposed him to the elements and calcinated his skin.

Carnival: Street Dancing

This vignette recalls my Ati-atihan street dancing experience with Augusto on January 16, 2000.

Augusto left the room to announce that it was time to street dance. He stooped a little and held his headdress to fit his bedroom door. Ayan na sya! "There he is!" one of his friends from Manila exclaimed in Tagalog after seeing how made-up, coiffed, and dressed-up Augusto was.

Augusto commanded in Aklanon that "all of us should now go out for the procession" and join the musicians who had already started playing in the street. We passed the dining area, marked by a couple of five-foot jars Augusto had bought from itinerant Muslim traders from Mindanao.

When Augusto walked towards the middle of the street, the musicians played louder and Augusto's many onlookers started clapping on the wayside. To get a quick look at him, his neighbors hurriedly left their houses and business establishments. Some of the members of the Chinese merchant family abandoned their grocery store. He waved at all of them, and assumed his position—at the front and center of his group.

Bathed in sunlight, and as if poised for a very long flight, Augusto started dancing, and led them towards the plaza. A group of women rushed towards the group to have a photo taken with Augusto. He placed his bejeweled hands on top of the shoulders of one of the women, and welcomed them to his carnivalesque fold.

After nine hours of street dancing around Kalibo, only breaking for lunch and light snacks on the sides of the streets, I met Augusto once more. The bamboo sulu, *torches carried by some of the group's members, made it quicker to locate Augusto in the throng of people about to be covered by nightfall.*

At six o'clock in the evening Augusto was as resplendent as the transformed Folies Bergére chorus girl I saw early in the morning. His body elegantly held the countless accoutrements and dizzying array of trinkets. The flickering street lamps and the handful of torches illuminated his body. His sequins, beads, precious and semiprecious stones, and fake and real jewelries glinted in all directions. His rhinestones on the high-heeled pink shoes sparkled against the asphalt streets.

After giving me a quick hug, Augusto said to one of his servants, Patukaea eon ninyo do Mambo No. 5 pagkatapos. *He decided that "Mambo No. 5" should be played after the ongoing theme music of* Hawaii 5-O. *I jumped into the ongoing fray, beside Augusto, into this fast-beat music from a TV series bearing the same title that highlighted my childhood years in Kalibo in the 1970s.*

Upon the instruction of Augusto, two versions of Lou Bega's "Mambo No. 5" blasted from the back. The musicians played its tune with their drums, trumpets, and xylophones as if there was no tomorrow. His relatives and servants on top of the jeepney with loudspeakers played the song's recorded Filipino version; its tune was exactly the same, but its lyrics had been changed to Tagalog. Bega's upbeat combination of Afro-Cuban and hip-hop melded with the song's localized, Filipinized lyrics. The two live and recorded versions enveloped the group. Suddenly everybody was waiting for the music's five-beat rhythm supplied by the professional musicians in concert with the taped music as "one-two-one-two-three."

After the chorus came the music's bridge, and the musicians played this part with more gusto. The servants turned the speakers up louder on the jeepney. Some of the onlookers dashed in to dance with the group. In this heightened atmosphere, Augusto developed his cha-cha-cha, unleashed a renewed energy that allowed him to move vertically forward and back, and to turn at the beginning of every cha-cha-cha. He full turned, spotted efficiently; the elaborate costume and the high-heeled shoes proved not to be barriers in his dancing. Until the music ended, he alternated between the basic cha-cha-cha of forward-and-back and its much more complex turning version.

The music changed to "Happy Days Are Here Again," reminiscent of the U.S. colonial period. Augusto shifted his footwork to a 4/4 tempo to fit this imported music that Kalibonhons rearranged for drums and xylophones.

At around nine in the evening, with that colonial music inching him forward, Augusto reached the cathedral. Augusto went right away inside the church, dipped his right hand into a bowl of holy water, genuflected before the altar, and knelt on one of the pews. Outside the cathedral, the noise and the fun were slowly diminishing. Not bowing his head as usual to steady his headdress, he looked up to the altar where the Santo Niño was. He made a sign of the cross, and stayed quiet for a moment to say a prayer. Away from his music and dancing space, he kept his "female" body still, fervent in posture and seemingly pious in thoughts. His accoutrements were intact, motionless, but sparkling like tiny stars under the cathedral's yellow lights.

This vignette closes the circle of Augusto's transgendered performance for the Santo Niño. In the street dancing that was synonymous with a carnival event—its time accented and atmosphere intensified to the extreme—Augusto found his ultimate expression of faith. Through his excessive "female" body, he danced the *panaad* he had been observing for decades. He paraded his Folies Bergére chorus girl body and imbued it internally with sacrality and unknowingly made it ooze with campiness. Against the background of the carnival, he danced this double corporeality, which was still recognizably Augusto and always took on a foreign self with a fey sensibility.

The carnival offered Augusto a non-quotidian frame in which to transgender his faith, to temporarily become a "woman" so as to innocuously announce his being an *agi*, and to provide some laughter to the Santo Niño and His many faithfuls. While it opened the floodgates of inebriation, excess, and transvestism, the carnival set in motion the two webs of meanings: *panaad* and sacred camp. It was the carnival frame in the Ati-atihan, the third web of meaning, that in the end allowed Augusto's "female" body, which he took the trouble to make up and dress up, to kneel in one of the pews of the Kalibo Cathedral to be left alone all by him/herself, to be momentarily lost in prayer.

Such choreography of gender-tweaking and authority at a time and space that are outside the everyday resonates with the carnival as described by Mikhail Bakhtin. My observations are inspired by his two major works: the earlier *Rabelais and His World* (1968) and the later *Problems in Dostoevsky's Poetics* (1984). The carnival offers participants limitless possibilities to be different from, or even to be complete

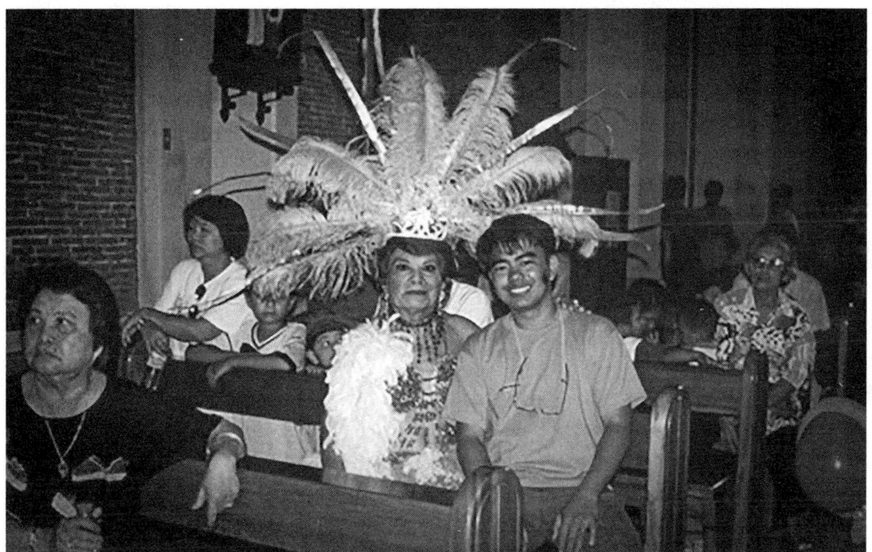

Augusto and friends participating in the parade.

opposites of, their ordinary selves. In the carnival everyone has a place and share in the feasting: the rich and the poor, the powerful and the powerless, and the heterosexuals and the homosexuals. This special realm that is fraught with inversive behaviors and the promise of being an Other is what Bakhtin calls carnival or carnivalesque. Since the status quo allows the participants to do a "cartwheel" of themselves, the carnival is like a catharsis where the masses can summon up bodies they keep hidden in the quotidian. To disembody their pent-up selves is to cast an explosion of extraordinary signifiers into this transient universe, and to claim signifieds that mattered most to them.

In response to the question of why his transgendering should not be seen as sacrilegious, Augusto would say, *"Ginasugtan man ni Monsignor para magkasadya kita."* "It is allowed by Monsignor so that we all can have fun." He danced away with this permission as far as he could, into the land of his fantasy in order to embody a "female" self he could only prepare for and dream about in the everyday. In this imaginary universe, Augusto corporealized what the public appreciated: year after year he transgendered himself and convinced the church that the doors of the Kalibo Cathedral should be kept wide open for "her." Augusto pushed the boundaries of Kalibo's Roman Catholicism, demonstrating how tolerant it could be in its accommodation of each and everyone's excesses,

how soft towards class and gender differences, and how accepting of
the fantasies adherents wished to experience at the moment.

The carnival leads to a diffusion of authority, and Augusto seized some
of this. In the front and center of the line, Augusto became a "female"
leader, who determined his group's music and dance steps. The festival
participants centered their attention on Augusto as he and his group
illuminated and energized their path with their bamboo torches, irides-
cent costumes, blasting musics, and dancing bodies. Augusto composed
a kind of choreography for the group and for the others, who were
affected by his group's inversive qualities and decided to jump from
the wayside. He performed acts of extraordinariness as his choreography unfolded, igniting all sorts of signifiers to explode in his midst. He
laced together the costume, the music, and the dance steps to be one
with the carnival spirit. In this state of exalted, double being, Augusto
hoped that he would be transported closer to the Santo Niño, or better
yet, that the Santo Niño would be affected as well to join him and his
cohorts in their street dance of praise.

His eighty-year-old self carried his costume with the panache of a
young ballerina and the conviction of a devout Catholic from morning until well into the night. He rhythmically defined his performance
with a cacophony of music that was both anachronistic and contemporary. "Happy Days Are Here Again" from the country's colonial past
was no longer a song about the U.S. Great Depression of the 1930s,
but was newfangled to become a melody of fun and laughter for the
Kalibonhons.

Augusto climaxed his street dancing with his favorite Latin music for
that year, "Mambo Number 5," created by Lou Bega, an artist born in
Germany who has a Ugandan father and Italian mother. On the asphalt
streets, Augusto fitted his moves to this music that Bega originally composed for salsa dancing. His marrying cha-cha-cha with Bega's salsa
music was so infectious that the crowd did not mind the disparity, a
mismatch, which on the ballroom dancing floor would have been automatically judged as a non sequitur. Augusto stepped forward with his
left foot, did a right-shoulder half-turn with his right foot on the next
count, and finished with a pas de bourée to face back front. His high-
heeled shoes elevated his dancing body and made his turns, which were
as smooth as the countless *soutenu, chaînes*, and pirouettes I remember
he danced before his ballet students, all the more challenging. Even
though he had to hold his torso straight to keep erect the towering

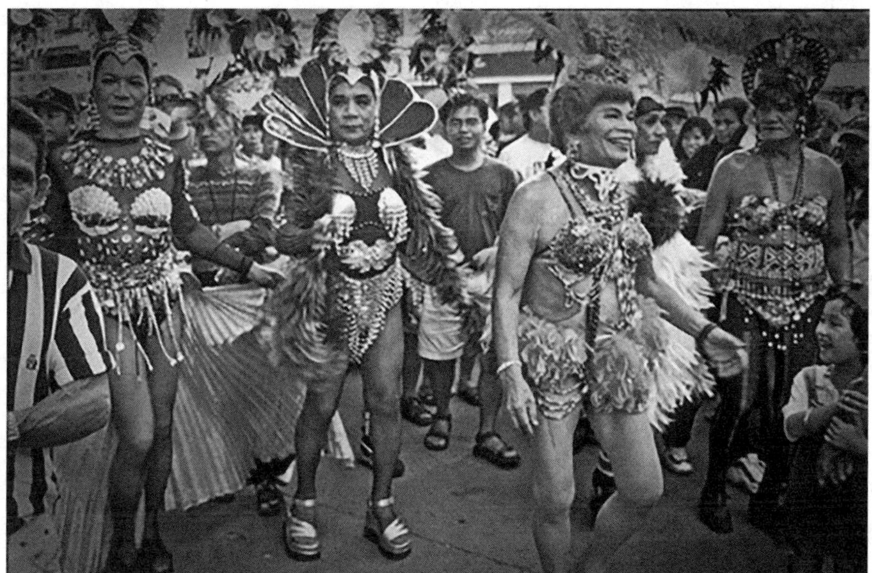

Augusto and Patrick inside the St. John the Baptist Cathedral in Kalibo.

headdress, he still found the freedom to oppose continuously his arms with his busy feet, to snap intermittently his bejeweled fingers, and to sway demurely his feather boas-covered hips. He repeated these steps until the music faded out to segue into another music of his choice.

Nonetheless, in spite of this newfound authority, Augusto had always subsumed himself to the Santo Niño, and at the end of the day he took repose in the cathedral. He did not dance to unseat the power of the Santo Niño but rather to confirm it all the more.

Every time Augusto covered his face with makeup and slipped on the different parts of his costume, he departed from his quotidian self and entered a new carnivalesque self. After partaking in a sumptuous meal, when the last of his guests had left his home that night, Augusto called his helper, Ambo, to help him find the tens of hairpins stuck around his headdress, and to unhook his feather-boas tutu and beaded bustier. Augusto reminded Ambo to hook carefully his headdress and the soft tutu on the nail just above the many images of the crucified Christ, and to store the bustier back in the Carnation box under his bed, below the Santo Niño statuettes. Ambo then left the room quietly. I followed him to leave Augusto alone to take off his wig, to slip off his spandex thong and panty hose, to stack his jewels inside a case, and to smear his face with Ponds Cold Cream to erase his thick Japanese-made *kukuryo* and U.S.-made Max Factor makeup. When his servants were about to turn off the lights, I left Augusto to retire in his yellow-walled bedroom, with his many figures of the smiling Santo Niño, the crucified Jesus Christ, and the beneficent Virgin Mary. It was in that room littered with the many parts of his costume, hooked and tucked away in several corners, in the sacred presence of those devotional figures, that Augusto ended his outpouring of feminine and exaggerated energy which left him spent corporeally but overjoyed spiritually.

What Augusto additionally made more tangible was how agentive, or following the parlance of the Philippine studies scholar Sally Ness (1992), how "resilient" cultural bearers could be in their ability to take on different bodies in response to competing historical and religious forces that infiltrate their ordinary and extraordinary festival lives. It was a resiliency that ultimately made his undulations to the music so infections, and his iridescence against the bamboo *sulu* torches and under the cathedral's yellow lights difficult to eclipse. Indeed, as Martin Manalansan theorizes, and paraphrasing him, Augusto played with the world and authored himself to make sense of his sexuality and his Roman Catholic upbringing. In the floating signifiers that comprised the Ati-atihan carnival, Augusto wended his transgendered body to produce a sea of signifieds. His faith in the Santo Niño and the mischief and gender ambiguity of the Holy Child served as Augusto's rudder—keeping him, his *agi* identity, and his fiercely fabulous choreography on a steady, dancing keel.

Note

An earlier version of this essay appeared in *Aklanon Lens*, January 2007.

Bibliography

Alcedo, Patrick. "Remembering Augusto Diangson: A Santo Niño Dancer." *Akeanon Lens*. (January 2007).
———. "Sacred Camp: Transgendering Faith in a Philippine Festival." *Journal of Southeast Asian Studies* 38, no. 1 (February 2007): 107–32.

Bakhtin, Mikhail. *Problems of Dostoevsky's Poetics*. Trans. Caryl Emerson. Minneapolis: University of Minnesota Press, 1984.

———. *Rabelais and His World*. Trans. Hélène Iswolsky. Bloomington: Indiana University Press, 1968.

Ness, Sally Ann. *Body, Movement, and Culture: Kinesthetic and Visual Symbolism in a Philippine Community*. Philadelphia: University of Pennsylvania Press, 1992.

Militarism, Violence, and Critiques of the Neoliberal State

This chapter brings together various progressive Filipino activist groups whose work tackles multiple forms of exclusion and oppression faced by Filipinos in Canada and in the diaspora that are perpetuated by patriarchy, homophobia, transphobia, and sexism. As the contributions that follow demonstrate, some of their political stakes include—but are not limited to—immigration and labor, transgender violence, and LGBTQ rights which have become a recent focus of these organizations as they see the importance of intersectional politics in bringing about systemic change and justice to some of the most pressing social and political problems facing diasporic Filipinos. While critiquing the shadows of U.S. imperialism in the Philippines and the institutional racism of Canadian society masked as neoliberal benevolence, these contributions highlight the leadership of queer Filipinos in the Left Movement in Canada, and in particular, the vision and vital interventions of Filipina lesbian women at the forefront.

Radyo Migrante's Trans Day of Remembrance

Interview with Mithi Esguerra

On November 20, 2014, Radyo Migrante CHRY 1055, a Toronto-based Filipino community radio show, marked the 2014 Trans Day of Remembrance by highlighting the case of a trans woman named Jennifer Laude who was murdered by U.S. Marine Private First Class Scott Pemberton on October 11, 2014, in Olongapo, Philippines. Producer Rhea Gamana interviewed Mithi Esguerra of GABRIELA-Ontario (an organization committed to the promotion and defense of the rights and welfare of migrant Filipino women in the province) on the ongoing struggles of LGBTQ individuals in the Philippines, the neocolonial tensions of the Philippines-United States Visiting Forces Agreement, and the continuing fight for transgender rights. The following is a transcription of the inter-view by Lean Laygo and Ysh Cabana.

RG: I am with Mithi Esguerra of GABRIELA-Ontario, and she will discuss with us how LGBTQ issues are linked with social issues in the Philippines today. Please welcome Mithi Esguerra and thank you for gracing us here at CHRY. But first, please tell us what GABRIELA-Ontario is and please give our listeners a backgrounder about the situation of our LGBTQ compatriots in the Philippines.

ME: Good day Rhea and our listeners at CHRY. Thank you for having me here today. GABRIELA-Ontario is an organization of Filipino women here in Ontario. Our mandate is to advance the rights of Filipino women in relation to advancing the rights of Filipino people as a whole. So we are advocating for genuine national liberation in the Philippines and genuine democracy as a solution to the current economic, social, and political problems in the Philippines today.

I'd like the listeners to know that I speak as an ally of the LGBTQ community and not as somebody with lived experience as an LGBTQ individual. I say that because somebody from the LGBTQ community would give a different insight and approach to the issue that we are talking about today.

You wanted me to talk a little bit about what the situation is like for LGBTQ individuals in the Philippines today. It's hard to describe it exactly in just one statement. I was reading earlier today that there was a survey that was done that ranked the Philippines as one of the most gay-friendly places in the world, and it's based on the opinions and responses of the people who were surveyed. It was based on how the majority of the respondents agreed with the statements that gay people should be respected and accepted in society.

Those may be the opinions of individuals, but on the more struc-tural level there is definitely room for improvement in terms of the protection of the rights of LGBTQ people in the Philippines. In terms of antidiscrimination laws, there are laws in place against discrimina-tion in employment and the provision of goods and services, but these are not nationwide laws. Same-sex marriage is something that's been a topic of debate in recent years. There's been a lot of strong oppo-sition from politicians and also a lot of strong opposition from the Catholic Church in the Philippines. There have even been attempts by some lawmakers to put forward a law banning same-sex marriage.

In the media, you see LGBTQ individuals who are more visible but in my opinion, they just occupy a niche in pop culture. Like, in the fashion and entertainment industry they're highly regarded. In movies and TV shows we see them, but more in comic roles. So there's still a lot to be done in terms of raising awareness on sexual orientation and gender identity issues.

But there has also been an increase in advocacy on the part of organizations formed by the people from the LGBTQ community itself. The first organization was actually formed in 1994; it was called Pro-Gay Philippines–Progressive Gays of the Philippines. This was a group that was formed not only to bring forth the issues of identity but also in response to the economic changes that were happening at the time in the Philippines, which was the value-added tax to goods and services. Essentially, it was like the goods and services tax and the harmonized sales tax here, but it was something that was going to be a huge burden to working people, so this was something that a lot of people in the Philippines rallied together to oppose. It was something that affected our brothers and sisters from the LGBTQ community as well, so they organized around it.

Since then, a lot of other groups, primarily in universities, have been formed.

There was a political party that was established in the last elections in the Philippines. You also see pride celebrations that are happening in the Philippines now, but definitely there is still a lot to be done. Even in the language that is used in discussing matters of sex orientation and gender identity, you'll see that it's quite limited in comparison with the terms that we have here in North America that reflect the spectrum of gender identities. So essentially there's still a lot of room for exploration on that issue in the Philippines.

RG: Speaking of lives, let's move on to the case of a transgender named Jennifer Laude who was allegedly killed by U.S. Marine Private First Class Scott Pemberton on October 11 this year. Please tell us about that and how it is connected to the very much talked about Visiting Forces Agreement (VFA) that has existed in the Philippines for a very long time.

ME: Jennifer Laude was a trans woman, twenty-six years old, who was found dead in a hotel room in Olongapo city. She was found leaning against the toilet bowl of the hotel room with bruises all over her body, and it was discovered from the autopsy that her death was because of drowning—she was drowned to death. The last person seen with her based on eyewitness identification was a U.S. soldier named Joseph Scott Pemberton.

A case was filed against Pemberton on October 15, but he did not show up during the preliminary investigation on October 21. He is currently being held in Camp Aguinaldo, which is a Philippine military facility, but he's being held there within the Joint U.S. Military Advisory Group facility or JUSMAG. It's a U.S. body that provides advice and training to the Philippine military, and that is something that was established many years ago in the U.S.-Philippines military agreements.

The case of Jennifer has once again brought to the forefront the debate surrounding the presence of U.S. military troops in the Philippines. U.S. military troops have had a long history of presence in the Philippines because of the mutual defense treaty between the Philippine government and the U.S. government that was signed in 1951. Under the terms of the mutual defense treaty, both countries are to give each other military assistance in the event of threats to the national interests of either country.

There were military bases in the Philippines until the agreement expired in 1999. But after that, the Visiting Forces Agreement was put into place; it was an agreement that set up provisions for a U.S. military presence in the Philippines without the presence of actual bases, but it also allowed U.S. troops to be stationed in the Philippines for indefinite periods of time. Now there's the Enhanced Defense Cooperation Agreement (EDCA), which has been put into place to supposedly enhance—based on its name— the cooperation between the two countries' military forces. It sets out provisions for a rotational presence of U.S. troops in what they call "grid locations," which are essentially military facilities in the Philippines.

The relation between these U.S.-Philippine agreements and the murder of Jennifer Laude is the fact that it was a U.S. soldier, Joseph Scott Pemberton, who was in the Philippines—he was participating in recently concluded joint military exercises as part of the VFA. The fact that he is now being held in a secure facility protected by the U.S. military also shows the flaws in the military agreements where U.S. soldiers who are in the Philippines are able to commit human rights violations with impunity.

RG: I mentioned this to you just before we started this conversation. There was footage of one newscaster who said, "Why are there some people who are trying to make this case of Jennifer Laude political? Why not simply show sympathy to Jennifer and to her family?" What can you say about that?

ME: I've read a lot of commentary about the death of Jennifer, and some people are saying that these leftist organizations are taking advantage of her death to put forward their agenda. When people say we're putting a political spin on this issue, they're referring specifically to the fact that we're raising the issues of the VFA and the EDCA. Like I said before, the murder of Jennifer by a U.S. soldier happened in the context where all these unequal agreements between the Philippines and the United States are in existence.

Some other people are even saying, "Well, you know, Jennifer could have been murdered by anybody else. It just so happened that he's an American soldier. So that's why your organizations are able to put forward your political agenda." But Jennifer's case is not an isolated case, and there have been instances before when Filipinos have been murdered by American soldiers who are on Philippines soil because of joint military exercises. For example, in 2002, the Philippines government was waging a war against supposedly "Muslim extremist terrorist groups." But there were a lot of civilians hurt in the operations that the government undertook. And at that time, there were also joint military exercises where U.S. soldiers are not supposed to engage in combat but an individual named Buyong-Buyong Isnijal was shot to death by an American soldier. Eyewitnesses attested and identified the American soldier who shot him.

In 2006 Suzette Nicolas, who is better known in the media by her alias "Nicole," was raped by a U.S. soldier with the assistance of a few others. That was such a long process. But Nicole was able to keep strong and actually speak out in public to go through the whole legal process. These murders happened because of the presence of U.S. troops in the Philippines that were allowed by the treaties.

So Jennifer's murder is not an isolated murder. It's political because the Philippine government is allowing these human rights violations to take place without much effort to pursue justice for the victims because it's protecting its own interests. In fact, the VFA and EDCA are currently in place to supposedly help in the modernization of the Philippine military and to make it more effective in responding to instances of threats to national security and to provide humanitarian aid in cases of natural disasters or other crises in the Philippines.

But what we've seen in the past years until now is that the military aid coming from the United States is being used by the Philippine government to target the people who are critical of the latter. It is being used to crush what the Philippine government terms an insurgency but is actually the people's movement. You've seen how the Philippine military has been implicated in the murders of human rights activists, student leaders, and journalists who have been critical of the government. But the training coming from the United States and the military assistance are being used for that purpose. Or in the case of Buyong-Buyong Isnijal, some military personnel are actually active participants in whatever combat operations are being carried out which end up injuring innocent civilians. In this process, it's those people or groups in Philippine society who are already relatively powerless, like people from peasant communities, women, children, and LGBTQ individuals, who are most often the casualties of these attacks on people's rights. To the Philippine government, that's just mere collateral damage in the war against the so-called insurgency.

Like in the case of Jennifer Laude, a lot of progressive and nationalist organizations have said that her murder once again proves that the VFA should be abrogated. But the response from President Benigno Aquino III is that one simple incident doesn't mean a whole treaty should be abrogated. Also, his response to the demands or the suggestion by some that he should attend the wake of Jennifer Laude was so insensitive and undiplomatic. He said "I generally don't attend the wake of people I don't know." And he tried to expand on it: "I don't want to be a burden to the family by attending there." Some people were saying "Ok, fine. He doesn't necessarily have to attend the wake. But he should, at least, have had a more sensitive response." For me, his response just shows that there's really a completely disregard for the lives of ordinary people. The protection of the state interest, the interest of the ruling class takes precedence over the lives of people like Jennifer Laude.

Of course, observers, or the people who've analyzed Jennifer's body, say that there is evidence showing that it was murder committed in the heat of rage. There is evidence to conclude that it was a hate crime because Jennifer was a trans woman. There is a lot of violence perpetrated against trans people and against LGBTQ individuals, and it's important for people to learn about this. As you know, there are other groups that are saying "Never mind the political issue, never mind the issue of the U.S. bases. Let's just look at it from the lens of identity. It's a hate crime, that's all it was. Let's not consider the aspect of U.S.-Philippines relations in the matter anymore." I don't think those two things should be separated because there is an issue of power relations, not just among the dominant groups in Philippine society. Also, trans people are already disadvantaged because of their gender identity. But in a country like the Philippines, where the majority of the population are struggling to make ends meet and there are only a ruling few enjoying economic and political privileges, that means the majority of LGBTQ people are also within those disadvantaged sectors. So they are already disadvantaged in terms of gender issues. But the struggles that they face are made worse because of those two intersecting problems. So those two issues of gender and class cannot be taken apart.

RG: Final message to us for today on Trans Day of Remembrance.

ME: There is a campaign in the Philippines to seek justice for Jennifer. We, in GABRIELA-Ontario, are participating in this campaign. We want the legal process to be thorough as it should. We want the suspect to be held accountable for her murder.

What we also want to bring to people's attention is that the issue of Jennifer's murder is something that needs to be looked at from all sides. Like what I've been saying before, there definitely needs to be more awareness raised on the issue of trans people, more discussion, more understanding of their issues. There need to be more structural changes in order for the rights of trans people and others from the LGBTQ community to be protected so that they don't have to be subjected to hate crimes. But there also needs to be critical examination of the policies that are put in place in terms of foreign relations, specifically relations between the Philippines and the United States.

We are firm in our stand that the Visiting Forces Agreement should be abrogated because it's supposed to be a mutual agreement that would bring mutual benefits. But we know, these two countries are not starting on an equal footing. Then, the majority

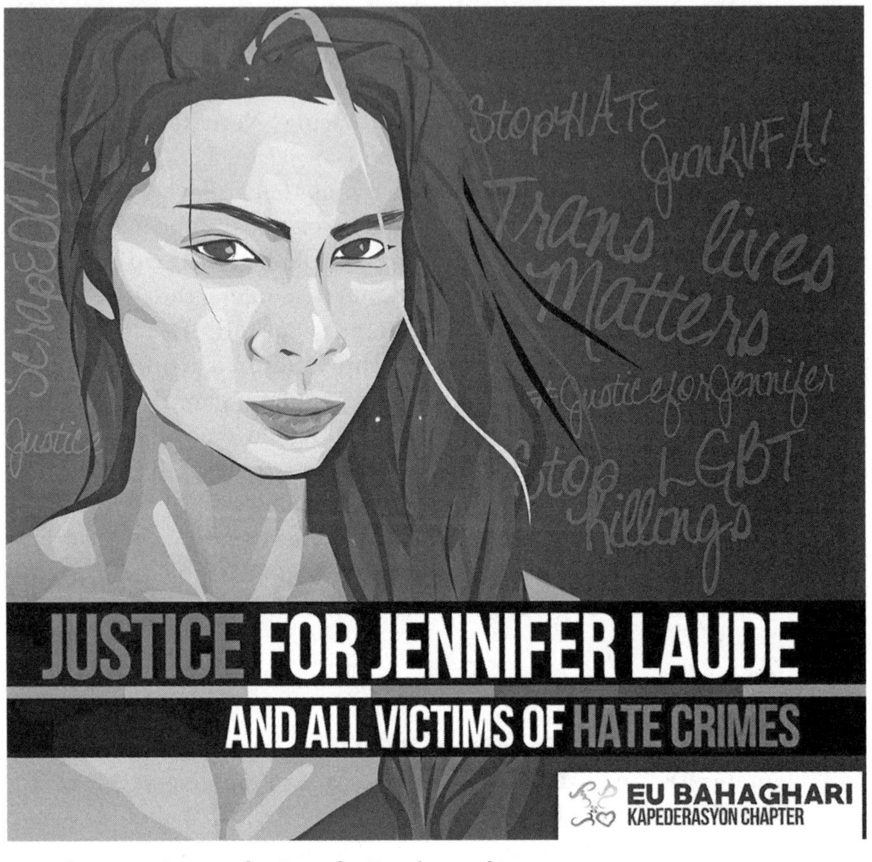

Kapederasyon, Justice for Jennifer Laude graphic.

of the Philippine population are not benefiting from that. It's a very big issue.

We commiserate with the family of Jennifer Laude and the families of other trans people who have lost their family members because of hate crimes. We also commiserate with the families of those whose children, mothers, or fathers have become victims of human rights violations by agents of the Philippine state or U.S. soldiers in the country, for that matter.

We encourage people, because there are so many factors to consider, to contact us and we'd be more than willing to shed more light upon these issues.

RG: Thank you Mithi of GABRIELA-Ontario.

Out Now! U.S. Troops, Out Now!

Anakbayan Toronto

Out there, there is too much that the mainstream media have published; out there, it's been a taboo topic. If you're still trying to figure it out, this is the best time to stand up for justice. Jennifer Laude's murder case is not an isolated one-off. There is a history of brutal crimes involving U.S. troops as they conduct war games in the home front.

With much love and acceptance of our sisters and brothers from the LGBTQI (Lesbian, Gays, Bi-, Transsexual, Queer or Questioning, and Intersex) community, Anakbayan Toronto unites with the global alliance of mass organizations in solidarity with the family and supporters of Jennifer Laude, a twenty-six-year-old transgendered woman who was tortured, as evidence shows, and brutally killed in an Olongapo lodge on October 11, 2014.

Coming from different backgrounds, we work in solidarity with different sectors in addressing issues such as gender-based violence while at the same time claiming our stake in calling for justice for the poor, the marginalized, and the oppressed peoples.

We are in the thick of the conversation where the aspects of sexual orientation, gender identity, and expression (sogie) have been singled out to conclude that it was a hate crime done by a certain Marine Pfc. Joseph Scott Pemberton. But in the context of the Philippines as a client state of the United States, ethnicity, nationality, and class should have been scoped out in the pursuit of the case, or any case involving the U.S. military, for that matter.

Though the Subic naval base officially closed in the 1990s, crimes against Filipinos at the hand of the predator U.S. military persist. Laude's death came about at the end of the joint military exercises under the Visiting Forces Agreement (VFA) as ratified by the Philippine Senate in 1999. In 2006, Lance Corporal Daniel Smith was slipped off to American custody despite the court sentence that he was guilty of the rape of a Filipina and should be confined in a Philippine jail.

Americans never left the country, as pointed out more recently with Washington top officials and the local puppet government clamoring to sign the Enhanced Defense Cooperation Agreement (EDCA), which permits an unlimited number of U.S. soldiers to put up their bases anywhere in the archipelago.

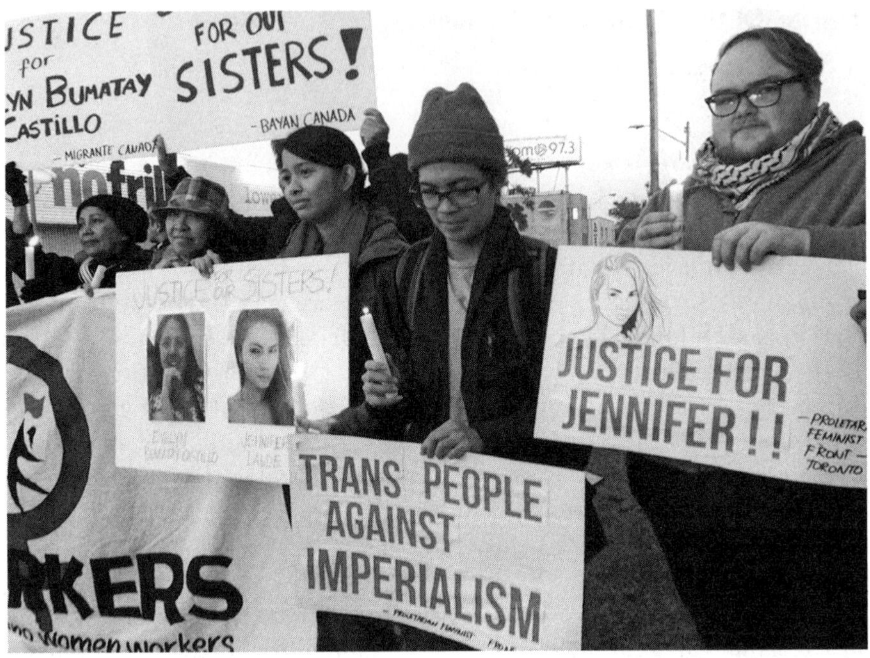

Members of the Toronto chapter of Anakbayan, a comprehensive, national democratic mass organization of Filipino youth, at a vigil for Jennifer Laude.

Clearly, there is a significant and concurrent growth of atrocities where there is a large military presence. The VFA and EDCA have not only violated Philippine sovereignty, but agreements as such act to legally protect U.S. troops from being prosecuted and punished for gross human rights violations in the country.

We call on the U.S. authorities to turn over the American Marine to the Philippine government for further investigation of the incident. We urge the Philippine government to act swiftly, and provide transparency in accordance with the proper legal process of its law. Furthermore, the B. S. Aquino government must stop defending so-called foreign alliances, which are skewed and only serve to protect the vested interests of the U.S. imperialists.

"My heart goes out to the family and friends of Jennifer Laude. With the ongoing colonization of the Philippines, the threat of violence is never too far, especially for queer and trans women. It is time for the U.S. military to leave the Philippines and it is time for U.S. imperialism to end now!" says Anakbayan Toronto member Zenee May Maceda

As a progressive Toronto Filipino youth organization, we are joining the call to all Filipinos around the world to intensify the demand to scrap the VFA and recently signed EDCA, and the complete expulsion of U.S. troops from Philippine soil.

It is widely ackowledged that the escalation of the U.S. imperialist presence sustains the systemic deprivation of the already imperiled sectors of society. Just as migrants', women's, and children's lives matter, transgender lives matter too.

Junk VFA and EDCA!

Down with U.S. Imperialism!

Immediate Justice for Jennifer Laude!

The Toronto chapter advocates around Philippine issues and those affecting the Filipino community in Canada. We work with other Filipino and non-Filipino organizations with similar aims and objectives.

Two Stories of Murder

Lui Queano

1. Jennifer Laude, Transgender

He was draped in love on that night.
Peace written all over his face
He had no reason to fear
None to mar
His feeling of pleasure and solicitude
He must have felt like a quiet stream
Or sea shore
Or purling brook caressed by the wind,
A mirror looking up at the wide sky
But that was also the night of treachery and murder
When a bloodhound American soldier
Killed you, Jennifer Laude
Stuffed your head into the toilet bowl
Until you choked to death
Every fibre of your body twisting and shaking to the end
Before you were clobbered, beaten up,

Punched in the nape and throat
Pounded hard even as the night watched in horror
A thousand punches must have broken
Your face to a pulp
Now suffused with thick blood,
At the hand of the brute,
All under protection of the Visiting Forces Agreement.
Riding on the Enhanced Defense Cooperative Agreement
While meekly watched our imperialist puppet of a government
Who hardly had balls to bring the killer to court,
Even as the masses of our people loudly rallied
And cried out for justice
When will justice ever be served,
Alight on the grave of Jennifer?
Where will justice come to compensate
Every unimaginable beating and torment that you received.
For it was not only you that was slain,
Our country, too, was severely violated, lost its sovereignty,
The VFA surely benefited only the visiting forces,
As our government stood impuissant to enforce its laws
On the American behemoth,
Soon, there was no murderer to persecute,
The criminal flown away with no one to take responsibility
As in times past;
Because our country, Jennifer Laude
The country you loved might as well have lain with you,
Long battered by dark forces, imperialist oppression,
Yet, the struggle of the oppressed masses will continue
Inevitable like hurricanes venting its fury against foreign domination,
As freedom is won, justice will be served in the end
To all who have given up their lives or fallen victims in the struggle.

2. Evelyn-Bumatay-Castillo, Caregiver

You were driven to a foreign land
In pursuit of the dream you could not hold in your hand
Unknown to the loved ones you left home,
Every dollar remittance that you made
You paid dearly with your own person,

Your own self-esteem and dignity peddled in the open market
Brazenly crafted with the government Labor Export Policy,
You had a tag pinned on you,
Like a common commodity peddled off to foreign bidders,
Primed for your caretaker job by your TESDA training,
Obsequiously diplomatic, readied to serve the foreign master
But fate had been harsh to you
There was a day when your picture was splattered over pages of
    newspapers
You were brutally killed, your body about to be burned
You became fodder for rumor mongers
Robbed of your dignity,
You were portrayed unjustly, your morals denigrated
Truly, no well-meaning capitalist
Would save you
Except the women of your own class who sympathized,
Brought to light your experiences of untold oppression.
Your dignity is the dignity of all women,
The exploited class,
Despoiled of dignity.
You were also Mother,
You were also sister,
You were wife who shared responsibility with your husband,
Who gave birth to loving kids,
You always had a space in your heart
For those who needed comfort and caring,
Those with wounded hearts.
No one understands why till now your brutal death
Has not found justice.
        —Translated by Nonilon Queano

Dalawang Kwento Ng Pagpaslang

Lui Queano

1. Jennifer Laude, Transgender

Balot siya ng pag-ibig nang gabing iyon
Kapayapaan ang nakasulat sa kanyang mukha

Walang dahilan ang pangamba sa kanyang dibdib
Walang dahilan
Upang gambalain kanyang ligaya.
Payapa siyang batis
Payapang pampang at
Sapang ininuman ng hangin
Salaming nakatunghay sa malapad na langit
Ngunit gabi din iyon ng traydor na pagpaslang
Berdugong sundalong kano
Ang kumitil sa iyo, Jennifer Laude.
Nilublob ka sa inidoro
Hanggang doon'y panawan ng buhay
Kumisay-kisay bawat iyong himaymay
Bago yaon'y kinulata, binugbog
Sinapok, sinikmuraan
Hinampas hanggang matulala ang gabing payapa
Waring libong suntok na lumanding
Hanggang ang iyong mukha'y
Namuong mamad sa dugo
Sa kamay ng halimaw.
Sa ngalan ng kasunduang Visiting Forces Agreement
Sa ngalan ng Enhanced Defense Cooperative Agreement
Sa ngalan ng imperyalistang gobyernong
hindi sa iyo umalalay
Sa ngalan ng walang katarungan't hustisyang isinisigaw
Ng buong sambayanan
Anong hustisya ang daratal
Dadapo sa puntod mo Jennifer?
Anong katarungan ang makakamit
Sa bawat tinanggap na hagupit
Sapagkat hindi na lamang ikaw ang pinaslang
Kundi ang bayang kinamkaman na din ang soberanya
Sa mga kasunduang nagsasabi:
Kapag ang mga sundalong kano ay lumabag
Sa sagradong saligang batas ng bansa
Walang pagkakasala o mananagot sa kanila
Dahil ang bayan mo Jennifer Laude
Ang bayan mong mahal ay bangkay ding nakaburol
Pinaglalamayan ng daluyong
Daluyong na siyang papaslang sa impeng dayo

Titindig lalaban ang dantaong inaping sambayanan
Hanggang hustiya, hanggang katarungan'y manaig
Sa lahat na pinaslang ng mga anak ng bayan!

2. Evelyn Bumatay-Castillo, Caregiver

Itinaboy ka sa malayong bayan
Upang katagpuin ang mailap na kapalarang
Hindi dumapo-dapo sa iyong kamay
Lingid sa iyong iniwanan,
Sa bawat padalang dolyar
Kapalit nito'y ang iyong pagkatao
Dignidad na inilako sa malayang palengke
Ng ekonomistang programang Labor Export Policy
Nilagyan ka ng tag ng iyong gobyerno
Inihandang paninda sa mga among dayuhan
Dakilang caregiver mapagkakatiwalaan
Tadtad sa treyning ng TESDA
Diplomado at sinanay para sa dayuhang amo
Ngunit sadyang madamot ang tadhana
Isang araw ng linggo laman ka ng pahayagan
Pinaslang bago tangkaing sunugin
ang iyong bangkay
Kung ano-ano, kung sinu-sino
Nagpiyesta sa iyong kwento:
Tinatakan ang iyong dignidad
Tinawaran ang iyong pagkababae
Sadyang walang mabait na kapitalista
Ang magsasalba sa iyo
Kundi kapwa uring kababaihan
Ilantad sa madla ang iyong kaapihan
Ang dangal mo'y dangal ng kababaihan
Uring pinagsamantalahan
Uring tinanggalan ng dangal
Ikaw na Ina din
Ikaw ay kapatid din
Ikaw na asawa't katuwang
Ikaw na nagluwal sa mga anak
Ikaw na laging may puwang

Upang magbigay ng yakap
Sa mga sugatang puso
Ikaw na ngayo'y pinagkaitan
Ng hustisya't katarungan!

Past Gains and New Beginnings: LGBTQs in the Filipino Canadian Left Movement

Congress of Progressive Filipino Canadians

The first Filipino Canadian lesbians, gays, bisexuals, trans, and queer (LGBTQ) consultative forum held in Canada, titled "Strength, Struggle, Stories: LGBTQ National Consultative Forum," took place in Vancouver, British Columbia, on October 14 and 15, 2014. This forum was organized by the Philippine Women Centre of British Columbia under the auspices of the Congress of Progressive Filipino Canadians (CPFC), and with the support of the Department of Gender, Sexuality and Women's Studies of Simon Fraser University. This event marked a milestone in addressing the need to discuss various issues that concern queer Filipino Canadians' experiences in the community and the broader Canadian society. It highlighted the important roles that LGBTQ Filipino Canadians play in continuing the efforts to resist the rapacious attacks of neoliberalism and imperialism on racialized and marginalized communities, and the implications these have on the Filipino Canadian community, particularly the LGBTQ one.

The two-day forum provided a venue and space for LGBTQ Filipino Canadians to openly discuss and share stories of marginalization perpetuated by patriarchy, homophobia, transphobia, and sexism. The narratives shared in the forum underscore the persisting systemic discrimination and social exclusion of many Filipino Canadian LGBTQs based on class, gender identity, and sexuality. As a result, Filipino Canadian LGBTQ participants collectively drafted the following plan of action to advance their interests and concerns:

> To connect and build networks with other LGBTQ, LBGTQ of color, and people of color organizations
>
> To document and historicize the experiences of LGBTQ Filipinos/as in Canada

> To acknowledge and critique the societal, political, and economic factors that affect LGBTQ Filipinos/as in Canada
>
> To create and foster spaces of dialogue, participation, and involvement for LGBTQ Filipinos/as and their allies
>
> To advocate for the diverse LGBTQ Filipinos/as' concerns in all aspects of Canadian society—legal, social, political, economic, and cultural

Filipino Canadian LGBTQs and the Congress of Progressive Filipino Canadians

The formation of the Congress of Progressive Filipino Canadians (CPFC) signified a new beginning in the Filipino Canadian Left movement. At our first congress held in Montreal, Quebec, on May 1–2, 2010, the CPFC united on fifteen-point concerns[1] that outline an overall program to help build the socialist movement and socialism in Canada. One of the concerns included in this declaration is the concern on LGBTQ—"The rights of LGBTQ against violence and all forms of discrimination to a life of dignity and secured existence." This concern demonstrates that upholding and advancing the struggles of LGBTQ Filipino Canadians is an indispensable component of the overall work of the CPFC and its member organizations, namely the Philippine Women Centre (PWC), the Filipino Canadian Youth Alliance (FCYA), and SIKLAB, a Filipino Canadian workers' organization.

LGBTQ Filipino Canadians are an integral part of the history and ongoing struggles of the progressive Filipino Canadian Left movement. Leading up to CPFC's formation, Filipina lesbian women were pivotal in forming and sustaining the Philippine Women Centres (PWCs) in British Columbia and Ontario. They provided the leadership in the PWCs' educational campaigns and initiatives in leading the ongoing movement for genuine women's rights, human rights, and the genuine development and liberation of Filipina women in Canada. One campaign that has started since the 1990s and continues today is the campaign to scrap the racist and anti-woman Live-in Caregiver Program (LCP), now called Canada's Caregiver Program. Filipina lesbian women, along with other women, also conducted various community-based research on the situation of Filipino mail-order brides in Canada, the de-skilling of Filipino nurses and their fight for accreditation, the housing needs of Filipino caregivers, and economic violence perpetuated against them. They investigated cases of prostitution and the sex trafficking of Filipino women; and also joined rescue operations of Filipino caregivers who experience abuse and violence from their employers.

From past to present, Filipino Canadian LGBTQs involved in the CPFC and its member organizations lead in advocating for the issues facing the Filipino Canadian community at large. LGBTQ members embraced the community's struggles and have been at the forefront in advancing these struggles. CPFC's intersectional analyses of race, class, gender, and sexuality are direct products of their efforts. Given the mainstream LGBTQs' lack of emphasis on the class struggle, the CPFC gives utmost importance in situating the LGBTQ struggles within the larger revolutionary anticapitalist and working-class movement. Filipino Canadian LGBTQs in the CPFC assert their important role in helping build a movement towards socialism in Canada, conscious that the struggle for genuine LGBTQ liberation is fundamentally a struggle against class, women, and racial oppressions.

Discussions from the LGBTQ National Consultative Forum

Based on the consultative discussions, the LGBTQ Filipino Canadian situation is largely defined by the overall situation of the Filipino Canadian community in Canada. Now the third-largest visible minority group in Canada numbering over 600,000, the Filipino community has been largely shaped by federal labor programs, such as Canada's Caregiver Program (CCP), formerly the Live-In Caregiver Program (LCP), and the Temporary Foreign Workers Program (TFWP). Moreover, the Philippines is the number one source of temporary foreign workers in Canada and to date, more than 100,000 Filipina women have come through the LCP/CCP. These programs funnel the majority of Filipino workers into Canada and relegate Filipinos to Canada's reserve army of cheap and disposable labor. Although not formally documented, there is a growing visibility of LGBTQ Filipinos in these federal labor programs. These programs thus situate LGBTQ Filipino Canadians within the overarching context of Filipino im/migration and settlement in Canada wherein Filipinos are systematically denied full participation and entitlement in all aspects of Canadian society.

LGBTQ Filipino Canadians share the same experiences of professional de-skilling and nonrecognition of previous educational attainments with other Filipino Canadians. As a result, Filipino Canadian LGBTQs expressed concerns about being wedged into low-paying, insecure, and unstable employment with limited upward labor mobility. While sharing similar experiences with the broader community, the discussion reveals that LGBTQ Filipino Canadians also contend with their particular struggles based on their gender identity and sexuality. Participants expressed concerns around bullying, lack of social support, and sexual racism as well as being targets of anti-immigrant sentiments from white LGBTQ Canadians. Other issues brought out were bullying in publicly funded Catholic schools, queer health and reproductive rights, and intensifying violence against LGBTQ youth of color.

Moving Forward: Filipino Canadian LGBTQ Organizing and Anti-imperialist Solidarity

The national consultative forum served as a starting point for Filipino Canadian LGBTQs to unravel critical aspects of Filipino Canadian LGBTQ realities and experiences. Based on the discussions and the resulting plan of action, we, LGBTQ Filipino Canadians in the Congress of Progressive Filipino Canadians, aim to pursue the following:

> Hold echo Filipino Canadian LGBTQ consultative forums in other Canadian cities.
>
> Continue to educate, organize, and mobilize the Filipino Canadian community and Filipino Canadian LGBTQs to challenge temporary labor migration schemes that lock transnational workers into a constant cycle and varied state of permanent impermanence.
>
> Be at the forefront in the fight for "genuine settlement and integration" along socialist lines, demand to end these temporary labor migration programs, and advocate for permanent immigration as a solution.
>
> Strengthen support and solidarity with Indigenous peoples, including two-spirits peoples, in their struggles for self-determination, sovereignty, and healing by continuing to be critical of Canada's history, legacy, and continuing colonialism and imperialism of Indigenous peoples, lands, and nations.
>
> Bolster our links, support, and solidarity with our existing networks of LGBTQ people of color and anti-imperialist organizations both locally and internationally, such as True Colors Coalition (TCC), a Filipino LGBTQ political organization based in the Philippines.[2]
>
> Intensify community organizing work from a LGBTQ, socialist, anticapitalist, antiracist, and feminist standpoint to combat

the pervasive dominant culture of neoliberalism on LGBTQ communities that commercializes and profits from LGBTQ identities as well as perpetuating sexual racism through the degradation, exoticization, and objectification of LGBTQ of color bodies.

Be vigilant in protecting established laws, policies, and human rights protections fought by LGBTQs in Canada (e.g., same-sex marriage, human rights protections for gender expression and identity) while at the same time, being critical on how neoliberalism can impinge on LGBTQ rights.

Develop community-based Filipino Canadian LGBTQ educational resources and hold consciousness-raising workshop series on LGBTQ issues that will aim to combat conservative, machismo, misogynist, patriarchal, homophobic, and transphobic values embedded within the Filipino Canadian community and the broader Canadian society.

Continue to foster spaces of dialogue, participation, and support of LGBTQ Filipino Canadians in the CPFC and the broader Filipino Canadian community in order to empower LGBTQs to achieve their full potential as individuals as well as leaders in the Filipino Canadian Left movement and the broader Canadian Left.

These steps are just the beginning as we forge our growing strength and unwavering resolve to bring about genuine social change. We, as progressive Filipino Canadian LGBTQs, will continue to take part and be at the forefront of our community's struggles. We know that our contributions as progressive LGBTQ Filipino Canadians have made past and present gains possible, and will continue to do so in the years to come.

Congress of Progressive Filipino Canadians, 2016

Notes

1. Creating and Nurturing a New Path for the Progressive Filipino-Canadian Community, http://www.magkaisacentre.org/cpfcdeclaration 2010/.

2. The True Colors Coalition is a member organization of the Kilusan sa Pambansang Demokrasya (Movement for National Democracy). It was formed after the death of Jennifer Laude, a trans Filipina woman murdered

by a U.S. military serviceman, Joseph Scott Pemberton, on October 11, 2014. The True Colors Coalition and its sister organization, KAISA KA, a Filipino women's organization, spearhead the "Justice for Jennifer Laude Campaign." TCC.

Education, Activism, and Performance
Filipino Community Organizing and HIV/AIDS

This section foregrounds the activism of Filipino Canadian community members during the HIV/AIDS epidemic in the 1990s. In particular, it acknowledges the work of queer Filipino/a community members who mobilized the arts as a form of public pedagogy in order to promote HIV/AIDS awareness and education. One such effort was the production My Grandmother and I. *Written by Lani Montreal in the early 1990s at the peak of the HIV/AIDS epidemic,* My Grandmother and I *is a play that centers around the death of Dino, a Filipino Canadian gay man who passes away due to an AIDS-related illness. Dino's relatives are in deep denial of his homosexuality and the reason for his death—all but his sister Marissa and his grandmother, who represents a connection to Philippine spirituality and precolonial traditions and to whom Dino appears as an apparition from beyond. Foregrounding the Filipino immigrant experience in Canada in the 1990s, the play grapples with multiple discourses, such as Indigenous rights, racism, homophobia, transphobia, living with and mourning in the wake of HIV/AIDS, and issues of colonialism and globalization—all from an intersectional perspective. The heaviness of the issues addressed in the play is counterbalanced by the humor and melodrama that is characteristic of Filipino cultural valence. For these reasons,* My Grandmother and I *represents an early and important contribution to the queer Filipino/a archive in Canada and acts as an artistic harbinger for the intersectional politics of present-day scholarship and cultural production in the field.*

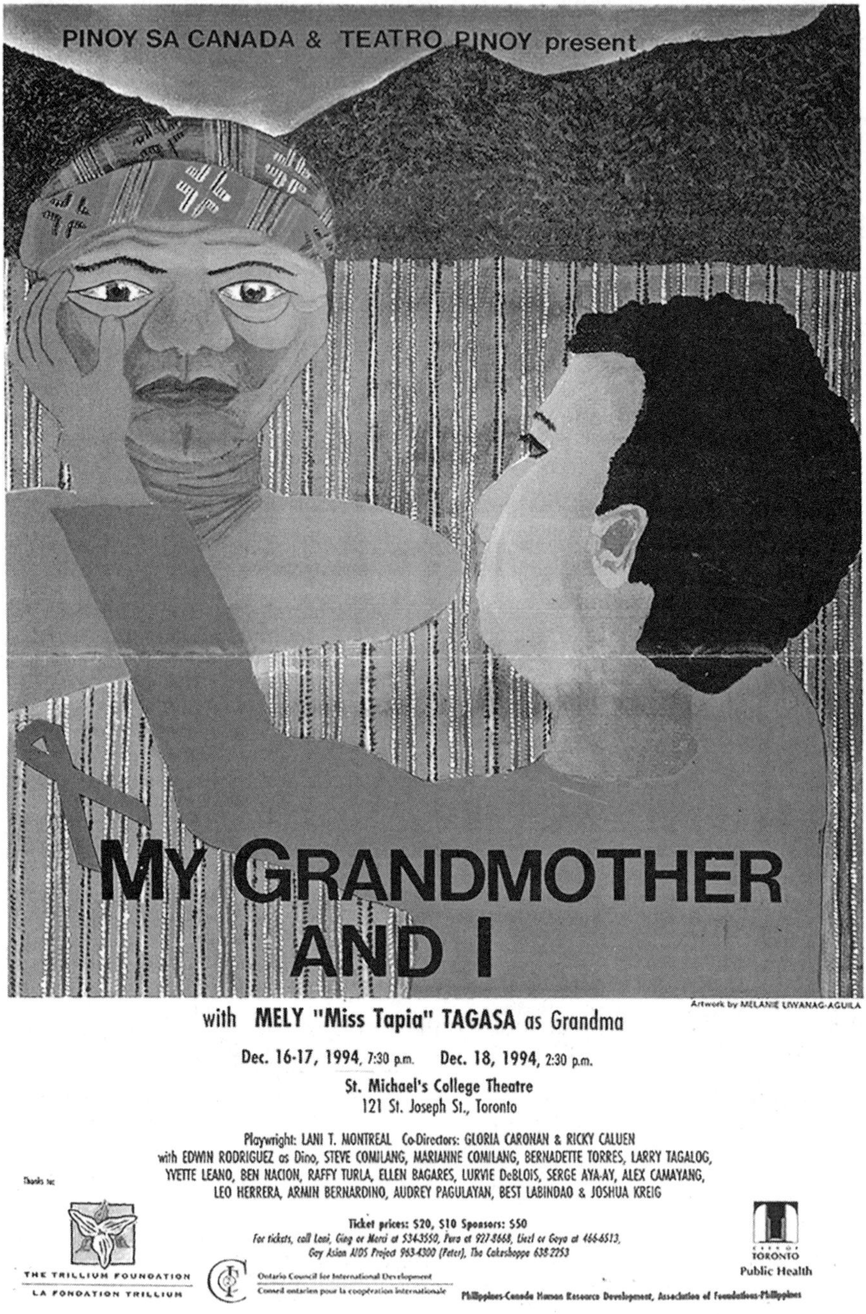

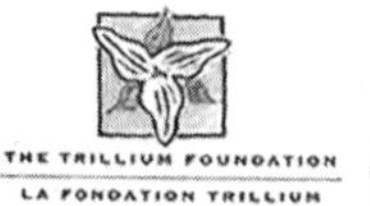

Poster for Lani Montreal's *My Grandmother and I.*

My Grandmother and I: A Play by Lani Montreal

CAST:

Grandmother   About sixty-five years old, Lola (Apo) came from the northern part of the Philippines to Canada when her daughter migrated here to become a nurse. She is Indigenous and received education from the American missionaries, which is why she is fluent in English, although with a proud and heavy accent. Her wisdom came from the mou   ntains and the old-growth forest. (Mely Tagasa)

Dino   Twenty-five years old. Born and raised in Canada, Dino no longer speaks Tagalog or Ilocano or his ancestors' dialect. He is gay and has only begun to accept himself for who he is when he is afflicted with AIDS. (Edwin Rodriguez)

Marissa   Nineteen years old. Bright-eyed and cheery, Marissa is also a straight-A student. She was the only one who accepted her brother's gay identity. When her brother died, Marissa was devastated. She has a native boyfriend whom her father does not approve of. (Marianne Comilang)

Nanay   Nurse. Mrs. Ramirez came to Canada in the 1970s. She studied in Manila and herself experienced discrimination for being a minority. She turned away from her culture because of the pain of discrimination only to discover that it exists everywhere. (Bernadette Torres)

Tatay   Mr. Ramirez met Mrs. Ramirez in the hospital. He was sponsored by his family to come to Canada in the 1970s. He is a lowland Filipino with traditional patriarchal values about family. (Steve Comilang)

Ken   Dino's white lover. Compassionate. (Joshua Kreig)

Jessica/Jessie/Jesus   A drag queen. Dino's close friend. (Larry Tagalog)

OTHERS:

Anito	Woman deity. Strong character. (Yvette Leano)
James	Marissa's native boyfriend. Pensive. (Amadeo Velasco)
Uncle	Retired general in the Philippine Army. Homophobic.
Chris	Dino's friend. Muscular. Straight-looking. (Ben Nacion)
Tina	Cousin. Regular teenager. (Ellen Bagares)
Rick	Cousin.
Aunt Tessie	Lesbian. Mid-30s. (No speaking lines) (Yvette Leano)
Grace	Aunt Tessie's lover. (No speaking lines)
Doctor	(Bill Etzkorn)
Priest	(Serge Aya-ay)
Tribal chief	(Serge Aya-ay)
Diwata	Strong character. (Yvette Leano)
Stranger	Malevolent spirit. (Joshua Kreig)
Aunt Ludy	Uncle's domineering wife. (Lurvie DeBlois)

Other friends of Dino's, closeted and out gays and lesbians.

Relatives of the family.

ACT 1 SCENE 1: DINO'S DEATH

House curtain still closed. In a hospital intensive-care unit. A flurry of clinical sounds. Doctor and nurses inside the cubicle are trying to revive a patient. Voice over.

> **DOCTOR:** We're losing him . . . We have a code blue . . . Get the defib!!! Move back (*nurses echo her words*) . . . Okay, ready, charge . . .

Flatline. Sounds die down.

Center stage lights up. Nanay is seated on a sofa while Tatay paces anxiously. Marissa holds Grandma's hands, their heads bowed. All are expecting news from inside the ICU.

Doctor comes out. Nanay and Tatay rush to meet him.

DOCTOR: I'm sorry. We tried everything we could to save him.

NANAY: We want to see him.

Doctor leads everyone to the cubicle except Grandma, who asks to be left alone. Doctor approaches Grandma and holds her hand and tells her about what happened. Grandma bows her head in grief.

Voice-over of Nanay crying out loud. They come out of the cubicle, Nanay buries her head on her husband's chest. Marissa also embraces Nanay and Tatay. Ken walks to Lola and then to Marissa.

TATAY: Tahan na, Nanay.

Nanay escapes from Tatay's arms and runs to Lola. Tatay stands awkwardly, not knowing what to do. He is macho and wouldn't show tears.

NANAY: Ma, they said they tried everything to save him.

LOLA: But he didn't want to be saved, Josie.

NANAY: Ayan na naman kayo, There you go with your superstitions. This is not the time to make those comments, Ma. (*Tries to help Grandma up*). Halika na. Let's go home. We—we have to make arrangements for the funeral.

Grandma is somewhat in a daze. Marissa and Ken comfort each other. Grandma mumbles softly as she looks back to the cubicle. Lights gradually dim.

LOLA: He didn't want to be saved. Daytoy iti kaya't iti, Apukuk.

SCENE 2: THE ENCOUNTER

Transition to afterlife. In a forest area, Dino awakes and in a daze finds himself in front of a strange old woman. Spotlight on stage left.

DINO: Where am I? Who are you?

ANITO: You are on sacred ground. I am your spirit guide, Apo Kalai-ngan, and I was sent by Apo Kabunian.

DINO: Apo Kabunian? Is that the same Supreme God my Grandma has talked about?

ANITO: Yes, Dino. You know, Dino, your body may have perished but we, your ancestors, think your spirit is not ready for the afterlife. You carry with you so much baggage. Didn't you know you had to travel light on this journey?

DINO: I know, Apo. But no one wants to take this burden I carry with me.

ANITO: Well, you have to go back and leave it on earth where it belongs. Burn it if you must. It won't be easy, we know. Your spirit could roam the earth forever.

DINO: But how do I get rid of this baggage, Apo?

ANITO. You will have to find help. We will allow you to show yourself to one person whom you think has the most wisdom and the greatest capacity to assist you in this mission. Choose wisely.

Quick blackout. Lights on stage right. Lola's bedroom. Her room is decorated with memorabilia from the north, including a photo of Macliing Dulag, the hero of Chico Dam, hanging on the wall. Lola is about to retire and go to bed. Goes about fixing blanket when suddenly she hears a voice calling out to her.

DINO (*voice over*): Lola, Grandma . . .

GRANDMA:(*Startled*) Is that you, Marissa? (*No one replies. Dismisses the thought and goes about preparing herself. Dino calls out again. This time he appears and taps Lola on the shoulder*).

DINO: Lelang . . . Apo (*affectionately*) It's me, Dino.

Grandma tries to brush off the hand of Dino. She peers at him. Dismisses what she sees and suddenly realizes it's Dino! Grandma stifles a scream.

GRANDMA: Apo Santa Maria!

Grandma runs to the door, carrying with her a blanket. Scared of what she saw, she wraps blanket around her. Dino goes to her and tries to calm her down.

DINO: Calm down, Lola.

GRANDMA: But I thought you were dead! No ay al-alia (*tries to scream again*)

DINO: Don't be scared, Grandma! It's really me, Dino!

He takes her to a chair and massages her back. Not looking at him, Lola is calmed by Dino's caress. Then she realizes it's her dead grandson. She tries to scream but no voice comes out.

Dino starts to sings an Ilocano lullaby, the one she used to sing to him when he was small.

DINO: Dong, dong ay. si dong ilay, isinalidumay, dong ay . . . silay . . . si dong ilay . . .

GRANDMA (*loosens up and tries to touch Dino as he sings*): Sikagayam, Dino. It's really you. You did not die after all (*embraces him*).

DINO: No Lola, I was sent back by my spirit guide, Apo Kalaingan.

GRANDMA (*absentmindedly*): The dark spots on your face— they are gone. And you gained weight. You don't have diarrhea anymore? Dios iti agngina, Apo Kabunian. Does your mom know? Has Marissa seen you? They miss you so much, Dino. Miss you so much. (*Hugs her grandson*) You seem cold. Malammin ka (*puts blanket around him*)

DINO: I miss you too, Grandma. But I am . . . dead. (*Grandma's eyes widen as she tries to scream again, but Dino covers her mouth.*)

DINO: Only you can see me. (*Grandma calms down, resigned.*)

GRANDMA: Why? Apay?

DINO: Because I chose you.

GRANDMA: But why? Don't you know I have hypertension? You should have chosen Marissa. You almost gave me a heart attack (*realizes something*). Ay amukun . . . You've come to take me with you, ha? Well, tell them I'm not ready . . . I haven't even used my senior's pass for half-price movies yet. You promised to take me to . . . to . . . this movie. What is that movie again?

DINO: *Jurassic Park*, Grandma.

GRANDMA: Oh yes, *Jurassic Park*. But no, your friends are more important than this old grandma of yours. You kept saying, Grandma, you'll love *Jurassic*. It's a very nostalgic movie. It's about old things coming back to life . . . (*absentmindedly takes her blanket in her hand*). Then you also promised to give me a nice blanket because the one I have is all worn out. I kept waiting and waiting, then you got sick, then you . . . (*she cries*). Is that why you have come? To take me?

DINO: No, Lola. You see, when I died I found myself in this beautiful forest where I met this strange person. It was just like the story you told me before about how our elders will meet us in the afterlife and how there will be no more pain. Besides, I chose you because it was you who had told me that the dead sometimes roam the earth with the living—and spirits and humans are supposed to coexist peacefully.

GRANDMA: But that is Mount Apuyo, my child, I thought the spirits would never find their way in Toronto. They will get disoriented with the subways, cars, and the CN Tower. It happens to me all the time.

DINO: But you know, Grandma, there's another reason I chose you. It's because you are the kindest, most understanding person I know. Nagpintas pay!

GRANDMA (*flattered*): Ay, pudnu de ta. That is why you and Marissa are so goodlooking. You took after our side of the family. But wait, did you get to see Apo Kabunian, the Supreme God?

DINO: I didn't get that far, Lola. But I will not tire you anymore. You have to rest. You have to rest. You have a long day tomorrow. And please, don't wear black at my funeral, Lola. Not unless you accessorize with chains and leather. Just kidding.

GRANDMA: But Dino, what is this burden you speak of? How can I help you?

DINO: Later Lola. You better get some sleep. We'll talk again.

GRANDMA: Will I see you again? What did you want me to wear at your funeral?

DINO: Your traditional dress. The one you wear at the caravan. I love the colors. (*Dino starts to leave and goes back to the closet.*) Bye . . .

GRANDMA: Okay ngarud . . . But, Dino . . . Dino . . . (*runs to open the closet, but Dino isn't there.*)

Blackout.

SCENE 3: THE WAKE

Funeral home. The whole stage is lit. Stage right is the funeral parlor. Candles, flowers on the side. Sofas. Everyone (about seven people) is in black or other dark colors except Lola, who comes in with Marissa and her native boyfriend, wearing her authentic bright-colored Igorot dress. Entrance is on stage left. She holds her head high even as the guests eye her curiously. Nanay notices them coming into the funeral parlor. Smoking lounge is also on stage left.

Nanay talks briefly with Tatay in a hushed voice. She hurries toward Lola.

> **NANAY** (*discreetly*): Mamang, kababain ka? Why didn't you wear black? (*grabs Marissa by the hand*) And you, Marissa, why did you bring James here? Your father is going to get upset. Both of you (*Marissa and Lola*)—If anybody asks any questions, Dino died of pneumonia, okay?

She acknowledges James, who also greets her with a shy nod.

> **MARISSA:** Everybody knows that no one dies of AIDS. Only of AIDS-related illnesses. You should know, Mom, you're a nurse.

People react to the mention of AIDS.

> **NANAY** (*loudly*): Band-AIDS? Apay anak, you got hurt? I got Band-AIDS in the car. Let's go outside and get them.

Tatay notices the commotion. He approaches. Meanwhile, Lola has gone over to look at her grandson.

> **TATAY:** What is all this? You (*calls Marissa, points a finger at her. Berates her in a controlled soft voice*), why did you bring that boy here? I told you I don't like to see him around. He's bad news, and I should know. I always see people like him in the hospital drunk and crazy.

James overhears, approaches them.

> **JAMES:** I only came to offer my condolences, Mr. Ramirez. He's my friend too, you know. But I'm leaving now . . . See you later, Marissa.

Nanay tries to stop James together with Marissa. James hurries out. Marissa turns to her father.

MARISSA: If you hate native people so much, you shouldn't have married Mom.

She walks toward the casket, leaving her father flustered. Tatay hurries after Marissa, but just as Tatay is about to raise his voice, Lola raises her hand as if to say "silence." Tatay is taken aback.

Grandma puts her arm around Marissa and they both gaze sadly at Dino's face. Nanay calms Tatay down. People whisper, and some approach to give condolences.

A relative has a videocam. People are gloomy, but when they notice the camera focused on them, they pose and smile.

Ken enters the room. The man with the camera follows him. People steal glances at the handsome blond hunk. He approaches Nanay and Tatay, embraces Marissa and Lola. He looks so macho. Then, upon seeing his dead lover, he breaks down and cries.

NANAY (*to the woman sitting beside her*): They were so close.

TATAY (*to the man beside him*): They were like brothers.

Nanay and Tatay turn to each other with suspicious looks. Two young men behind them—Chris and Joey—give each other knowing looks. One makes a signal to the other to go out of the room. Chris approaches Ken and whispers something, gestures to the door. Ken nods his head. They go to stage left, the smoking lounge entrance. One lights a cigarette and offers it to the other.

Uncle asks permission from his wife to go out to smoke. Just mime. Uncle looks like a stereotypical military officer. He goes to the smoking lounge and asks for a light from Chris and Joey. Kids play around. People go in and out.

AT THE LOBBY

UNCLE: So, is Dino a good friend of yours?

CHRIS AND JOEY: Yes, sir. I'm Chris and I'm Joey.

CHRIS: You must be Dino's uncle—the one in the military.

UNCLE (*proudly*): Yes. I'm actually a lieutenant colonel. I flew in from the Philippines for this occasion. His father and I grew up in Pangasinan, where as you know, the President of the Philippines was born . . . I came to offer my brother some support. (*Boasts*) We're staying at the Sheraton. We did not want to inconvenience my brother.

The three shake hands. Small talk.

JOEY: Oh, yes, he certainly spoke about you.

UNCLE: Really? I'm flattered. Have you ever been to the Philippines, boys?

CHRIS: Oh yes, sir. In fact I spent Christmas at my friend's place at 690 Retiro Ave.

Chris snickers with Joey.

JOEY: I went there two years ago, sir. Remember, Chris? (*He winks at Chris.*)

UNCLE: You boys sound like you'd make real good soldiers. You know, we could always use those hard muscles of yours. You'd love it in the field, boys. It's always action, action, action!

Guys look at their flexed muscles.

CHRIS: Well, we work hard on them, sir. Like you said, sir, we want action, action, action!

UNCLE: You said you were friends of my nephew, are you by any chance . . . (*dismisses the thought as he looks at their macho physique*) IMPOSSIBLE!

JOEY (*shrugs*): Well, apparently, you haven't met the Village People!

UNCLE: What's that, boys?

The men snicker.

BOTH: Nothing.

UNCLE: It's just that, Dino—he's a little too soft. Not like you guys. I kept telling his Dad to bring him to the Philippines so I can toughen him—make him into a real man—you know what I mean?

CHRIS (*sarcastically*): Frankly, sir, we don't have any idea what on earth you 're talking about.

Uncle seems nostalgic. He gestures like he has a gun in his hand and he's about to shoot it. Talks and aims imaginary gun toward the audience.

At the parlor Tita Ludy, Uncle's wife, is getting restless. She keeps look-ing at her watch.

UNCLE: There's nothing like the feel of a gun barrel in your hand, the cold steel hard against your palm, your index finger on the trigger, aching to release all that power!

JOEY (*sarcastic*): I can feel the same power and excitement from a less deadly, but more explosive weapon, sir. And it's probably just as hard.

The two guys laugh amusedly. They tap each other on the back affec-tionately. Uncle looks at them suspiciously. He stands up, his suspicion confirmed, and ditches his cigarette.

At this point Tita Ludy stands and goes to the entrance to the smoking lounge. She overhears Uncle.

UNCLE: Mga malas sa buhay! ! ! Mga bakla . . . Hmmp . . .

Tita Ludy calls out, irritated.

> **LUDY:** Nanding, bien a'qui! ! What's keeping you?

> **UNCLE:** Yes, dear, I'm coming . . .

The two guys laugh some more.

> **CHRIS:** Can you believe that guy? Is he from the Middle Ages or what?

> **JOEY:** Don't delude yourself, Chris. People like that are a dime a dozen. I'm going to the washroom, wanna come? (*Goes to left*)

> **CHRIS:** No thanks, I'll go out and buy some more cigarettes. And behave properly, girl, we're at a funeral.

Chris goes back to the parlor to get his coat and then exits to the right.

A young bored couple go out to smoke and talk in the lounge. They stand in front of the funeral room. Marissa was going to follow them, but as she steps out of the door, she overhears them talking. She stays by the door and listens more.

> **RICK:** I heard he's gay and died of. . . . Well, you know. That's his lover over there.

> **TINA:** That's not true. I know our cousin Dino, he's so charming with girls. He couldn't be gay. No, he couldn't be. Could he?

> **RICK:** Oh, you're so blind. And you probably didn't know that Aunt Tessie is a lesbo and that she's living with another woman. Didn't you see her? She came with her lover. The nerve!

> **MARISSA:** Should it matter that my brother was gay? Or that Aunt Tessie is probably the only relative we have who has a good relationship?

> **RICK** (*embarrassed*): Marissa, we didn't know you were there.

Marissa talks to Girl.

MARISSA: Should it matter that your cousin was gay, Tina?

Tina cries and tries to bury her head on Rick's shoulder. Rick moves back. Tina is angry at Rick for pulling back.

TINA: Dino would never do that. He always knew how to make us girls feel better. (*To Rick*) Get out of here (*faces Marissa and cries more*).

Rick goes back inside the funeral parlor.

MARISSA: My brother IS gay, you know.

TINA: Did he die of AIDS complications?

MARISSA: Yes, he did die of . . .

TINA (*cuts her off*): I guess that was what he was always trying to tell us when he said he was different. Sayang (*sobs more*)!!

MARISSA: What are you so sorry for?

TINA: Myself? You know. . . . (*whispers*)

MARISSA: You what? You have a crush on Ken? Well, you better look somewhere else, Tina.

Tita Ludy goes to the washroom located at the smoking lounge.

Marissa and Tina are laughing. They go back inside the parlor. Tita Ludy comes out of the washroom just as Jessica enters in full regalia (with feathers and all). He just came from a show and didn't have time to change. His mascara is smeared so that he looks like a distraught clown. Tita Ludy and Jessica bump into each other. She shows disgust at Jessica. She refuses to let him inside the parlor. She blocks his way. They look like they're playing a game in mime. It could be that they find themselves wearing the same outfit and are outraged.

JESSICA (*angry*): Let me in!! I said let me in!

Marissa hears him. She goes out to the lounge.

MARISSA: What's going on?

LUDY: This (*looks at Jessica*) thing is insisting to get in. It said it knows you and Dino.

MARISSA: Jessica!! (*To Tita Ludy*) Yes, Tita, SHE is our friend.

Ludy is still angry and puzzled. She goes back inside and vents her anger on Uncle. Through mime she urges him to take her home. Uncle talks to Tatay to let him know that they are going back to the hotel. Jessica embraces Marissa. Tita Ludy looks at Jessica as they leave. She can't stand him.

JESSICA (*somewhat upset*): I found out during the rehearsal. Why didn't anyone tell me?

MARISSA: I'm sorry, Jessica. Everything happened so fast. We didn't get to call everyone.

JESSICA: But he is—was—my best friend, Marissa.

He's about to step inside the room.

MARISSA: I know, I know, Jessie. But if I were you, I wouldn't go in just yet.

Jessica hesitates. He becomes resigned.

JESSICA: I understand. Why don't we have coffee outside and wait till everyone has left, then maybe I can pay my respects.

MARISSA: Sounds like a good idea to me. Wait, let me get my coat and tell my mom, okay.

Marissa goes inside the funeral parlor to get her coat. The rest of the stage darkens. Spotlight on Jessica.

JESSICA (*he starts to sing to the tune of* **Cabaret**): What good is sitting alone in the dark, when your friend just died of . . . (*tries to see the humor in the situation*) Let's see, how many more friends will I lose this year? (*counts by plucking feathers on his stole*) There's Steve, and Sheena, and Romy, and . . . and . . . (*can't go on, and cries silently*).

(*To himself*) Dino, Dino. Why did you leave me? We were in this together . . . Remember when my parents kicked me out and you took me in? Two fucking fag Flips stranded in this cold unfriendly place? We came from two countries but didn't belong anywhere. Who would want two fucking fag flips, anyway?

(*Smiles, remembers good times*) I remember when you asked me to teach you Tagalog. You wanted so badly to fit in—in our own community until you found out what people were saying about us. Bakla, binabae, dimonyo, mga tinamaan ng lintek . . . They spilled out those words with so much hatred in their eyes. (*Gets sad*) Man, they treated us like we weren't even human. And they said they were Christians! (*buries head on his arms*) Come to think of it, that's probably why they wanted to screwcify us.

Dino appears from the dark and gently touches Jessica's hair. Jessica feels it and tries to hold the hand. But Dino leaves, disappears if possible.

Marissa comes in with her coat and with Ken. The stage lights up again. Marissa touches Jessie's head.

JESSICA (*catches her hand*): Marissa (*surprised*) it's just you.

MARISSA: Oh, excuse me. Were you expecting Prince Charming? Well, here he is (*shows Ken*).

Ken and Jessica embrace. Onlookers are disgusted. They go back inside the funeral room. Some leave.

JESSICA (*smiles*): No, it's just that I just thought . . . (*shrugs his shoulders*) Forget about it.

MARISSA (*as they were leaving*): Did my brother just make his presence felt to you? Be afraid. He just might spring on you from inside the closet.

KEN: Well, Dino knows I'm scared of ghosts.

Their voices fade as they leave the stage, which is slowly darkening.

JESSICA: Oh, I get it. Dino out of the closet. I can't believe you just made that insinuation about your brother, Marissa.

MARISSA: Why not? I used to tease him about being a closet queen (*giggles*). Oh, he wouldn't mind.

Dino appears like he wants to go with them. Stage lights out as he reaches out his hand.

SCENE 4: 'SUSMARYOSEP

Moments later. Funeral home. The three—Jessica, Marissa, and Ken— come back. There are no more people except Tatay, Nanay, and Lola. Father is repulsed by Jessica's presence. He ignores Jessica's greeting. He stands up as Jessica approaches the casket. He is going to confront him but is stopped by Ken.

KEN (*kindly*): So, sir, when are you going to have Dino's body cremated?

TATAY (*distracted for a while*): Cremate? Oh, no. Of course not. We're Catholics, we don't do that sort of thing. . . . Besides, he didn't die of a contagious disease. We don't need to burn his body.

KEN: But sir, that's what Dino said to all of us before he died, that his body should be cremated and his ashes thrown over Mount Apuyo in the Philippines.

TATAY: He's going to the Philippines, but not in ashes. He will be buried there beside my father in La Loma, Quezon City, not Mount Apuyo.

NANAY: I thought we talked about this before? We will just bury him here. It's too expensive to bring his body home. That will cost over $10,000. Where are we going to get that kind of money?

TATAY: God will provide.

Jessica leans over to kiss Dino's forehead. Tatay notices this and stops him.

TATAY: You, whoever you are. Stop that! You will desecrate my son's body. . . . Haven't you freaks done enough? You infected him with your blood and now . . . Get out.

JESSICA: But Mr. Ramirez. Don't you recognize me? (*Removes his wig*) I'm Jessie, Dino's best friend.

TATAY (*recognizes him*): Hesus? Ikaw ba yan? 'susmaryosep! What is this world coming to? Does your Dad know about this?

JESSICA (*finds an excuse*): I'm an actor, sir, remember? We have a show and this is just my costume. And please, sir, stop calling me Hesus. Jessie na lang po. You don't want people to think you're taking the Lord's name in vain.

TATAY: Naku, Jesus. Jessie na kung Jessie. But you shouldn't be choosing roles like that. It's so degrading for a man to be playing women's roles.

NANAY AND MARISSA: What did you say?

LOLA: Agtal na kayo amin! Can't we have a little respect for my grandson?

ACT 2 SCENE 1: GRANDMA AND DINO MEET AGAIN

Lola and Dino in Lola's bedroom situated stage right.

DINO: Lola, tell me about that legend again. That story when the strangers came and brought illness to a tribe.

LOLA: This is a legend told to me by my great-grandfather. He said that a long time ago, our people lived happily in the lowlands . . .

Stage left, a silent legend (mime) unfolds. Tribal music plays up (wind instruments and drums).

LOLA: There was enough food for everyone and people were kind to each other. There was a lot of love then, you know, Dino. Not like today, when there's so much violence coming out of that noisy box we call television. Before, there were no radios or TV, people talked to each other more.

Mime depicts a tribal community (men, women, and children) from the time they rise, work in the fields, tease each other.

LOLA: Then one day, a stranger came to the village. He was pale and looked sick. The people took him to the Babaylan, the priestess. She performed many rituals to heal him, but he was still delirious. She was about to give up when finally he became well . . .

Mime portrays Lola's story.

LOLA: Nobody suspected he was a—lalaki nga gamud . . .

DINO: A warlock, Grandma.

GRANDMA: Yes, that's it, a warlock. He stole the children's native tongue so that they no longer speak their language but the stranger's. They could no longer understand their parents. Families were broken. The stranger brought illness and discontent.

One day, he brought out a beautiful blanket. It was woven with threads of silver and precious gems that glittered in the sun . . . Everybody who looked was dazzled.

People, under the spell of the stranger, longed for the blanket. They did not want to share anymore. They did not recognize that the blanket was Apo Diwata, the goddess, under the spell of the evil stranger . . .

On the left side of the stage the actors continue to portray the legend.

LOLA: The man raised the beautiful blanket and its brilliance outshone the sun. The people of the tribe tried to reach out for the blanket. When someone finally pulled down the blanket, the tribal folks tore into it like wild dogs. Apo Diwata cried out, each tear turning into a gem. But the people did not hear her and finally when the blanket was torn into many pieces, the piece that held her mouth spoke. It said: "Because of this mistake, you people will suffer. You will be sick with wanting for as long as you do not discover the roots of your discontent." There were those who escaped to the mountains when they sensed something wrong about the pale-faced man. These people remained generous and kind. They didn't want what the sorcerer offered. But the people who were left behind were cursed to dig for gems and silver. They no longer cared about each other. When someone got sick, they left them to die. They were cursed to work hard. Their hearts became heavy with wanting, but they can't have what they want until they find out why they want it.

Actors on the left stage freeze. Lights dim.

DINO: That sounds like Toronto to me, Apo. People just working and working. People just wanting and wanting . . .

GRANDMA: Dino, (*pauses*) tell me about this burden of yours. You said you have chosen me, but how can I help you? (*She's exhausted at this point and just wants to sleep.*)

DINO: Remember, Grandma, when I told you about that dreaded disease? You, Marissa, Mom, and Ken were probably the only ones who were really supportive. The rest seemed to have abandoned me, even Dad. Just like in the legend when the sick were left to die.

Dino notices Lola, who has fallen asleep.

DINO: But Grandma, I know you just made up that beautiful story for me.

Dino kisses her forehead and covers her with the blanket.

DINO (*in a whisper*): You used to do this for me, Lola, remember? (*Notices the old, worn woven blanket, from the Philippines. He shakes his head and smiles.*)

He moves carefully so as not to wake his grandma. He goes back inside the closet. Lights dim. Short blackout.

SCENE 2: THREE GENERATIONS OF WOMEN

Morning. Same room. Dino steps out of the closet. Lola is still asleep.

DINO: Wake up, Grandma. It's morning.

LOLA: Did you sleep well?

DINO: If I did I wouldn't be here.

LOLA: I keep forgetting that you're dead. Is this what they call Alzheimer's? Oh my God, I have it. I'm imagining you, ngarud?

DINO: No, Lola. I was sent here, remember? Ay, lelang nga bakit!

LOLA: Ah, don't be disrespectful ha. Ah ag-al-alwad ka!

DINO: Sorry.

LOLA: Dino, I dreamt you told me about your burden. Is it heavy? Nadagsen aya?

DINO: Grandma, it is the heaviest thing I've carried in my life. I never even felt how heavy it was until I got to the other side.

LOLA: Why don't you give me some of that weight, my apuku?

DINO: It's too heavy even if we carry it between us, Lola. We have to find a way to share it with everyone—then it won't be so heavy.

Marissa knocks on the door.

MARISSA: Grandma, is someone there with you? Can I come in?

LOLA (*startled*): Come in. Sumbreka, ay aguray ka, Marissa.

Lola tries to push Dino inside the closet. Marissa comes in and catches Lola shoving something with her hands.

MARISSA: What are you doing, Lola? I thought you were speaking with someone.

LOLA: I'm practicing our dance, anak. (*Continues shoving Dino. Dino backs up inside the closet, smiling. Lola looks like she's dancing*) There's going to be a fund-raising at the Community Centre and our group is sponsoring it. Mekkatuy, I'll teach you.

MARISSA: Okay . . . (*Imitates Lola's dance*) This is fun . . . Did you do this all the time in Mount Apuyo?

LOLA: Not all the time, Marissa. Only during harvest time, or weddings, or when a warrior dies and the tribe decides to avenge his death.

MARISSA: Dino would tease me big time if he sees me dancing like this.

LOLA: Oh, but he knows this dance, too. Remember, he even wore a g-string once and joined the Caravan when you were this small.

Grandma holds her hand to thigh-level.

MARISSA: Oh, yes. I remember that g-string. Dad wouldn't let him wear it to go trick or treating. (*She imitates Dad's stern voice.*) He said, "Dino, don't argue with me now, you're going to catch a cold if you wear that."

Marissa smiles as she remembers. Dino slowly comes out of the closet and listens.

MARISSA: Halloween—that was Dino's favorite holiday . . . I remember the look on Daddy's face when Dino and I swapped clothes for Halloween. Dino wore that pink little tutu I used for my ballet recital . . . and I wore the Superman costume Mom and Dad gave him for Christmas. Dad almost had a heart attack when he saw us!! He refused to come with us so you ended up coming, remember, Grandma?

LOLA: I remember that. . . . Dino and I would spend so much time making his costumes. Last year, we were making the orange monster costume when I asked him, "What are you supposed to be, anyway?" and he said—

Marissa cuts her off angrily.

MARISSA: HIV! The monster that was killing him.

Marissa starts to cry. Grandma calms her.

GRANDMA: Come, come balasang ko, let's sit down.

MARISSA: Grandma, I can't believe he's gone . . . This isn't fair! There were so many things he wanted to do . . . He wanted to start a support group in the community for people with AIDS . . . He wanted to keep marching so that someday gays and lesbians will be treated equally . . .

GRANDMA: It was just like when your Apo died, my husband. He was also in the middle of a fight when they shot him . . .

MARISSA: Who's they, Grandma?

GRANDMA: Evil men—with guns, goons, and gold—they wanted to trap the river, destroy the trees, and flood our sacred burial land—so they can build dams for electricity . . . for the rich people and big business . . . They wanted to take land away from us. And land, my apuku, is what nourishes life.

MARISSA: How could they do such a thing, Grandma?

GRANDMA: They look down on us because we're not like them. We did not give up our old ways—the tribal ways. They called us—bagtit—crazy. Taong bundok—savage mountain people. Ah, but they could not bring us down. We fought back.

Grandma takes Magiting's photo off the wall.

GRANDMA: This is your uncle, my cousin, the brave Magiting Alay-ay. He is the greatest chieftain who ever lived.

MARISSA: Oh yeah, Dino told me about him. He was killed during martial law for trying to stop the building of the dam, right? Did we really have a hero for a grand-uncle, Grandma?

GRANDMA: Of course. Our tribe has a warrior tradition. Like when those men tried to build that dam on our land, the women and children, your mom and I marched to the construction site and hid all the tools.

MARISSA: Seriously? I didn't know you were such an activist, Grandma. Now I know who Dino took after.

GRANDMA: They stopped building the dam then. But now, your Aunt Gemma wrote me that they are starting again— because of this Philippines 2000. Hah! (*stands up and raises her chest against an imaginary enemy*) Haan nga agtal na iti ili! Our people will be ready for them.

MARISSA: Your story sounds very familiar, Grandma. It's the same story James told me about how the native people were displaced and continue to be discriminated against in North America. You two should talk sometime . . .

GRANDMA: It seems life, balasang ko, is a never-ending struggle. Even when one warrior dies, the fight goes on.

Marissa laughs but then suddenly turns pensive.

GRANDMA: Oh, apay? What's wrong?

MARISSA: I just remembered Dino, Grandma. The last Halloween we spent together was at the hospital. He made a joke about wearing a diaper . . . by then, he had lost control of his bladder . . . and he was so thin—not even fifty pounds. He said "Look, Marissa, this is my Halloween costume—I'm a talking baby skeleton." The next day, he—he went into a coma . . .

Marissa cries. Just then Nanay knocks.

NANAY: Ma . . . Ma . . .

GRANDMA: Tahan na (*in Ilocano*), balasang ko. Open the door, it's your mama.

Marissa wipes her face. Grandma notices Dino listening. She shoves him inside the closet again. Marissa opens the door.

NANAY: What are you doing here? I thought you had gone to the funeral parlor.

MARISSA (*notices Grandma dancing*): Oh, Grandma is teaching me their tribal dance.

LOLA: It's OUR dance, anak. The spirit of the tribe lives in you too, it runs in your blood. It always will.

NANAY: She's Canadian, Ma. She and her brother Dino were born here. They've never even been to the bundok!

MARISSA: That's why I've been saving money, Mom. So I could go there.

NANAY: What? How come I didn't know about this? This is what I hate about Canada. Your kids turn eighteen and they think they can do anything!

MARISSA: Mom, Dino and I never told you, but we've had this plan for a long time, and now that he's gone, I feel more strongly that I should go—to scatter Dino's ashes over the Mountain Province.

NANAY: You can't go. Besides, your Dad and I have decided that we're gonna . . .

LOLA: We're going, Josie. Dino wants his ashes to meet the earth that nurtured his roots.

MARISSA: Grandma?

NANAY: So, you've been planning this with the kids.

MARISSA: It's the first time I heard it too, Mom. But I don't mind having Lola for company. That'll be cool.

Lola starts packing her bags as the two are arguing.

LOLA: Oh, yes. It's cool in the mountains. . . .

NANAY: Listen to me. There's nothing for you there. This is where you belong. We've made a home for you here. (*Turns to Grandma*) What are you doing, Mamang?

Tatay is about to knock when he overhears Marissa's angry voice. He eavesdrops. The door is slightly ajar.

MARISSA: Sometimes, Mom, I don't really feel that this is home. Dino and I, we've talked about this so many times before. We grew up, not liking who we were. In school, our classmates taunted us, called us names. We didn't even know who we were . . . You didn't know, but one time, Dino tried to kill himself . . .

Nanay gasps. Grandma stops packing.

MARISSA: I came in just before he could jump off the chair with a rope around his neck. We kept it from you and Dad. We knew you had problems of your own . . . If you only knew how badly he was hurting inside.

We didn't fit in because of our color. What Daddy thought about James and his people, people thought about us. They just have other names for us, other ugly ideas. But they're all painful just the same . . . And even in our own community, Dino had to keep his true identity hidden or else they would make fun of him. Others who suspected did . . . Even you were ashamed of him because he was . . .

NANAY (*interrupts even before she can say the word*): He was confused, Marissa. Your brother was a very troubled young man. He didn't know what he was doing. And we were not ashamed of him.

MARISSA: Yes, you were. You and Dad. You didn't even let his friends in the community and our relatives visit him at the hospital because then they would know he had AIDS.

NANAY: We didn't want him to get hurt. We were only protecting him, Marissa.

MARISSA: Maybe you mean yourselves, Mom. Maybe you mean our community. You were protecting yourselves against him because he was strong. Because he knew what he wanted and he worked hard to get it. Dino just wanted to be himself, not what people expected him to be.

Silence. Each one starts thinking about her own problems. Suddenly Marissa and Nanay start talking at the same time about their own personal hardships. As they talk they move to opposite corners of the room and face the audience. Once in a while they face each other.

This is a fast exchange.

NANAY: You think that you kids had it difficult?

MARISSA: You say I'm Canadian because I was born here—

NANAY: When I came here I got a job as a nurse, but the patients always looked down on me.

MARISSA: —but people always treated me like I came from somewhere out of space.

NANAY: Some of them demanded to have a white nurse.

MARISSA: They would ask if I knew how to speak English. Tell me I should be good in math because I'm Chinese—

NANAY: I didn't even have my family here.

MARISSA: —and if they found out I'm Filipino they'd say, "Oh, we have a domestic who's Filipino. Is your mom a domestic?"

NANAY: I endured the winters that were so long and lonely.

MARISSA: We had no Filipino teachers.

NANAY: My supervisors were always white. I never quite understood why they never promoted the Filipino nurses.

MARISSA: Our history wasn't taught in school.

NANAY: I said, maybe our accents are really bad. We studied very hard to gain a Canadian accent.

MARISSA: And then Dino, he tried to be the same as the boys in school.

NANAY: We would always say EH? at the end of each sentence so maybe we'd sound more Canadian.

MARISSA: But he was different and I was different so we got stuck with each other, and with other people who were treated differently.

NANAY: Then I had you and Dino and I said ah, these kids, they will be Canadians through and through.

At this point they face each other.

MARISSA: It was hard to get summer jobs. It was hard to make friends.

NANAY: They were born here.

MARISSA: We were born here

NANAY: They are the same as white Canadians.

MARISSA: —but we weren't treated the same.

NANAY: They will not be victims of discrimination.

MARISSA: We were victims of discrimination!!

LOLA (*starts getting worried. She brings them together*): Husto daytan. Agtal na kayo amin. Enough, both of you. Enough. (*Looks at the closet*) I think I know what you mean, Dino.

Nanay and Marissa embrace each other upon realizing they had similar experiences. Lola comforts them. Tatay is moved. Then, they chorus.

MARISSA AND NANAY: Why didn't you tell me about this?

LOLA: I'm going to get a glass of water.

NANAY/ MARISSA: No, Mamang/Grandma, you don't have to.

LOLA: What do you mean I don't have to? I'm thirsty.

Nanay and Marissa laugh. They sit on the bed and start to talk and apologize to each other. Lola catches Dad eavesdropping, just as he is turning his back on the door.

LOLA: Tino . . . so you heard?

TATAY: Yes. (*Pauses. He seemed ashamed of himself for eavesdropping. That's so un-macho. He tries to find an excuse.*) I couldn't help it. I was about to knock when . . . I just needed to ask Josie to. . . . (*Suddenly angry*) Ah, what's the point? So I wasn't a good father to Dino. It's too late to do anything about that now. He's dead, for God's sake!

LOLA: In your own way, you were. It's never too late, Tino . . . Florentino, haan pay nga na odi . . . (*She hurries into the kitchen.*)

Dad sits on the sofa with a faraway look on his face. He wants to go inside Grandma's room but he hesitates. He appears angry with himself for being so macho, so insensitive to his family's needs.

TATAY (*angry at himself*): But it is, Mamang!

LOLA (*ignores him*): But you know, you were not such a bad son-in-law.

Tatay touches her hand and then buries his face in his hands in confusion. Lola goes back inside the room.

LOLA (*mumbling*): Haan pay nga na odi . . . (*in Ilocano*)

Lights out.

SCENE 3: THE UNBURDENING

Back to the funeral. It's Dino's interment today. Many people have come. Dino was well-loved because of his community work. Many people didn't know he was gay. The priest prepares for the service. Ken is seen standing at the smoking lounge. Chris approaches.

JOEY: We see each other again. (*Sarcastically*) Refresh my memory. Where was the last time? At Rosar's Funeral Homes or O'Connor? Funeral homes are getting to be much of a gay hangout, wouldn't you agree?

KEN (*annoyed*): I wish you wouldn't be so casual. That was Dino, my lover, your close friend.

JOEY: I'm sorry . . . But you must admit, this is not the last funeral we'll meet at. In fact, I met my current partner at one (*smiles*). . . So how has it been with you?

KEN: Not too good . . . My T-cells are down and I have a lesion on my stomach. It might be my funeral you're going to the next time . . .

JOEY: So, who's being casual?

KEN: I comfort myself with the thought that maybe Dino and I will see each other in the afterlife. I miss him so much, you know. (*He breaks down.*)

Dino comes in along with the guests. He listens to the conversation. They don't see him.

JOEY (*comforts him*): We all do. But Ken, do us a favor. Don't die yet? We have a lot of work to do. First, we have to stop giving these funeral parlors so much business!

KEN (*smiles*): That only works for those who don't have it yet. What about those who have it? What about those who would rather catch AIDS because no one cares about them anyway? No one gives a damn.

JOEY (*angry*): We will make them give a damn! But as Dino would say, we have to start somewhere.

Chris takes out condoms and brochures from his pocket, shows them to Ken, who smiles and shakes his head.

The priest goes to the lectern at the base of the casket, facing the audience. He prepares for the service. Lights dim at the smoking area.

PRIEST: In the name of the Father, of the Son, and of the Holy Spirit . . . We are gathered here today to mourn the loss of our beloved brother Dino Kinow-od Ramirez. I see that he has many friends from the community . . . (*He clears his throat as he looks at Dino's gay friends.*)

I would like to read a passage from the book of Luke, chapter 23, verses 44 to 49. Jesus's death is witnessed by his friends.

(*He reads:*) All his friends stood at a distance, so also did the women who had accompanied him from Galilee and they saw all this happen.

(*Looks at audience:*) You see, there was nothing his friends and followers could do as they saw Jesus dying on the cross. But their presence spoke about their great love for him. Sometimes, it's all that matters.

Is there anyone from Dino's family who would like to say a few words about the deceased?

(*Grandma goes to the lectern.*)

LOLA: There was no one like him, my beautiful Dino. He always knew how to make me laugh. When I was sad and missed the place where I was born, Dino—he would listen to me tell all those stories about the mountains. He never tired of listening—that boy. He would always say "Grandma, you're the best history teacher in the world . . ."

He wanted to go there to the Philippines . . . to pay respects to the elders and meet his relatives . . . to see what life is like for them . . . (*Pauses*) What can I say about Dino that you did not know about him? (*People start whispering*) He was the kindest, most loving person. But he also knew how to fight—like a true warrior. . . . (*Her voice is sad*) He is here now. His spirit is restless . . . Addatuy iti apukuk . . . We have to help him find peace . . . Tulungan tayo tapno agtal na isuna . . .

Grandma is led back to her seat by Marissa. Tatay comes forward. He talks with a quivering voice.

TATAY: Oh yes, Dino knew how to fight. He was stronger than any of us. When he was lying on his bed at the hospital, he said "Dad, you don't have to tell our relatives and friends to come here. I know you don't want them to know I have—I have—AIDS." (*Audience reacts*) I feel ashamed of myself—

Nanay tries to interrupt.

NANAY: Tino, you don't have to. . . .

TATAY: No, I have to, Josie.

She holds out her hand, and Tatay takes it as he speaks. Stage dims. Spotlights on Tatay and on stage left Dino, looking sick.

TATAY: It's true, I am ashamed of myself. I let him die without seeing his friends, people who love him.

DINO: I told you, it was enough that you were there. Dad and Mom, Marissa, Grandma, Jessie and Ken . . .

TATAY: Maybe, if he knew that people cared about him in spite of the choices he made in his life, in spite of his illness, maybe he would still be here with us.

DINO: Dad, do you remember when I introduced you to Ken the first time?

TATAY: I remember when he introduced me to his friend Ken. He seemed to be telling me something . . .

DINO: I wanted to share with you, Dad, that I had found the person with whom I wanted to spend the rest of my short life— the way you found Mom.

TATAY: That he has made a choice and that I should respect it . . . But I wasn't listening . . .

DINO: And when I spoke to you about AIDS, you just couldn't believe it could happen to us—to our community. You were ashamed to see me marching on the streets with my queer friends . . .

TATAY: But this syndrome—this AIDS—it's deadly . . . I never believed Dino when he said it could happen to our community . . . I thought it's supposed to be a white person's disease. . . . But Dino WAS right. It IS killing our children . . .

DINO: I couldn't tell you then that I was sick with AIDS . . . Your shame weighed down on me and until now it has kept me from lifting off the ground . . . (*Breaking down*)

TATAY: He kept his illness from us . . . To spare us from the pain . . . Even as he himself was drowning in pain. The shame and silence choked him—probably more than AIDS itself . . .

DINO: I was waiting for you to get the cue. You knew how angry I was that people couldn't care less . . . It's a gay disease, they say . . . Punishment from God for prostitutes and drug abusers . . . Don't you think it's blasphemy that they think that the God you worship is so cruel . . . so judgmental? That certainly wasn't the God you or even Grandma taught me to believe in . . .

TATAY: I couldn't get the cue even as he was campaigning for people to start doing something about it. To start getting educated. To start caring about people who have it . . .

DINO: I couldn't even convince my own family . . .

TATAY: And he couldn't even bring his own father to say the word . . . (*his voice breaks*) I'm sorry, Dino . . . Please, forgive me . . .

DINO: I forgive you, Dad.

Spotlight on Dino out. Normal lighting on funeral stage. Marissa approaches Tatay and Nanay. Marissa and Tatay look at each other. Tatay embraces her . . . Nanay embraces both of them . . . The priest, obviously shaken, clears his throat. He loosens the collar of his habit. He talks but his voice squeaks. People start getting restless.

Voice-over on stage left. Have a neon light if possible saying "Shadowland."

VOICE-OVER: Once again, ladies and ahem, Ladies (*audience laughs*). Shadowland's hottest queen . . . Miss Jessica James . . .

Spotlight on Jessie in drag, sitting dramatically on a stool, holding a mic.

JESSIE: This is for you, Dino . . .

Music up. Woman version of "In My Life." Jessica lip-synchs with so much emotion as priest speaks.

PRIEST (*having regained his composure*): Let us pray, all powerful and merciful God, as we commend Dino, your servant, in your mercy and love . . . Blot out the sins he has committed in this world, he has died. Let him live with you forever. We ask this through Christ, our Lord . . . Amen.

ALL: Amen.

The priest blesses the casket, after which the men in the family, including Uncle, come forward to carry the casket . . . They bring it down the stage and parade it . . . The people follow the casket in twos . . . They go down the stage, then back and exit just before Jessie finishes the song.

Spotlights out after the song.

ACT 3 SCENE I: ENCOUNTER TWO WITH ANITO

Everything is dark. Suddenly spotlight finds Dino standing before the Anito . . . He is covered with a blanket.

ANITO: So have you unloaded your baggage?

DINO: I believe so, Apo. (*Pauses*) Frankly, I think we still have a long way to go to fight homophobia in our community and see the commonalities between that and racism but . . .

ANITO: Wait a minute . . . Homo-what . . . Rey who?

DINO: Oh, I thought you knew everything!

ANITO: That's Apo Kabunian.

DINO (*looks at audience*): Cool, I get to lecture a god. (*To Anito*) Okay, homophobia is when people treat another person with disrespect, hatred, or fear because he or she loves someone of her or his own sex. With racism—you just change the last words with—"Because of the color of their skin or ethnic origin." There are many reasons why these things happen, Apo—but mostly it comes from being ignorant and being unwilling to share power . . .

ANITO: Hmmm . . . power. That's another big word, my child . . . So are you ready to start on your journey to meet Apo Kabunian, the Supreme God?

DINO: Can I just say good-bye to my family please? I was so proud of my father. I didn't think he could say those words. I need to let him know that I forgive him . . .

ANITO: Oh, he knows . . . Intan, we have to go . . .

DINO: Please, Apo? Okay, okay—just my Dad . . .

ANITO: Hala, ngarud, go. . . (*Exasperated*)

Lights out.

SCENE 2: CHRISTMAS WITHOUT DINO

Pasko. Nanay is arranging things in the living room, she is rushing to prepare for a party. Marissa is talking to James over the phone. Grandma is reading a letter from the Philippines. She is reacting to the contents.

MARISSA (*talking to James*): No, James, my Dad doesn't mind. I've asked him if I could invite you over for the party and he said okay. Yeah . . . Uh-huh . . .

NANAY (*to Marissa*): Make sure you call everybody, Marissa. You know, Jessie, Chris, Joey, and Ken. Don't forget your Tita Tessie and her friend, Grace.

MARISSA (*over the phone*): Gotta go now, James. (*To her mom*) Can I call them later, Mom? I still have some packing to do. Grandma says my cousins can use some of my old sweatshirts in the province . . .

GRANDMA (*to Marissa*): Your Aunt Gemma is excited to see you, Marissa. She said she's going to teach you to speak Ilocano when we go there.

Marissa peeks at the letter that Grandma shows her. Tatay enters from the basement with Marissa's suitcase.

MARISSA (*dismayed*): It's in Ilocano! (*To Tatay*) Great, you found my old suitcase. (*Takes the suitcase to her room. Exits.*)

NANAY (*calls out*): Marissa, don't forget to call everyone and tell them to come at seven.

MARISSA (*backstage*): Yes, Mom. I'll do it from my room, okay? Grandma, can you please help me choose what clothes to bring?

GRANDMA: Okay. I'm coming. (*Exits to Marissa's room. Puts letter back in envelope.*)

TATAY (*to Nanay, nostalgic.*): It was a mess in the basement. Dino never did get around to cleaning it . . . I better do that while I'm on leave . . . (*on his way back*)

NANAY (*tries to stop him. Strongly*): You have to stop this, Tino. You have to let go. I don't think your son wants to see you blaming yourself for things that happened in the past . . .

Tatay sees truth in what Nanay says. They break down and embrace.

NANAY: Tino, listen to me. Dino's friends are coming. They're part of the family now. If you think we hurt our son so badly, then let's make it up to his friends, to his extended family. Hala, start making your famous fruit salad.

TATAY (*sad*): Oh no, not the salad. That was Dino's favorite. Remember, he used to pester me to make it when he was young . . . When he and I were still talking. (*Smiles*) He would even watch me make it. (*Shrugs*) There's no need to do it now. Not the salad, no way.

NANAY: Ano ka ba naman? It's Dino's pasiyam, his ninth day and it's also Christmas, what could be a more special occasion than this?

TATAY: O sige na nga. (*Jokes around*) Prepare the chopping board for the master chef!

Nanay laughs. They are startled by a noise coming from Grandma's room. Dino comes out of the closet, trips over some clothes hangers. He takes the blanket from his shoulder and leaves it on the bed.

TATAY: What was that? (*Rushes to Grandma's bedroom*)

NANAY (*follows him with her voice*): Hay, si Mamang. She probably left the window open again. She can't stand the cold, but she can't stand being locked inside the house. She says it's too oppressive.

Tatay sees Dino's spirit. He is totally shocked and speechless.

DINO: Good-bye, Dad, and thank you.

Dino embraces his father. Tatay is too shocked to respond. Dino steps back and his spotlight goes out. Tatay looks around and believes he has seen a ghost.

TATAY: Good-bye, son.

Blackout. Christmas party music up. People talking. Tatay and Ken are singing a duet. A flurry of sounds. Laughter. Prayers.

SCENE 3

Prayers. Last few lines. Marissa leads prayers. The whole family is present, including friends. Some are coming in from outside. Some standing. Some kneeling. Everyone is in colorful attire. Marissa goes to the closet and looks inside. Puzzled and then she laughs to herself.

> **MARISSA:** This we ask through Christ our Lord . . .

> **EVERYONE:** Amen . . .

Marissa and youngsters kiss the hands of the elders.

> **NANAY:** O mangan ta. The food is going to get cold!

Party atmosphere.

> **KEN:** Hey, I like this. Did you make this, Mrs. Ramirez? What's it called?

> **NANAY:** Tessie made that. It's called dinuguan. . . . and don't tell me to translate it into English.

> **JOEY:** I'm sorry, but I have to go soon, Mrs. Ramirez . . . My friend Jim is in the hospital. I don't want him to spend Christmas Eve alone.

> **NANAY:** Ganon ba? O, eh, bring some food to the hospital, Joey. We have so much . . . I know how bad the food is at hospitals . . .

> **JOEY:** He'd really appreciate this, ma'am. He misses Filipino food so much . . .

Music up and under (two seconds).

> **MARISSA:** Seriously, I think we should start that support group for people with AIDS and their families—right here in our community. That was what Dino wanted to do . . . You have one in your community, right, James? How did you do it?

Voices react—"That's a good idea" attitude.

> **TATAY** (*tapping a glass with a spoon to get people's attention*): I want to make an announcement. Josie and I decided that Dino's ashes will be scattered in Mt. Apuyo . . .

Chris opens the champagne bottle. People cheer.

> **KEN:** Let's make a toast to Marissa and Grandma, for a meaningful journey to the Philippines.

Party atmosphere throughout. Everyone is saying Merry Christmas to everyone else . . .

> **JESSIE:** Hoy Marissa, bring a letter for me, ha?

The others tease him. "Is that for your boyfriend?"

> **MARISSA:** Sure, Jess, anytime . . .

> **JOEY:** Careful Marissa, he didn't say if it's attached to a microwave.

People laugh . . . Pinoy humor. People urge Tatay to sing à la Elvis, and after much prodding he obliges . . . Tatay sings. Fades out.

Grandma backs out to her room as she listens to Tatay singing inconspicuously. She goes inside her room.

SPLIT SCENE. *Light on party scene is gradually diminishing. Sounds slowly fade. The light on Grandma's bedroom is on. She comes in, notices the closet door is slightly ajar. She checks inside to see if Dino is there. She is dismayed. She feels sad.*

> **GRANDMA:** Dino, Dino . . . (*She looks under the bed.*) Stop hiding from me, Dino . . .

She sits on the bed, notices the blanket for the first time. She wraps it around her shoulders. She cries too for the first time. He is really gone.

Then she is quiet. Meanwhile, merrymaking continues . . . Oblivious.
Spotlight on Grandma.

GRANDMA: Yes, be at peace, my apuku. Be at peace.
(Ilocano too?)

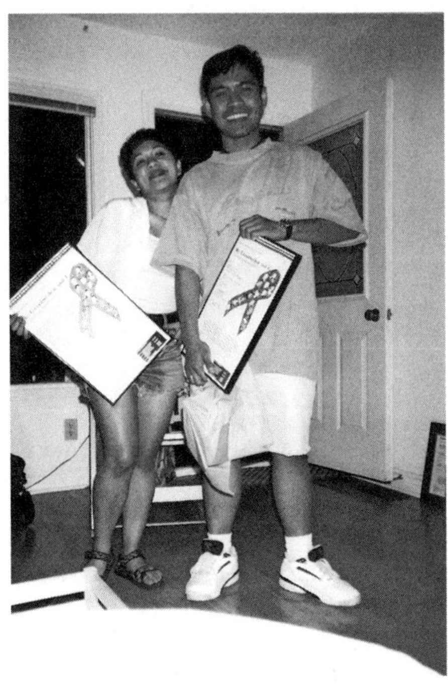

Still frame from a video recording of
My Grandmother and I.

Transgressing Borders, Generations, and Taboos:
Lani Montreal reflects on *My Grandmother and I*

RD: What inspired you to write this play? Was there a specific context which led to the writing of *My Grandmother and I*? Could you describe that time for us?

LM: It was Carmencita "Ging" Hernandez's idea to produce a play featuring a grandmother and a grandson in response to a call to raise awareness on the issue of AIDS/HIV. I was ready to write brochures, facilitate workshops, and devote some issues to the topic, but Ging thought a play would probably be more effective. I agreed and well, it turned out to be more fun, too. At the time, numbers we got from reliable HIV/AIDS organizations in Toronto showed that Filipino-Canadians were among the hardest hit among Asian communities. We felt we needed to do something! We organized workshops and invited community members to talk about it, and that's when we realized it's more urgent than we thought.

RD: Why did you choose a story with an intergenerational component, or a story which discusses the tensions/connections between three generations in a family (a grandmother, her children, and their children)? Do you think generational stories are important for Filipinos?

LM: As for the choice of Grandma as main character, it is quite common for immigrant Filipino couples to petition their parents to live with them once they are settled. When the couple has children, the grandparents are counted among the main caregivers. I remember having a discussion with Ging about the way grandparents and grandkids connect, sometimes on a deeper, more nonjudgmental level. There is no pressure for the grandparents to "shape" their grandchildren, as this is seen as the parents' job. They are only there to care for them and provide guidance as necessary. This, I think, loosens the tension between the two generations.

Yes, generational stories are important for Filipinos because it is an acknowledgment of our complicated cultural identity. I think that as Filipinos abroad, our identity is defined by the mainstream, so there is a struggle to create our own identity within our families, to hold on to traditions and ideas and impose them upon our children even though they may not work in our new environment. At times, these ideas alienate us from each other, instead of bringing us together closer. In the workshops we had with community members, they shared these feelings and thoughts and so the play is like holding a mirror to our community, to allow us to see how we were hurting each other and what we can do to change things.

RD: We were struck while watching the play that it had an educational component, which specifically talks about racism, power, homophobia, etc. So, who were your intended audiences? Do you think educating them was an important element of how the play was written?

LM: It was my first play and I wasn't sure if I was going to write another one; and so there was so much I wanted to say! Seriously, though, I just wanted to show how these issues intersect. My intended audience was the Filipino-Canadian community, whose homophobia stemmed from colonization that brought the Catholic religion to our people. On a personal level, my intended audience was my own mother, to whom I wasn't yet out as a bisexual woman. At the time, AIDS/HIV was a taboo issue. It was not something that happened to "us" and so "we" should not talk about it. The play was part of our campaign to raise awareness on the issue, and so including the educational component was important. This was also how we were able to get much-needed funding from the local and provincial governments.

RD: How was the play received, by the Filipino community, and by other audience members?

LM: I would say it was well-received. We always had a full house when we premiered at St. Michael's College and then at the bigger Betty Oliphant Theater. We also toured it to Montreal and Vancouver. The LGBTQ community always came out in support. In fact, our production volunteers grew in number. The community press wrote positive reviews. Other LGBTQ groups from other immigrant communities talked about doing something similar for their own communities.

RD: The play also featured many cosmological worldviews (from Indigenous knowledge, to Catholicism, etc). Could you speak more about what inspired you to feature these different worldviews?

LM: When I was in the Philippines, and even when I lived in Toronto, I was very much involved in the Indigenous people's rights movement. They are the most oppressed sector in the Philippines (and elsewhere where colonization is a historical reality); their lands and resources taken away, their culture belittled, appropriated for profit, and/or destroyed. I wanted to show parallels between their experience and the experience of LGBTQ within the community, who persist and proudly stand despite the oppression.

I'm not sure if you want to include this anecdote, but we met with members of a Philippine Indigenous group based in Toronto whose Indigenous ancestry can be traced from Benguet, Ifugao, Bontoc, Apayao, and Kalinga, to talk about the play's references to Igorots and Ifugaos. They expressed concern about the characters being an Ifugao family, saying they are already being negatively perceived by the Filipino community and then to add the stigma of AIDS and homosexuality? In respect and because we understand where they were coming from, we decided to create a Filipino Indigenous group with its own set of values and beliefs—more like a composite of Indigenous groups I had met and written about as a young activist and journalist in the Philippines—but still based in the northern part of the Philippines. It was good in a way because it gave me some freedom to create stories. That's how the Legend of the White Devil came to be, which was an allegory for colonization.

RD: Related to the previous question, was the *babaylan* an important figure for you? If so, in what way?

LM: Yes. Many stories exist about the *babaylan*, but as a child I just remember seeing a photo of a weathered Filipino or Indigenous woman in one of my history books captioned, "babaylan—spiritual leader and healer," but that was it. A piece of historical anecdote. I wanted to know more about her. I can't remember anymore where I found the information, but I learned that when the Spanish came they refused to meet with women and instead looked for the men. The women were invalidated and later on cast out as witches. Later on, I associated the women healers I encountered in my life with *babaylan*s. I dislocated my ankle (and other movable parts) a lot as a child and my parents would always bring me to a bone setter or *hilot*, who "fixed" what was broken with massage and herbs. I do believe they were descended from the *babaylan*s.

RD: Why was the Philippines an important space for the play as well? At some points in the play, you cover mining in the Philippines, the effects of globalization, etc. What inspired you to discuss these issues that are specific to the Philippines?

LM: Well, I migrated from the Philippines and, aside from writing for Pinoy sa Canada, I was also part of the group called PSG—Philippine Solidarity Group. We aimed to promote and raise critical awareness of the Philippine struggle for political and economic justice. It is important for us to show how these issues intersect. Many of the problems that the Philippines continues to face stem from our colonial history—the colonizers never left, it seems. They just became multinational companies and a few wealthy mestizo families that drain our resources and leave poor and struggling Filipinos with no choice but to find better opportunities abroad.

RD: Looking back, more than two decades later, what was most rewarding about writing *My Grandmother and I*? Do you feel like it still has resonances today?

LM: The most rewarding thing about *MGI* is the way it brought people together to work toward a common cause: to raise awareness about AIDS/HIV for the purpose of creating a safe and caring environment for people with HIV/AIDS. Friendships extended beyond the show and we created a safe space for people to come out and be themselves. Support groups were formed or members joined groups that already existed. It was also a safe space to disagree and participate in the discourse on the issues we raised in the show. After I left in 1997, it was painful to hear about production members being HIV-positive or passing away from AIDS, but I'd like to think that because of the production, they did not suffer alone. I do believe that while there is more tolerance now, homophobia and transphobia still exist.

Queer Elsewhere
Fabulosity and Futurity on the Horizon

Martin F. Manalansan IV

When I was asked to write an afterword to this anthology, I felt a little uneasy. An afterword seemed more like a wrap-up, a denouement, and a final statement. What I offer below is more of an anti-afterword because it leaves things open rather than providing final closures. The various orientations of the text toward an "over there" and an elsewhere make it more like the beginning of a reverie, snatches of dreamlike sequences and meandering thoughts.

This text starts off as a personal reflection, using the memory of a friend as the primary takeoff point. But then, while I sought an arrival or a final destination for this unwieldy text, I became more enamored with its energetic and itinerant quality. Perhaps more than ever, this afterword strongly suggests that we refuse teleologies or preset blueprints to futures, and to freely experiment. This is the ethos of this text, which tries to approximate the ebullient exploratory spirit of this collection, and the conference I attended, "Diasporic Intimacies."

Not Here, Not Now

I often think about my childhood friend Boyette. I remember that he used to have this instant sparkle in his eyes when he would talk about going "abroad." I used to tease him as someone who just daydreamed of moving away because I guess we all felt that the Manila of the 1970s was just dreary and boring. He would talk about what he would do when he gets "there"—the shapeless, formless "abroad" that seemed to be brightly lit and hued like the Technicolor movies from Hollywood. Playing in the snow, eating ruddy apples, and later, as we matured into our teens, he would talk about cavorting with exotic handsome men, blonde guys, swarthy ones . . . just not the ones that used to be around us—always calling us the B word. Not bitch. But *bakla*. The word would hurt our ears and pride. The word has a harsh glottal stop. The final "a" almost sounds like a choking sound. Maybe I am mistaken. I am not a linguist. Nor do I have reliable memories these days. But one thing is sure; Boyette did not get to go abroad. He was murdered. I hate to write about this. After spending the summer of my junior year out in my parents' house in Bataan, I came back to a new school year to be virtually slapped with the devastating news. I never saw that sparkle again. His eyes were closed when I viewed him lying inside his casket at the school chapel.

Those were the 1970s. Living in the shadows of the Marcos regime, the weird cadences of martial law, political assassinations or "salvagings," pageantries, opulence, poverty, violence, anger, sadness, mourning . . . I could go on and on with a long concatenation of images, sounds, and emotions that make up a good part of my life, my teen years when I was green both in terms of innocence and of envy of other places, other peoples, and other times. Like Boyette, I longed to move away. Away from all these things that were in what was my "now." Like Boyette, "abroad" became more than a word, more than a state of being, and more of this slow but steady force that seemed to stretch my guts into different directions, a feeling, an ache, an ardent yearning to leave or just disappear.

I came to America in 1984 at the cusp of a couple of upheavals. A few months after I arrived, People Power brought down the regime of Ferdinand Marcos. Just a short time later, I started learning about this thing call GRID that eventually was renamed AIDS. Again, there was a trail of deaths, mourning, violence, political maneuverings, and other things that made me rethink, so if I am now abroad or in the "there" of my dreams, why I am still feeling those familiar pangs of longing? As I watched many of the new Filipino friends I met slowly die of AIDS, I was filled with a kind of trepidation. Maybe the "there" of my dreams wasn't all that I thought (together with Boyette) it would be. Maybe longing is all I have. All that queers will ever have. Maybe we should all just quit. At that same moment, I realized that I have other things to worry about and I should not just wallow in pitiful mourning and be only focused on death.

Many of the things I read in queer studies (some of which I admire) these days have this rather disturbing fascination with death. While I clearly recognize the ways in which death tracks and marks queer life, I do not subscribe to thanato-philic or necro-centric frameworks. I believe in a vitality that pivots on impossibility, mess, and hope—a combination that I believe is productive of a fabulosity or fabulousness that can animate a life force, a way of being that while being immersed in the gritty banal violences of the now and everyday can also uplift, reorient, and redirect our gaze, composure, and bodily energies towards working through challenge, enabling survival, and opening up moments of exuberance and hopefulness.

Claiming the Impossible: Saying Yes

In 1988, I was preparing for fieldwork on a topic that I thought would be a strategic choice that would help me land a job in academia, the study of Islamic education in Sumatra, Indonesia. But my plans changed radically. In the middle of what is typical graduate school hysteria, a report from the San Francisco Department of Health indicated that there was a dramatic two hundred percent increase in AIDS cases among Asian and Pacific Islander gay men or men who have sex with men. The news grabbed me in the same visceral way as the death of Boyette did years before. The statistics seemed clinical when set against the weekly news of Filipino gay men with AIDS that I knew in New York City. Some had been admitted to hospitals for varying illnesses or infections; a few were still standing around but were often hiding in their apartments. A few more were so ill that they were deemed to have "no hope" and were preparing to die, oftentimes alone. Those with families had to contend with their kin's shenanigans. One person in particular, a scion of a prominent Filipino family, came down with AIDS and his mother, a well-known socialite, was rumored to have been telling people that her son was a "drug addict" and he was not sick but just needed assistance in going to the supermarket and of all places, the opera.

I realized at that point that I was not about to spend a year in another "there"—in Sumatra—and devote a good amount of intellectual and emotional energy to studying a "safe topic." I was not about to stand still like I did in Boyette's wake—peering into a screened-off scene of death. I had to do something. Nervously, I told my adviser that I was changing my topic and field sites from Islamic education in Sumatra to Filipino gay men in New York City. My kind adviser just nodded and sighed. He said I should do what I wanted, but I might never get a job. In short, without him telling me directly, I was committing career suicide.

Without thinking much about my future career options, I set myself to conduct fieldwork in New York City where I have family. I applied for a job at the Gay Men's Health Crisis, which was then and still is the biggest private AIDS nonprofit organization in the world. In 1989 there was a massive tidal shift in the pandemic. No longer were gay white men (mostly middle to upper middle class) the primary group being affected by HIV. Particularly in the northeast, the new groups being affected were women, newborn babies, IV drug users, and "men who have sex with men" from working-class, immigrant, and racialized/minority communities. I was part of a big batch of employees from various backgrounds who were recruited by the agency to help assist in dealing with the challenges brought about by these dramatic demographic changes.

Working from 1989 to 1995, and then moving to APICHA or the Asian Pacific Islander Coalition on HIV/AIDS, also in Manhattan, I learned many lessons that I have never really written about. First, it was clear that the HIV/AIDS pandemic brought gay men (forcibly or not) out into the open, for better or for worse. These coming-out or forcing-out episodes, which played out in so many narratives of pride and healing, also inadvertently opened up new questions about sexual identity and categories. As I started my own fieldwork with Filipino gay men in New York City and in nonprofit work dealing with working-class and immigrant clients, "gay," which was for many of us then a solid, stable identity, became frayed if not wobbly in the face of the many life stories of immigrant and minority men. What was originally a study of AIDS and gay Filipinos widened and opened up to include a critical consideration of identities, everyday life, survival, and beauty.

At first, people thought that I was minimizing or watering down the devastation of AIDS and HIV on the community, but I had to argue that at the heart of various dilemmas of Filipino gay immigrants was not just the horrific conditions of the disease, but the multiple challenges and strictures presented by racism, poverty, legal documentation, gender performances, and many others. Such strictures were never isolated or discrete; rather, they bleed into or intersect with one another. In other words, the perceived effeminacy of Filipino and other Asian queers was a product of cultural perception but was also constituted by racist assumptions about Asian men as failed masculinities. Another example would be the fact that mainstream gay consumer lifestyles were beyond the reach of many working-class Filipino queers so they cannot fully participate as full "gay" citizens, especially at a moment when gay as a category was being pegged as a manifestation of the idealized lives of middle-class white/Caucasian single gay-identified men or when the category "gay" is linked to specific consumerist behavior.

Gay is popularly seen as an identity category that people should rightfully assume based on their sexual orientation or sexual object choice. As an identity, gay is often assumed to something akin to taking on a new dress that fits. But clearly, as the works in this anthology argue, gay is a racialized privilege if not, often an impossibility. To assume the facile taking on of gay identity is to deny the contradictions inherent in the structural realities about gay selfhood and community. Erased or sidelined from popular and dominant gay visual culture, Asian queers in general and Filipino queers in particular were attempting not only to gain visibility and representation in the American gay mainstream, but also to think of alternative ways to be queer and not necessarily "gay." Here I am signaling my shift in the use of "gay" to "queer" to signal a turn to a cultural dissidence based on necessity. Many racialized queer people wanted to embrace the redemptive promise of "gay through rights discourse," several Filipinos were content and quite correct in reclaiming *"bakla"* not merely as an identifier but as a counterpoint to the hegemony of gay especially in the failure of gay politics and community not only to be inclusive, but to be self-critical in the ways in which "gay" has been stabilized despite the fact that racialized and marginalized subjects like Filipino queers who are herded into the gay "slot" do not fit comfortably in their prescribed designation. This is especially true since queer Filipino lives, bodies and predicaments are located in dissonant or incongruous ways to the demands and sensibilities of being gay. So what is to be done?

I was part of the founding group that established *Kambal sa Lusog,* which was an organization of Filipino queers (although we did not use the term) trying to think about what it means to face off with an emergent gay "establishment" or mainstream. When applying for grants, we were questioned as to why we even felt the need to come together as Filipinos and whether in fact we were ghettoizing ourselves from the "community." Some members were all about "liberating" other Filipinos from the closet and from the chains of tradition. They even talked about bringing gay liberation to the Philippines. Several of us asked these gay liberationists why they thought that coaxing our compatriots to come out of the closet was helpful, if not practical. In addition, we asked them why they thought anyone needed "liberating." Those questions motivated us to think more expansively beyond the categories of "gay" and "lesbian." We thought critically about why some of our members have become what was then called "transsexual" and why they felt they needed to stay away from our gay and lesbian-focused group; even *"bakla"* did not resonate with them anymore. Those were the early 1990s, when transgender as a category had not yet gained social traction, but we were questioning the very premises that brought us together. Despite all these barriers, the organization did manage to do some fund-raising, volunteered in numerous AIDS activities, and had multiple socials and workshops, including a Santacruzan at (what was then called) the Gay and Lesbian Community Center. More than these, the very questions that initially brought us in were the basis for interrogating our mission, which seemed at some point to be both energizing and limiting.

Kambal eventually disbanded. Now, from the vantage of a new era in the twenty-first century dubbed as "post-gay" or even "post-queer," my involvement with *Kambal* and the AIDS nonprofit world was a way to say "yes," to accept the challenge of facing and actively engaging with the "now." It is not that I suddenly woke up from the stupor of "elsewhereishness." Rather, I took those pangs of longing as a motivation and a fulcrum for acting upon the present. The present was not something I needed to escape from but to work on. The two phases in my life—one in the Philippines, and my life in America during the 1980s and 1990s—were not divergent periods, but rather interconnected ones, with one set of years leading to another. While set in two different sites in a migratory life, both periods were all about dreaming, of exuberantly imagining the "not here," that is, not about the disappeared present but one that combines gritty realities with a sense of longing for things on the horizon, the "not yet here," but with a steady foot planted on the realities on the ground. It is the doubleness of both claiming and resisting the "here" and the "now" that enables new encounters and new ways of being. It is this combination of hopeful exuberance and stark pathos that I believe is the stuff of queer migrant world-making. This kind of world-making was evident in *Diasporic Intimacies*.

Claiming an Elsewhere: Embodying Filipino Queer Activism and History

What does it mean to establish a way of life, to create worlds and meanings, claim spaces, rights, obligations and debts? What does it mean for Filipinos scattered in more than a hundred countries across the world make sense and establish survival tactics in order to make it through and survive? I think of the various ways in which creative communal efforts are deployed in various events and settings both in commonplace and spectacular sites. The *Diasporic Intimacies* conference and the anthology that came out of that event are evidence of survival tactics. This anthology's itinerary is a strong evidence of the varied kinds of embodied tactics and strategies that are mapped into the lives of Filipino diasporic communities everywhere.

The essays in this anthology that devote their energies to confronting history are the temporal and spatial unfoldings of departures and arrivals, points of origins and destinations, roots and routes. These various essays, poems and other genres are not only narratives of who, what, where and when, but more importantly, all the works in these anthologies are sites of training, of creation and of fostering critical sensibilities that enable queers to engage with the world more effectively. Filipino Canadian queer history is as much about discontinuities as it is about continuities. Diasporic distance creates multi-stranded complex relationships with family and nation. *Balikbayan* boxes are filled not only with material bounty but also weighed down by the obligations and duties of the normative, despite nostalgic intentions. These trouble the very idea of origins as wayward trajectories do not necessarily lead to a developmental and teleological path. Rather, their waywardness can lead to constant flux and temporary settlements. These unconventional experiences demand a deflection of an essential provenance such as unproblematic kinship with precolonial queer figures such as the *babaylan*. Instead, this anthology fosters a devotion to the cultivation of new sensibilities and creative activism.

It is no big wonder that a considerable number of the works gathered in this collection are about cultural production and the work they do as activism and as a major part of the creation of new critical sensibilities. From poems to visual images, these works are about queer immigrant aesthetic rooted and routed in the travels and settlements of Filipino Canadian queers.

Aesthetics as a discipline and branch of philosophy is clearly about the training of the senses. The works contained in this anthology are about understanding the messy power of the body and its various capacities such as senses, emotions, feelings and affects. Apprehending a picture is no longer just a visual task but can also be haptic. Listening to a song is as much about the skin as it is about the ears. What this means is that queer Filipino Canadian artistic and cultural productions are about more complex and unruly ways of seeing, touching, tasting, hearing and smelling as well as to understand the various embodied ways of knowing. Cultural productions do something. They create discordant atmospheres and moods. People are affected by them. But what do these works have to do with the politics of diasporic and queer lives? Passions and other energies or capacities are essential to insubordinate political visions, material action, and imaginations. What we can imagine as politically and materially possible are vitally shaped by cultural productions. Such works are about extending, transgressing and delineating the boundaries and borders of our everyday lives. Poems, pictures, movements, and all the other products of what we call the "arts" are really catalysts for engaging with the world, of acting upon the world.

The participants in the *Diasporic Intimacies* conference and the contributors in this volume are offering not just works to be read but rather they are tools or more appropriately triggers in enabling and encouraging radical thoughts, alternative behavior or attitudes and progressive ways of being in the world. In other words, the conference, this anthology and the cultural productions are themselves embodied acts of taking on a world that has caused pain, suffering, joy, exuberance, loneliness and happiness—the messiness of queer diasporic life. One can call these objects from the conference and this anthology as activism incarnate, of things that do something—to create a world, a space that one can call, at least provisionally, Queer Filipino Canada. This is an elsewhere that is not merely located in here and now but also projected to the future, a space that not yet but will be.

Queer Filipino Canada: Prospects and Possibilities of an Elsewhere

As I finish this essay which I think of as a movement between biography and community, I think of all the other queer Filipinos dreaming and trying to find their ways through the maze of migration—departures, returns, settlements, unsettlements, and the infra-ordinary task of "moving on." Having spent most of my life now in the United States, I have been curious to test the extent and limits of my own thoughts about queerness and Filipino-ness.

Attending the "Diasporic Intimacies" conference afforded me a window on the various struggles and dreams of queer Filipinos in Canada. The conference itself was not just a pioneering effort at community-building but was more than that: it was a claiming of things that heretofore have been deemed impossible. Beyond the struggles of visibility and inclusion, the panels, presentations, and performances were directly struggling with not just LGBT inclusion but rather with the very terms and conditions of what makes inclusion even thinkable and relevant, of why inclusion is limited. The conference examined to what extent queer Filipino Canadians can move beyond the discourses of rights to a struggle to define legal personhood that is not abstracted from the realities of race, gender, sexuality, class and nationality; to create new appropriate queer archives and not just to rely on established ones; to examine modes of attachments and desire instead of just passively accepting them, and to question happiness, fulfillment, and the very terms of being Filipino, Canadian, and queer.

I strongly believe efforts like the "Diasporic Intimacies" conference are very instructive to Filipinos (both queer and non-queer) in Canada, the United States and in other spaces of the Filipino diasporic elsewhere. The efforts of the conference organizers and participants are emblematic of what it takes to come together even at a moment of political apathy, homonormative consumption, and privatized desires. "Diasporic Intimacies" was not just an event but an intervention into the malaise and quagmire of early twenty-first-century LGBT and queer politics. Despite an otherwise staid, complacent, and often smugly contented group of constituencies, the conference and this book can be seen as a sparkle, a glint in the eye of young Filipino queers who are excited and hopeful at the prospect of better things and times on the horizon, of the not yet here, of shimmering futures and of things about to bear fruit. These are lofty ideals and dreams indeed, but they are what we would need as fuel and sustenance as we set forth in our travels to the elsewhere and beyond.

CONTRIBUTORS

Melanya Liwanag Aguila is a first-generation Canadian of *pinay* descent. She graduated from OCAD University's integrated media program in 1999. She has contributed to the lives and history of the queer Philippine diaspora through hosting social events and activities; connecting art, activism, and people; and supporting diversity in the Philippine community.

Jodinand Aguillon is a transnational multidisciplinary artist and entrepreneur. He is currently the executive director at Pineapple Lab, an arts and performance hub dedicated to finding innovative ways to showcase the works of Filipino art makers, international artists, and collaborators. He is the founder and former artistic director of the performing arts collective HATAW, a set designer, a wardrobe stylist, and a visual merchandiser. Aguillon combines mediums and integrates vocations, folding together varied experiences to create from a unique perspective.

PJ Alafriz is from Abra, Philippines, of Indigenous *Tingguian* descent. Alafriz came to Canada through the Foreign Domestic Movement in the 1990s, and quickly became an important community organizer. Alafriz has organized numerous collectives in Toronto with a specifically queer following, including *tibo* basketball, *Pardz* Nights, and Babaylan events.

Jo SiMalaya Alcampo is an interdisciplinary artist born in Manila and raised in Malvern in the heart of Scarborough. Alcampo currently lives in Toronto. Her art practice integrates storytelling, installation-based art, and electro-acoustic soundscapes. Alcampo has developed community arts projects with various groups, including queer youth, consumer-survivors of the mental health system, and migrant domestic workers. In 2010 she graduated from OCAD University with a B.F.A. degree in integrated media. Advisors in OCAD's Indigenous visual culture program inspired her to reconnect with her roots.

Patrick Alcedo is an associate professor in the Department of Dance at York University, where he is also the graduate program director. He holds the government of Ontario's Early Researcher Award and is the artistic director of the forthcoming, "Luzviminda: The Philippines Dances for Canada 150," a dance concert featuring folk, modern, contemporary, and urban dances that have helped define Filipino identities in Canada. His writing has appeared in the *Journal of Southeast Asian Studies* and in anthologies published by Palgrave Macmillan and Playwrights Canada Press. With Sally Ann Ness and Hendrik M.J. Maier, he is the editor of *Religious Festivals in Contemporary Southeast Asia*, which was nominated for the Thirty-Sixth National Book Award in the Philippines. He is also the director, writer, and producer of five documentary films. In 2013, his *Ati-atihan Lives* was nominated for Best Documentary at the Gawad Urian Awards. In recognition of his achievements in dance studies and ethnographic research, he won the prestigious Selma Jeanne Cohen Fund for International Scholarship on Dance from the Fulbright Association of America in 2014.

Anakbayan Toronto is a Filipino youth group that seeks to build a progressive movement to engage, organize, and mobilize fellow youth and students around the interests of poor and working-class communities in the Greater Toronto area. The group works to link local struggles to the conditions and popular movements for Philippine national democracy with a socialist perspective. It is also a regional chapter of Anakbayan Canada and an overseas chapter of Anakbayan Philippines.

Christine Balmes was born and raised in Quezon City and Ilocos Sur in the Philippines. She immigrated with her family to Canada as a youth. It was while pursuing Asian studies at the University of Michigan that she first learned how to play *kulintang*. She has devoted most of her adult life to working in and with the Filipino Canadian community as an educator, artist, and musician. She is currently a youth and parent support worker as well as a member of Kapwa Collective, a group of artists, healers, and critical thinkers who aim to bridge the narratives of the Filipinx and the Canadian, the Indigenous and the diasporic.

Benjamin Bongolan is the newcomer family settlement services coordinator at the 519 Community Centre. In this role, he works with LGBTQ convention refugees, newcomer youth, live-in caregivers, and families by offering weekly programming and one-on-one support. Bongolan's work focuses on LGBTQ newcomer accessibility, leadership, safer spaces, and immigrant youth well-being. He also maintains partnerships with the Philippine government through their representative offices in Toronto to support caregivers and overseas foreign workers. He is a graduate of the University of Toronto with a B.A. in political science and history.

Constantine Cabarios was born in Paniqui, Tarlac, and immigrated to Toronto with his family in 1975. He currently shares his home with his loving partner of fifteen years and their cat, Mabuhay. He is a registered social worker who works as a mental health counselor for the AIDS Committee of Toronto, providing clinical counseling to a diverse group of gay, queer, bisexual, and gender-fluid men. He also teaches part-time at Seneca College. As a Filipino Canadian, he has been shaped by his lived experiences as an immigrant and racialized queer man while bearing witness to the effects of HIV/AIDS, mental health challenges, and substance use.

John Paul Catungal is a tenure-track instructor in the Institute for Gender, Race, Sexuality, and Social Justice at the University of British Columbia (on unceded Musqueam territory). His research broadly concerns the racial, sexual, gender, settler colonial, and transnational politics of community organizing for health, education, and social services in Canadian urban contexts. His dissertation research on the queer of color geographies of ethno-specific AIDS service provision (University of Toronto, 2014) was awarded the Governor-General's Gold Medal for Academic Excellence. Along with other publications, he coedited *Filipinos in Canada: Disturbing Invisibility*.

Eirene Cloma is a multi-instrumentalist and singer-songwriter trained in classical, Latin, and jazz guitar. Her sound combines her musicianship with soul, jazz, and pop influences. Eirene was the session guitarist for Kimmortal's debut album, *Sincerity*, released in December 2014. Eirene is one-half of the queer pop sibling duo the Lonsdales. Eirene was born and raised on unceded Coast Salish territory. Prior to moving to Tkaronto in 2014, she served in the Candian Armed Forces for eight years and deployed to Afghanistan and Cyprus. Her experiences as a second-generation Filipinx settler, veteran, and transmasculine queer shape her artistry and advocacy.

Roland Sintos Coloma is a professor of Cultural Studies in Education and chair of the Department of Teacher Education at Northern Kentucky University. Previously he was a faculty member at the Ontario Institute for Studies in Education of the University of Toronto, where he taught the first courses on Asian Canadian history and theorizing Asian Canada at the university. His research interests include history and cultural studies; race, gender, and sexuality; curriculum, policy, and teacher education; and Filipinx and Asian diasporas. His publications include two edited books: *Filipinos in Canada: Disturbing Invisibility* and *Postcolonial Challenges in Education*.

Congress of Progressive Filipino Canadians (CPFC) is the national center of organizations dedicated to educating, mobilizing, and organizing progressive Filipino Canadians and their communities to struggle for genuine settlement and integration. The CPFC is committed to building the socialist movement in Canada as well as the global antiimperialist support and solidarity movement. They bring together the cooperation and participation of other Filipino Canadian progressive groups and individuals and seek to unite and coordinate with other progressive groups and individuals outside the Filipino community. As CPFC commits itself to genuine settlement and integration along the process of helping build the socialist movement in Canada, it stands and fights for concerns such as human rights in civil, political, economic, social, and cultural fields against class exploitation and national and state oppression; enhancing women's equality, development and human rights; making the youth count in Canada's future, especially the right to education and employment; supporting the rights and welfare of temporary and migrant workers, and upholding the rights of LGBT against intolerance, violence, and all other forms of discrimination, and to a life of dignity and secured existence.

Michelle Cruz is a social worker by day, a musician after hours, a mom 24/7, and lover of life for forever.

Joanna Delos Reyes is a Filipina-Canadian artist, musician, and community worker based in Tkaronto. Influenced by her lived experience as an immigrant, and privilege to travel, she is interested in the intersections of (im)migration, identity, place, and the built-environment. Attracted to the noises of the everyday, the experimentation of post-punk sound, and guilty grooves of '90s girl bands, she brings a lil strangeness and a lot of sweetness to the studio. Constant thing-doer and collaborator, she plays with noh-wave experimental metal noise rock band and performance art collective Yamantaka//Sonic Titan and celestial R&B *kulintang* ensemble *Pantayo*.

Robert Diaz is an assistant professor of transnational feminisms, globalization, and sexuality studies in the Women and Gender Studies Institute, University of Toronto. His research, teaching, and community work focus on the intersections of Asian diasporic, postcolonial, and queer studies. Diaz pays particular attention to Filipino/a cultural practices as these are affected by, and affect, histories of empire. His writing has appeared in the *Journal of Asian American Studies, Signs, GLQ, Women and Performance*, and *Plaridel*, as well as in anthologies such as *Philippine Palimpsests: Essays for the 21st Century* and *Global Asian Popular Culture*. Diaz's book, *Reparative Acts: Redressive Nationalisms in Queer Filipino Lives*, is forthcoming from Temple University Press. In it, he examines Filipino popular culture from the 1970s onward as he charts the links between nationalisms, redress, and queer acts of resistance. Diaz is ultimately committed to seeking equity and social justice for those most marginalized. He has thus collaborated with many community organizations in Toronto, foregrounding needs of racialized, queer, Indigenous, and differently abled communities.

Mithi Esguerra is currently the chairperson of GABRIELA Ontario, an organization of Filipinas working to advance the Philippine struggle for national freedom and genuine democracy, while at the same time addressing the local struggles of Filipinas in Ontario. She arrived to Canada in 1994 as a teen and has been involved in grassroots organizing, political education, and advocacy work since then. Her initial involvement was with the Philippine Solidarity Group of Toronto, an organization of Filipinos and Canadians that sought to mobilize support for issues of human rights in the Philippines. As she experienced the struggles of a first-generation immigrant youth, she became involved in organizing Filipino youth around issues of family reunification and identity. Her community organizing experience since then has also led to to work with live-in caregivers and migrant workers.

Kat Estacio is a musician, artist, and enabler of creative culture in Tkaronto. Her work speaks to the intersectional meeting of narratives as a diasporic queer woman of color, expressed through supposed contradictions of nostalgia and decolonization. She is a founding member of Pantayo, an all-women Filipinx *kulintang* gong ensemble, and is one-half of Sharps Lab, a tattoo and sound-art collective. Kat's solo music blends drifty experimental synth tones with the soft percussive timbre of *kulintang*, a departure from the more rhythmic stylings of the larger outfit she shares in Pantayo. A strange hypnotic world unfolds that is both starkly daunting and deeply inviting: https://soundcloud.com/kat-estacio.

Katrina Estacio is a Filipinx-Canadian immigrant settler from Manila currently residing in Mississauga. Her work is inspired by her interests in environmental sciences, translations, event logistics, materials production, and gong playing. She is a sensi-queer who thrives in communities that are conducive to creativity, efficiency, and critical thinking. Katrina likes organizing her calendar, and in her free time she can be seen doing twin-related activities or traveling to watch her favorite football club.

May Farrales is a Ph.D. candidate in geography at the University of British Columbia. Her work includes thinking through how sexualities articulate at the nexus of the gendered, classed, and racialized subjectivities of Filipina/o Canadians and is concerned with the ways in which sexuality, race, and gender relate to different forms of colonialisms. Farrales lives with her family; she works and studies on the unceded and traditional territories of the Musqueam, Skxwú7mesh, and Tsleil-Waututh peoples (also known as Greater Vancouver).

Kapwa Collective is a group of Filipino Canadian artists, critical thinkers, and healers who work across different academic and applied disciplines. The group believes in the values of inclusivity and accessibility, and works toward bridging narratives between the Indigenous and the diasporic, and the Filipino and the Canadian. The group also facilitates links among academic, artistic, activist, and other communities in Toronto.

Sean Kua is a Filipinx-Canadian composer, classical pianist, vocalist, and songwriter extraordinaire. They are a beautiful, complex, brilliant queer that tells their story through poetic, earnest, rageful music. Find their music at seankua.bandcamp.com.

Marissa Largo is an artist, an educator, and a Ph.D. candidate in the Department of Social Justice Education at the Ontario Institute for

Studies in Education of the University of Toronto. Largo's doctoral project, "Unsettling Imaginaries: The Decolonial Diaspora Aesthetic of Four Contemporary Filipino/a Canadian Artists," explores the ways in which the work of Filipino/a Canadian visual artists act as assertions of marginalized subjectivities in Canada. In 2013 she was awarded the prestigious Joseph-Armand Bombardier Canada Graduate Scholarship from the Social Sciences and Humanities Research Council of Canada. Her artwork and curatorial projects have been presented in museums and galleries across Canada.

Martin F. Manalansan IV is an associate professor of anthropology and Asian American studies and the head of the Department of Asian American Studies at the University of Illinois, Urbana-Champaign. He is an affiliate in the Department of Gender and Women's Studies, the Global Studies Program, and the Unit for Criticism and Interpretive Theory. Manalansan is the author of *Global Divas: Filipino Gay Men in the Diaspora* and the editor or coeditor of four anthologies: *Filipino Studies: Palimpsests of Nation and Diaspora*; *Cultural Compass: Ethnographic Explorations of Asian America*; *Queer Globalizations: Citizenship and the Afterlife of Colonialism*; and *Eating Asian America: A Food Studies Reader*. He has edited a special issue of the *International Migration Review* on gender and migration and more recently, a special issue of the *Journal of Asian American Studies* entitled "Feeling Filipinos," as well as publishing in journals such as *GLQ, Antipode, Cultural Anthropology, positions: east asian cultural critique*, and *Radical History*. Among his many awards are the Ruth Benedict Prize from the American Anthropological Association in 2003, the Excellence in Mentorship Award in 2013 from Association of Asian American Studies, the Richard Yarborough Mentoring Prize in 2016 from the American Studies Association and the Crompton-Noll Award for the best LGBTQ essay in 2016 from the Modern Language Association.

Julius Poncelet Manapul was born in Manila in 1980 and immigrated to Toronto in 1990. He attained his B.F.A. in 2009 from OCAD University, followed by a one-year residency in Paris. He earned a Professional Art Studio certificate from the Toronto School in 2011 and completed his Masters of Visual Studies and earned a Sexual Diversity Studies Certificate from the University of Toronto in 2013. His work has been presented in galleries and art centers in Toronto, London, Paris, and Berlin.

Casey Mecija is an interdisciplinary artist and musician, a community organizer, and a Ph.D. student in the Women and Gender Studies Institute at the University of Toronto. There are two experiences that guide her artistic practice: being a singer/songwriter, and being an arts educator. In tandem with her graduate studies in arts education, sociology and equity, and postcolonial theory, Casey aims to create art that signifies the complexity of her personality and desires.

Lani T. Montreal is a queer Filipina educator, writer, performer, and community activist based in Chicago. Her writings have been published and produced in Canada, the United States, the Philippines, and in cyberspace. Among her plays are: *Nanay, Panther in the Sky, Gift of Tongue, Looking for Darna, Alien Citizen, Grandmother and I*, and *Sister OutLaw*. She is the recipient of the 2015 3Arts Djerassi Residency Fellowship for Playwriting, the 2008 3Arts Ragdale Residency Fellowship, and the 2001 Samuel Ostrowsky Award for her memoir "Summer Rain." She was a finalist for the 1995 JVO Philippine Award for Excellence in Journalism for her environmental expose "Poison in the River." Lani holds an M.F.A. in creative writing from Roosevelt University. She teaches writing at Malcolm X College, one of the City Colleges of Chicago, and writes a blog called "Fil-in-the-gap" (filinthegap.com). She lives (and loves) in Albany Park, Chicago, with her multispecies, multicultural family.

Pantayo is a Toronto-based all-women gong ensemble whose music is grounded in the *kulintang* music traditions of the Maguindanaon and T'boli peoples of the Philippines while exploring the possibilities of *kulintang* as influenced by their identities as settlers on Turtle Island ("North America") and as diasporic Filipinas. Members are: Christine Balmes, Eirene Cloma, Michelle Cruz, Joanna Delos Reyes, Kat Estacio, Katrina Estacio, and Marianne Grace Rellin. Past notable projects include performances at the Music Gallery's X Avant Festival, Wavelength Festival, and a collaboration with YAMANTAKA // SONIC TITAN for an award-winning video game soundtrack for Severed (Drinkbox Studio). Their full-length debut album will be released in 2017.

Fritz Luther Pino is a registered social worker and a Ph.D. candidate in the Department of Social Justice Education at the Ontario Institute for Studies in Education of the University of Toronto. He received the Social Sciences and Humanities Research Council Doctoral Award for his dissertation project on older Filipino gay men in Canada. He also received the Ontario Seniors' Secretariat Provincial Grant for his Website Development Project, an online resource for seniors, gerontologists, social workers, and healthcare providers. Pino was born and raised in Cebu, Philippines, where he received his bachelor's and master's degrees in psychology. He migrated to Canada in 2007 with his parents and siblings.

Lui Queano lives in Toronto and belongs to a family of musicians and writers. His poems have been published in several literary publications, including the *Cultural Centre of the Philippines Anthology*. He was a member of Galian sa Arte at Tula, a progressive writers group organized during martial law, and Bagong Dugo, a political satire group composed of theater artists and writers formed during the People Power Revolution of 1986. His collection of poems *Engkwentro* was published in 2005. A chemical engineering graduate from Saint Louis University, Queano is also a registered engineer-in-training under the Professional Engineers of Ontario.

JB Ramos is the main instructor at Combat Science: Warrior Arts of Asia, a Filipino martial arts school based in Toronto that was established in 2003. In addition to studying with world-recognized masters and grandmasters in the Philippines, Ramos has successfully competed in several international events and competitions, including advanced combat sport *eskrima* (full-contact stick fighting). As a martial arts teacher and longtime LGBTQ activist and supporter, Ramos recognizes the need and importance for self-defense instruction for non-martial artists as well as for the LGBTQ community. Hence, Ramos regularly promotes the Filipino martial arts in all its forms through demonstrations, workshops, and self-defense programs working with various community organizations throughout North America and the Philippines. Aside from teaching, JB Ramos is also a certified Use-Of-Force instructor, a student of traditional healing arts from the Philippines, and a casual writer.

Marianne Grace Rellin is a queer Filipina immigrant born and raised in Manila and now based in Scarborough, a culturally diverse suburb of Toronto. She works in programming, marketing, and communications for the visual and community arts sectors. Her work as an arts manager and musician focuses on empowering the margins and deconstructing Western systems of thought.

Patrick Salvani/Ms. Nookie Galore is a genderqueer, pansexual, hairy Asian, Filipino panda Queen and Horror Storyteller. She's like you. But better. He/She/They/Anything but "Bro" is the FatherMom to the largest and longest standing Queer and Trans People of Colour Community show, *The Drag Musical*. Their artwork has been profiled in *CBC Arts* and in the documentary *No Fats, No Femmes, No Asians* and showcased at the *Art Gallery of Ontario's First Thursdays*. Their new Horror Drag Cooking Show *Sarap* has been featured in the Mayworks Festival of Working People and the Arts, the Rhubarb Festival, and the Allied Media Conference; it will soon be a film made in partnership with Audre's Revenge Film Production Company. Patrick/Nookie believes in Community. Some people suck but there's always good lipstick for that.

Lisa Valencia-Svensson is an award-winning documentary film producer based in Toronto. Her first feature-length documentary, *Herman's House*, won an Emmy for Outstanding Arts and Culture Programming and was nominated for a Canadian Screen Award, the Donald Brittain Award for Best Social/ Political Documentary. Her second feature, *Migrant Dreams*, won the Canadian Hillman Prize and a Canadian Association of Journalists Award. It premiered at Hot Docs, where it was a Top Ten Audience Favourite, and screened at DOXA, where it received honorable mention for the Colin Low Award for Canadian Documentary. She associate-produced several films, including *The World before Her*, which have garnered Emmy nominations and Canadian Screen Awards, have been broadcast internationally, and have won awards at festivals including TIFF, Tribeca, Hot Docs, and IDFA. Her passion is for film projects that explore issues of inequality and social justice. She has also been involved in Filipino, Asian, and queer cultural and political organizing in Toronto off and on for more than twenty years.

Kim Villagante (Kimmortal) is an independent artist and creative powerhouse based on unceded Coast Salish Territory (Vancouver, British Columbia). As a queer Filipinx woman of color, she explores themes relating to love, healing, ancestral connections, and community empowerment through an eclectic mix of soul, indie-rock, rap, hip hop, and experimental. She often brings unexpected instruments into her live sets, including the ukulele or glockenspiel. After graduating from UBC in visual arts and art history, she became immersed in theater, community activism, and art projects while recording her debut album, *Sincerity* (2014). Festivals she has performed at include Canadian Music Week, the Kultura Filipino Arts Festival (Toronto), New West Pride Festival, and the Queer Women of Color Film Festival (San Francisco). She has opened for artists Shad K, Azizi Gibson, Gabriel Teodros, and Lal.

INDEX